IRAN

Published under the Auspices of THE NEAR EASTERN CENTER
University of California, Los Angeles

Political Development in

a Changing Society

by Leonard Binder

University of California Press

Berkeley and Los Angeles

1 9 6 2

University of California Press
Berkeley and Los Angeles
Cambridge University Press
London, England
© 1962 by The Regents of the University of California
Library of Congress Catalog Card Number: 62-14944
Designed by Frank J. Lieberman
Printed in the United States of America

To the Memory of

My Mother

Preface

This book is part of a newer tradition of studies of non-Western political systems. In its general conception and its concern with logical presentation it reflects its intellectual origins and the aspirations of a growing group of political scientists to break away from a fruitless formalism and to reach for that essence which we all know and feel to be the really "political." It is not only the political that is essential to our purpose, however, for this is not a work in philosophy. We are concerned here with the political life of Iran, with distilling that residue which is the true meaning of being an Iranian, guided both by values and by worldly goals. If an understanding of the truly political is a philosophical exercise, grasping the real Iran is an active pursuit compounded of study, experience, and empathy. These are the two elements, strongly stamped with a personal impress, that we have attempted to compound in a communicable conveyance of knowledge.

It is to be hoped that, in escaping from one kind of formalism, we have not fallen into another and emptier one. A theoretical framework is what one can make of it empirically, and naught else but intellectual autism. For political scientists and those who would understand what political scientists are about, we have made our framework explicit and have attempted to justify the procedure that has been followed. All of that will be found in the first chapter, where it is offered with appropriate diffidence and apologies to those who hold that the main body of the exposition must stand or fall, not in the relationship of theory and fact, but in the degree that meaning is configuratively conveyed from mind to mind. The latter are right, of course, as far as they go.

It is well to bear in mind, however, that our purpose is understanding, in its most comprehensive sense and in neither the formulation of policy nor the explanation of yesterday's events. Where circumstances have permitted, both references to things and the tenses of verbs have been brought up to date. But this is only to avoid the taste of dryness in an analytical reconstruction of an admittedly changing political system.

As in every study of this sort, this one too is only superficially the work of one person. In a deeper sense, many have contributed both to its formulation and its content. But I am constrained to limit the specificity with which acknowledgment may be made, and this for three reasons: limitations of space, the dullness of memory, and the fear that some measure of undeserved responsibility may be attributed to those who were so generous with their time and so patient in their explanations. It is, therefore, no mere formality when I insist that sole responsibility for the judgments and opinions contained in this volume rests with the author.

The slow germinating kernel of the theoretical scheme which informs this study was first implanted by Sir Hamilton Gibb, University professor at Harvard. My interest in Iran, and the beginnings of my presently deep admiration for the remarkable people of that country, were the direct consequence of the stimulating teaching of Professor T. Cuyler Young, an old Iran hand and the chairman of the Department of Oriental Studies at Princeton University. The field research upon which this study is based was made possible by a generous grant from the Comparative Politics and Near East Committees of the Social Science Research Council, but the financial is the least of the ways in which I have benefited, both from the activities of these committees and from the highly talented staff of the Council. Important assistance was also received from the Research Committee at UCLA, and from John Smith, formerly librarian at the Institute for Administrative Affairs at Tehran University, and now public librarian at Santa Barbara. I am similarly indebted to many Americans who served in Iran during and before my own stay there, to Professor Richard Gable of the University of Southern California for an exceptionally good preresearch briefing, to Professor Wayne Untereiner of the University of Indiana for frequent discussions in Tehran, to Bert Blosser, then Information Officer at USIS in Iran, and to the staffs of the United States Embassy, the Public Administration Division of ICA in Iran, the Governmental Affairs Institute, and the Institute for Administrative Affairs.

In Iran, wherever I turned I was met with warm friendship and eager assistance, so that I fear I can hardly do justice to all those who helped. I shall, therefore, single out only a few, symbolically, and hope the rest will understand my predicament. I am grateful for the assistance of H. E. Hussain Ala minister of court; Dr. Manuchehr Eghbal, former prime minister; Asadullah Alam, leader of the Mardum Party; Dr. Nasratullah Kassemi, former minister of state; and Professor A. A. Siassi, dean of the faculty of arts at Tehran University. To Professor Purhumayun, director of the Institute for Administrative Affairs, I owe a special debt for greatly facilitating my work through the provision of a semiofficial base of operations.

Above all, I am grateful to a number of Iranian citizens who became interested in my research through personal friendship, and through whose constant companionship I was enabled to see things as they did. There is no way that I can repay the help of these people, nor can I even say that I have accepted their views. Nevertheless, I am also bound to thank especially a teacher, an assistant prosecutor, an oil company employee, a lawyer, an assistant professor, a graduate student, and a young mujtahid.

All of the conventional reasons why authors thank their wives apply in this case as well; but how much more significant is their application, when it involves a year's foreign residence and all the attendant disruptions to home and the education of the young. I am grateful for the cheerful management of these things and for the fact that there was enough spirit left over so that we could share the deeper experience of Iran.

L. B.

Chicago

December, 1961

Contents

ONE

A Strategy for

the Study of a

Whole Political System

WHAT IS A REVOLUTION?

Two young men came to see me. They sat down and engaged in a discussion. One of them spoke thus, "I have read your writings. Your words are correct, but we are very far from our goal if it is to be approached by that road; in this country we need a revolution . . ." The second one, supporting this view, said "You want to make things right by gradual improvement. We, the youth, move fast; we believe that we must improve things rapidly by a revolution."

So long as I gave no answer they spoke to one another thus, "Yes, we are backward, we must be swift."

I said . . . " 'Revolution' is one of those words which fall easily from the tongue and which is used without any clear meaning being understood from it.

"If I should ask you 'What is a revolution?' I know that you would be nonplussed. In any case, you who desire to make a revolution, have you ever planned one, have you ever prepared the ground for one?"

*They said, "No. Our goal is to elucidate a theory, we
don't make plans in such haste." I said, "From your argument
I am compelled to tell this popular folk story: A man went
one time as a guest to the house of a friend. The host asked,
'Would you like to have some melon?' The guest thought
that his host had some melon which could be brought to the
table. He said, 'Bring some. I will have a little.' The host
answered, 'I will tell the servants to bring some if there is
any.'*

*"You have said the same thing. You are not pleased with
a way which has been opened and by which efforts have been
made for years, and through which some progress has been
achieved. You are not pleased because the end goal is distant." [1]*

Like the two young men who approached Ahmad Kasravi
in his Socratic splendor, we are not planning a revolution in Iran,
nor even in the comparative study of politics, but we would like
to theorize about both. Kasravi's answer, it must be remembered,
does not deny the possibility of a revolution; his view is, rather,
that he has all the answers already, so that theorizing is superfluous. Such will doubtless be the response of those who are falsely
complacent about the present capacity of the science of politics,
who will urge that theoretical digressions and analytical arrangements of observations are superfluous and distorting. I am
reminded of the complaint of one earnest fellow in a heated neigh-
borhood meeting, to the effect that strict adherence to parliamentary procedure was obstructing progress. In the ensuing bed-
lam, all sense of direction and of purpose was lost with the
elimination of procedural order—but each speaker was happy
in the belief that he was somehow saying something of significance. This experience has its parallel among students of
the politics of foreign areas, each of whom may have something
of significance to contribute, but who have not been able to
combine their efforts to ensure a measure of cumulative progress
in resolving issues that stubbornly persist through changes of
personnel and changes of constitutions. In theorizing about a
revolution, rather than planning one, we admit that we do not
have all the answers. Instead, we are attempting, by this selfconscious preoccupation with procedure, to make it clear which
answers we have and which we don't have. In much the same

---

[1] Translated from Ahmad Kasravi, *Inqilab Chist?* (Tehran,
1336), p. 10.

way, it is also hoped that it will be clear where we have erred through naïve procedural lapses and where there are lacunae of an empirical nature. We invite correction of both kinds.

To introduce attempts at the construction of theory by a form of justification appears to be an incipient custom. This introductory chapter will therefore depart but little from the current trend. No new reasons for the importance of theory will be offered, nor does it seem appropriate any longer to reiterate the charge that no one is concerned with theory. Instead, we will face frankly the fact that the construction of a theory requires justification because, insofar as it is general, it necessarily out-reaches empirical findings by far. It even stands in comparative isolation from the limited accumulations of middle range theory. This isolation not only weakens any claim for special attention to any particular effort; it also renders more likely the chance that each effort at the construction of general theory will stand apart from every other. For those who are primarily interested in empirical research, and for whom the guidelines exist in the work of their predecessors, it is easy, perhaps wise, to disregard these fledgling efforts, leaving it to future generations to reinterpret the findings of the political scientist of today in terms of the theory of tomorrow. But there are some research fields in which it is impossible to draw such a comparison between the usefulness of empirical research of limited scope and the construction of general theory. There are also certain fields in which there are no standard studies to be continuously revised, and no established categories to be filled.

These fields can be defined both geographically and substantively. The new nations and the developing nations locate such fields of study in a geographical sense, but the substantive fields emerge out of the new questions that are being asked in these areas, and to an increasing extent, now, in the older stamping grounds of political research. The new questions are concerned with the nature of political change, the effect of economic development on politics, the relationship between administration, culture, and politics, and the connection between ideology, communication, and politics. When faced with the task of having to answer questions of this kind, with regard to the countries of the developing areas, the researcher is doubly perplexed. Not only are there few studies which deal with the problems adequately; usually there are very few studies by political scientists on the country of his interest, or none at all.

The problems of the would-be specialist in one of the developing areas are not mitigated by the relative isolation of the study of ideology from that of political parties, of administration from the study of interest groups, and of law from propaganda and communication. His field is essentially comparative government, but the usual run of work in this subdiscipline has not attempted to integrate the findings of those in the other subdisciplines. The area specialist might, therefore, be the strongest critic of contemporary political science—if he had something better of his own to offer. In most cases he does not have, but because he finds little in the rest of political science to serve his needs, he tends to borrow freely from other disciplines.

Our justification of this attempt at theory construction does not reject the charge that we are not ready for general theory yet. It simply stresses the fact that, without even the flimsiest of general orientations, little can be done in the study of the developing areas. The second point is that this orientation ought preferably to be one that is calculated to render the results of such research intelligible to other political scientists, even if not necessarily to area specialists of other disciplinary persuasions, rather than the other way round. One could expatiate greatly on the untoward results of the development of the new would-be disciplines of area studies, or of "overseasmanship" and the like; suffice it here to say that the exponents of these specialties have rushed in where more cautious political scientists fear to tread. If the more firmly based social science disciplines have been dragged to the brink, that is owing to the urging of newer converts who have felt the inadequacy of these pseudo disciplines during their training, and who now seek the support of their colleagues in rehabilitating the social-scientific, as opposed to the literary or technical, aspect of their field of interest.

Neither area studies nor overseasmanship are without plausible theoretical bases, though these dimly perceived bases are rarely made explicit and are almost never subjected to testing. The first concentrates upon the unique culture of the area and assumes that certain essential elements of that culture will modify the impact of all new forces brought to bear on the geographical area. The second concentrates upon the technical problems of transferring culture, and upon cultural change. The obvious relationship of the two renders it all the more astonishing that they have been pursued quite independently, with the language and literature people following the one, and the public administration people following the other. A most interesting analysis might be made of the reasons for the lack of communication between the exponents of deep cultural understanding and those of the technology of one-way culture transmission, but it is the more difficult to explain why both have tended to treat lightly the potentially systematizing contributions of political science, anthropology, sociology, economics, and psychology. It is obvious, however, that these two new specialties, each in its own way, have attempted to cope with all of the social phenomena of the developing areas without regard to the central core of social science knowledge. Each has been able to throw light on the problems of the developing areas, but each lays down a challenge to the very concept of universal social science disciplines, as well as to the aspiration toward a practical and communicable research methodology. Area studies require that a person steep himself in the "culture" for a long period of time; but overseasmanship requires an endless store of "inside dope." That a person armed only with intelligence, with the central concepts of a discipline, and with a willingness to work, can learn something significant about the developing areas is not explicitly denied, but it is blandly ignored. On the other side, there have been a few attempts to apply concepts (and even sweeping theories) to these countries, attempts made by highly respectable social scientists who have disregarded the possibility that their conceptual apparatus may be culture-bound. On the whole, I think that these courageous formulations have had more relevance than those of the area specialists, though they lack the firmness of similar work done on Western countries. Nevertheless, the fact that preliminary efforts appear to have been fruitful strongly suggests the value of adding the theoretical framework to linguistic and historical training, for field research.

Nor is the issue merely that of asking a significant question. Policy-oriented questions are being asked about these countries with increasing regularity and urgency, but they are not the kind of questions which lead to any cumulative body of knowledge. The same, or similar, questions may be asked every month or every year without making the answers any easier to give or any more accurate on each succeeding occasion, nor, one might add, any more relevant to what is happening in the developing areas. The real issue appears to be the establishment of a framework which will produce problems for basic research, the product of which will, in turn, provide an increasingly firm foundation for the making of policy choices. We assume that such a framework will not differ for each country of application, though we cannot prove this assumption a priori. Moreover, it is a long step from the provision of a framework which may discipline research, and thus avoid the random approach, to demonstrating its adequacy in relating and explaining both dependent research findings and the random accumulation of "facts." Not only do we assume that the framework will be changed while taking that step; we also assume that theory, until it unequivocally experiences its moment of truth, may be determined more by the values of its proponent than by the phenomena which it intends to explain. But it is also the usual case that the broader the theory the less capable are we of devising tests to judge its validity. Generally, the value of a broad framework is limited to the explanation of why certain questions were chosen for research. Without doubt, the very phrasing of the questions depends upon an explicit, or implicit, frame of reference which permits the logical transfer from theoretical statement to operational definition.

Ultimately, however, the postulation of a general theory depends upon the prior assumption that a variety of social phenomena can be understood, not simply in their relationship to one another, but that the relationships among social phenomena are regular enough to be given to logical statement such that a relatively small body of rules can be extrapolated and applied to a relatively large number of cases. As yet, this assumption is a matter of belief, but it is questionable how widely the belief is held. Viewed in this light, the difference between those who are "for" general theory and those who are "against" it is a more or less metaphysical one; and it may be assumed that the more readily empirical data may be related to general theory (or theories), the more widely will definitions of the discipline differ. The most difficult position of all, perhaps, is that of the middle range theorist who fails to make explicit the relevance of his work, beyond the correlation of a number of variables. Still, it must be admitted that the philosophical underpinnings of middle range theorists do not appear to differ from those of people who apply themselves to general theory; moreover, the intellectual interaction between the two has been fruitful. The middle range theorist often has the advantage, in being able to demonstrate empirically some of what he says, but the general theorist attempts to construct the overarching ideological explanation of the relevance of the work of others, or, too often in political science, the explanation of the irrelevance of the work of others.

But these are generalities, and we have some special pleading in mind. The special plea for general theory, with regard to the developing areas, has already been made. This plea was based on the inadequacy of the usual descriptive categories applied to Western political systems, and on the inapplicability of the few theorems relating those categories. Furthermore, the dominant intellectual influences guiding research in the developing areas appear to militate against an eventual *ausgleichung* between the methods and categories of political scientists at home and abroad.

This need may be less laboriously fulfilled by establishing new categories, rather than by devising some sort of general theory. Recently, we have seen such an effort in the work of Almond and the Comparative Politics Committee of the Social Science Research Council.[2] The work of this group has not only borne useful fruit; it has also stimulated many others to do some thinking on these problems. The functional approach that Almond has adopted has resulted in a large forward stride, by means of the device of generalizing what appeared to the theorist to be the broad classes of political activity found in Western political systems. These classes of activity are derived neither logically nor empirically (except as that term may be used in the loosest sense); and so we may ask why these and not others? There is no answer to this question, because it is impossible to restrict the number of analytical categories into which complex social acts may be classified, except through making explicit the metaphysical foundation which permits abstraction of qualities from behavior, and which justifies limiting the scope of interest. It does no good to dogmatize that a classification scheme is unacceptable without a supporting theory, for the former may be the condition of the latter. Nevertheless there can be no special value in trying to use a scheme simply because it exists, and even the group of authors who attempted to apply the Almond scheme judiciously avoided remaining within its limiting framework or, in the case of the "governmental functions," made it clear how insignificant has been the effort to apply the traditional categories of Western political science. The weakness of the scheme is evidenced in the fact that the joint work permitted the suggestion of several descriptive generalizations but few theoretical hypotheses, and these generalizations, too, were not derived from the logical relationship of the "functional" categories. Moreover, the more systematic effort to draw conclusions went off into uncharted territory which the original categories do not include.[3]

---

[2] Esp., G. Almond and J. Coleman, eds., *The Politics of the Developing Areas* (Princeton, 1960).

[3] *Ibid.*, the final chapter by J. Coleman.

These remarks should in no wise be interpreted as asserting the incorrectness of Almond's scheme, for manifestly there is no sense in which a number of loosely connected analytical categories can be "wrong." Until the categories are qualified by empirical definitions which can be correlated with one another, anyone who so desires can apply them, in any political system, as he sees fit. The categories are broad enough, and no doubt are ambiguous enough to be universally applied. This sort of unreasoned applicability does not recommend their use above those categories which seem more relevant to the problems of the particular country under study, and hence do not appear to do more than sensitize the researcher to areas of political activity which he might not notice. Ultimately, however, the scheme will be accepted as a framework only if it lends itself to the analysis of specific systems as well as to problems of comparison, and only if the implicit assumptions of the scheme accord with the theoretical assumptions of individual researchers.

In the latter regard, the most important claim made for the seven-function scheme is that it lends itself to the analysis of whole political systems. Whether there is any powerful reason for dealing with whole political systems, rather than with the presumably more manageable parts of systems, is a matter which we shall have to take up. But at first glance it seems obvious that the very concept of a whole political system presupposes a general theory, whereas a simple grouping of significant categories lies at the other end of the road of scientific development. It is valid enough to start at either end, according to the exponents of general systems theory, but it is probably useful to keep in mind the distinction between the two. Hence, if one attempts to approach the study of politics through the study of whole systems it appears that some conception of the nature of *the* political system is indispensable. And it is in this light that the implicit assumptions of the Almond seven-function theory may be considered.

The real problem turns on the use of the terms system and function. In its broadest sense, a system describes any collection of elements which the observer decides to relate in terms of his own analytical purpose. The system may or may not have a "product" (e.g. integration, adaptation, decisions, stability, etc.). Action going on within the system, or upon it, need not be purposefully directed at maintaining the system or at producing anything. Nor can we assume that changes in any part of the system will necessarily cause changes in all, or in any other parts of the system. As an analytical construct, such a system is a subject of empirical study in order that the interdependence of its components, if any, may be discussed.

A more specific subcategory of the concept system is one for which the existence of "inputs" and "outputs" are postulated. The primary meaning of these terms requires the further distinction between the system and its environment and the notion of boundaries, for the inputs are changes induced from outside the system, and outputs are actions upon the environment. Even this distinction between system and environment is an analytical one, though in the case of living organisms the boundaries appear to be very clearly marked. The "outputs" may be looked upon as the product of the system.

Organic systems, whose tolerance for change is limited, suggest another type of system in which the interaction of the components is easily lent to description as adaptive or directed at maintaining the system in being. There would appear to be systems which simply change but do not go out of existence, except in the most cloudy of analytical senses. A "revolutionary" change in a political system (wherein we must take theoretical account of revolutionary forces, too) is a case in point.

The possible relationship between the action of the components of a system and the continued existence of the system itself leads us to the problem of functionalism. Presumably, activity which is necessary for the maintenance of a system is functional activity. This is the sense in which functionalism is used in sociology and in anthropology. There are differences of emphasis in these two disciplines, however, for sociologists usually speak in wider theoretical terms of types of activity which are functional for any social system, or for the social system, but anthropologists are more concerned with the functionality of particular practices, or customs, for the maintenance of a concrete social or cultural system. A third approach, prevalent to some extent among both sociologists and political scientists, neglects the idea of system but retains the principle of functionality. Merton, who is the stanchest exponent of the later sociological view, uses this idea to classify diverse social activities in terms of their impact on concrete social structures (groups, classes, demographic categories, societies) much as do some anthropologists for cultures, but he admits the possibility of dysfunctionalism, and he insists that functionality must be determined empirically.[4] The political scientists who use this term without reference to a system are usu-

---

[4] R. Merton, *Social Theory and Social Structure* (Glencoe, 1949).

ally comparative government specialists, who deny the utility of formal institutional (constitutional) categories and seek others to describe what governments do or what happens in politics.[5] The polity, or the social sphere of political activity, is often described as a system, but the use of the idea of functionality is not related therewith. Emphasis is, rather, on what is done in a political system, that is on the political functions. That Almond's "system" is clearly of the latter type is borne out by his references to the older concept of political functionalism, as set down in the *Federalist Papers*. The executive, legislative, and judicial functional triad is rejected on empirical, rather than on conceptual, grounds. This functional approach is also described as a behavioral orientation which further substantiates the view here taken that emphasis is upon devising descriptive categories, rather than classifying behavior in terms of the analytically defined or empirically discovered processes of a system, or in terms of the maintenance of the system in more or less unchanged form, or in terms of the impact of behavior on the various structures or components of the system. In fact, the only relevance that the term "system" can have in Almond's framework is with reference to the supposition that a limited number of functions (Sc. types of behavior) comprise the political system. But it is empirically unfeasible, if not logically impossible, to limit the variety of categories into which such behavior may be classified without the aid of the analytical limitations and synthetic facilities of a priori theory. It is for this reason that Almond's "seven-function system" (really neither functionalist nor a system), despite its advance over institutional description, may be praised as interesting or perceptive, without compelling further attention. It will be useful, indeed, to those seeking a better way to define the problems they want to study, but it cannot serve as a foundation for the study of whole political systems. The relative lack of use of the seven categories by Coleman, in the last chapter of their joint book, is a warning in this regard. In order to study whole systems we need a statement of what the political system is, even if unaccompanied by an elaborate set of descriptive categories. Hence our second special plea is that general theory will facilitate the postulation of comparative categories for widely divergent systems, that without such theory any proposed arrangement of categories is in danger of remaining logically unacceptable or

---

[5] Functionalism, as a comparative method in political science, also refers to institutional comparisons, as opposed to the "country by country" approach.

incommunicable (it will not be understood), and that without general theory it is impossible to approach the study of whole political systems.

The theoretical justification for the study of whole political systems is by no means self-evident nor unequivocal. The strongest argument we have is, in fact, a negative one. It is widely agreed that social phenomena are extremely complex subjects of study given ultimately, perhaps, to reduction to the interaction of organic molecules. The problems involved in moving from the chemical to the biological to the physiological to the psychological and on to mass sociological phenomena staggers the imagination, but it also sustains arguments which exclude complex social questions from attempts at scientific treatment. The negative argument which is put forward by exponents of general systems theory is that the very difficulty involved in seeking to reach the smallest irreducible element of social behavior compels us to seek uniformities of scientific weight at some higher level of complexity. The optimum level of complexity is apparently a matter of choice, for there is no a priori method of distinguishing subsystem from system, and system from a more complex combination of systems. Hence the components of a system are designated in a fairly arbitrary fashion, but the usefulness of any such designation depends upon what can be said about the relationship between those components.

As we have suggested, it is insufficient to use the term political system instead of state, country, government, or politics, without further specification, and we intend to be more specific. It may well be that the particular definition of a whole system which will be used in this work is narrower than that suggested by the wide usage which this term enjoys, but that would appear to be the inevitable result of designating any finite number of system components. Yet this limitation is necessary if we are to describe the things that go on "inside" the system (i.e. the way in which components are interrelated) as well as the effect of environment on the system.

In this regard it may be well to refer to three recent attempts to deal with uniformities to be found among whole systems.[6] In

<hr>

[6] Coleman, *op. cit.*; S. Lipset, "Some Social Requisites of Democracy: Economic Development and Legitimacy," *American Political Science Review*, LIII/1 (March, 1959); and K. Deutsch, "Toward an Inventory of Basic Trends and Patterns in Comparative and International Politics," *American Political Science Review*, LIV/1 (March, 1960).

two of these, no attempt has been made to define the political system, while the third implies the "seven-function" system which has been briefly commented on earlier. Leaving aside the question of whether the statistical data used in these comparisons are really comparable, it is apparent that such data refer to elements outside of the political system itself (by any definition), for the "working" of the systems concerned was correlated therewith. The descriptions of the systems themselves, and even of important parts of these systems such as legitimacy or interest group autonomy or competitiveness, were taken for granted. The suggestiveness of all three efforts is beyond question great, but they lead us rather quickly to ask for a theory which will more clearly indicate the connection between particular environmental conditions and the behavior of particular components of the political system. They also lead us to question whether the system itself must always be seen as the dependent variable, in relation to every area covered by the statistical questionnaires sent out by various United Nations organizations. If regularities are found, then the reply might be "who cares?" But they have not been found, or else they are based on such broad generalizations about whole groups of systems as to require some greater precision in describing whole systems and classifying them. Before we can assert the correlation of two factors we must have more or less good information about the behavior of both of them. If economic development is to become the independent variable par excellence, then we must seek at least equally reliable information about dependent political changes.

The mere existence of this data on economic development, demographic change, and communications points to some of the uses to which similar information on political behavior might be put, as is attested by the attraction of these three eminent scholars to such examination. Their efforts encourage us to seek some way of dealing with whole political systems, even as the pressure of events and the existing pattern of international relations compel us to try to understand the "maker" of foreign policy. Foreign policy is made in the name of the state, and while not all political behavior is directed at international ends, the study of foreign policy appears to pose the most comprehensive questions of all. That is, it suggests that there are a group of factors which must be considered together, before any understanding can be achieved. The word "understanding" is used advisedly, for the whole of the rethinking going on in the field of comparative government is based on the feeling that we have not been comparing the same kind of things, that is, components which are functionally diverse. Before we can compare phenomena of the same class we must first make certain qualitative judgments about the relevance of observed phenomena to the whole system. First, let us understand the system as a whole if we can, and thus perhaps we can weigh the import of those factors which are given to empirical measurement. It is from this point of view that we have attempted to set down a broad statement of approach to the study of whole systems that is both spare and simple, but that appears to permit the communication of a qualitative understanding gained during field observation.

Our preference for analysis of whole political systems compels us to seek some means of categorizing not only the component parts of the political system but types of systems as well. Obviously the distinguishing factor among diverse systems will be the differential operation of the various components, dependent in turn upon the differences in the structures upon which the functional components depend. But before elaborating our conception of these structures and functions, it seems appropriate to leap ahead and assert that in concrete political systems structures and functions may exhibit a greater or lesser degree of unity or integration. The concept of integration suggests parallels with the integration of the action system or with that of a cultural system, perhaps even that of the personality. The essential meaning behind these applications of the term is the same: the integration of thought and action, of ideal and practice, of the legitimate and the actual. This state of integration suggests a kind of utopia, except that it admits the possibility of many utopias, without openly judging between them. Integration in these senses is the goal of social and psychological engineering, its definition and measurement is the goal of social science. If ethics and politics are a single discipline, a single universe of intellectual discourse, then the comparative study of politics is as surely based on the recognition not only of this intimate relationship but also on the discernible experience of diverse ethical systems standing in juxtaposition to diverse patterns of political behavior. The problem of the integration of ethics and politics is a moral one, but it also depends upon our ability to perceive relationships between philosophical abstractions and concrete human acts.

Even if we assume the possibility of finding parallels between the ideal mental constructs of a just social order and the multifaceted "reality" of human acts, can we validly assert that a body of ideas is not only logically but philosophically consistent, that a bundle of repeated acts signifies a comprehensible and explainable unity, and, most difficult of all, that there can be a patterned relationship between that body of ideas and that bundle of acts? The problem is, again, one of the validity of abstract classification. It is the observer who imposes a unity on the discrete objects which he perceives or understands. In this manner we assert that there is a unity between the prevailing beliefs about what is the legitimate source of authority and the behavior of those adhering to such beliefs. This unity goes beyond the conscious attempts of individuals to integrate their beliefs and their behavior. Belief and behavior are not simply mutually interdependent variables, but each is part of complex processes that extend beyond the individual, beyond his life span, and in part even beyond the sphere of social relations. The two disciplines of philosophy and the sociology of ideas do not really interpenetrate; they set boundaries for one another, and in so doing indicate the limits upon the integration of belief and behavior. These limits, in turn, are the source of the ever present tension which permeates all relations among rational human beings. But if we are allowed to hold that we perceive the unity of a body of ideas, on the one hand, and on the other the unity of a bundle of acts, taking neither as necessarily prior, may we not similarly seek out the concrete situations in which both unities exist among the same people? Should we find this coexistence of unities, we would be able to make limited statements about the consistent configuration of beliefs and political behavior, and insofar as configurations of this type exist over time we might speak of an equilibrium. In their generality, beliefs and political behavior comprise an analytical system which is, by definition, always in equilibrium. But when we refer to specific beliefs and specific behaviors in the perceptible world of continuous change, we must focus our attention on degrees of malintegration of ideas, of political behavior, and of each with the other.

Obviously, in human affairs there is constant conscious effort to bring about greater integration, as that desideratum may be perceived by those concerned, but we necessarily discern only greater or lesser degrees of integration upon each discrete observation. We are faced with arrangements which are never exactly the same and never precisely repeated in another time and place. How is comparison possible, among a multitude of unique systems composed of beliefs and acts? The difficulty of the task is not to be minimized, and our solution is but a frail device. Starting with the assumption that beliefs about the legitimacy of social order are of the same mental stuff as are our analytical abstractions of behavior, and that they are more amenable to rational understanding than our limited perception of behavior, we hold it reasonable to construct abstract models (as few as may be possible, for reasons of economy) of static configurations of beliefs and acts against which concrete systems may be compared. Thus we characterize system types by their dominant conceptions of legitimacy, but bearing in mind that beliefs and acts are essentially different, and not logically transferable to one another, we assume a certain degree of malintegration. How much malintegration? Of what sort? For answers to these questions we cannot, obviously, have recourse to utopian derivations from political philosophies, which do not provide for the regularity of their own inapplicability to human affairs; instead, we must attempt to construct these out of historical systems which have asserted the legitimacy of one or another or our model belief systems (in approximation, of course).

In Iran, as we shall see, there are several different concepts of legitimacy coexisting in a single system, and there are several different types of political behavior apparent to the observer. Ideological confusion leads to the exploration of a variety of political strategies, so that the expected malintegration of the system is compounded. Moreover, for the participant in the system, whose perception is both physically and mentally limited, there may be very little or no relationship between legitimacy and political behavior. This is the phenomenon of political alienation.

These two basic elements of the political system are not merely juxtaposed in the mind of the contemporary Iranian (or American); they interact with one another. Their interaction is not at the level of mutual control. It is a partial and discontinuous interaction in which only certain types of behavior specifically call forth ideologically malintegrative consequences, or, indeed, formal reaffirmations of existing legitimacy. It is these types of behavior, organized and institutionalized in political processes, challenging or maintaining the legitimacy of an existing distribution of values, which comprise for us the political system. Politically invisible changes are important and relevant, but they are a part of the environment of the system, just as the rising cost of living in Iran is environmental and a teacher's strike systemic. Even a silent, cautious, inner rejection of the system by an alienated clerk is systemic, while his inability to find a better paying job is environmental. Let us try, then, to describe in more specific terms the components of our system and to see how it may be possible to distinguish systemic from environmental factors. We start with a basic definition.

The study of politics is the study of the legitimization of social power. Power is a relative concept, existing only in situations involving social interaction.[7] It is impossible to separate the concept of social power from that of even the most routine of social interactions. The impact which the overt behavior of any single individual has upon the behavior of any other single individual can be seen, depending upon one's standpoint, as a power relationship as well as a social relationship. The fact that the behavior of an individual is at least in part causally affected by the behavior, past, present or anticipated, of other individuals or groups or institutions is the foundation of this most elementary conception of power.

It will be readily noticed that this description of the elementary power situation owes much to the basic component of the theory of the action system.[8] There, however, the system is held together by the hypothesis that the behavior of the individuals concerned conforms, within limits, to their respective expectations, expectations which have been learned in a complicated and lengthy socialization process. This unit of social interaction has, therefore, an element of mutuality and equilibration in it. For the theory of the social system, the question of whether the respective responses are qualitatively and quantitatively equal is relatively unimportant, but for political science this difference is crucial, since it determines the power relationship between the two actors.

Not all kinds of social power are of interest to the political scientist, which is to say that not all kinds of social power are kinds of political power. Only that social power which has relevance to the action of persons in governmental roles is political power. In the case of a highly developed society, it is not difficult to discern which is and which is not a governmental role. Reference here is to a group of institutions (or institutionalized roles) that are often generally described in a constitutional document, and to any other subordinate institutions established through their agency. In underdeveloped or primitive societies, where the division of labor or role specification has not reached an advanced

---

[7] See C. J. Friedrich, *Constitutional Government and Democracy* (rev. ed.; Boston, 1950).

[8] T. Parsons and E. A. Shils, *Toward a General Theory of Action* (Cambridge, 1951).

level, it is necessary to define governmental roles in terms of the actual functions performed by persons, either in their diffuse capacities as individuals or in one of their special capacities. These functions are usually the making or interpretation of law, the application of law, and the enforcement of law.[9] Interpretation of law is here understood to comprehend the equivalent of a legislative process, wherever the law is presumed to have come from some higher source; both interpretation and application, however, can refer to adjudication and administrative regulation. It is recognized that these functions may have an ultimately decisive effect upon the allocation of authority, security, wealth, and prestige within a society.[10] Perhaps it may also be appropriate to see in the action of government the definition of the social and territorial limits of the polity.

We have characterized political power by its potential effect on what David Easton has called the authoritative allocation of values, without at the same time restricting the type of behavior itself.[11] The effect of the power relationship is of greater concern than its actual observable content. But in taking this position we do not intend to restrict political behavior to such obvious, but often unfruitful, categories such as voting, making speeches, or signing petitions. There is a far more subtle level of social relationships at each level of group association or institutional organization which will determine the kaleidoscopic shifts of influence, control, inhibition, and support. This is the stuff of social psychology, or reference group behavior, of the theory of socialization, and of the impact of primordial sentiments.[12] It is not easy to classify all of the various types of relationships that are relevant here. In fact, a relationship of any kind may be significant, but in each culture and each system those kinds which are of greatest significance will stand out. Furthermore, there will be different kinds of relationships which are more significant than others, in regard to the allocation of certain values. Harold Lasswell has constructed an admirable theoretical statement of this feature of power, in his distinction between base values and scope values, and Robert Dahl has applied a similar insight in demonstrating

---

[9] Almond and Coleman, *op. cit.*, p. 17.

[10] In the sense of Lasswell's *Politics: Who Gets What, When, How* (1936).

[11] D. Easton, *The Political System* (New York, 1953).

[12] E. Shils, "Primordial, Personal, Sacred, and Civil Ties," *The British Journal of Sociology*, June, 1957.

that the attribution of power to an individual has reference to a specific kind of value, rather than to all values at all times.[13] In other words, power is not really an attribute, except insofar as it is a continuous reassertion of a relationship between persons who are differently situated with regard to personality, skills, status, and roles, within a culture which values these things differently.

There are difficulties in Lasswell's approach, resulting from his attribution of power to persons controlling certain base values and his tendency to fall into the language of quantification. These difficulties are not essential, however, if we bear in mind that the attribution is a logical consequence of the abstract classification of power types and is but a shorthand method for describing only certain characteristics of certain real persons. It is a logical correlate of discourse in terms of social classes, roles, and occupational groups. This is a point to which we shall return. Quantification may similarly be discussed if it is kept within the logical bounds of a relational and situational frame of reference, which we shall presently attempt to do. What concerns us here, however, is to point out, if briefly, the importance of the cultural context.

Taking Iran as our example, we note that the specificity which Lasswell sought is not applicable to all systems. In Iran, ascriptive status is more important than acquired skill or achievement. Furthermore, ascriptive status has a wider application in terms of scope values than is implied by Lasswell's one-to-one scheme. The grouping of the Parsonian pattern-variables comes immediately to mind, as an elaboration of this point.[14] In Iran, the important base values appear to be age, courage, agnatic relationship, eloquence, apparent shrewdness, and landed wealth. Here, to a far larger extent than in the industrialized democracies, we find Persians attributing power to individuals, not only as a consequence of ascribed status but also as a function of what is loosely known as personality. Just what enters into this description is a fine subject for empirical study, and we have simply attempted our own interpretation, in listing what appear to be the most significant base values.

Let us go back to the problem of the qualitative-quantitative aspect of the respective responses of the participants in our elementary power relationship. Remembering that this relationship is significant only insofar as it bears upon those in governmental roles, the qualitative aspect resolves itself into two modes, in that

---

[13] R. Dahl, "The Concept of Power," *Behavioral Science*, II (July, 1957).
[14] T. Parsons, *The Social System* (Glencoe, 1951).

its impact is either direct or indirect. If indirect, we shall call the resultant situation simply part of the environment of the political system. The resultant, having a direct impact on government, may be further differentiated in terms of whether the two actors (*a*) have combined forces for a common goal, or (*b*) have coöperated for complementary goals, or (*c*) have hindered one another in pursuit of situationally conflicting goals, or finally (*d*) have opposed one another in pursuit of some mutually exclusive goal. The quantitative aspect has several modes, involving time, intensity, and number of objectives, but above all it concerns the question of whose power is greater. Superiority in such a power relationship must be analyzed in terms of the four possible qualitative variations of the resultant having a direct impact on government. Hence, that individual has superior power (*a*) who directs more of the action of the two toward the common goal, or (*b*) whose particular goal is the one sought by both in cases of complementarity, or (*c, d*) who most effectively hinders, opposes, or inhibits the action of the other. It is possible also to conceive of a case where the complementarity of goals in such that the goal of one has no impact on government, or has only an indirect effect. In such a case, the other, whose goal is directly related to government, is the more significant, but the relationship may be understood in the same manner as above. A similar case would be that in which the one derived some direct affective benefit from coöperation with the other. Many more cases could be elaborated, but enough have been presented to illustrate (1) the importance of the content of social interaction (as opposed to its symmetrical character) for political science, and (2) that this content is relational and situational.

Thus far, we have argued the importance of attempting to analyze whole systems; we have asserted the validity of treating systems as more or less integrated units, in terms of their dominant pattern of legitimacy; and after establishing the importance of the logical dichotomy between belief and political behavior, we have sought to understand the nature of the political act in its most elementary and least structured form. Our problem is now to work back from the elementary power relationship to the global concept of the political system. We seek the nexus between power and legitimacy, but as we move on we will also be marking out the components of the system, that is, the sort of things which ought to concern anyone engaged in an analysis of a whole political system.

As we attempt to work our logical way from elementary

power relationships up to the characterization of a whole system, it should be borne in mind that power relationships do include both cultural and moral valuations (if the two are separable) though not necessarily of the order of the ideas which legitimize the political system as a whole. One of our interviewees who abruptly interrupted our conversation on democracy to curse and strike his servant for a purported affront to our dignities was obviously not aware of the contradiction between his views on the whole polity and his management of his household. It is difficult, even if warranted in all situations, to make all of one's personal relations accord with one's political ideas, because of the disparity between the dynamic personal relationship and the legally defined formal political relationships which are the subject of legitimizing doctrine. The Persian businessman who so extravagantly flatters the bureaucrat or subtly mentions his family connections may not realize how his behavior conflicts with the spirit of the constitution of Iran or the spirit of Islamic law. He is doing what he has learned is the right thing. Few are those of such vision, or who hold such strong civil sentiments, that they can see the relationship between everyday acts and political arrangements or, seeing them, are disposed to make them accord. At any rate, moral considerations and notions of political legitimacy are related, but they are not the same thing and are not of the same analytical order. Nevertheless, just as the exercise of nonlegitimate power must tax the capacity of a political system, so will behavior of the same order, though it may not be immediately recognizable as a demand upon government, appear to vaguely contradict the legitimacy of the political system itself. Such indeed, is the major theme of this study, and it reflects the manner in which both political pessimism and confusion about the source of legitimacy of the present regime in Iran are reinforced by the daily dealings of the members of the partially "modernized" urban lower middle and intellectual classes.

Having distinguished the moral aspect of elementary power relationships from the concept of the legitimacy of the whole system, and having, in turn, re-related the two dynamically, rather than philosophically, we have reaffirmed the need to find some analytical means of moving from the smallest unit of the political system to its largest and most comprehensive characterization. To put the matter in terms of the field researcher's most vivid experiences, if he is fortunate he will authentically grasp the nature of personal relationships and note, in Iran, their extreme ambiguity outside of the family itself. He will also have read about political instability, near revolution, and occasional resort to violence. His task of understanding politics in Iran is to draw the lines of logical interdependence between these two.

It is a manifestly impractical research strategy, however, to attempt to piece together the literally millions of changing personal relations that comprise the political system. Nevertheless, as Douglas Ashford has so sensibly pointed out, everybody is part of the political system, even the inarticulate peasant or tribesman, if only by virtue of his just being there.[15] But even the physical scientist who, at least until recently, sought to isolate the irreducibly smallest unit and to discover its characteristics, in order to analyze more complex arrangements, does not treat each electron individually. Analytically, an electron or a molecule of air or a drop of Omar Khayyam's wine are all electrons, all molecules of air, all drops of wine, under the same conditions. When we speak of our units of analysis in these terms we are guilty of some ellipsis, but we joyfully do such violence to the individual in order to better grasp his problem of living in civil society.

There are really two somewhat disparate ways of treating large numbers of personal relationships as constant and theoretically manipulable units. The concept which corresponds to the first of these is called the class, and it describes a number of relationships which are configuratively identical. The second concept is the group, which refers to relationships that are themselves diverse but that stand in a fairly constant total configuration.

This is not the place to enter into a prolonged consideration of all the things that class can mean; for our own interests, there are but three aspects of the general concept that are most relevant. Leaving finer distinctions aside, class can refer to any collection of persons having some single common characteristic, or it can refer to persons having certain characteristics in sufficient measure to objectively justify the application to them of a commonly accepted idea of social class. The first type of class is so broad that it comprehends the second, as well as what are known as "categoric" groups or "demographic" groups, interest associations, and institutional groups such as the military, the bureaucracy, or the clergy. The use of the second concept depends upon first agreeing upon the nature of a social class, in theory, or devising an empirical definition thereof. The third aspect of the general concept, and the most important here, is that in attempting an

---

[15] D. Ashford, *Political Change in Morocco* (Princeton, 1961), p. 5.

economical description of power relationships in a political system we are free to choose between classifying persons in terms of types of power relationships and attempting to discover the types of power relationships which appear most frequently among those who are part of an "objective" social class. In our description of classes in Iran we have chosen the latter for the following reasons:

1. to render that part of our analysis more or less parallel to our discussion of organized groups by maintaining our focus on real structures of power relationships, rather than abstracting certain aspects of these;

2. to economize, as well as remain within reach of, the concrete, since any culturally rooted concept of class involves a collection of relational potentialities (in Lasswell's terminology, a number of base values); and

3. to retain in our description of power structure some relevance to ideologies and political programs starting from assumptions about social stratification.

The concept of social class, in its particular cultural form, is, therefore, most useful as a descriptive category, but it cannot comprehend all significant social differentia. In our description of social power structures in Iran, we have not been restricted to classes but have also included categoric groups, as well as variously organized primary, secondary, and party groups. Categoric groups come close to fulfilling the loose requirements of our first alternative definition of persons characterized by having identical base values, regardless of "objective" class membership. But in what sense do common language, common racial origin, common sex, common age level, common geographical location, common religion, even common occupation, such as farming, form a power base? There are two ways in which we can justify using categoric groups in the manner of social classes and interest groups, even if not in a precisely parallel manner. The first justification accepts certain ideologies at face value and agrees that for certain purposes all the members of a category have a single interest and are capable of working together to satisfy that interest. The second would rather see those categoric groups in a passive sense, as limiting the formation of other groups or limiting the construction of an ideological consensus which does violence to the "selfhood," or primordial sentiments, of persons so categorized. It will be noted that the dividing line between categoric groups and social classes is not a sharp one, nor need it be. In our own treatment of power structures in Iran we have used all the categories that seemed relevant to the fullest description of the kinds of power and existing concrete power structures in that country. We have used demographic groups, have referred to contemporary notions of social stratification, and have attempted to construct a stratification scheme which combines occupation, education, institutional affiliation, and prevalent ideas of social class in Iran.

The second way of treating large numbers of personal relationships, that of the organized group, is the more significant in Western industrialized political systems and is characteristically of less importance the more traditional the political system. Nevertheless, a great deal of attention has been paid to this aspect of power structure in Iran, for two reasons. The first is that in an essentially traditional system such as Iran a fairly complete picture can be given; and the second is that, starting from a fairly complete description, it will be possible to gauge the changes which may occur in the future.

The important difference between organized groups and classes is that all the members of the group do not control identical base values, do not have identical interests, are not continuous members, and, in contradistinction to certain demographic categories, such as tribesmen or villagers, may have other affiliations. While these limitations appear to render the group less important to the resolution of political problems, the formal continuity and legitimacy of the group as a political actor actually renders the group a more significant category than the class. This significance is somewhat vitiated in Iran because, as we shall see, secondary interest associations are often not continuous in their action and often are not legitimate or are of doubtful legitimacy. Furthermore, they are frequently subordinated to the interests of traditional leaders, and their techniques are informed by the dominance of cliques (that is, primary groups) and their peculiar modes of decision making in Iran. The result is that secondary interest associations, institutional groups, and even political parties are best understood as the borrowed institutional settings or arenas in which primary group politics and parapolitical conflicts are worked out.[16] In our description of these groups we have tried to maintain this sort of emphasis, but the elaboration of prevalent political techniques is dealt with more directly in the discussion of the political processes or the dynamics of the Iranian political system. Because we have been concerned with Iran as a transi-

---

[16] The term "parapolitical," in its present use, is borrowed from D. Easton.

tional system, the section on the bureaucracy and the military have been treated separately from the rest, and along with the cabinet, in order to stress their role in the modernization of Iran. Nevertheless, even in this special treatment of what we have called the machinery of rationalization an attempt has been made to describe its traditional aspects.

These considerations compel us to face up to the important distinction between the power relationships within groups and those between groups, and thus warrant a more formal statement thereof.

In most political systems, power relationships which have a significant impact on government are those of groups rather than individuals. Nevertheless, an analytical framework similar to that employed above can be applied to the interaction of groups with persons, and groups with other groups. Regardless of whether a group is a permanent hierarchically organized collectivity or a temporary and loose collection of persons, it will be found to be made up of a number of power relationships, when seen from the point of view of political goal orientation. Insofar as any group engages in purposeful action having an effect upon government, all the primary relationships within that group will have a political power dimension. The combined resultant of these relationships may be called a power structure, and that structure will have a profound effect upon the nature and efficiency of the group's political action.

The most difficult factor in theoretical extrapolation from individual to group behavior is the problem of motivation and its intimate connection with personality. We have not taken up this problem, in discussing the elementary power relationship. Insofar as we have found the basic element of power in the resultant of a unit of interaction, motivation and personality are relevant only as anterior causes. Proximate causes are to be found in the overt behavior of the actors themselves. If we are concerned with a continuing power relationship involving many persons, or persons having critical decision-making roles, motivation and personality become important variables affecting group solidarity and rational decision making. (Rational decision making is here taken as aimed at the maximization of authority, security, wealth, or prestige for the individual, the group, or the whole society, depending upon the individual's solution of the role conflict in which he happens to find himself.) However, the relationship between group formation, aggregation, and the diverse motivations of group members depends partly upon such structural factors as the general level of education, cultural patterns, social class, and role patterns. Rational decision making at the politically critical level is similarly dependent upon organizational structure and the degree to which an achievement, as opposed to an ascriptive pattern, is institutionalized in the important sense that the most powerful group to which the individual is attached will or will not long tolerate either irrationality or the subordination of its interests to those of a smaller group or to those of the individual, in a decision-making position.

But levels of political participation, awareness of interest, group solidarity, and the full exploitation of opportunities for influencing governmental decisions (access) depend also on the nature of the issue in dispute, on the scope of the application of the decision, and on the political techniques employed by political leaders. Rational decision making, too, depends upon factors such as the limits of access and the authenticity or completeness of information. Even these explanations fail to account for political participation which is primarily based upon displaced affective motivation.

Insofar as leadership is concerned, this objection is not very serious, because of the controlling factor of group organization and the balancing of interests of those who "create" the leader. The objection becomes more serious where the political system is unstable and where large numbers of people are detaching themselves from traditional values and may attach themselves to a charismatic leader.[17] Such situations are transitory almost by definition, and until institutionalized may be regarded as generalized attacks on the legitimacy of the social and political systems. Consequently, they may be described as unstable states of other systems, or as the equivalent of conditions of low awareness and limited information, once the successors of the charismatic leader have achieved legitimacy. It should be remembered, however, that the preëxisting structure of power relationships is never entirely destroyed in such a transition, even though the behavior of the truly charismatic leader is not directly dependent upon the organization and control of the group.[18]

The problem of rank and file participation which is affectively

---

[17] For the application of this "Weberian" term, see D. Apter, *The Gold Coast in Transition* (Princeton, 1955); and D. Rustow, *Politics and Westernization* (Princeton, 1956).

[18] This use of the term "charismatic leadership" differs from that of E. Shils, "Concentration and Dispersion of Charisma . . ." *World Politics*, XI/1 (October, 1958).

motivated is relevant to an explanation of why certain individuals accept the roles of party or organization militants. Otherwise, this problem is reducible to (*a*) elementary power relationships, (*b*) socialization of reference group orientation, or (*c*) cultural patterns involving a high level of "joining" and political action.

Two conclusions emerge from this brief discussion. The first is that the power structure of politically oriented groups is not merely the sum of a random collection of elementary power relationships. The elementary power relationship, as herein described, is not controlled by its time dimension, and the essential character of a group lies in the very persistence of the power relationships which it connotes. This persistence arises not only from the immediate resultant of social interaction, but also from learned interests, reference group identifications, education, and so on, and also from the nature of the issue posed to the government. The second conclusion is that the members of a group are variously motivated and that not all the causes of membership and coöperation are to be found in intragroup power relationships, nor even in the action undertaken by the group. The group is neither a constant nor is it entirely comprehensive. Social groups do not comprehend all of the activities of their members, and individual members may "belong" to more than one group. Therefore, the internal power relationships of any concrete group will have only a limited qualitative-quantitative relevance of the kind described. However, in any group which persists over a period of time there is a strong tendency toward the formation of a stable hierarchy, toward the institutionalization of a number of leadership, administrative, and communication roles, and toward the emergence of a concrete oligarchical leadership of real persons. This sort of institutionalization, perhaps coupled with policy continuity, is the key to the connection between power structure and group persistence, despite membership turnover.

To attempt to flesh out all of the relevant factors elaborated with examples from Iran would be to anticipate what will follow in succeeding chapters. Our principal point here has been to indicate the general limits on the utility of the concept of the organized group as a political phenomenon and to suggest the cultural and situational determinants of its disparate utility in particular systems. We have also attempted to justify using this higher level of political generalization, despite our understanding of the political in terms of the individual. It may still be useful to suggest, even in only a preliminary fashion, that in Iran the structural factors of general level of education, cultural patterns, class structure, and role patterns all militate against the formation of many functionally specific groups and against even moderate measures of control by members of the group over their leaders. Similarly, political participation, awareness of interest, and group solidarity outside of the traditional group are all low, and access is greatly restricted. This condition accords with the relative narrowness of interest in issues placed before government, the extremely limited scope of most governmental decisions, and the preference for, and greater efficiency of, personal and particularistic political techniques. In general, the system is characterized by an absence of authentic information at all levels and by a great profusion of rumor among politically aware groups that are deprived of access. The inability of the present group arrangement to care for the political needs of those who identify themselves in terms of secondary interest associations does, of course, prepare the ground for more diffuse self-conceptions which reject the whole system and are amenable to charismatic leadership of even a low quality.

In moving from the power relationships within groups to those between groups, which themselves vary along the scales of organization, solidarity, and comprehensiveness, we may return to a previously omitted special case of the elementary power relationship for some elucidation. It will be remembered that the quantitative aspect of the elementary relationship was defined very much in terms of the four possible variations of the qualitative aspect. These four logical possibilities were all derived from the identification of the elementary power relationship with an interaction situation. There seems to be no relevance between this scheme and the quantitative aspect of the power relationship of two persons who do not interact with one another. The answer to this objection will have an important bearing on the problem of intergroup power relationships.

If we assume, in this special case, that we are concerned with two individuals, neither of whom holds a critical position, and for whom political interaction is highly unlikely, then the power relationship between the two is insignificant, even if the use of the term here has a remotely meaningful sense. If, however, we are comparing the power relationships of John Smith with those of Sam Brown, rather than the relationships between these two, then we are concerned with the power structure of two social clusters which may or may not include one or more variably organized groups. This circumstance involves only a static power comparison which may be useful in classification. We may say that what we are comparing are the respective facilities of two persons for the maximization of political value. When, however, we move to comparisons of the power of groups or persons holding critical positions, we discover a dynamic relationship of great importance to a concrete power system. Even when we are concerned with groups which do not seem to be either coöperating or in conflict, we actually have a relational situation, because the political values which each seeks will be either compatible or incompatible with those sought by the other. The possible incompatibility of these values arises from their limited availability in any concrete system. If the goals of the two groups are compatible, then their relationship is complementary, as are their political activities. It is this complementarity, or conflict, which makes their activities relational; that is, they are engaged in more or less indirect interaction. The power of these groups is therefore the resultant of this interaction, which may be integrated by other groups or by the government in a concrete system. Similarly, the power relation of the two individuals who are not directly interacting in our special case, or who do not seem to be either coöperating or in conflict, can be defined with respect to the same limitation in the availability of political values. But except in the case of a very small polity, this relationship is insignificant. It follows, then, that every individual and group engaging in purposeful action aimed at the maximization of political value is interacting with all others in a single power system, the limits of which are defined by a government.

It will be noted that we have glided from the explanation of power as a resultant of direct interaction, and have intruded the idea of relative ability to elicit gratifications from a government. This ability is partly dependent upon respective structures of power, but it is not merely the resultant of the interaction of these structures, for the desired response is not that of the actors in conflict, but of the government. It is, moreover, possible to imagine that, if left to their own devices, the two groups in conflict might resolve their differences in a manner other than that chosen by the government. In order to explain this phenomenon we must either have recourse to an explanation of power as ability to move a government, or we must regard the action of government as a mechanism for the resolution of complex interaction sequences which might result in the cessation of all interaction between the groups concerned—or which might result in a solution by violence. Governmental action is not always required to resolve differences between groups or group leaders, and in some cases it merely confirms the existing power relationships. That is, we may find systems in which direct bargaining or direct dominance-submission relationships exist, along with those in which the government acts to resolve the issues according to established rules. In the last instance, the power relationship is conventionalized, but it is at bottom cognate to the kind of power relationship described earlier. The conventionalization of a power relationship involves accepting power to move a government as the equivalent of power to control the behavior of the opposing group, or even of the whole society, at least for a time. Without such conventions it would be impossible to include geographically distant groups in a single system, or at least to maintain a high centralization of planning and administration. In this regard it is significant to note that where decentralization prevails, direct bargaining is more frequently found. In any case, in setting limits to the system, the government also defines the limits of available value and thus sets the conditions under which noncompetitive striving of diversely interested groups is posed as a political issue.

It is often extremely difficult to determine the real power relationship of indirectly interacting groups; thus the development of an adequate classificatory system is necessary, for purposes of comparison. Furthermore, in the absence of a comprehensive set of rules for the dynamic working of a power system, we shall have to be satisfied with descriptions of power structure and power facilities. Power facilities must be understood in terms of conventional, normal, and theoretically universal types of human motivation and in terms of institutionalized role patterns having a cultural-value dimension. The description of the power structure of a particular group is a feasible if difficult task, and social scientists have been developing a catalog of useful descriptive terms, as well as a number of empirical generalizations relating to the dynamic character of such structures. Working from these foundations, it should be possible to arrive at reasonable approximations of dynamic power relationships throughout the system. It must be stressed, however, that the comparative, rather than relational, analysis of power can be meaningful only insofar as it may be referred to the dynamic relational framework. Power is a relationship, but power facilities and intragroup power structure are no more than inferences about power relationships. It is essentially this kind of comparative analysis of power structure in Iran that we have delineated in chapter four of the present study.

What we have discussed thus far is not a complete description of a power system that is at the same time a political system.

The interaction patterns of diverse groups, in a concrete political system, are not nearly so fluid as might be indicated by the foregoing. Though it is extremely difficult to determine the power relationships of all the elements in the system, certain relationships are more or less known and permanent, and others may be evidenced from time to time, in specific events. Even as in instances of elementary social interaction and more complex forms of association, so in intergroup relations, power relationships tend to become institutionalized. The institutionalization of such power relationships is most importantly accomplished by what we ordinarily call government. The structure, personnel, and legal procedures of what are usually known as governmental institutions lend permanence to certain aspects of the existing pattern of power relationships in any polity. This permanence, or institutionalization, is what we shall call legitimization.

The function of government, then, is the legitimization of power in a political system, and the limits of such a system are set by the effective performance of this function. A power relationship which one seeks to make permanent through the action of a government is a political power relationship, the classification of the actions which may lead to such legitimizations being a classification of the political processes and techniques prevalent in any concrete system.

This definition contains some difficulties. There is the question of whether a government is the only legitimizing institution. In the sociological sense this is not true. Certainly power relationships are institutionalized in the family and the tribe, in a business firm and in a charitable association, in a professional association and a church, in a labor union and a political party. It is also true that much of the allocation of authority, security, wealth, and prestige in a society is accomplished through the interaction of these groups. However, none of these power relationships have legitimacy throughout the whole political society, unless so recognized by the government. Strictly speaking, in a highly developed polity having a justiciable constitution, every power relationship is theoretically illegitimate except those recognized by law. Thus we have two kinds of power in our political system, one legitimate and one nonlegitimate. Legitimate power may further be analyzed in terms of whether the form of its legitimization accords with its objective character. Nonlegitimate power may be subdivided into that which has no bearing on legitimated power or the working of government; that which has an indirect bearing, in the sense that it tends to widen the gap between real and legitimate power; and that which has a direct bearing, in the sense that it seeks legitimization in order to alter a nonlegitimate relationship or to bring the form of a particular legitimization into closer conformity with the real relationship. Nonlegitimate relationships having only an indirect bearing on government are environmental factors. The reason why a power relationship that has been legitimized may differ from the legal statement thereof is that the real power relationship is a dynamic one and may have diffuse or nonmeasurable aspects, while permanence and specificity are characteristic of the legal statement. Nevertheless, this difference remains a factor affecting only the efficiency of the system, until such time as an attempt is made to alter the legal situation, that is, until an issue is "created." [19]

Earlier, we stressed the law-making and enforcement actions of government as the most relevant to the legitimization of power. These actions do not exhaust the means of legitimization in the hands of the government. In addition to law-making, law application, adjudication, and law enforcement, there are many other ways of granting legitimacy which are not quite so formal. Furthermore, the kinds of legitimizing actions which may be used vary from system to system and are one of the bases of differentiating the types of systems. Other methods of legitimizing power include consultation with bureaucratic or legislative organizations, delegations of quasi-legal powers, inclusion in religious or quasi-religious-patriotic ceremonies, audiences or informal meetings with the head of the state, the granting of symbolic honors, inclusion in councils with power to adjudicate or arbitrate disputes not involving the government, the appointment of key persons to administrative posts, election to political office of interested persons, official repetitions of stylized and value-laden imprecations, or decision by referendum or plebiscite. The specific means utilized in any polity may be in part specified in a constitutional document, or they may depend entirely upon the institutionalization of cultural values.

The particular point of view presented here is in moderate conflict with two others: that politics is concerned with the authoritative allocation of values for a whole society,[20] and that values, including legitimacy, are allocated by the political process

---

[19] See J. A. Schumpeter, *Capitalism, Socialism, and Democracy* (4th ed.; London, 1954), esp. Part IV.

[20] Easton, *op. cit.*

in such a way that the functions of government are not to be differentiated from the functions of groups or of individuals.[21] Emphasis on the authoritative allocation of value, insofar as "authoritative" is stressed, approaches our notion of legitimacy. However, the authoritative statement is not only the product of political interaction, but its effectiveness is also a product of such interaction. This view insists that the legitimization is psychological, rather than symbolic, and it fails to distinguish the legitimization from its implementation. The second view has been objected to on the valid ground that it does not differentiate between value allocations that are politically relevant and those that are not.

The theoretical utility of all three views does not lie in their being true, in the sense that they accord with some sort of reality. Their utility lies only in that they make various aspects of politics more intelligible. The present view has been preferred because it seems to come to grips with the problem suggested by the controversy over whether most political scientists have been led astray by legal superficialities, while a few have seen the light. The problem lies in the dichotomous nature of political phenomena, and the solution lies in establishing a systematic relationship between both aspects thereof. Instead of avoiding the issue by emphasizing one or the other aspect, it seems most sensible to grasp both horns of the dilemma.

There are other problematical dimensions of the activity of government. The legitimization of certain power relationships does not exhaust all the functions of government. Leaving aside activities bearing on foreign affairs, it is apparent that governments or governmental agencies are often engaged in certain kinds of relationships comparable to those of private associations. Most governments also engage in activities calculated to maintain both their own existence and the existence of the structure of power relationships which they legitimize. Consequently, empirical investigation may show that governments (as well as groups) perform political functions and not legitimizing functions solely. It may even be difficult to distinguish empirically between the political and legitimizing aspects of governmental action. Furthermore, the complexity and multiplicity of modern governmental institutions within an advanced polity may lead to contradictory actions arising partly out of intragovernmental power relationships and partly out of uncoördinated policy determinations.

If we abstract the legitimizing function from the general con-

---

[21] H. Lasswell and A. Kaplan, *Power and Society* (New Haven, 1950).

cept of government, we may say that any power relationship for which legitimacy is sought is a political relationship. For any social scientist, power which does not seek legitimization may be a proper subject for empirical research, but for the study of the political system, its relevance to legitimization is of crucial significance.

The legitimization of power has been compared to the institutionalization of value patterns in social roles, but the mechanisms of the political institutionalization of power relationships are not the same. The outstanding feature of the legitimization of power is that it is accomplished at a specific time and continues for a similarly measurable period. The formal procedure of legitimization is an empirically determinable evidence of the resultant of a more or less complex power relationship. It is also a fact that such legitimization may have a profound effect on the nature and continuity of the relevant power relationship. Consequently, the political system is composed of two elements which are closely integrated in mutual causality: power relationships, and legitimizing actions backed by the dominant control of coercive force.

These two elements may be seen in an input-output arrangement. The power relationships are the inputs that create the legitimizing act, and the act in turn tends to reinforce existing power relationships, or to change them. However, many power relationships are continually resulting in many legitimizing acts, not all of which are compatible with the rest. Furthermore, the impossibility of accurately describing a power relationship in a legitimizing act, and the common tendency to exaggerate, leads to the transformation, rather than the rigidification, of the power relationship. Finally, new power relationships are continually emerging at the political level from the geographical, economic, social and cultural background; and this background is constantly setting limits to the possibility of actually transforming power relationships into the form in which they have been legitimized. It is these systematic inefficiencies which result in repeated reviews of the legitimacy of power relationships and, more importantly, in system maintenance activity on the part of the government which does not seem to be directly related to group conflicts. Other institutions or groups may also engage in system maintenance activity, but this may be more properly seen as an aspect of the normal power relationship. For governments, however, this action takes one of two major empirical forms: an attempt to bring real power relationships into conformity with existing legitimizations, or an attempt to revise legitimizations in terms of existing or some preferred power relationships.

In the case of system maintenance activity, we are not always dealing with resultants of broad power relationships among important groups, for the institutions we usually know as government tend to acquire a functional autonomy independent of the legitimization of power relationships. They are also much more sensitively oriented to external forces, and they are more immediately concerned with the physical and administrative problems of the effective enforcement of a formalized power relationship. Thus, we may find various governmental organizations engaging in activity calculated to increase the efficacy of legitimizations. Such activity, while not necessarily motivated by identification with the interest of particular nongovernmental groups, will surely affect their power relationships. Again, these activities can take the form of a series of legitimizations, or of politically functional activity comparable to that engaged in by nongovernmental groups.

Action which is directed at achieving the legitimization of a particular power relationship, or that which is directed at manipulating power structures with a view to future legitimization, is politically functional activity. While such activity may involve the allocation of security, wealth, or prestige, its allocative character does not make it functional. Most theories which stress allocation, in analogy with economics, consider power a value which is allocated, rather than as a cause or determinant of the allocation of value. But as we have seen, legitimization does not allocate power, nor is it the only way in which security, wealth, or prestige are allocated. The distinction between legitimizing activity and allocative activity hardly seems worth making, in regard to a primitive system, although it is analytically possible. In more advanced systems, however, it is obvious that certain kinds of individual and group action would not exist were there no centralized institutions of legitimization. Within any system having differentiated institutions of government and, of course, well articulated cultural values, the performance of political functions becomes highly stylized; in some cases it even approaches a sort of ritual.

The performance of these functions is a kind of bridge between actual power relationships and legitimizations. The existence of this bridge is important in reducing the discrepancy between these two, because one of the major political activities is the restatement of the power relationship in a manner in which it can be acted upon by the government. This is what is normally meant by presenting a formal demand to government in the form of a petition or a legislative proposal. In addition to such formal restatement, the power relationship becomes transformed into the more concrete form of votes, memberships, protest meetings, strikes, coalitions, bribes, or bargains. Thus the political function involves not only an adjustment to the established patterns of legitimization but also a resourceful exploitation of complex and diffuse power structures, of prevailing culture-based ideologies, and of the attitudes, social relations, and interests of persons in governmental roles. In the same manner that the pattern of effective legitimization is dependent upon functionally political activity and upon the relative inflexibility of power relationships, so are these environmentally rooted power relationships altered, to some extent, by the flow of legitimizations and by the canalizing tendency of the established forms of political activity, and so also is such politically functional activity limited by power relationships and purposefully adjusted to the character of the legitimizing function.

Stylized political processes are the specific forms in which the political function has been institutionalized in a particular system. Even where these processes are not themselves legitimized, there are usually a set of empirically discoverable practices that are engaged in with a high degree of regularity by persons and groups interested in legitimizing a power relationship. These processes do not correspond to Almond's fourfold classification of political functions, but they may involve elements of each. Thus, attention to specific processes helps us to distinguish between the political function, systemically conceived, and broad classifications of political activity.[22]

The combination of the various classes of political activity that are found in stylized processes depends upon the actors involved, their value-oriented techniques, the issue at stake, the

---

[22] In our use, "politically functional activity" is essentially a behavioral definition of the political system. The behavior referred to is functional only, in the sense that it is an observable representation of the analytical construct "political system." Insofar as function implies purpose, the purpose of such activity is analytically defined by the definition of the political system. See A. R. Radcliffe-Brown, "On the Concept of Function in Social Science," *Structure and Function in Primitive Society* (London, 1952). Later on, we shall have occasion to use the term "dysfunctional," but there it will be used as in some sociological works, to refer to the impact of concrete or objectively defined behavior on a specific system or type of system. Throughout, a distinction between *the* system and *a* system must be maintained.

extent of the formalization of the process by previous legitimizations, and the general level of economic, communications, and bureaucratic development of the system itself.

The use of the threefold classification of traditional, conventional, and rational systems will be explained below, but it is apparent that these three may be differentiated in terms of the major types of processes found in each. Athough no single type of process prevails throughout any concrete system, the classification of types of processes as (1) bargaining, (2) polyarchal, and (3) hierarchical, seems to correspond with the three types of systems referred to. These three types of processes have been explained as (1) control of leaders by leaders, (2) control of leaders by non-leaders, and (3) control of nonleaders by leaders.[23]

Once the existence of stable processes can be discerned, closer study will usually reveal that even these processes are carried forward through patterns of discrete political acts which vary from system to system to a greater extent than do the political processes, but which are fairly constant for any particular system. These techniques depend upon much the same things as do the processes in which they find their places, but also, in significant degree, upon the personality and motivation of the individual actors involved. In dealing with political techniques, we approach a level of political behavior that ties in with the basic interaction situation producing our elementary power relationship. Because political techniques persist through superficial changes in constitutions, or in the incumbency of governmental offices, even sometimes through important systemic changes, they can be taken as factors governing the behavioral orientation of individuals.

Our system, then, is comprised of power relationships which are exploited in a limited number of ways, in order that legitimizations may be won. A perfectly efficient system would be one in which all power relationships are immediately and accurately translated into legitimizations. Such perfection is impossible to attain because, first, power relationships are expressed only in limited ways, in order to win legitimizations; second, because any particular array of legitimizations limits the kind of power relationships which may be recognized, and third, since the legitimization is a verbal and at least somewhat rationalized statement of the power relationship, it cannot match the flexibility of a power relationship. Behavior and words or verbal descriptions can never be exact equivalents. This same discrepancy occurs again between

---

[23] R. A. Dahl and C. E. Lindblom, *Politics, Economics, and Welfare* (New York, 1953).

the statement of legitimacy and its administrative application. To some, it has seemed more logical to omit the statement of legitimacy or to subsume it as relevant only to the extent that its terms were behaviorally represented in administrative implementation. But this procedure neglects the behavioral consequences which arise from the cognition of the discrepancy between power realtionships and legitimizations, such as everywhere exists to a greater or lesser extent.

To this basic analysis we shall add two simple overlapping typologies. The first of these is a threefold classification which is based upon certain differences in the structure and functioning of particular systems, from the point of view of ideology or system legitimacy. The second typology really designates two widely separated points along a continuum representing a secular trend in the quantitative change of certain structural and functional parameters. For analytical purposes, these two typologies and five classes are treated as distinct categories, but the typologies are understood to be dynamically related and the first three types are not meant to exclude hybrid types (that is, a more highly differentiated typology with many more types). The purpose in developing these two overlapping classifications arises from the generally accepted view that system change in the ideological sense, involving the array of legitimizations, is by definition instability, but that any other change which is somehow accommodated within the existing framework of techniques, processes, and legitimizing operations is by definition stability.

The three terms of our system-legitimacy classification are traditional, conventional and rational. Change from one of these systems to another is generally called instability. The two ends of the continuum are simply called underdeveloped and developed systems. Quite arbitrarily, it seems to be agreed that movement from one extreme to the other does not entail "real" system change or instability, if it does not also include a change in system legitimacy. With as much validity, one may insist that "real" change occurs only within the framework of the second classification, but it is more than likely that there is a good deal of overlapping between both. That is, empirical investigation will probably reveal that only certain types of ideologically defined systems can be correlated with development.

The traditional system follows closely the relevant Weberian ideal type. It is characterized by patriarchal leadership, by the haphazard delegation of authority, and by religious justification of the acts of government. Two patterns of ideology may be applied, patterns that are not mutually exclusive. The first is based upon a belief in the inscrutability of God's will and a prescientific notion of causation. Hence, the existing order of society is accepted as preordained, and insofar as possible its origin is referred to the distant past. The second is a more complicated notion of patriarchal absolutism which urges the responsibility of the king to God alone. Should the king fail to uphold "the law," he will be punished, perhaps by rebellion, but more likely in the next world. A wicked ruler is also a visitation of divine punishment upon a sinful people, and rebellion is opposition to the will of God. The second view depends, as does the first, upon a notion of a preordained social order, but it admits of deviations from the ideal, as a consequence of sin.

Ideologically, then, the traditional system has no plan, nor is it ever very clear when power and legitimacy do not coincide, that is, when unauthorized "power" is asserted. There might be conflicting claims of emperor and pope, or of king and nobles, or of Abbasid and Fatimid and other caliphal pretenders, but these affected only a limited group of persons, and the pattern of specific legitimizations practically not at all. In fact, the forms of system legitimacy in each opposing case were closely parallel. Victory for one side and defeat for the other world seem to be very much like the simple alternation in office of political parties in the United States. There was a sufficiency of alternation among these contenders to suggest that the changes which have beset those systems did not arise by design and forethought.

The most important forms of legitimization, under the traditional system, are delegation of authority, consultation, contractual agreements, the grant of audiences, honors or rewards, marriage, and the like. The processes often fall into the pattern of seeking appointments, using "pull," or lobbying, the institutionalization of access in consultative and administrative bodies, and system maintenance through (especially) religious ceremonials.

The following is a list of specific processes to be found in less developed, more traditional, systems and is actually drawn from observation in Iran: the system maintenance process which may be found in religious ceremonials, but is also manifested in controlled democratic or constitutional ceremonials, paralleling the electoral and legislative processes of conventional systems; the system challenging process empirically manifested in generalized protests, boycotts, and work or service stoppages; the process of the selection of the incumbents of all governmental positions; the consultative (as opposed to the deliberative activity of the "conventional" legislative) process; and a distinctive "lobbying" process which owes its special character to the institutionalization of most important points of access in legislative and administrative roles, in such a manner as to overshadow conventional legislative and administrative activity.

To generalize from the political system of Iran, traditional techniques tend toward diffusion, almost camouflage, of the political goal itself. The applicant for a license or a position may attack the government, or have an article slandering a recalcitrant official published; a guild of bakers may close their shops to cope with strong competition; a professional association may convert itself into a political party; an aristocratic landowner may donate large amounts to the religious hierarchy. In contrast to such highly diffuse patterns, kinship ties or regional patronage systems may be explored for specific "favors." Where elections take place in such a traditional system, a curious blend of conventional and traditional techniques occurs, with prayer meetings being used for party speeches, or Westernized politicians posing as religious ascetics. Competing candidacies represent traditional aristocratic rivalries, or a family feud over village leadership, or an age-old competition for control of a craft guild. Street demonstrations and the employment of "goondas" or "chakokesh" or "hooligans" are some of the more highly specialized techniques in these areas, where communication and aggregation are weak or erratic.

In underdeveloped countries such as Iran, where the support for traditional authority is weak and where the legitimizing functions are more traditional than conventional, assassinations, *coups d'état,* and the cultivation of charisma point to greater concern with "personal power," loyalties, or "character," rather than with conventional processes. Consequently, in underdeveloped traditional systems party formation may be a relatively short-term technique for protecting a special interest, or it may be part of the system maintenance process. And street demonstrations can be both system maintenance or system challenging in purpose. The use of goondas may serve to get legislation passed or to quiet newspaper criticism within a more general "lobbying" process or a process of personnel selection.

The specific techniques are characterized by bargaining, as in arranging for the supply of troops, winning administrative office, making feudal contracts, arranging marriages, and paying bribes; though there is often room for the representation of grievances and the receipt of redress. Structures of power relationships are fragmented and compartmentalized. Primary groups, and ethnic groups or demographic classes, are the dominant reference groups. Patriarchal leadership permeates these structures, and each leader is a bargainer with every other one, both for himself and his followers. Associational groups are few, though guilds of numerous kinds and lay religious groups are often found. These leaders are no less patriarchal, but in most cases they enjoy their leadership as a result of a combination of heredity and royal favor. There are, in fact, numerous examples of a hereditary dual leadership of village headmen, guildmasters, town qadis (judges), and even wazirs, whose alternation in power depends primarily upon bargaining and higher governmental or royal convenience. In many ways, the same emphasis upon primary group affiliation, patriarchal leadership, and particularistic-ascriptive role orientation is characteristic of the major institutional groups such as the bureaucracy, the military, and the clergy (or ulama), though the division of labor and special skills required by the goals of these organizations makes them easier to rationalize.

Because they are lacking in a plan and have a strong tendency toward accepting events as the will of God or the way of the world, these systems can accommodate mild challenges, such as a change of dynasty or the claim of the leader of some robber band to ennoblement. The stability of traditional systems may be described in terms of a neutral equilibrium.

As already suggested, the conventional system is the equivalent of a working constitutional democracy. The relationship between constitutionalism and democracy is not an improvement upon democracy, in the moral sense, but is a practical modification of democracy in an undemocratic direction, in the interest of making it work. Hence constitutionalism is a limitation of democracy, rather than a limitation of government. Because, as modern democratic theorists point out, all men are neither good nor rational nor absolutely equal, ideal democracy cannot work. The contemporary discussion of whether democracies can survive in the present world is, in a sense, a discussion of how much more ideal democracy must be conventionalized by further constitutional limitations. The severity of ideological disagreements about democracy arises from the tendency to justify constitutional limitations by the use of democratic arguments.

It is thought by some that intolerance of ambiguity and paradox is both a sign of immaturity and a symptom of the authoritarian personality. In an ideological sense, it would seem that such intolerance is a heritage of the age of reason, for traditional systems can easily blame divine whims for social and political paradoxes. Ideal democracy is as much a logically consistent ideology as is Marxism, and possibly as immature or authoritarian. Totalitarianism is not necessarily as logically consistent as ideal democracy; witness the ideological inconsistencies in Nazism and Fascism. Both of these had their atavistic elements, which may account for the limited parallel with traditional ideologies. It may be the case, further, that the noted intolerance of ambiguity and inconsistency among the Westernized classes in the new nations of the Middle East is due more to the influence of Western rationalism than to the patriarchal-authoritarian culture of these areas. Their notion of democracy has also been of the more logical systematic variety.

In our Western democracies, on the other hand, constitutionalism has been the rule, and apologists for our system have praised the acceptance of ambiguity as mature, and as the only true democracy.

The conventional system is one in which the pattern of power relationships is recognized as fluid, and change is generally viewed with favor. Emphasis here is upon conventionalized procedures for achieving the legitimization of new or changed power relationships. These procedures, and even the legitimizations themselves, are recognized as lagging behind the real state of affairs and as approximating, but never exactly reproducing, the likeness of actual power relationships. Despite the possible existence of a broad consensus on ultimate values, there is a general refusal to admit of man's capacity to know the Good in any particular case. Because of this orientation, there is a great deal of tolerance for the pursuit of self-interest and for deviations from the ideals of liberalism, democracy, and constitutionalism. Nonlegitimized power relationships are condoned, but in themselves are not considered as adequate claims to legitimization. Freedom is conventionalized as the freedom to act politically, so as to affect the legitimacy of some power relationship, rather than as the freedom from the inevitable entanglement of power relationships. Laws themselves are not taken as something of ultimate value, rather, as temporary compromises between power relationships existing in some part of the polity and the imputed interests of the whole. The absence of any firm assumptions about the place of any group in society sustains its pluralistic emphasis and justifies the interest of all groups in the relations of all others. The goal here is relative justice, rather than absolute justice.

The legitimizations in the conventional system follow the familiar patterns of legislation, adjudication, and administrative decisions, but they also include consultation, coöptation for administrative purposes, subsidization through tax relief or tariffs. The usual processes include the electoral, the legislative, the judicial, and the administrative, in both their formal and their informal aspects. Political techniques include campaigning for office, lobbying, the formation of associations, propaganda, and the like; throughout which one finds polyarchal tendencies predominant. Polyarchy, or the distant control (within broad limits) of leaders by followers, is most apparent within the structures of power relationships. Primary groups and demographic classes are generally less important, or where significant are felt to be so incongruent that they are organized and are run along the lines of common interest groups. Interest associations are rationally organized, in accordance with formally democratic principles, but the iron law of oligarchy generally holds sway, so long as the major demands of the group members are met. Institutional groups tend to be highly rationalized, hierarchical, complex, and relatively efficient organizations whose members are indoctrinated in the belief that they must not interfere directly in political affairs.

A distinctive characteristic of the conventional system is that wherever it prevails, groups standing between the government and the individual do not define all the power relationships of their members, nor do they dominate their members. Furthermore, such systems tend to exaggerate the independence of the individual by restricting the legitimacy of group leaders and by legitimizing the power of the individual through the convention of the general election. The general election is a convention, of course, because it assumes that every voter is equal and that he casts his vote uninfluenced by any external pressure. Nevertheless, the free election by secret ballot does give some outlet to nongroup-oriented interests which are not directly effective between elections. The individual is of systemic importance in all three systems, but only in the conventional system is this recognized, even exaggerated. Consequently, we find that the criterion of legitimization in a conventional system more nearly approaches the complexity of reality, that its conventions are more comprehensive, and that they are limited only by the fertility of the human imagination. Pragmatism tends to be a dominant characteristic of the conventional system.

The rational system, by contrast, seeks absolute justice and shuns compromise. It insists upon an ideal pattern of power relationships, to be legitimized, as occasion may require, by the exponents of the logical extrapolations of some theoretical ideal.

It is assumed that the nature of the ideal society may be known to man through his reason or through his senses, and that only those who have seen the light may perform either political or legitimizing functions. Tradition is rejected for offering no rational justification of its fixed legitimization of power relationships, while "conventionalism" is rejected as being either hypocritical or lacking in any rational order. In the rational system, power relationships and legitimizations tend to be equated. Legitimizations are taken to represent the real and the desired state of affairs, and there is a tendency to see in power its own justification; otherwise it would be impossible to approximate rationality in a political system.

The legitimizations in the rational system are in the form of administrative regulations. The relevant processes are those of a hierarchical organization, where the business of reporting, planning, budgeting, coördinating, granting promotions, and the like is crucial. The techniques actually employed in a highly rationalized system are not too well known, although absolute obedience, and slowdown or absenteeism, are the logical extremes. Some bargaining seems to exist between superiors and subordinates within the hierarchical framework, but the administrative spirit permeates the whole. Structures of social power exist in the same variety, but ideally, all are hierarchically organized and established on a territorial or occupational basis. Primary groups and demographic classes are but grudgingly recognized, if at all (note, though, the peculiar nationalities problem of the Soviet Union and its "territorial" solution). Associational groups are adjuncts of administrative organizations, and are controlled therefrom. Institutional groups are thoroughly hierarchized and rationalized, and their permanent leaders (except possibly the clergy, for we have no extant example) are identical with the highest legitimized authority in the system.

In order to suggest the ways in which the preceding classification can be used for a comparative description of political systems, the accompanying "Paradigm of Political Systems" is presented. This graphic simplification does not add to what has gone before, but it is offered here hopefully, with the thought that it may clarify and summarize.

It is fairly obvious that most traditional systems, in the twentieth century, have acquired some of the paraphernalia of the conventional systems. Some of them hold elections, many more have cabinets, and nearly all have established regulatory agencies and a centralized judiciary. The conventional systems,

PARADIGM OF POLITICAL SYSTEMS

System Characteristic	System Type		
	Traditional	Conventional	Rational
Legitimizing myth of the system	Arbitrary ordination of the order by God	Social contract or majority will; procedures rather than ends	Ends emphasized in framework of a collective welfare concept; extreme belief in the applicability of reason to human affairs
Example of form of a specific legitimization	Delegation of authority	Parliamentary legislation	Administrative regulation
Effectiveness of legitimizing acts in controlling power relationships	Erratic	Temporary	High
Operational character and applicability of legitimizing act	Persons	Time and circumstances	Secret, subject to abrupt reinterpretation
Functional processes	Bargaining	Polyarchy	Hierarchy
Examples of legitimate processes	Consultation	Elections, representation	Democratic-centralism
Type of activity aimed at effecting a legitimizing act	Bargaining,	Bargaining among leaders of secondary groups	Bureaucratic techniques
Type of activity aimed at altering power relationships	Bargaining, force	Polyarchy	Regulation and suppression
Differentiation between the two preceding	Little	Great	Moderate
Manner in which government engages in politically functional activity	Bends legitimizing act to accord with new power	Attempts to act and speak for welfare of the whole polity	Interprets and applies rational ideology as conditions require
Governmental techniques as part of the system-maintenance process	Use of nonrational symbols, coöption of new persons	Procedural symbols, law	Ideology, suppression
Character of administrative activity as parallel of political processes	Uncoördinated	Decentralized	Centrally coördinated
Positive techniques (tending to make the system more efficient)	Gift, bribe, petitioning for redress	Political participation	Obedience
Negative techniques (tending to make the system less efficient)	Holdout in bargaining	Quiescence as a form of protest	Slow down, absenteeism

SYSTEM CHARACTERISTIC	SYSTEM TYPE		
	Traditional	Conventional	Rational
Nature of power structures	Fragmented, compartmentalized	Flexible and shifting within limits	Hierarchical, territorial, occupational
Access and applicability of legitimizing acts	Limited in terms of persons and variable in substantive scope	Unlimited as to persons variable as to scope	Access sharply limited in terms of persons but applicability is unlimited, substantive scope is as comprehensive as possible
Information in the system	Low, uncontrolled	High, uncontrolled	Limited, rigidly controlled
Economic development and social mobilization	Low	Medium to high	Low to high

too, retain certain traditional myths which may be manifested in the selection of personnel for offices, in the availability of education, in the establishment of a church, or in the retention of royalty. The rational systems usually pay lip service to democratic ideas, but they shun the democratic conventions. Nevertheless the appearance of conventionalism is retained; deliberative bodies are elected, and there is the assumption of equality before the law. Less frequently, and Iran is one of the important exceptions, examples of a cross between a traditional and a rational system may be found. Here, tradition has been rationalized by the close subordination of aristocracy and corporative "concessionaires" to the personalized source of legitimacy, and by the identification of that source with a more logically ordered set of values than that of the existing order.

One need not probe deeply into the historical origins of these hybrid systems to learn that they cause confusions about the legitimacy of the system, as well as about the legitimizations produced. Legitimacy confusions do not in themselves create instability, so long as legitimizations accord more or less with power relationships. We must bear in mind, however, that legitimizations do not include administrative implementation and that power relationships include reference to the availability of information. Consequently, when legitimizations do not accord with power relationships, administrative implementation must be extremely efficient, either backed by a great deal of force or so adjusted in individual circumstances as to render as few persons as possible aware of the consequences of the legitimization in question. Where legitimizations are narrow in personal or substantive scope, implementation problems are less significant; but where far-reaching changes are to be brought about, as in countries seeking to modernize, the administrative problem may be formidable and high awareness will almost inevitably result. A similar situation exists where important changes in the structure of power relationships occur and are not recognized in new legitimizations.

We turn now to the distinction between developed and underdeveloped systems. Generally speaking, traditionality and underdevelopment are found together. The correlation is not logically necessary, but is explainable. On the other hand, both conventional and rational systems tend to be developed in comparable, though not undifferentiated, ways. Since the two ends of our scale are roughly opposites, we need describe only one of them.

The usual indicators of development, or modernity, are: education and literacy, industrialization and the division of labor, communications and transport, health and sanitation, bureaucratic and military rationalization, scientific and engineering achievements, the restriction of religion to a narrower social sphere, increasing mean income, the broadening of so-called middle-class groups, the formation of contractually organized limited interest associations, increasing mobility in social and vocational and geographical spheres, and a generally increased emphasis upon universalist-achievement role orientations.

These are all correlates of development, but political development itself must be described in terms of the impact of the incremental change in these factors upon the components of the political system. Without such a statement of the relationship between the two we will have no theoretical foundation for seeking out the causal relationships between such changes and political changes.

Economists usually define development in their own terms. While admitting all of the correlates we have listed, the essential systemic criteria remain increased efficiency, increased complexity, changes in the allocation of the factors of production, and changes in the kind and amount of value added to raw materials. By increased efficiency, reference is simply to increased output for the same quantity of input. Increased complexity is represented by the division of labor, economic interdependence, a money economy, lengthier and costlier production processes requiring long-range planning, coördination, and market predictions. Development also implies, as a result of technological changes and savings investment, a relative decrease in labor and an increase in capital, per unit produced. New kinds of value are added as increased labor becomes available for the provision of services such as distribution, packaging that is pleasing, and prestige-conferring salesmanship.

Our notion of political development is similar to the economists', but it is stated in terms of the political system. A developed system is more efficient, in the sense that power relationships are more often translated into legitimizations and less frequently left outside the political sphere. This is often described as the increasing scope of government. Furthermore, the means of winning legitimizations are better defined, or at least the forms of legitimization are fewer and more definite. Consequently, developed systems tend to be more efficient in that the probability of a prolonged discrepancy between power and legitimacy is less likely, in a developed system. Another aspect of this efficiency arises from the fact that conflicts of interest between noninteracting groups are more readily comprehended. In other words, the developed system is more efficient in that more issues become political more easily.

It is not necessarily more efficient in the sense that there is a stable adjustment of power relationships and legitimizations, because the system also becomes more complex. Complexity is partly the necessary consequence of the efficiency described, that is, of the greater load carried by the political system. But it is also the result of the less direct character of the political processes. In a developed system, politically functional activity requires greater planning, better organization, larger resources, and certain technical skills. This complexity is best evidenced in the operation and scope of institutional groups. The bureaucracy, especially, increases in size, in specialization and the division of tasks, and in the professionalization of its personnel. The military and other security forces also increase their ability to use violence, so that the potential for control over other structures of power relationships by these two institutional groups increases greatly. Another change arises in the form of legitimizations sought. Legitimizations are no longer stated in terms of persons and their descendants, but in terms of occupational or regional groups, and for limited periods and limited purposes.

In underdeveloped systems low incomes, low literacy, faulty communications, technological stagnation, and all the rest set an upper limit to the levels of political information intruded into the system. But the structure of power relationships restricts access and political participation, and fatalistic ideologies justify resignation and tacit consent. In developed systems, there is a tendency toward the formation of new groups to represent all kinds of interests; and information and access, even administration implementation, tend to vary with perceived deprivation or gratification and the intensity of that perception. Information and access vary directly, though administrative implementation varies indirectly with deprivation and gratification intensity. Where the deprivation implied by a legitimization is widespread and severe, there will be a tendency to mitigate it somewhat in its implementation. These tendencies do not always work themselves out, however, for they too can be controlled by effective military and bureaucratic activity. The point here is that it cannot be assumed that in a developed system deprived groups will do nothing, or that interested groups will long fail to seek special benefits.

Having now set forth the basic framework of our political system, and having elaborated three system types and the criteria of political development, we next turn to an examination of the relationship between these three theoretical statements. Through this examination we shall try to support the following hypotheses, in their application to Middle Eastern systems:

1. that underdeveloped systems are more vulnerable to environmental factors than are developed systems;

2. that development has been first induced in contemporary systems by environmental factors;

3. that the primary systemic causes of change are the result of dysfunctional system maintenance activity;

4. that once this process is begun the tendency toward positive equilibration causes it to snowball;

5. that despite great confusion about the legitimacy of the system itself, a vaguely democratic ideology of cultural and social change is accepted by both revolutionary and anti-revolutionary forces;

6. that developing systems may branch off toward hierarchical types or toward conventional types, as in the Western democracies;

7. that this branching depends primarily upon the differential rates of economic, political, and administrative development, and only secondarily upon the will of the governing elite (whether traditional or revolutionary) to establish effective Western institutions; and finally,

8. that the relative ease of achieving administrative develop-

ment suggests that the transition to a Western type of democracy will become, at best, a tactical matter to be decided upon by particular governments.

Looking back to our statement of the political system, it appears that there are three ways in which changes can occur. Assuming that we are concerned with a system which is traditional and underdeveloped, the first source of change would be environmental. This is the most important source, because we have found traditional systems to be low information systems. Consequently each of the compartmentalized power structures, including institutional groups and aristocratic elites, are relatively unaware of events taking place within other structures, or outside the territory under the control of the government. Environmental changes have two major forms, the usual and generally understood form of international pressures, and the analytically environmental changes in the previously listed correlates of development. The second may be caused by the first, but may also be caused by population movements resulting from "acts of nature" and the like. The second may also be caused or intensified by systemic factors, as we shall see. The changes which we have designated as the correlates of development are environmental, simply because they do not represent power relationships directed at the achievement of legitimizations. By contrast, international pressures are not wholly environmental, for the demand for economic concessions by foreign citizens supported by their governments is precisely parallel to similar demands by citizens. On the other hand, cultural influences, foreign markets, imports, and technical assistance are clearly environmental. In discussing Middle Eastern states, we cannot ignore the special case of foreign conquest and imperial control which brings with it a relatively complete, if temporary, transformation. Regardless of whether the original impulse came from foreign conquest; foreign economic influences; foreign cultural, religious, or technological influences; the direct involvement of foreigners as participants in Middle Eastern political systems; or all of these together, the result for most Middle Eastern states has been a secular (but erratic, for any short period) increase in each of the correlatives of development.

Another source of change arises from what might be called normal system eccentricity. By this term, reference is made to the necessary deviation of legitimizations from the power relationships they are supposed to legitimize. The normal process of conflict resolution ought, theoretically, to lead to gradual and almost imperceptible change. Under ordinary circumstances, this gradual change is seen as mere adjustment within a stable state. With regard to traditional systems, these changes are within the accommodative range of their neutral equilibrium. Nevertheless, some cultural crisis can bring about a sharp realization of the existing divergence of legitimized power relationships from the generally acknowledged ideas of system legitimacy. Such an ideological revulsion may be the catalyst which facilitates what we have called the correlatives of development becoming politically significant, in the immediate sense of being manifested in power relationships which demand new legitimizations. Even without such an extreme development, normal system eccentricity under appropriate environmental conditions, can lead to legitimizations which, when challenged, cannot be sustained by favored groups. The appropriate environmental conditions may be supplied by a benevolent foreign power, or even by a protective international organization. Nevertheless, in a traditional system the mere inefficiency of its processes can cause extreme divergences which are not challenged. In the Middle East, with government by both nonlegitimized war lords and overlegitimized caliphs, nearly all of these situations have obtained.

The third type of change is also systemic, because it arises from dysfunctional system maintenance activity.[24] The changes which are entailed in this type of activity may originate from an imperial authority, as well as from an indigenous government. For the Middle East, the latter is the more significant, so we shall use it in our discussion. It is a commonplace of Middle Eastern history that the governments of this area were challenged, both militarily and economically, by the more highly developed European governments. Foreign concessionaires and creditors demanded improved administration, and at times they took over certain administrative organizations. Access was won for foreign missionaries, and prevalent notions of justice, legitimacy, and morality were severely challenged. The response of these governments, especially those of Turkey and Iran, but of Egypt as well, was to modernize the army and rationalize the bureaucracy. Educational reforms were made, and there followed new taxes requiring improved control over production. In more recent times, these governments have moved into direct industrial production, and

---

[24] See note 22. In this context, i.e., with reference to a specific system, dysfunctional refers to the unstabilizing effect of policies, or of other political behavior. It is not the same use as that implied by the referral of politically functional behavior to *the* political system.

even into the formation and direction of secondary "interest" groups; they have guided religious education, and have instituted universal military service. Though logically unnecessary, most Middle Eastern governments have also adopted, at least outwardly, parliamentary institutions.

The extent and order of these innovations is not here so important as the fact that such changes were made in order to preserve traditional systems. If we conceive of the system in neutral equilibrium, and as a shallow cylinder rather than a sphere, so long as the cylinder is moved along on its curved side it is stable. But if it should be tipped toward its base it becomes shatteringly unstable. This is the direction of the system maintenance activity which has been described, and it is obvious that this activity forces the pace of political development while providing but partially for its environmental prerequisites. Furthermore, the traditional system is incompatible with the developed system. To maintain the traditional system against external challenges, wholly new structures of power relationships are created in a short time. Areas which were never the subject of legitimization become matters for political concern. Another entirely new idea of system legitimacy, perhaps more than one such idea, is appealed to by traditional elites. And the idea of planned change affecting every aspect of social and cultural life becomes firmly implanted.

The coexistence of several ideas of system legitimacy leads to a condition that may be called legitimacy confusion, a type of paradox that we have found to be contemned by the "moderns" in the Middle East. In reality, it is not the moderns who are intolerant of such political ambiguity, for the younger relatives of the traditional elite show all of the maturity that Western democrats might desire. The challenges come, rather, from those who have been given new ideas through development, individuals who have demanded some effective legitimization of their newly proclaimed equality. Such internal challengers have won more severe control from traditional governments, and the challengers have engaged in technique exploration. These techniques have ranged from literary club meetings to nationalist movements in exile, to party organizations, to street demonstrations, to secret conspiracies, and on to infiltrations of the army and the bureaucracy. In general, traditional governments have tended to become more rationalized and hierarchical, while revolutions have occurred where new alternative elites have won control of those two most important instruments of rationalization, the army and the bureaucracy.

Where there has been imperial control, in the Middle East, it has been only as an interlude, and not even then has there been any appreciable divergence from the model here developed. Neither, as yet, does there seem to be any significant difference between the basic nature of the specific system change in the countries of revolutionary governments and in those nominally traditional regimes which have moved resolutely along the path of rationalization. Turkey may be an example of the importance of a revolution in stabilizing the system and perhaps guiding it toward conventionalism. Iran, however, is an example of a system in which the same goals are sought, by some at least, without a sharp break in system legitimacy. Egypt stands between the two, having had its revolution, and it now declares its direction to be democratic, but not necessarily of the constitutional variety of the West.

These divergent examples can still be dealt with by means of a single model, assuming only that we start with a government which is responsive to a small elite having effective control over the military, the bureaucracy, and associational groups. The intervention of a charismatic interlude, after a revolution, may or may not be a prerequisite for the creation of a feeling of community, or a devotion to the nation; but let us assume, further, that an adequate substitute can be found.[25] What, then, is the possible path of the transition from this point on to a (conventional) democracy or to a rationalized system?

This is surely a complicated problem, but it may help if we reduce it to three general issues. The first is that of the socialization of key personnel in new roles. The second is concerned with capabilities, that is, the resources of the system in relation to the effective demands made. And the third is the issue of institutional efficiencies.

For the transition to democracy, socialization in new roles comprehends not only the appropriate indoctrination of the military and bureaucratic elites, of representatives and association leaders; it also involves the creation of a broad ideological atmosphere in which the military and the bureaucracy will cease to regard themselves as the guides and leaders, and through which representatives and association leaders will respond to the in-

---

[25] For a discussion of some of the issues involved see my "Islam, Arabism, and the Political Community in the Middle East," a paper presented at the ACLS-SSRC Middle East Conference, October, 1961; also N. Safran, *Egypt in Search of Political Community* (Cambridge, 1961).

choate demands of their respective constituencies. While it is patent that these changes can only come about where there is a wide diffusion of power, the impact of development upon the traditional systems of the Middle East has resulted in the greater concentration of power.

Be that as it may, a second prerequisite would appear to be the actual practice of working the democratic institutions associated with representative government and pressure politics. Even the working of these in a tentative manner, such as under a colonial government, depends upon a relative confidence that there are resources available to meet new demands that may arise. It may be noted in passing that while Middle Eastern economies can be further developed, the task is long and hard and the eventual possibilities are limited.

The issue of institutional efficiencies is the test by which Western democracy will, in the final analysis, be found to exist. As Professor Haas has pointed out, the mere provision of institutional means of resolving certain conflicts and of encouraging coöperation between divergent groups may be found to have pragmatic value for those concerned.[26] We begin with a generally favorable attitude toward democratic institutions, and it is likely that the discovery of a pragmatic value will soon enough lead to the kind of end-value attachment thereto found in Western democracies. This attachment will be limited to the group benefitted, and if the aforementioned researches in European integrative institutions are valid for other situations the phenomenon of "spill-over" may occur, with these groups demanding that still other tasks be delivered to the procedures of democratic institutions. Spill-over appears to be a particular manifestation of the earlier mentioned notion of system eccentricity.

Spill-over sits in well with Mayo's view that one can do no more than keep trying. That is, since the prerequisites of democracy are little known, one can only try these institutional devices until they are found to work. Mayo quotes another authority to show that democratic institutions have had moderate success in non-European countries only when they have been imposed from above.[27] System eccentricity works more slowly, perhaps, than spill-over, but the mere acceptance of democratic institutions, even if only formally, makes the idea plausible. Guided democracy would seem to have much in common with both the

---

[26] E. Haas, *The Uniting of Europe* (Stanford, 1958).

[27] H. B. Mayo, *An Introduction to Democratic Theory* (New York, 1960), p. 293.

effect of system eccentricity and spill-over, being no more than a specific application of the two more general ideas.

What we have been suggesting is that the transition to democracy depends upon the willingness and the ability of the military and bureaucratic elites of Middle Eastern countries to reject their own institutional orientations and to decide rationally and consciously to establish and work certain democratic institutions to some extent. Doubt has been cast upon this possibility for two reasons: first, that it is difficult to conceive of these elites, who at present are becoming socialized in hierarchical roles, suddenly changing in order to act polyarchal roles; and second, that Middle Eastern governments do not appear to enjoy the resources necessary to requite all the demands that have been created or will be created by development. Nevertheless, our pessimism is only moderate, for there are a number of loopholes. In the first place, it is not impossible that hierarchically imposed stability, coupled with education and the formation of broad interest associations, may permit the moderation of demands to accord with existing resources. Secondly, stable, rationalized government will permit a more orderly development of resources than has heretofore taken place, and such government has already proven its ability to win greater quantities of foreign aid. Thirdly, some of the oil producing countries can be developed to a considerable extent. Fourthly, and most important, both Turkey and Egypt evidence some tendency for members of the military and bureaucratic elites to move to important positions both in private industry and in political parties or interest associations. As yet, this tendency is slight, and where there is extensive government control it is unlikely to mean very much. Nevertheless, as development proceeds and full control of industry, commerce, and finance evade Middle Eastern governments, one may expect a wider diffusion of power and the growth of attitudes appropriate to the working of a conventional system. Some further comfort may be taken from the fact that the military in these countries are neither professionally, ideologically, nor socially clearly differentiated from civil servants, professional intellectuals, and other members of the thin middle class. There is some evidence that they conceive of themselves as members of the intelligentsia and as the vanguard of the people as a whole. If this attitude is strong enough, it further enhances the likelihood of successful spill-over.

It has been suggested that the military are, in fact, the vanguard of the middle class, rather than of the people; but the problem is that the middle class itself, by any definition, is small and largely organized in hierarchical organizations under the government.[28] Furthermore, the top military in Middle Eastern countries have many cliquish tendencies and have been especially favored by both traditional and revolutionary governments. Again, it is hard to conceive of their practicing a degree of self-denial which would permit the transition to democracy.

Thus far, we have discussed the transition to democracy as though there might be little difference between the position of revolutionary and traditional-rational systems. If past experience is any criterion, it might be argued that it is, in any case, the fate of persisting monarchies to undergo the Middle Eastern style revolution which skims off the top layer and leaves the top military and bureaucracy in charge. There is no inevitability about these things, however, and it behooves us to consider what are the chances for democratic government in these countries. In a recent article, Lipset has suggested that democratic institutions are more easily sustained where elements of the traditional legitimacy are retained.[29] This makes good sense, in that the wide diffusion of power necessary to a conventional system would seem to be guaranteed by the judicious extension of both procedural and substantive legitimizations to newly articulate groups, by an enlightened but self-interested elite. More especially, there may be greater likelihood of a multiparty system and of effectively alternating governments.

This approach is highly problematic, in the Middle East. The reasons for the difficulty of application there are as follows: First, antitraditional revolutions have taken place and have been generally approved by the Westernized classes throughout the area. Second, revolutionary governments have been notably successful in their foreign policy dealings. Third, for Arab monarchies, traditional legitimacy has been severely shaken by the phenomenal growth of the Pan-Arab movement. Only in Iran can the shah serve as a symbol of national unity for Persians. Fourthly, the traditional elite in Middle Eastern countries is not an hereditary aristocracy with an ideology of service. Finally, it may be too late to revive traditional legitimacies in a form that will permit

---

[28] See M. Berger, "The Middle Class in the Middle East," in W. Z. Laqueur, ed., *The Middle East in Transition* (New York, 1958).

[29] S. M. Lipset, *op. cit.*

the broad sharing of power because of the growing dominance of ideologies of revolutionary social and cultural change, in which government is to play a central role.

This is not the place to elaborate on this view, yet I think it significant indeed that such widely divergent writers as Maududi of Pakistan, Kasravi of Iran, Aflaq of Syria, and Nasser of Egypt have such similar notions of revolution.[30] All insist on the need for fundamental changes. For all four, revolution means not merely the seizing of power, it is also the changing of people's beliefs and behavior. Lipset saw some of the prerequisites of democracy in economic development, as well as in the hazardous historical resolution of certain major problems, so that interest cleavages were nicely balanced by fundamental ideological unity. Where events have turned out otherwise, "democratic parties of integration" have refused to play the game of conventionalist politics.[31] In the Middle East, at the present time, interest cleavages are not so well articulated, and ideological differences (even if they are not very solid ideologies) dominate the field. The difference in the Middle East, though, is that a diffuse ideology of social and cultural revolution is spreading wider, and a more or less homogeneous but disunited elite of middle and lower middle class origins is gaining increasing control. These people assert that the revolution they have in mind will lead automatically to democracy, a thesis which Lipset wrongly attributes to Lerner, but rightly rejects.[32] What Lerner held was that modernization leads to the creation of the contemporary participant society, or what we might call the developed system, though it need not be democratic.[33] On the other hand, if it is not to be democratic, we have already noted that there must be a compensatory control of the flow of information, of access and technique exploration, and of the interplay of the structures of power relationships in the system. But we have also drawn attention to the limited resources of Middle Eastern governments and may conclude, not without some hesitation, that they haven't the physical ability to assert full totalitarian control. If this is true, then we may make

---

[30] Abu'l Ala Maududi, *The Process of Islamic Revolution* (Pathankot, 1947); Ahmad Kasravi, *Inqilab Chist?* (Tehran, 1336), and *Mashruteh* . . . (Tehran, 1335); Michel Aflaq, *Fi Sabil al-Ba'th al-Arabi* (Baghdad, 1953); and Gamal Abd al-Nasser, *Egypt's Liberation* (Washington, 1955).

[31] Lipset, *op. cit.*, p. 95.

[32] *Ibid.*, p. 82.

[33] D. Lerner, *The Passing of Traditional Society* (Glencoe, 1958). See quotation and note 26 in Lipset, *op. cit.*

a comparison between the condition of contemporary Middle Eastern systems and the divine-right monarchies of premodern Europe. Following Lindsay, we find that in terms of doctrine these states were potentially totalitarian, and the degree of administrative control which they achieved was sufficient to lay the basis of national unity.[34] Nevertheless, administrative efficiency was insufficient to prevent the Reformation, modern science, and capitalism, from implanting the foundations of individualism and achieving the legitimization of nongovernmental structures of power. In a sense, Middle Eastern governments are better situated, for they are not burdened with a divine-right theory, and they do make obeisance to democratic ideals. It should further be remembered that even revolutionary parties in the Middle East are not tightly knit ideological organizations.

To sum up, the problem of the transition to democracy appears to be compounded of three related "developments." The first is political development, or the creation of a participant society. The second is administrative development, in the broad sense of permitting an expansion of the scope of governmental activity.[35] The third is economic development. For a transition to democracy to take place, it may be suggested, aside from unique events of the kind Lindsay and Lipset discuss, that economic development must precede administrative development. The reasons for this order are by now obvious: Economic development increases the wherewithal to requite demands; through political development demands are increased; and administrative development helps to provide more efficiently for these demands while the bureaucratic hierarchy is limited and is directed by the participant public. In the Middle East, the staging of these three developments has been reversed, even though, as in the West, all three have been proceeding simultaneously. According to Middle Eastern theories of democracy, it is possible to reverse the order of these developments, for both economic and political development can be brought about by the administrative apparatus. If we grant that military officers and civil servants can overcome their own role orientations, and if we agree that the key to the successful application of this reversed theory is to establish democratic institutions from above, then the transition

---

[34] A. D. Lindsay, *The Modern Democratic State* (New York, 1947), pp. 73 ff.

[35] Similar ideas are expressed by Lindsay, *op. cit.*, C. J. Friedrich, *op. cit.*, and K. Deutsch, *The Political Community and the North Atlantic Area* (Princeton, 1957).

to democracy depends upon the resources at the disposal of Middle Eastern governments, and at the same time upon the tactical choice of Middle Eastern elites as to the appropriate time for allowing democratic processes to work themselves out without administrative interference.

There is also a third alternative, one that Lipset suggests is typical of many transitional societies and that Lerner holds to be the situation in the United Arab Republic, and that probably characterizes Iran at the present time. This third alternative is where political development outruns both economic and administrative development. The response of Middle Eastern governments, as suggested, has been to press for administrative development. The consequences of their failure would be so undesirable that Western observers can only hope for the successful application of the reversed democratic faith of Middle Eastern leaders.

TWO

Legitimacy,

a Rational-Traditional System

THE POLITICS OF IRAN are unique in many ways. It is not that similar political phenomena have nowhere else appeared, but that Iran recapitulates within living memory most of the varied political experience of all the Middle East. In Iran, these experiences, compounded of nearly all that the rest of the Middle East has known, have not yet been resolved, and the future there remains uncertain. Furthermore, the majority of the Iranian people are united in a language not shared with other countries (Afghanistan, excepted) and in a nearly exclusive religion. Consequently, the study of Iranian politics recapitulates for us much that lies buried in the past of Egypt or of Iraq, yet reveals much that is distinctive.

In its constitution, the oldest document of its kind still in effect in the Middle East, Iran demonstrates some of the first timid stirrings against autocratic government in this area. In Reza Shah, Iran had its own slightly tarnished Kemal. In the present ruler of Iran, at least some of the time, we find a throwback to the traditional monarchy. Its people, too, still evidence nearly every stage of Middle Eastern development, from its small tribes and backward river people of the Helmand through the great seminomadic "federations," the poverty-stricken peasantry, the easy-going townspeople, and the striving and sophisticated two million residents of Tehran.

Iran has let nothing pass. All that is unique and all that the country shares with its Middle Eastern neighbors remains to be seen and felt today. The visitor who stays but to see a little and to talk to only a few may with equal justification report that Iran is a constitutional monarchy, a tyranny, a nation state, a theocracy, an aristocracy of one thousand families, an oligarchy of the greatest landowners and most influential generals, or a charming, wonderful garden of the most complete and utter chaos. Little has been lost to history, yet none of what remains seems real. Iranians have not yet chosen their future path, although the way has been prepared for them. And while they hesitate, they halfheartedly breathe life into a government that is as full of contradictions and inconsistencies as is the history of the country itself. The government of Iran is a living fossil. It has life; but no one, neither shah nor minister, neither military man nor bureaucrat, and certainly not the intellectual, wishes it to remain as it is. Yet the author of the present work is grateful that he has been permitted to see it as it was.

The impermanent nature of the Iranian political system is best illustrated in the variety of coexisting and competing legitimizing formulae and patterns of political activity. Here, the primary concern is with the legitimizing formulae, as statements of what the system ought to be or might be. And so this discussion will be followed by a description of the machinery which has been developed and directed toward realizing the synthesis of legitimizing ideals preferred at the present time. The weaknesses and strengths of this machinery depend only in small part upon the task they are meant to perform; for the rest, they are the product of the social and political elements which they are meant to change. These elements, then, the concentrations of social power and the ways in which this power is legitimized, will be surveyed. After giving special but brief attention to the problems of economic development and international pressures, the factors making for instability, and the prospects for the direction of future change, will complete the exposition.

The current collection of legitimizing myths, because it is plural, is incapable of being realized through the existing machinery of rationalization except insofar as that machinery itself fails to operate in accordance with the more obvious goals of its establishment. Inconsistency of both ideology and administrative implementation of policy are not in themselves unbearable, nor do they necessarily lead to change; however, there are a number of secular trends, including economic development, urbanization, and communications modernization, which are poorly managed by the machinery of rationalization. From the latter there arise increasingly insistent demands for change and for consistency.

We commence with a discussion of legitimizing formulae, rather than with an analysis of the social bases of power or a description of the ways and means of legitimizing power in Iran, because these coexistent but divergent formulae include ideas about both of these areas. The modern educated Iranian, in any case, will derive all sorts of conclusions from a statement of legitimacy by which he will tend to judge what he sees around him. Today, in Iran, this judgment is almost universally negative, for as we shall see, none of the alternative legitimizing formulae accords with reality, and there are glaring discrepancies which are obvious to all. The weight of attitudes rejecting the system are rooted in the recent history of Iran and in the gradually awakening aspirations of many classes and groups. The individual seeks increased income, higher social status, security, the ability to plan his future, and the ability to identify with the past and future glories of his nation. He seeks an end to shameful backwardness, disease, and ignorance, and an end to hypocritical appeals to conflicting ideals, an end to double standards of justice and value distribution, and an end to all those forms of authority legitimized by tradition. The individual wants all these things, yet remains very much a traditional himself, and in his ambivalence he rejects the system but not all of its manifestations. He demands that others recognize his rights as individual or citizen, but he takes advantage of any small perquisite afforded him by the rejected system; he may even work the system to the best of his ability while soothing his conscience by righteous verbalizations. This is the educated, modern, urban, male Iranian who reads the history of his country as a series of failures or hypocritical maneuvers.

Here, in present-day Iran, is not merely the sacred nation beleaguered and harassed by feudalism and imperialism, awaiting but the moment of freedom to release its energies. Here is a nation that has not ruled itself in historical times, that has had an alien religion imposed upon it, that has twisted that religion in order to cheat its Arab tormentors, that can boast no military hero, that is beset by the superstitions of its dervishes, that has been deprived by its poets and mystics of all will to change its fate, a nation where no patriot is untainted by self-seeking, where every public figure is identified by the foreign power he is said to serve, and where no one speaks the truth. The modern Iranian may deny the glories of the past or not, but he knows that the validity of the monarchy rests upon the complicated events of not more than forty years ago, that the effectiveness of the constitution of 1906 is extremely limited, that the integral nationalism of the interwar period ended in tyranny, foreign occupation, and ignominious surrender. He is aware that the aristocracy has never served the country selflessly, that the religious authorities are fearful of egalitarian social change, and that the present attempt to synthesize all these elements in a single legitimizing formula persists only at the expense of compromise and inconsistency. With his aspirations aroused, though as an individual he is unable to realize them, the modern Iranian equates inconsistency with hypocrisy, and the failure to deliver gratifications with corruption and inefficiency. In the face of five coexisting legitimizing formulae, he rejects them all and either seeks some extreme solution or sinks into despair.

The five formulas are monarchy, aristocracy, theocracy, nationalism and constitutionalism. All are current issues. The monarchy was attacked, limited, transformed, and renewed, during the last half century. Despite these developments, it is smilingly affirmed or heatedly denied that Iran is ruled by one thousand families. The aristocracy has coöpted new elements, and titles have been dropped, but it remains essentially a tribal and Qajari group with an admixture of Pahlavi cronies and *nouveaux riches* from the bazaar. The religious authorities have been deprived of much influence, and many of them openly reject the present regime, yet they have resisted modernization both within and without their institution. Their remaining influence is often exaggerated; still, all agree that the average Iranian is religious. The extreme nationalism of Reza Shah has been replaced by the "negative nationalism" of Musaddiq or the "positive nationalism" of the shah; nevertheless nationalism remains a central issue of Iranian politics and ideology. Nationalism can justify anything, but its authenticity must be established by its opposition to imperialism; that is, it must be anti-American, anti-Soviet, or neutralist, in addition to being anti-British. Iran's constitution, despite serious amendment, remains in effect. Few criticize the document, but nearly everyone affirms that it does not determine current practice, even though it should.

MONARCHY

THE IDEA OF MONARCHY has a long but not unvaried history in Iran. As might be expected from the history of monarchy elsewhere, the earliest conceptions of kingship did not allow of absolutism. The ruler was bound at once by obligations to the religious authorities, to the aristocratic families who chose him or acknowledged his leadership, and to the polity, if not to its people. Even as the idea of the caliphate developed, under the influence of Eastern imperialism, the obligations of the ruler were elaborated, though his responsibility was referred increasingly to God and the hereafter. Orthodox Sunni theory developed a short-lived tendency to justify the deposition of the ruler by a vague public authority, should he contravene the conditions of his office, but the more practical minded of the Iranian school preferred to understand revolution or military defeat as the result of either royal or popular impiety. This same Iranian school emphasized statecraft and warned of the dire consequences of inattention to duty upon the stability of the dynasty. In time, however, early Irano-Islamic political thought became permeated with both Greek philosophical and Shiite ideas. The weight of these twin influences may be found in the identification of the philosopher-king and the imam. Nevertheless, it would seem that such extremely absolutist conceptions were repeatedly mitigated by a minor theme that included both Neoplatonic ideas and Islamic notions of the constituent functions of the people of loosing and binding. This minor theme recognized the practical impossibility of finding a philosopher-king, the role of formal religion in obtaining obedience and order, the possibility of "mixed government" based on the coöperation of the king, the military, the bureaucracy, and the ulama, as well as the obligation to provide for the general welfare. With the rise of the Safavids in Iran, there was an effort to rearrange these elements so as to identify king and ulama, and the military and the bureaucracy. The Safavid shahs posed as the imams of the age and tried to assume the prerogatives of the philosopher-king. The Qajars, however, were more closely identified with the military, but the ulama, at many levels (but not at the top), were identified with the bureaucracy. The court, while not disdaining the support of many ulama, authorized both the bulk of the religious classes and the groups from which they drew their major support, even as they increasingly claimed absolute power. The claim of the Qajars to kingship was not based upon their imamate, but rather on their choice by God through the events of history, the justice of their reign, and their piety. The idea of the constitutional limitation of the monarchy was imported from the West, but was acceptable to some of the ulama as in keeping with the Islamic conception of the sultanate. Later, however, Reza Shah's attempt to institute a republic was opposed by the ulama as un-Islamic, but this was probably due to the recent example of Turkey, rather than to any intrinsic attachment of Islam to kingship. Since the accession of Reza Shah and the succession of his son, republicanism had not been much of an issue until the last days of Musaddiq's prime ministry. Musaddiq himself had demanded that the king reign and not rule, but it was Hussain Fatemi and Dr. Shayegan who demanded a republic after the 25th of Mordad.

Kingship, consequently, has a long and distinguished tradition in Iran, but it may be subjected to a variety of interpretations. It may be seen as a national cultural tradition, as an Islamic institution, as a legal institution defined in the constitution, or as the apex of a highly stratified social pyramid. For most of the people of Iran it has always been there, and they cannot conceive of any other form of government. For the favored classes it is a constant source of reward. For the dissatisfied moderns, however, it is an anachronism acquired by usurpation and maintained by violence, corruption, and foreign intervention.

Government spokesmen, during these last five years, speak of the shah in terms of unabashed adulation. Iran has progressed because of the wise and inspired leadership of the shah. The prime minister has called himself the slave of the shah. The leader of the opposition has defined the differences between the two official parties as competition in the service of the shah. The shah himself has proclaimed that monarchy is the only suitable form of government for Iran, and the ministry of court made the preparations for the celebration of the 2,500th anniversary of the Iranian monarchy during the year 1339 (1960). A newspaper statement put it, rather unhistorically, that for 2,500 years the monarchical tradition of Iran had remained unbroken. The Tehran cynics, too, tell us that everything is done by the will of the shah.

It is quite clear, despite all that may be said of the imperial tradition (dowlat-i-shahanshahi) of Iran, that the monarchy has been severely shaken during the present century by (a) the constitutional movement, (b) the regency during Ahmad Shah

Qajar's minority, (c) Reza Shah's attempt to establish a republic, (d) his nationalism, (e) his forced abdication, (f) the antagonism of many aristocratic Qajars to his successor, Muhammad Reza Pahlavi, (g) and the flight of the shah from Iran in Mordad 1332 (1953). Contemporary prepossessions with reaffirming the monarchy are to be seen as a reaction to these events, and more especially as a desperate effort on the part of the present incumbent of the throne to stabilize his position, in the face of powerful opposition and firmly rooted counterideologies. It must be noted, however, that kingship has usually been justified on the basis of some other good in Iran, and that only now is it justified tautologically. Emphasis upon its traditional basis has meaning only when tradition is passing.

From these general statements about the monarchical tradition of Iran, it is most difficult to determine the entire machinery of government and the structure of society which this legitimizing formula explains. The shah is identified with the state, and it is apparent that the primary duty of bureaucracy, judiciary, and army is to serve the shah. But the logical consequences of the general conception of the dowlat-i-shahanshahi have not been worked out. Instead, it is treated as part of a complex ideological, historical and social synthesis. This is to say, that the monarchical theory is understood to be inadequate. The image of the shah as the benevolent, sympathetic, wise, and efficient administrator is quite overshadowed by the image of a distant, cold, formal dispenser of arbitrary decisions. Nationalism, independence, industrialization, literacy, health, security; all such policy objectives are subordinated to the rule that from the marble palace goeth forth the law. During the last five years, insofar as has been possible, politics has been made a simple question of whether one is for or against the shah.

The monarchy is an institution, but the shah is an individual. The personality of the incumbent of the throne has an important bearing on the place the institution holds in the Iranian political system and upon the manner in which it is currently justified to the people of Iran. On this matter it is impossible to do more than speculate at a distance, yet some of the statements of the shah and those in contact with him are very revealing. The picture we get from these sources is of a sensitive young man who was completely dominated by his father. The affects of the thoroughgoing atmosphere of authority and duty in which he grew up cannot be measured, but they were significant, especially in that the shah has bitterly complained about these very conditions, has insisted that he cannot rule like his father, and is known to be far less ascetic than his father. Reza Shah made the monarchy, insofar as it was an effective institution during his time, but Muhammad Reza Pahlavi has been made by the institution. Moreover, he succeeded his father when his predecessor was forced to abdicate, and in those first years of his reign he frequently heard his father attacked (in the very majlis Reza Shah had appointed, too) as a dictator and a usurper. His own views were often disregarded, and he was compelled to accept aid from any quarter, the Qajar aristocracy, the ulama, and the army, although large numbers of each of these classes rejected him while others wished to use him for their own ends. Little loved, little feared, little respected, and at the same time fearful of the military, upon whom he most depended, the young shah could not but compare his position unfavorably with that of his father. The culmination of these circumstances occurred, perhaps, in the attempt on the shah's life, in 1949. By his own description, the shah was left standing alone with his would-be assassin, dodging and weaving while his bodyguard and his fawning courtiers fled. No one would risk his life to save the king. It is not surprising, then, that the shah now trusts so few people, or that he is at once cynical about protestations of loyalty and demanding of ever more extreme manifestations of personal devotion. There are few people, indeed, who can speak frankly and critically to this monarch. Political insecurity is complemented by personal insecurity.

ARISTOCRACY

THE "THOUSAND FAMILY" FORMULA for explaining Iranian politics often rings true, even though it is but an oversimplification. It is undoubtedly true that a great deal of political influence is wielded by a few families, while many more who have some wealth and notoriety are treated with great deference. Social, political, legal, and economic inequality are characteristic of modern Iran and are deeply imbedded in the everyday behavior of all classes, even those most opposed to the present regime. All educated persons recognize class distinctions and adjust their speech and manners in accordance with these preconceptions. It is also assumed, almost without exception, that one's political influence will vary in accordance with his social position or his connections with others of higher position.

Iranian aristocracy is not a monolithic institution. Its various elements include tribal leaders, owners of large tracts of land, descendants of the Qajar clan or of their more prominent servants, descendants of honored and outstanding religious dignitaries, friends and servants of Reza Shah, and a few people who have exchanged commercial wealth for landed wealth, though the latter group are increasing in number. It is not entirely clear how many whose wealth is exclusively commercial or industrial have been assimilated by the highest levels of the aristocracy, but money, and not merely land, counts for much nowadays in Iran.

In Iran, landownership is the traditional basis of deference and influence, as well as wealth; but with some exceptions, the landowning group has usually changed with the advent of a new dynasty. The aristocracy might therefore be defined as the family, or military and bureaucratic supporters, of the shah. The present dynasty, dating from 1925, did not greatly change the personnel of this class. In fact, one of the supposed aims of Reza Shah was to suppress the Qajar aristocracy in instituting a new national monarchy. Titles were prohibited, but they were transformed into last names. Qajar influence was to be obliterated, and the new elite were to be military officers, administrators, university professors, and professional and technical experts. These revolutionary aspirations, however, were not realized.

The first step backward was Reza Shah's acceptance of the crown. The republic never came into being, and the people of Iran were never permitted to participate in their own government. A president, of course, is elected, while a shah need not renew the mandate of heaven. Stranger, however, and as yet unaccounted for, was the fact that Reza Shah rather quickly made his peace with the aristocracy. Some of the wealthy landowners were victimized, and many more were simply excluded from public life. Nevertheless, many titled Qajars continued to serve Reza Shah, to be members of the majlis, and to hold important administrative positions. Reza Shah even took a Qajar princess as his second wife, though he barred her offspring from the succession. Thus, despite the appearance of new elements among the elite; the military, the bureaucracy, and the professional and technical classes remained essentially of the former aristocracy. The self-made man is still a rarity in Iran, and military or religious service still, as in past ages, offers the best chances for mobility. In addition, many of those who rose to power, fame, and fortune with Reza Shah followed his example and married their children into the aristocracy, or bought land, or both. The religious classes, as is well known, were most severely repressed; nevertheless, many whose religious pedigree went back many generations, and who had land or family connections with the aristocracy, fared not so badly, provided they did not openly oppose the shah.

The Qajar aristocracy has had to coöpt some new elements, but they are, under Muhammad Reza Pahlavi, even more influential than before. They run the state machinery, to a very large extent, and they are the beneficiaries of state policy to a significant extent. One says the same thing, whether he argues that the state ought to be run by the aristocracy or by the talented and educated. Talent is hardly recognized, unless one has an academic degree, while advancement to the highest places is reserved for those with a large stake in the system. Reza Shah's administrative state and the aristocratic tradition of Iran have made their peace with one another.

Muhammad Reza Pahlavi was compelled to accept things as he found them. His majlis was divided and outspoken, at his accession. When the Allies marched into Iran, in 1941, his army had lost its discipline, its esprit, and its ability to control affairs. Temporary coalitions of influential persons were formed to pass legislation, to profiteer, to win bureaucratic office, or to win membership in the majlis. The shah had to play the game, if he was to stay on; he had to patronize all those who would support him in return. He had to return, or at least promise to return, the lands confiscated by his father. He had to appoint as prime minister the particular nobleman pressed upon him by the majlis. And, until after Musaddiq's overthrow, he grasped at such straws as the small fascist-like parties, goonda leaders, and wellborn but not well educated ulama. Since Musaddiq's downfall, there has been much talk of economic development, of administrative improvement, of positive nationalism, of universal literacy, and the like. But through it all one may discern a persistent tendency to choose among the mediocre, the socially acceptable, and the nonideologically oriented, in the filling of key positions. In short, the aristocracy still controls the most important military and bureaucratic positions, and many of the majlis and senate seats are also held by members of the aristocracy.

It must be stressed that there exists no clear definition of an aristocrat and no well-articulated theory of aristocracy. In the minds of average educated Tehranis, an aristocrat is, above all, one who held a title under a previous dynasty or one who is descended from such a person. Usually, he will have large holdings in land, and in addition some commercial, industrial, or possibly banking investments. He and the members of his family will almost certainly hold high administrative, judicial, or military positions, and he will enjoy access to the highest places. In general usage, however, the term aristocrat may be applied to any influential person of good breeding and substantial education. Hence "aristocracy" becomes a synonym for "the privileged class." The theoretical justifications of the privileges of this class, insofar as these are expressed, has reference to the older, traditional Iranian idea of a stratified society in which each class has its particular function to perform. The task of government is to keep everyone in his place and to give each his due. The privileged class is made up of the men of the pen and the sword who serve the state. Land is the basis of their income, and absentee landlordism is a necessary complement of their presence in the capital and of their service to the state. Holding some sort of government position is a mark of honor and a means of institutionalizing access and influence, even though the salary involved may be inconsequential. This ideal picture has been somewhat marred by the bourgeois temptations in such highly remunerative operations as urban land speculation and banking, or, during the last war, in light industrial manufacturing. The privileged classes, therefore, typify the elite of diffused economic interests of underdeveloped countries, rather than a well-defined interest group. Politics, too, in so far as it is legitimate, is no more than the familial rivalries of temporary groupings of this class.

No class of persons, and especially one so loosely structured and of such diverse interests as this, can be conceived of as a mechanically operated unit. Personality, family history, education, opportunity, and more, will affect the behavior of each individual member, and the factors tending to institutionalize "appropriate" aristocratic behavior grow steadily weaker. The aristocrat's place is not ready for him, when he comes of age. He must get a Western-style education; he must supplement his income from land, as land is further subdivided through inheritance laws or threatened by talk of land reform; he must find an appropriate government job, even though the government, for several years now, has prohibited hiring civil servants. Above all, he must attach himself to friends who will put in a word for him at the right time and place. If anything goes wrong he will criticize the system which does not recognize his education or value his talents, or acknowledge the service of his family, or value him as a person. He may become a member of the "opposition." He may become a reformer. Perhaps he will write an article or a book. There is even a chance that he will become a revolutionary, though there has been only one Musaddiq.

Despite the unique experience of Musaddiq, there are many of the privileged class who would try to change many things, or who might seek to exchange privilege for permanent, even unlimited, power. The older ones would bring back the good old days when a quiet conference of a few insiders could settle many problems. The younger ones would wipe out petty corruption and achieve the highest degree of efficiency. But these alternatives fail to take account of political realities, especially that of the shah's position and personality. The aristocracy must pay for its privileges by loyal obedience and by manifestations of love, even adulation; but it must not seek power. No noble cabal can make policy, and no young blueblood can create an efficient organization of his own. None of the privileged is to be alienated, but neither are the privileged to have complete security and independence. Delegated power is to be neatly divided, the incumbents of all but a few key positions are to be changed with reasonable frequency, and obstreperous youngsters are to be given pleasant but innocuous places; above all, preference must be given the mediocre, the obedient, and the satisfied. Persons who may rock the boat are neutralized by placing them in some middle-level position. It is not surprising, then, that even the privileged classes complain.

RELIGION

THE MAJORITY of the population of Iran adheres to the Shiite faith, and this branch of Islam has been the established religion of the country since the accession of Shah Isma'il, the first of the Safavids. Originally, the Shiites were the party of Ali, the son-in-law of the Prophet, and they claimed his right to the secular succession as caliph instead of Abu Bakr, Umar, and Uthman. This claim was rationalized by reference to a disputed designation of Ali by Muhammad, to a disputed interpretation of the laws and customs of inheritance, and by the exceptional qualities of Ali, who it is claimed was the most wise, God-fearing, courageous, sinless, and humble of the companions of the Prophet. Whatever may have been the appropriate rationalizations of opposition to the early caliphate, it is apparent that the innovation of the caliphate and the restriction of tribal independence, as well as the new concentrations of wealth and the revolutionary distribution of status, ill-accorded with the simple and egalitarian teachings of the Prophet. Ali, as fourth caliph, failed to win over the whole of Islam, and his oldest son, Hasan, accepted a pension and retirement in Madina. The younger Hussain was killed in a futile attempt to rally the army at Kufa to his side. Despite the failure of the Shiite movement, but to some extent because of the "martyrdom" of Hussain, Ali and his descendants became the symbols of recurring demands for utopian justice and equality. Shiites of all kinds (and the Kharijites as well) refused to accept the practical compromise of the caliphate as the institutionalization of the secular components of prophetic charisma. Not only were dissatisfied groups attracted to Shiism, but secret societies were formed and missionaries were sent out to convert the populations of areas relatively inaccessible to the control of the caliphate at Damascus or Baghdad. Thus even today we find Shiism among Arab tribes who remained nomadic and who were compelled to continue the old raiding in order to keep body and soul together; we find it also among non-Arab converts living in the larger towns and among the tribesmen of the mountainous marchlands, villagers in isolated valleys, and tradesmen and artisans in the larger cities. Shiism not only took hold in distant Ifriqya, Yemen, Bahrain and Dailam; it also penetrated the heart of the caliphal lands, as Baghdad grew weaker. Nevertheless, none of these peripheral concentrations were able to win exclusive authority or to reunite the Islamic empire. The Qarmathians were suppressed by a temporarily reinvigorated caliphate, the Dailamite Buyyids were replaced as "protectors" of the caliphate by the Sunni Seljuqs, the Fatimid caliphate of Egypt was snuffed out by the Sunni Ayyubids. As for the Zaidi imams of the Yemen, they were never powerful enough to venture forth out of their isolation. However, Shiite messianism and millenialism permeated Islamic thought, entered folk religion, blending into the semi-mystic beliefs of border tribes and merchant and artisan classes.

Two major forms of Shiism developed, one an activist revolutionary creed which insisted upon some living exemplar of the true faith, either an imam or his designee, who was descended from or who succeeded Ali, and who was the rightful ruler of the world and interpreter of the law. Examples of this branch are to be found today in the imam of Yemen, the sultan (imam) of Morocco, and the agha khan of the Isma'ili Shiites. The other branch, known as the twelvers, or Ja'fari Shiites, differ in their acknowledgement of the true line of succession, in that they do not insist upon open rebellion, and they believe that the last of the twelve imams is now hidden and will reappear to bring justice to the earth at some unappointed time. The twelfth imam was succeeded by four "lieutenants" who interpreted the law with full authority for their followers. This period was known as that of the lesser occultation and direction of the Shiite community, then, as the "specified agency." After the four "lieutenants," and the failure of the fourth to designate a successor, there commenced the "greater occultation" and the direction of the "general agency," executed not by a specific person but by the whole body of the ulama.

The failure of the fourth lieutenant to designate a successor parallels the Sunni view that Muhammad designated no successor, and the Ja'fari Shiites are thus left in the same sort of predicament. Having no immediate spokesman for divine authority, Shiites and Sunnis both must have recourse to interpretations and adaptations of the law of the Qur'an and to traditions of the Prophet (and the imams) which, despite the extensive learning and piety that sometimes accompany them, must be regarded with an element of doubt. Similarly, it is only the imam or some specified agent who can be accepted as the ruler of the world, for the general agency of the learned and pious could not easily be referred to government.

Nevertheless, the Shiites retained strong monocratic tendencies even in questions of legal interpretation, in addition to a decided preference for a living leader. From these two predilections there emerged the notion of the propriety of following the "most learned" among the ulama, and recognizing the authority of those who have reached the highest degree of learning to reinterpret the law on the basis of their own understanding and in terms of the problems of the day. The Shiites, unlike the Sunnis, have not acknowledged the unfailing authority of the founders of schools of interpretation, but each individual must decide which living mujtahid to follow—that is, who is the most learned and pious, or at least the most learned, of those accessible to him. However, it should be quite clear that learning is not acknowledged to be passed on by heredity, though prestige is.

Consequently, it is possible to discern two Shiite themes regarding the proper government of Islam. The first is that the imam, directly descended from Ali and by divine grace exhibiting all the qualities of the philosopher-king, must rule and will unfailingly institute the kingdom of God on earth, if he is accepted by all men as he should be. The second major Ja'fari Shiism political theme parallels the Sunni tradition, and in the absence of the hidden imam it would elevate a powerful, talented, and pious ruler who is guided and advised by the "general agency" of the imam or the Shiite mujtahids.

In the absence of any attachment to a stable and extensive government, Ja'fari Shiism was slow in developing its political theory. Most particularly was this so under the paradoxical hegemony of the Dailamite Buyyids, who at once patronized the Shiite ulama and "protected" the Sunni caliphate. Shiite religious endeavor was directed both at institutional consolidation at the academic level, and at expanding ritual and personal behavioral instruction at the local community level. Emphasis on the proper institution of theocratic government was uncongenial to the Buyyids, in their delicate political and military circumstances, nor were they willing to acknowledge either the legitimacy of the Fatimid caliphate or the political authority of the most learned of the general agency.

The ideological confusion of the Buyyid period reappears during the Safavid era. The Safavids of Sufi-Shiite antecedents, established the Ja'fari Shiite religion in Iran; they called themselves imams, appointed religious judges, and regulated the pious foundations (awqaf); they appointed leading ulama to official positions and patronized those of standing in the community; and finally, they accepted the advice and guidance of the most learned of the general agency, at least some of the time. We see, then, during the Safavid period, both Shiite legitimizing ideas in effect and unreconciled. The imamate of the shah was stressed among his sufi-inclined tribal troops, while orthodox, anti-sufi Ja'fari Shiism was imposed throughout the realm, with the aid of the madrassa-trained ulama.

The Safavids, of course, did not claim to be the successors of the pre-Islamic monarchs of Iran. Nevertheless, the near absolutism of the shahs was achieved by this confusion of legitimizing theories and by the close association of military and religious sanctions. This absolutism was passed on to the Qajars, but the claim of the shah to the imamate was dropped. The Qajars, however, played the role of Islamic rulers much as did the Sunni Ottomans. They patronized the religious authorities and sometimes asked and accepted their advice; they established official religious posts and appointed ulama to them; they appointed qadis and regulated waqfs; they built mosques and decorated shrines; they went on pilgrimages and had the leading ulama declare their wars holy. Some of the ulama declared their support of the Qajars to be conditional upon monarchical piety, rightdoing, and acceptance of guidance from the general agency of the imam. Others, however, referred monarchical responsibility to God alone, and preferred prudent obedience to disorder and rebellion.

Doubts developed, and the coalition of religion and monarchy became uneasy as Western influences increased. Western education was preferred above traditional training for government service, commercial and communications concessions were granted to foreigners, new taxes were imposed, and new forms of attire appeared. The commercial classes who supported the ulama suffered in competition with Western manufactures, the Baha'i heresy appeared, and news of Western political encroachments on Islamic lands filtered through from both East and West. The income, the prestige, and the influence of the Shiite ulama declined, and criticism of their inadequacy in dealing with contemporary problems appeared at the very time when Ja'fari Shiite theology, jurisprudence, and philosophy were achieving their highest development.

Much of the friction that these changes entailed was epitomized in the preaching and in the movement of Sayyid Jamal al-Din al-Afghani. He criticized Nasir al-Din Shah Qajar for admitting so much of Western influence; he called for modernization, efficiency, technology, and piety, to combat the West and preserve Islamic society. He called for reform within traditional Islam and for activism and selfless devotion from the ulama. Some of the ulama, and more of the very small middle-class intelligentsia, responded to his teachings. Politically, the attitudes engendered by the changes suggested above, by the growing institutional strength of the ulama, and by the reformist movement of Sayyid Jamal al-Din, were manifested in the Tobacco Regie incident, in the assassination of Nasir al-Din Shah, and in the Constitutional Movement.

These three important events have been discussed at length by both foreign and Iranian historians and participants, but suffice it here to point out that while some of the ulama were prominent in these actions against the Qajar dynasty, they never acted alone nor did they press for unfettered political power on the basis of a religious theory of political legitimacy. Not only were there many ulama who declared it sinful to disobey the shah, who had been appointed by God; those who disobeyed demanded no more than that he rule in accordance with Islam and seek the welfare of the Muslim community. Any explanation of the coöperation of the ulama, seeking to retain traditional values and social organization with the modernizing constitutionalists, must ascribe some of the blame to simple confusion. Some blame also attaches to the common desire to limit the absolutism of the Qajars, some to the ambivalence of the bazaar and aristocratic classes, and some to the diverse orientations of the ulama, attached to the court, and to those deriving support from, and having influence over, substantial but nonaristocratic citizens.

The diverse interests and ambivalent orientation of the constitutionalists, further confounded by foreign intervention, rendered the new reforms largely at naught. The ulama became politically divided, for the next two decades, some remaining stanch supporters of the court, some trying to work the constitution and the majlis in order to strengthen the independent influence of the general agency, and some of the younger and more adaptable, moving wholly into public life as politicians or publicists and striking out for modernizing reform of both religion and government. The first group adjusted their allegiance to whoever was in power. The second group compelled the enactment of constitutional provisions prohibiting legislation contrary to the rulings of the general agency, as represented by five officially designated mujtahids, and they also prevented Reza Shah from establishing a republic. It was the third group that became the most vigorous reformers, changing their turbans for hats and taking government jobs, or going into exile for extremist political activity. One of the latter, Sayyid Zia al-Din, led the coup that eventually put Reza Shah in power.

Vigorous political participation by the ulama did not save them from severe repression under Reza Shah. Traditional Shiite Islam was equated with all that was backward, shameful, unmodern and non-Iranian. Nevertheless, Shiism was not as rigidly suppressed as was Sunni Islam in Turkey. The Shiite faith was not disestablished, nor was the constitution officially suspended. The new civil law was declared to be based on Shiite Islam, and this was largely so. The financial resources of the ulama were restricted but were not completely eliminated. Waqfs were not taken from religious custodians if they had a clear title, nor were the proceeds of waqfs entirely diverted from religious purposes. Toward the end of Reza Shah's reign, an attempt was even made to regulate religious training and modernize the "general agency," though its nonpolitical nature was offered in explanation.

Reza Shah's forced abdication brought numerous changes. In the general reaction to his repressive rule, the ulama, too, raised their voices and demanded, especially, control of the educational system, of waqfs, and to a lesser extent influence in the legal system. A number of fundamentalist religious movements appeared, and certain ulama threw themselves vigorously into the political arena, joining erratically or selectively with the parties, the cliques and groups, the court, or the outstanding personalities that now struggled in a many-sided battle royal.

The young Muhammed Reza Pahlavi accepted coöperation from any who offered it, and was especially gratified by the adherence of those of prominent name and family. He, too, made some religious appointments, favored ulama or their offspring with jobs, pensions, and seats in the legislature, visited the shrines and distributed largesse through religious hands, rebuilt and refurbished the mosques, invited the ulama to visit him on Now-Ruz, and responded gracefully to requests for jobs and favors from religious quarters. It was during the present reign that the most learned of the general agency was established at Qumm in Iran, rather than at Najaf in Iraq, and this dignitary has been treated with the utmost respect and deference. In the majlis, too, it has lately been repeated that Iran is an Islamic state and that no law can be passed which is contrary to the tenets of the Shiite faith.

Despite this new atmosphere, all but a few ulama will admit, even to the foreigner, that the government of Iran is not Islamic. The shah does not take the advice of the ulama, and he is not personally pious, they say. Moreover, he has redoubled his efforts at modernizing, controlling, and depoliticizing the religious institution. The dignity of the most learned, his influence and his financial support depend upon his staying clear of politics and showing no enthusiasm for the monarchy. Nevertheless, the dangers of communism and secular reform are such that a prudent silence must be maintained. Consequently, the shah's claim to be an Islamic ruler goes publicly unchallenged, though the pretense is privately ridiculed by the religious classes themselves. Posters showing the shah and a Qur'an symbolize the duty of obedience to the pious ruler, and presumably they strengthen the loyalty of the simple, traditional, religious-minded masses. The younger intellectuals either deny religion or criticize it for passive support of the regime, while the ulama and their more religiously sophisticated supporters in the bazaar quietly but firmly deny the legitimacy of the regime.

NATIONALISM

AS A SYMBOL OF LEGITIMACY, nationalism is in less dispute than other symbols and is in less dispute than nationalism in some other Muslim lands. There is, however, the considerable problem of diverse interpretations of nationalism, some of which blend with one or another of the competing legitimizing formulae, other interpretations denying them all. Nationalism in all its manifold expressions, however, is ubiquitous among educated Iranians, and it is therefore all the more surprising that conscientious effort has not succeeded in turning up a single book attempting to set down the theoretical or other basis of Iranian nationalism.

Many of the so-called "objective" bases of nationalism exist for Iran, though as for all other nations, the firmness of these bases depends upon one's attitude and willingness to see exceptions. If one tries, he finds that Iran has a distinctive national history, a distinctive language, a distinctive religion, a distinctive literature, a distinctive art, and is even inhabited by a distinctive subrace. Emphasis upon these distinctive features, because they are not thoroughgoing, must lead to the anxious denial of contrary evidence. The Arab invasions and the Mongolian catastrophe did not break the continuity of Iranian history, for these barbarians were gradually civilized and assimilated. The linguistic minorities in Iran are inconsequential, or if not they speak Persian dialects, or at least are so Persian in other ways that it does not matter. Shiism is not only the true religion (or, some say, not necessarily the true religion); it is also the distinctive adaptation of Arab Islam to Iranian culture. The Sunni minority are primarily Kurds who, it is agreed, are racially and linguistically Iranian anyway. The other minorities are of no account except, of course, for the Zoroastrians, who are even more Iranian than the Shiites. No excuses have to be made for claims to Iranian excellence in literature and art, crafts and architecture; nevertheless one can discern among some moderns a tendency to reject the traditional art forms (though not so much traditional poetry) in favor of modern imports from the West. The distinctive racial characteristics of the Iranian people are not quite imaginary, though they are largely illusory; yet Iranians from the central plateau are taller, lighter skinned, or longer headed than their neighbors to the east or west. The underlying stock is held to be primarily that of the brown Mediterranean race, but enough of the long-headed, Caucasian, and Turkish blood has overlain this base to noticeably differentiate central plateau Iranians from Arabs, Turkmen, or Pakistanis.

Aside from the common denominator of these several factors, current nationalist attitudes lead to a variety of conclusions regarding form of government, policy, and foreign relations. The important place that historical tradition holds in shaping the nation permits shah, aristocracy, and religious groups to claim legitimacy for their positions, privileges, and influence, even in terms of modern nationalism. Such justification as is sought by these groups, however, is hesitant and partial only. It is more in the nature of an adjustment to a challenge, an adjustment accomplished by incorporating certain of the challenger's argument, and distorting the rest.

Supporters of the monarchy are at pains to point out the national traditional basis of that institution. Nevertheless, the posters which appeared on the streets on the anniversary of Musaddiq's deposition proclaimed the slogan "God, Shah, and Fatherland." Fatherland, rather than the nation, is the preferred symbol. In answer to the insistence that nationalism must be manifested in an independent foreign policy, in social and economic welfare, and in egalitarianism, the monarchy has produced the slogan of "positive nationalism." This term is meant to contradistinguish Iran's policies from those of the neighboring Arab countries and from the negative policy of Musaddiq. Iran must not cut off its petroleum nose to spite its nationalist face. Iran must coöperate with those countries that offer it aid. Iran must not follow a sterile neutralism while confronted by the threat of communist subversion or Soviet aggression. Iran must not embark on risky social adventures such as expropriating landowners and nationalizing large enterprises. Progress must be planned, slow, and steady. Above all, Iran must not change or shake its inherited institutions, which represent all that is positive and worthy in the national culture.

Few persons spontaneously discuss "positive nationalism," and when the subject is brought up even the members of the privileged class seem uneasy. The nationalist justification of aristocracy oscillates between vague references to tradition and claims that aristocracy is best able to serve the state. Among the younger members of this group, however, the talk is more often of administrative efficiency and its dependence on higher or technical education, of which they have a surfeit. Occasionally, the baneful effect of foreign intervention will be mentioned, or Musaddiq may be cited as the true symbol of nationalism, but most younger aristocrats will simply restate the basic thesis of Iranian nationalism, along with the hypothesis that all the prerequisites of greatness and progress exist, if only good, honest, educated and intelligent persons are put in charge in order to utilize them. The emphasis upon universalistic-achievement symbols is not the complement of nationalism, but the result of Western education.

It is not to be thought that many of these younger men are

in grave disagreement with their elders about the significance of family and descent, or about the rights transmitted by a noble, titled, or well-positioned ancestor. Last names often reflect descent from someone who played a prominent part in Iranian history, regardless of how the national historians judge that part. For that matter, the national historians, in sharp contrast to foreign historians, are surprisingly gentle in their judgments of the influential aristocrats of the past. So long as a man was powerful, so long as he had a part in determining affairs, he is treated as a hero. Part of the reason why this is possible, of course, lies in the fact that most of those engaged in the great issues of the constitution, or in the accession of Reza Shah, were wise enough to get on both sides of the issue, as circumstances required or permitted. From the older members of the aristocracy one gets the impression that they have a proprietory attitude toward the country, its history, and its culture, also toward the characteristics of nationalism, if one insists on them.

The attitude of the ulama toward nationalism is ambivalent in much the same way. The older ulama are certainly not nationalists. Some have attacked nationalism as a form of idol worship or *shirk* (associating others with the deity), but most would attack only the secular, modernizing nationalists. In general, one can say that the ulama are largely unmoved by nationalism as an ideological problem. Islam does not recognize differences of nation or race or language, but to say that Shiism is the religion of Iran and that Persian is the language of the leading Shiites is no more than the truth. Efforts are being made to reduce the antagonism of Sunnis and Shiites, and Arabic is the language of the Holy Qur'an, but one certainly feels most at home among Shiites and in speaking the Persian language. Furthermore, given the fact that Iran is the only Ja'fari Shiite country, the ideal of a Pan-Islamic state or of a revival of the Sunni caliphate can have little attraction for the ulama of Iran. Thus, in Iran more than in any other Muslim land, Islam flows along with nationalism, though even here the two are not identical. Insofar as nationalism merely affirms the distinctive language and religion of Iran, even insofar as it insists on national independence, it is acceptable to the ulama.

Monarchy, aristocracy, and religion have all attempted to accommodate the challenge of nationalism, but their efforts go largely unrecognized by those who call themselves nationalists. The roots of Iranian nationalism as a political movement do not go back very far. Until the rise of Reza Shah, and to some extent till this day, the issue has been more constitutionalism than nationalism. Nationalism, perhaps integral, romantic nationalism, was Reza Shah's ideal. Most Iranians did not take his efforts very seriously, either because they were not yet ready or because they were too sophisticated to accept its ideological enormities. Nevertheless, the glorification of the nation, the attempt to romanticize its history, the idealization of Zoroastrianism and the pre-Islamic empire, the partial effort to purify the language, the haphazard attempts to popularize folk culture and crafts, the revival of pre-Islamic architectural motifs, and the emphasis upon military power, athletic ability, discipline, heavy industry, and artistry, did lay the foundation for a wider awareness of the distinctive basis of Iranian nationalism.

This basis having been laid, and nationalism thus associated with all that was worth while in the pre-Islamic age but that was now corrupted, it was easy to relate nationalism to all that was inherently good in Iranians, even though it could not be released until the fetters of tradition were cut. As we have seen, Reza Shah did not succeed in cutting these fetters, and his fall was accompanied by the return of Britain and Russia and the advent of the United States to influence. Nationalism has therefore come to mean social reform, free elections, industrialization, land distribution, the exclusion of foreign influence, and the nationalization of petroleum, perhaps even of other natural resources. It also means ending corruption, reducing religious influence, opening careers to talent, achieving universal literacy, and maybe even recovering some long lost irredenta. The young, urban, educated men who call themselves nationalists find in these goals the logical consequences of the distinctive characteristics of Iran, and they judge others with reference to the same goals. The most important single symbol of this nationalism is still Dr. Musaddiq, regardless of whether he himself would have approved of each of these goals.

There are some special varieties of nationalism which emerged during the Musaddiq period and which still lie beneath, but close to the surface, of Iranian politics. These varieties may be conveniently grouped as those of the left, the right, and the middle. Leftist nationalism was best expressed in the publications of the Tudeh Party that were meant for the general public rather than for their own members. The Marxist orientation of the party was rarely exposed to public view; instead, heavy emphasis was placed upon national independence, democracy, and social equality. The Tudeh faltered badly on the question of oil nationalization, for they demanded only nationalization of south Iran oil, excluding that of the north in order to provide for a concession to the Soviets. The nationalist and anti-imperialist slogans of the Tudeh emphasized the importance of the workers and peasants, but the major appeal was to the young intellectuals. Yet the Tudeh did, however, succeed in reaching the industrial workers, and some peasants, at the same time appealing to the intellectual snobbery of the students with publications including avant guarde poetry, discussions of new western art, and philosophical tracts. They emphasized the evil results of the alliance of feudalism and imperialism, but the primer of modernization for most of their nonforeign-trained members was Kasravi and his outrageous iconoclasm.

Nationalists of the right came under the general heading of Pan-Iranists, of whom there were several small groups, specializing in streetfights with communists. These groups usually benefited from court support, though not continuously and not without reservation. Their appeal was greater among high school students than in the university, and their slogans and literature were largely nonrational appeals to activism, glory, self-sacrifice, blood, and soil. The influence of the Nazi and Fascist movements was marked. Military discipline was sought. Internal struggles for power were constant. Ceremonial and mystique were emphasized, and uniforms were a *sine qua non*. Anticommunism was as important as the Pan-Iranist objective. The latter was never very clear, sometimes threatening Afghanistan and Pakistan, sometimes coveting Iraqi and Turkish territories, and as occasion demanded emphasizing Iranian irredenta under Soviet control. These groups have dwindled, since the 28th of Mordad, and all but one have died. The remaining group is moderately active in criticism of the present regime, and they claim to be nationalist in the sense of appealing to the average young intellectual. Their leader was jailed for a three-week period, in 1959, as a demonstration of the mild displeasure of the government.

The nationalists of the middle now go under the name of the Iranian National Resistance movement, and they subtitle some of their clandestine publications as "In the Way of Musaddiq." Before Mussadiq's deposition, the middle might be identified as the followers of the Iran Party, the Toilers Party, and the Third Force Party. These three parties have now all been reduced to friendly conversation groups, and it seems that only some of the Iran Party leaders remain active in the Resistance Movement. The rest of the activists are younger people not among the disillusioned or cautious majority. These people also stress the alliance of feudalism and imperialism, but they do not entirely gloss over the danger of Soviet imperialism. They tend to be socialist, after a fashion, and have even drawn the Pan-Iranists over to their slogans in favor of limiting landholdings, nationalizing foreign enterprises, controlling larger domestic firms, controlling rents, and increasing the availability of (middle-class) urban housing. They also press for the restricting of urban land speculation, for increasing the wages of civil servants, for cutting out corruption, for equalizing opportunity, and for adjusting rewards to performance. This is the now familiar line of Middle Eastern radical reform, aimed at benefiting the lower middle class; it contrasts significantly with Khalil Maliki's (Third Force) advocacy of a west European type of socialism that seems entirely out of place in Iran. All of these people tend to be either anti-American or extremely suspicious of all things American.

There are other less vigorous and less popular nationalist tendencies abroad in Iran. For example, there is the Iranvij society composed of a few university professors and their friends, who are holdovers from Reza Shah's highly patronized but unhistorical and, from a scholarly point of view, questionable movement. They argue that the Arabs never conquered Iran; they say that Shiism is Zoroastrianism in Muslim clothing; they theorize about teaching literacy in six easy lessons, if their organic alphabet is adopted; but they hesitate to publicize their views widely because they feel that the public is not ready. The Fidayan-i-Islam, for all its religious zeal, had a strong nationalist streak too, seeking to purify the Persian language and reunite the Iranian-Shiite lands as well as to establish an Islamic government under an imam. This tendency, now greatly moderated, lives on in a few groups of younger semimodernized, educated men of major cities. There are also remnants of the followers of Kasravi, who meet occasionally and reprint his writings for distribution. These call themselves patriots, and they seek the salvation of their country in the purification of Islam and the establishment of true constitutionalism. Feudalism and imperialism are not so much the problems as are the superstitions and false faiths of imamism, sufism, impractical philosophical speculation, interpretations of the Persian poets, and the study of allegorical exegetics. Obviously, the work of Kasravi was largely negative, in that it shook the foundations of tradition for his young readers. His own "religion of purity" and his constitutionalism did not replace that tradition, but the way was opened for new secular ideologies.

At least one other group of a more exclusive and aristocratic membership considers itself to be nationalist. Its aims seem to be centered on improving the government of Iran by increasing efficiency and giving important positions to those who, like themselves, deserve to be so honored.

CONSTITUTIONALISM

LIBERALISM, PROGRESS, modernization, anti-imperialism, and nationalism are all freely confused with constitutionalism, in Iran, as is the more usual ideal of democracy. Iran has had a constitution since 1906, and an amplification of this constitution was codified in the Supplementary Fundamental Laws of 1907 and in the several amendments that have since been passed. Constitutionalism has thus become part of the background of the political scene. Those in power claim to be enforcing the constitution, or at least trying to make it work as it should, while those who deny the legitimacy of the present regime insist that the government is merely using the constitution as a façade.

The constitutional movement has been extensively treated elsewhere, though no definitive work on the subject exists. Similarly, works on the constitution itself exist, but none is exhaustive or even adequate. For present purposes, therefore, it may be sufficient to note that the original document of 1906 merely provided for the election of a national assembly (the majlis) from among six social classes, for the purpose of legislating for Iran. The Supplementary Laws added a number of important sections: the provision for review of all proposed legislation by a board of mujtahids, who would decide whether it was in accord with Islam; a general statement separating governmental powers in Iran into executive, legislative, and judicial; a section on civil rights; and another section on the rights of the monarch. Thus the foundations of Iranian constitutionalism are: the three principles of Shiite Islam, the monarchy, and the separation of powers. Neither civil rights nor the independence of the judiciary have become great issues, nor have they been realized in any approximation of the manner developed in Western constitutional countries.

It is patent that the crux of constitutionalism in Iran is neither more nor less than parliamentarism. The majlis is the symbol of constitutionalism, and the government has justified its policies by citing the fact that implementive laws have been passed by the majlis. The opponents of the regime say that the majlis has been hand picked by the court, and they cite the fact that the prime minister has told the majlis, in the same breath, that he is the servant of the shah and that they must pass the legislation presented to them. Members of the majlis and the senate stand very much on their dignity as representatives of the people; they may delay legislation, even for long periods when the government is not quite sure of what it wants; they may change minor provisions to serve their own interests; but in the end they are always obedient to the wishes of the government.

Elections in Iran have never been entirely free or fair. In the first fifteen years after the constitution was adopted, even under a highly restrictive electoral law, the majlis sat for little more than three years. From 1924, and more especially from 1928 to 1941, the majlis was the obedient and chosen instrument of Reza Shah. From 1941 to 1953 it was a divided, irresponsible, and venal collection of prominent persons who quickly defeated those governments that found no way of preventing their meetings. Since 1953— that is, since the fall of Musaddiq—the court has closely controlled both the majlis and senate. Even when the control was not great, the same sort of people were elected, though those who won their seats in the major urban areas tended to be at once more nationalist, more anticourt, and more antiforeign. Presumably, elections in the provinces were more easily managed by the local military commander, the *gendarmerie*, and the representatives of the ministry of the interior.

Although the majlis has at times symbolized the objective of limiting monarchical power, the cabinet has rarely been such a symbol. Some prime ministers have tried to do without royal direction, but until Musaddiq none on the basis of principle. In a sense, Musaddiq's government was that of the National Front, but after taking office he permitted the Front to languish, so that it all but disappeared. Nevertheless Musaddiq based his demand that the king reign and not rule, and he justified his demand for control of the army not on any principle of cabinet government based on party but on the principle of the separation of powers and the supremacy of the assembly. It may here be noted that Musaddiq was not in full control of the majlis, though many of its members were cowed by the Tehran mob; even at the height of his power he was unable to elect his own majlis. In any case, Musaddiq based his claim to supreme power on his choice by the majlis. To deal with the superficial aspects of this challenge, at least, the court encouraged the formation of two official parties to take the place of the traditional majority and minority in the majlis. The former prime minister, Dr. Eghbal, was the leader of one of these parties, and the head of the other is a stanch and loyal supporter of the monarchy and of Muhammad Reza

Shah personally. Thus the role of the prime minister as not only the servant of the shah, and/or as head of the government and/or leader of the majority in the majlis, has been worked into the system.

Constitutionalism, as presently maintained in Iran, is a farce. Even the newspapers, on Constitution Day, freely editorialize on how long the road still is to true constitutionalism and democracy —though foreign powers, or sometimes Musaddiq, are often blamed. Yet the continued existence of the majlis is confusing, and it tends to add to the growing unconcern with constitutionalism as a legitimizing and useful instrument of government for the people. The people of Iran, if one is to consider the overwhelming majority, understand monarchy and are either oblivious of the existence of the majlis or pay little attention to it. For others, knowing a member of the majlis, or perhaps becoming a member of that body, is rather helpful or is a much sought dignity. For the opponents of the regime, however, the majlis, as it now operates, is proof of the hypocrisy of the government. Indeed, it is the government, rather than the young modernized intellectuals, that stresses the importance of the majlis. The dissatisfied urban classes think more in terms of the necessity of a strong man, a Nasir or a Qasim or an Ataturk to solve their problems. It is remarkable that constitutionalism is only brought up to illustrate how bad the government is. No intellectual effort is being spent on the problem of how to make representative government work in Iran. No one but the members of the parties themselves even pretend to take such questions as those of party elections seriously.

THE PAHLAVI SYNTHESIS

ALL OF THESE VARIETIES of legitimizing formulae coexist, if somewhat uneasily, in Iran. Until or unless some revolutionary change occurs, all of those who are politically aware, in attempting to fashion some order out of confused reality, are compelled to conjure with each of the formulae and to put them into some relationship with one another. For those who oppose the regime, this task is somewhat easier, for they may juxtapose the false and the true, the bad and the good, the government as it is and as it claims to be. For the government, however, such a task is more difficult, for all of the formulae must be accepted as true, and all must be related in a single comprehensive synthesis.

The government attempts to synthesize, but its efforts are not very successful. Most often, one finds that five separate and distinct symbols or groups of symbols are appealed to but are not reconciled. The importance of the monarchy, of course, receives the greatest emphasis, and it is identified with the state and sometimes the nation. Aristocracy is not explicitly favored, but the privileged class, aspirants thereto and clients thereof, are taken as the representatives of the people. These are given seats in the majlis and are permitted to present welcoming addresses to the shah and prime minister, and their support of the shah is taken as a further legitimization of monarchy. A group of the prominent ulama in both the capital and the provincial centers serve much the same purpose in legitimizing the monarchy, from the Islamic point of view. The nationalism of Reza Shah and the efforts of the present shah to win a steel plant and extend the railroad system are examples of the resources exploited in order to lend nationalist legitimacy to the monarchy. Constitutionalism, too, is exploited for the same end, as all branches of the government stress the need for coöperation and concert in carrying out the shah's "progressive program." One need not belabor the fact that all symbols capable of eliciting some sort of favorable popular attitude are associated with the monarchy.

But this is flimsy stuff, even as is the whole game of propaganda and symbol manipulation in Iran today. Iran still awaits its communications revolution, even though Tehran itself has been in recent times politically volatile. The participant public, or at least those who are aware, are not easily swayed by propaganda, particularly when to be so swayed would make it infinitely harder to make rational decisions, even at the level of the problems of everyday life. If symbol manipulation alone were the method utilized to keep the present regime, it would have a short expectancy indeed. It is not the Pahlavi synthesis of competing legitimizing formulae which is the crux of the matter. This serves only to justify the existing paradox. The problem is really where the Iranian system is heading, and the real Pahlavi synthesis relates to where the shah and his supporters wish it to go.

As the Iranian political system exists today, it is primarily a traditional system. Its main pillars are a divine-right king, an aristocracy legitimized in a parliament, and an established religious institution. The working of this system will be examined below, but it must be stressed that tradition has been sharply altered by both constitutionalism and nationalism. Yet efforts to accommodate these two new elements, and suggestions that the functioning of the system is being altered more in the direction of conventionalism, remain only at the level of symbol manipulation and political tactics. In so far as the system is being consciously changed, even in so far as the opponents of the government wish to change it, it is being changed in the direction of a rational-hierarchical system. At the moment, Iran is in transition, and its political system may best be described as a traditional-rational system, the historical parallel for which may be found in the early monarchical states of western Europe.

The rationale for the dynamic tendency toward rationalization is to be found in the confluence of history, personality, and political exigency. The present dynasty of Iran may cite the 2,500 year history of the monarchy, but its own title goes back but 35 years. Reza Shah took the throne as a reformer, as a kind of Iranian Ataturk. He was to destroy tradition—that is, the traditional monarchy, the privileges of the aristocracy, and the prerogatives of the ulama—and build a new Iran. The formula for the new Iran was integral nationalism, centralized, disciplined, and near totalitarian. The difficulties in the way of Iranian progress and self respect were to be swept away by dictatorial fiat, and the new strong, loyal, honest, rational, obedient Iranian would emerge at a command. Reza Shah's failure has simply made the problem more poignant and has supplanted what is, elsewhere in the Middle East, the last basis of hope with a paralyzing despair.

Has the present shah abandoned his father's ideals? Has he rejected his father's goals? It would seem not. However, it is obvious that he could not proceed immediately in his father's footsteps, because of the conditions prevailing after his father's abdication. It also seems that he was temperamentally unable to use his father's methods at that time. The abdication of Reza Shah, foreign occupation, and the increased authority of the majlis simply served to reinvigorate tradition. Muhammad Reza Pahlavi took things as he found them, and perhaps naïvely hoped that he could achieve similar results by other means more congenial to his personality. In any case, he strengthened the elements of tradition against each of the extremists: those who would have a communist Iran; those who would return to the previous dynasty, or at least impose Qajar aristocracy control over the Pahlavi dynasty; those who wanted an Islamic state; and those who thought in terms of "real" constitutional democracy. Traditionalists and modernists alike opposed him, but in accepting whatever support was available from all classes, for whatever reasons, Muhammad Reza Pahlavi strengthened the traditional aspects of the Iranian political system. He tied some of the aristocracy and some of the ulama to the crown, but in so doing, and in the absence of full control of the machinery of government, he was powerless to pursue his father's goals. Rational policy had to be sacrificed to sheer survival.

Musaddiq did the rest. Musaddiq had been compelled by Reza Shah to withdraw from public life, and his strength lay in the fact that he collected behind him all the elements of opposition to the shah. But he also alienated, after a time, all the traditional opponents of the shah, and he carried into irreversible opposition the younger adherents of reform, rationalization, secularism, nationalism, and constitutionalism. He also carried into opposition all those who stood for the things that Reza Shah had said he favored. The traditionalists rallied around the king, and enough of the army did, too, to carry the day against Musaddiq, who refused to accept the logic of the situation he himself had created.

But consider the tragedy of Muhammad Reza Pahlavi, the son of Reza Shah, who was forced to accept the verbal loyalty of those whom his father had sought to destroy, who was now beholden to a small group of army officers whom his father had ordered about like new recruits, and who was now alienated from those with whom he had formerly felt great sympathy. However, there is no reason to believe that this was the result desired by the shah, or that he had rejected his father's aims. Nor is there any reason to suppose that the shah felt secure, under these circumstances, and after the trauma of Musaddiq.

The actions of the shah since the 28th of Mordad make sense only if we see in them the twin objectives of securing his position and fulfilling his father's ill-starred mission. These are twin objectives, because it is impossible for the shah's position to be secured unless he can achieve complete control of the administrative, judicial, and military machinery of the state. And it is impossible to do that unless the machinery is so organized that it can be controlled from a single command post; furthermore, it is useless to do so unless the machinery really controls the state, useless, that is, unless it controls the people of Iran. It might be possible to win security by some less thoroughgoing or extreme method, but it would be difficult to pursue a nonhierarchical course without first having to conjure with traditional opposition. The traumatic consequences of less thoroughgoing techniques put a premium on absolute security; moreover, this is the only available or feasible means of achieving the Pahlavi mission.

The Pahlavi synthesis of all five legitimizing formulae at the communications level is, then, paralleled at the level of practical policy. Tradition, comprehending the paraphernalia of aristocracy and constitutionalism with an admixture of religion, is balanced against rationalization aimed at realizing integral nationalism through a hierarchy of shah, bureaucracy, and military. The balance is a delicate one, and rationalization, too, is not without its risks. If less hierarchical control might result in aristocratic opposition, so might greater rationalization lead to subordination of the shah or his elimination by the military and bureaucratic chiefs. On the one hand, there is the specter of Qavam al-Saltaneh and Musaddiq; on the other, there is that of Razmara and Zahedi. Nor are the nationalists and the communists to be forgotten in their challenges, at present suppressed. There is little wonder, then, as we shall see, that the pursuit of rationalization and hierarchy is irresolute and cautious.

THREE

The Machinery

of Rationalization

THE GOVERNMENT OF IRAN is irrevocably bent on a policy of modernization and development. The ideological bases of this policy have already been briefly mentioned, and some of its political implications have been suggested. There are some parts of Iran into which the hope for a new and better life has not penetrated, but most reports confirm that these are becoming fewer and less important. There are classes and groups which are hesitant about admitting the unqualified virtue of modernization, but none reject it in theory. There are, of course, different ideas about what modernization entails, ideas which are freighted with legitimacy preferences and rationalizations of interests, but all those who have an opinion opt for change.

As in most parts of the Middle East, social change in Iran was initiated from outside its borders in a continuous historical process which began about a century and a half ago. Iran's response to foreign pressures, again typically, was composed of dissimulation, evasion, hostility, and partial surrender. The lesson of the organic interrelationship of technology and culture, of science and philosophy, of administration and society, and of ideology and politics was learned slowly and painfully. The legitimacy confusion which has resulted in Iran is the product of the interaction of these related aspects of human existence and of a variety of attempts to adjust matters by calculated political change. Institutional change has availed little except to create awareness of the pseudomorphic character of the Iranian political system.

As we have noted, legitimacy confusion, manifested in the incongruence of power relationships and legitimizations may lead to either administrative reform or the exploration of new political techniques by dissatisfied groups. To cite an Iranian example, the constitutional movement succeeded briefly because of a temporary coalition of diversely interested groups, and it culminated in establishing a new system legitimacy. However, almost immediately thereafter the legitimizing acts of the majlis were rendered ineffective by the defiance of its opponents, who were now encouraged by foreign support. The majlis tried to strengthen its control over the administrative apparatus of the state, but this attempt did not succeed. New techniques were explored, in the immediate post-war period, mostly emphasizing the use of force to win the objectives of the original constitutional movement. The Sayyid Zia-Reza Khan coup succeeded in establishing a new system legitimacy, and Reza Khan immediately proceeded to reform and rebuild the military and administrative services. His opponents were not permitted to explore new political techniques, except for secret conspiracies continued at great risk. After Reza Shah's abdication, though, many new techniques were employed, this time centering on the formation of ideologically oriented parties. Musaddiq, of course, succeeded in employing an entirely new technique of direct popular appeal through self dramatization. He did not succeed, however, in fully resolving the prevailing legitimacy confusion nor did he obtain the support of the security forces; and Muhammad Reza Pahlavi, since he regained control, has tried to reform the administration and tighten his control so that technique exploration might be eliminated.

The restriction of technique exploration, if efficiently pursued, involves much more than mere suppression of hostile groups. Political techniques are not limited to those forms of activity legitimized in formally instituted electoral or legislative procedures. There can be no a priori limitation of a literary group; and the enthusiastic demonstration of loyalty by the members of an underprivileged class can be politically functional, in the sense of seeking some sort of legitimization. Some Iranians feel that they are opposing the government by disobeying traffic laws, by withholding goods from the market, or by being overrigid in following regulations. Only the most efficient administration can cope with these techniques when silently coöperated in by large numbers of people.

Modernization and development put an additional premium on efficiency.[1] By common agreement, modernization and development are the responsibility of the bureaucracy and the government. This common agreement arises from divergent premises. Some hold that it is the government itself which has prevented modernization and so must be changed; some feel that powerful groups have diverted modernization to their own ends and must be restricted by government; some believe that lack of administrative skills and coördination have caused the high hopes of the past to be disappointed; others believe that the failure of Iran to modernize is due to the degeneration of Iranian culture and the false faiths and values that prevail, and that these ills must be remedied systematically and by force; still others feel that the investment, planning, and coördination necessary for modernization are such formidable problems that only a government capable of mobilizing all the resources of the country can solve them.

The common agreement on the importance of modernization, or at least change, is both a rejection of the existing system and a denial that beneficial change can grow out of it naturally. Therefore, if change is to be realized through the administrative apparatus, its personnel must be independent of their social and cultural environment. They must be separately educated, economically independent, and responsive only to the objectives of their organizations. The work of the various administrative organizations must be coördinated, and all must be controlled by a single pattern of priorities and standard criteria for the allocation of

---

[1] Regardless of whether an administrative organization is being used for social reform or to eliminate technique exploration, it cannot do without a measure of efficiency. For present purposes, it is enough to define efficiency in terms of the inevitable discrepancy between legitimization and power relationship. Administrative action can be identified in this context as governmental action following up a legitimization. (Even the decision to study a particular problem and devise a plan thereafter is a legitimization.) Consequently, administrative action is politically functional insofar as it succeeds in altering power relationships, and efficient insofar as it brings such power relationships into closer conformity to legitimizations. The lack of minimal efficiency, involving the inability to keep order or to supply the necessities of life, may cause rejection of either the society, the regime, or the government.

resources. The bureaucracy must comprehend the necessary skills and must be able to manage the facilities required for accurate statistical research, programing, and projecting the results of plans into the future. They must also be enabled to utilize, or develop, the technical skills involved in balanced economic planning.

The problem of efficiency may be related to two general issues emerging out of these considerations: one is the personnel issue, its recruitment, training, and professional orientation; and the other is the issue of organization, involving provisions for planning, clear lines of authority, division of tasks, supervision, responsibility, and coördination. The proper resolution of these issues might be called rationalization of the administrative system, and this involves converting it into an efficient hierarchy. This definition, however, raises two further questions: the first relates to control, and the second to the purpose for which the administrative system is to be changed. These are really two aspects of a single political problem. Must the administrative hierarchy be monolithic? What kind of political system is envisaged in the transformation of the administrative system?

These are political questions of the highest order. If the administrative hierarchy is multilateral, rather than monolithic, all the external points of political decision making must be tied together or efficiency will be lost. But technical efficiency without regard to political values is without meaning, for if a diffusion of political power and a conventional polyarchal system is preferred, then a measure of decentralization and some division into separate administrative hierarchies is efficient. On the other hand, if thoroughgoing social and cultural change is desired, how can the very groups which are to be changed be permitted to determine administrative objectives?

Prevailing values and aspirations negate the legitimacy of discrete power structures paralleling coöperating administrative structures, though something like this is now the case. It is also arguable that Iran has a dispersed administrative apparatus controlled by a single political command post. These are two conflicting interpretations of the present situation. The first interpretation coincides with either the aristocratic or the constitutional theories of legitimacy, while the second corresponds to the monarchical or nationalist theories. The coexistence of both tendencies has led to our classification of the Iranian system as a traditional-rational system.

The dilemma posed by the existing composite is enhanced by the twin monarchical goals of rationalization and security.

Rationalization is not merely a policy, but an ideology as well, and it renders pleas for technically efficient organization irresistible, given the assumption that empirical objectives are known or knowable through the application of unbiased reason.

Rationalization of the administrative apparatus, particularly under conditions where popular support is lacking, must be accompanied by a similar rationalization of the military and security forces and by their subordination to, or coördinated support of, the bureaucracy. This is one aspect of the security problem, but the other relates to the security of the shah himself. The history of absolute monarchy in the Middle East is replete with tales of the usurpation of power by military and bureaucratic leaders; and the recent experience of Middle Eastern and Asian countries is even more ominous. Rationalization, modernization, and development have brought military dictatorships to Egypt, Sudan, Iraq, Pakistan, and Burma. Indonesia varies only slightly from the norm, and Turkey somewhat more. Iran, of course, tended in the same direction at the time of Reza Shah, but now the wheel has turned full circle.

The shah can turn neither to conventionalism nor to rationalism without risk. The majlis exists, but it wields no real power; elections will be held, but they will not be free; the ministers meet often, but they are not a collegial body, united on policy. To change these patterns would be to invite another, one such as Musaddiq, to insist that the shah reign and not rule; or another Fatemi or Shayegan to opt for republicanism. Administrative reforms are continuously under consideration; some have been given legislative effect, but no decision for rationalizing the whole apparatus or for disengaging its personnel from the contemporary political process has been made. Two parties have been authoritatively recognized, and plans for reorganizing the ministries and installing a position classification and merit recruitment program are being developed at length. These two facts illustrate the two routes which may be followed. The relative lack of emphasis upon both, in the highest quarters, reveals at once ambivalence about the future, and preoccupation with short-range considerations.

If short-range goals are to be achieved, the existing administrative machinery must be used in accordance with its traditional mode of operation, or a new agency must be set up to bypass the problems of coördination and constant bargaining. If the long-range aim of rationalizing the administration is to be pursued, opposition will be manifested in bureaucratic sabotage of current programs and at least temporary chaos or the risk of a coup born of frustration with endless and complex inefficiencies.

The efficiency of Iranian bureaucracy is, therefore, partly a function of the degree to which the shah is capable of dealing adequately with all the parallel lines of administration reaching up to him independently of one another. Not only is the royal household or the ministry of court lacking in the necessary planning and coördinating machinery, but neither the plan organization nor the cabinet supply this need, except in small part. It is possible to discern some effort and greater aspiration on the part of the prime minister toward developing this machinery, but the shah has not given unqualified support here. There is also some impatience in military circles with both administrative inefficiency and lack of coördination, but the military leadership is by no means unified enough to press its views. The security and influence of the shah depend on his being a bridge between the civil and military services, as well as among the various branches of each. The price in terms of efficiency is correspondingly great. The result is that all recent reforms of the machinery of rationalization have been superficial and have not altered traditional bureaucratic patterns. Rationalization remains, therefore, an aspiration; and the transitionally traditional-rational system remains on dead center. Changes are occurring in the environment of the system, but they are not controlled, nor even measured, while the hierarchization of politics has not proceeded very far.

It is not merely a question of manipulating the administrative and security machinery. Resources, both human and material, are limited. The services boast a long history and a deep entanglement in the social fabric of Iran. Individual members of the services are themselves products of the ideological revolution of recent years, and many tend to withhold active support. The people of Iran, too, are not amenable to control by such means as now exist, they are both inaccessible to some parts of the machinery of rationalization and accessible to foreign influences. In addition, the proper management of modernization requires a nice adjustment of economic development, urbanization, education, communications development, and the like, as well as careful budgeting of limited financial resources. No one has yet learned how to make this adjustment without the occurrence of attendant political crises, short of imposing totalitarian controls. Nor has Iran yet begun to plan economic development, let alone coördinating such a plan with a desired adjustment of the factors mentioned.

Here our concern is not with all the ramifications of these problems, many of which will be referred to later, but with the machinery of rationalization as it exists. Our purpose is to examine the administrative resources which can be used in rationalizing the Iranian polity, before going on to assess the magnitude of the problem faced by this machinery, in the form of the present political system of Iran. This procedure emphasizes current policies favoring change, but it should not mislead toward the conclusion that this machinery is independent of the political system, even though it is already partially, and potentially wholly, dysfunctional to the existing system. The institutional form of this machinery had, by the middle of the present century, been almost entirely determined by reform and modernizing objectives. But it still operates largely on the basis of traditional standards. The meaning of rationalization in this context is obvious, but we must reëmphasize the fact that traditional operating characteristics are reinforced by the political system.

If any single issue has achieved the proportions of the efficiency-corruption preoccupation, it is the restricted basis of access and influence and the unequal distribution of political values which results. The legitimization of privilege by the present regime is one of the bases for its lack of support, particularly since it continuously asserts a contrary ideal. Such legitimization is manifested in politically functional, but legally deviant, behavior on the part of the bureaucracy. If theory and practice are to be reconciled, the whole administrative apparatus must be overhauled—an event which must be both the cause and the effect of a radical change in the Iranian political system. Paradoxically enough, such change is implied in many government development policies and in efforts to achieve greater control and regulation of interest groups, but the administrative machine remains incapable of coping with these responsibilities.

THE ROLE OF THE CABINET IN THE GOVERNMENT OF IRAN

IN THIS SECTION we will canvass the problem of whether or not the Iranian cabinet (within the broad context of the executive branch) is capable of carrying out the duties which have been imposed upon it by present political exigencies. In the main, these duties involve coördinating the increasing activities of a government bent on achieving economic development, so as to requite the demands of a population whose degree of political awareness is very nearly equal to the degree of its alienation from the present regime.

Specifically, we shall attempt to show that the present cabinet of Iran does not depart greatly from its historical predecessors, that its character and function are in no great measure determined by the constitution of Iran, that recent efforts to increase the power of the cabinet under Mussadiq were paralleled in earlier periods and have their parallel today, that these efforts cannot succeed without weakening the position of the shah, and that (even if the prime minister were given greater control over the cabinet) the prevailing procedures, subordinate administrative resources, and "culture" of that body will not allow for increased efficiency in carrying out its duties.

The Iranian cabinet is not capable of the coördinated planning and control required by high government policy. Its shortcomings are not due to any lack of application on the part of the ministers. It will be shown, rather, that the ministers spend a large amount of time in cabinet meetings and that they have evolved relatively stable procedures. The cabinet is, however, practically isolated from certain administrative organizations and does not appear even to try to perform any but those tasks traditionally accomplished in the cabinet or "divan" of the past.[2] Moreover, the Iranian cabinet has evolved a kind of micro-group culture of its own, comprising a strange combination of the prestige ranking and informal clique relationships that so often characterize small nonkinship groups in Iran. The evening meetings of the cabinet suggest also that these affairs have something in common with the more "socially" oriented *dowreh* (meeting) of the latter groups. In any case, this culture has militated against the consultation by strong prime ministers like Razmara, Qavam, Musaddiq and Zahedi with their cabinets; while it has drawn weaker ones into endless bickering and maneuvering in order to gain minimal coöperation and recognition of the primacy of the prime minister.

Historical developments have had a significant impact on the modern Iranian cabinet. Even, perhaps especially, the instability which has characterized this institution during the present century parallels that of earlier periods. Since Safavid times, the shah of Iran has always played a prominent role in the executive, but the degree of his direct involvement in policy making and ad-

---

[2] Because the cabinet of Iran is in part an imported institution and in part a descendant of indigenous institutions, the term cabinet will be used interchangeably with "executive" and "government," when discussing historical near equivalents.

ministration has varied widely. Generally speaking, the more closely
the shah has been associated with the business of government,
the less has been the authority of the prime minister and the more
restricted has been the administrative sphere of the cabinet. On
the other hand, whenever the shah has been more withdrawn
from governing, the cabinet has held a tighter control over affairs.
There has been another long-term fluctuation of power between
the prime minister (or his equivalent) and his cabinet colleagues,
which is partly to be explained by the personality and influence
of the prime minister. The rest of the explanation depends upon
a further fluctuation in the choice of cabinet members from among
those who are politically powerful, such as the tribal leaders or
nobility, or from among commoners of the technician variety.
The latter tendency has almost always been the result of efforts
at greater centralization, coördination, or reform by either a
powerful shah or a powerful prime minister. There has been another tendency to allocate authority and decision-making power
more on the basis of the individual concerned, and his political
support, than upon the formal position that he held. Consequently, there have always been a number of higher executive
positions or organizations which have existed outside the framework of the cabinet; sometimes these have been created by the
shah, sometimes by the prime minister, sometimes by the majlis
(though never really controlled by that body), and sometimes
forced upon the government by unofficial groups (principally
in earlier periods).

Alongside of these inconsistent tendencies there have been a
number of secular trends. One of these has been the increasingly
clear separation of the private household of the shah and the
central administration of the state. Another related trend has
been the impersonalization and professionalization of the civil
service, with some effort to extend this character all the way up.
A third trend has been the redefinition of the duties and the
more consistent acceptance of the position of the prime minister.
A fourth trend has been the understandable increase in the scope
of governmental functions, especially in the social welfare, economic development, and fiscal management fields.

In addition to these fluctuating tendencies and secular trends,
it may be well to keep certain other characteristics of the Iranian
executive in mind. One of the consistent features of Iranian
government has been the absence of civilian control over the
military, and the close relationship of the latter with the head
of the state. A second characteristic, despite concerted efforts at

coördinating the budgeting, accounting, and auditing functions, has been the absence of a centralized control over economic policy. Similarly, there is no centralized organization of personnel matters. A fourth characteristic has been the subordination of the judiciary to the executive. This last has always been partly true, even when traditional Islamic courts applied Islamic law, but during the present century, when even the restricted sphere of Islamic personal status law has come to be applied by secular courts, this is even more the case.

Ideological conceptions of the nature of the cabinet have undergone certain changes since the successes of the constitutional movement some fifty years ago. The educated classes no longer accept ministers merely as the servants of the shah or as the great lords of the empire, though ministers are still thought of as very lucky people, indeed. The constitutional documents of 1906 and 1907 have not clarified the position of the cabinet, though they have affected it. The specific provisions applicable to the ministers will be taken up below; suffice it for the present to remark that a good deal of ambiguity has resulted from a rather academic overemphasis on the doctrine of the separation of powers.[3] This overemphasis has encouraged the attitude toward ministers as merely chief administrators or high level technicians. Consequently, there seems to be a strong prejudice against the politicization of the cabinet, which in turn complicates the effort to place the head of the state above politics.

Any attempt to substantiate the preceding generalizations would require a full-scale study of the administrative history of Iran, as well as far better studies of Iranian political history than we now have. Here, no more than a few points of historical background will be offered, first to stress the dependence of present-day institutions on the past, and second to point in the direction of the kind of historical research which will be useful for further inquiry into Iranian political institutions.

It is a commonplace of Islamic history that the origin of the wazirate was in the government of the Sasanids.[4] This contention has not been proven unequivocally, however; and the

---

[3] *Supplementary Fundamental Laws*, Article 27; see also Qasim-zadeh, *Huquq-i-Asasi* (6th ed.; Tehran, 1334), p. 440.

[4] A. Christensen, *Iran sous les Sassanides* (2d ed.; Copenhagen, 1944); C. Cahen, "The Body Politic," in G. E. Von Grunebaum, ed., *Unity and Variety in Muslim Civilization* (Chicago, 1955), p. 146.

history of this office under the early caliphate is complicated, even after the period of the famous Barmakis.[5] Regardless of this "orientalist" problem, the position had been so far accepted, by the middle Abbasid period, that we find an entire chapter devoted to the wazir and his duties in one of the most famous Sunni expositions of the laws of Islamic government.[6] It was under the Seljuqs, however, and as a result of the efforts of the greatest wazir of all, Nizam al-Mulk, that the pattern of Iranian administration became most firmly established. The ideological tensions associated with the policies of Nizam al-Mulk are best exemplified, on the one hand, by the establishment of the Nizamiya academy, which borrowed heavily from the Islamic intellectual tradition, and on the other, by the well known *Siaset Nameh*, attributed to the great wazir, which stands four square on the contemporary recollection of Sasanid theories and techniques as mediated by the Samanids and Ghaznavids.[7] References to the wazirate by Sunni legists were certainly rare, but rarer still were those of Shiite theologians and legists. Consequently, even though the wazirate was accepted by the ulama, it was never clothed in any but the reflected religious legitimacy of the caliphate. With the decline of the political power of the caliphate, it is possible to infer the religious responsibility of the wazir as one who happens to hold power. But this has nothing to do with defining his position and function.

With the development of the wazirate under the Umayyads, the chief administrative posts were not clearly separated from the particularistic and diffuse role of tribal leadership. The similarity of the position of the Sasanid *vuzurg-framadhar*, who was often a leading member of one of the great tribes, should be noted. In this light the rise of the Barmakis may be seen as the high point of the effort of the early Abbasids to centralize and impersonalize their administration. A parallel effort was made to impersonalize the military, somewhat later, but with disastrous results. By the third Islamic century we find that both the civil administration and the military have been assimilated to the caliphal household, and that the caliph has lost effective control of both. The decline of the caliphal military forces opens the phase of tribal-militaristic

---

[5] S. D. Goitein, "Origin of the Vizierate and Its True Character," *Islamic Culture*, XVI (1942), 257.

[6] Al-Mawardi, *al-Ahkam al-Sultaniya* (n.p., *ca.* 1058).

[7] Nizam al-Mulk, *Siaset Nameh*, ed. and tr. C. Schefer (Paris, 1893).

invasions, each of which takes over the existing administrative apparatus, establishes a new dynasty, and subsequently attempts to depoliticize its military forces. In a sense, all of Islamic history, from the time of Harun al-Rashid, may be seen as a struggle of successive rulers to establish obedient, professional, and impersonal administrative and military structures. By and large, this struggle was successful with the bureaucracy for a time, but it was unsuccessful with the military, and at least in eastern Islam these two classes were drawn from different ethnic groups.[8] With the assimilation of the Mongols, the latter distinction became increasingly diffused, and under the Ottomans the ruling institution, hardly distinguishable from the "slave household" of the sultan, supplied both military and administrative leadership.[9] But under the early Safavids of Iran, the tribal-military basis of Shah Isma'il's support was also represented in the chief administrative posts, though Shah Abbas attempted to limit this dependence by substituting Caucasian slaves for Turkoman nobles. In addition to this attempt to alter the character and allegiance of his chief military and administrative personnel, he tried to shift revenue producing areas from the Mamalik to the Khassa bureaus, that is, from the control of provincial governors to that of the central administration.[10]

Under the Safavids, a more or less formalized council of ministers came into being, composed of up to eleven officials.[11] The first four of these and the last were the formal heads of military formations, so that the diffusion of functions is obvious. The members of the council were:

1. the qurchibashi (chief of the old tribal cavalry), who appointed the governors of the provinces; [12]

2. the qullar-bashi (chief of heavy cavalry armed with muskets, technically slaves of Christian origin), who was in charge of all the servants of the royal household; [13]

3. the eshik-aqasi-bashi (chief of the palace guard), who was master of official ceremonies and official doorkeeper; [14]

---

[8] Cahen, *op. cit.*, p. 147.
[9] Lybyer, *The Government of the Ottoman Empire in the Time of Suleiman the Magnificent* (Cambridge, 1913).
[10] V. Minorsky, ed., *Tadhkirat al-Muluk* (London, 1943), pp. 13, 14.
[11] *Ibid.*, p. 44.
[12] *Ibid.*, pp. 33, 46.
[13] *Ibid.*, pp. 33, 46.
[14] *Ibid.*, pp. 47, 118.

4. the tufangchi-aqasi (chief of the musketeers, mounted infantry of Persian peasant origin); [15]

5. the wazir-i-a'zam, who was in charge of all revenues from the Mamalik territories and from Isfahan, though he might inspect the Khassa accounts as well; [16]

6. the divan-begi, who was sort of a chief justice in charge of all the shari'a courts, responsible for the execution of all qadi decisions, and who presided over the high court of appeals (especially against administrative wrongs); [17]

7. the vaqi'a-nivis, who kept the official records of assemblies, put the shah's orders in due form, served as private secretary to the shah, and was in charge of similar subordinate officials in all the provinces whose reports were a major source of political intelligence; [18]

8. the amir-shikar-bashi, the master of the hunt; [19]

9. the mustaufi al-mamalik, who was possibly subordinate to the wazir-i-a'zam, and charged with the technical financial operations of accounting, auditing, and preparation of the budget; [20]

10. the nazir-i-buyutat, who was in charge of the Khassa revenues and the royal workshops; [21] and

11. the sepah salar, or commander in chief, who attended council meetings when some military campaign was under consideration.[22] The nazir, the mustaufi, and the master of the hunt are all recorded as having attended council meetings only in the last years of the reign of Shah Sultan Hussain.

It is quite clear from this recitation that even so sophisticated a policy making group was made up of the military leaders of both old and new formations, of finance officials, of court officials, together with the chief legal officer; that is to say, it included persons whose policy making functions were secondary attributes of their positions. Moreover, the unstable character of the membership and the overlapping of some duties indicate that function was a corollary of the trust and favor of the shah. The grand wazir was not described as the head of the cabinet, and so far was he

---

[15] *Ibid.*, pp. 32, 48, 118.
[16] *Ibid.*, p. 116.
[17] *Ibid.*, p. 119.
[18] *Ibid.*, p. 121.
[19] *Ibid.*, p. 120.
[20] *Ibid.*, p. 122.
[21] *Ibid.*, p. 118.
[22] *Ibid.*, p. 44.

from controlling all government operations that there is some doubt about his authority over the mustaufi al-mamalik.

The work from which this information was derived was intended to permit the Afghan conquerors of the Safavid empire to continue the same administrative system. Despite this effort, and despite the chaotic history of Iran during the remainder of the eighteenth century, we find the Qajars emerging with a somewhat more formalized and much better controlled ministerial apparatus than formerly. For one thing, the absolute authority of the shah over the ministers was established in principle.[23] For another, the Qajars had managed to exclude the tribal nobility from these positions.[24] However, the relations of the shah and prime minister, and of prime minister and cabinet were not well defined. Sometimes the prime minister was charged with the supervision of all departments; usually he was the equivalent of a modern minister of finance; and sometimes another minister of finance, or the mustaufi al-mamalik was appointed. But again, he was usually charged with matters of general policy, including foreign affairs.[25] Malcolm's interpretation of the situation prevailing at the beginning of the nineteenth century is worth quoting: "It is impossible to give an exact description of the duties which the Prime Minister of a King of Persia has to perform, these depend upon the degree of favor and confidence he enjoys, and upon the activity and energy, or indolence and incompetency of his sovereign." [26]

The Qajar shahs continued to maintain control over their ministers, and even left the post of sadr-i-a'zam, or prime minister, vacant for a six-year period. Nevertheless, with or without royal approval (and the issue is not clear) the composition of the cabinet, and hence the distribution of the major functions of government, increased in rationalization, and the power of the prime minister was enhanced. At the middle of the nineteenth century the composition of the cabinet is recorded as follows:

1. the sadr-i-a'zam,
2. minister of interior,
3. minister of foreign affairs,
4. minister of justice,
5. minister of public works,
6. master of the mint,

---

[23] Sir John Malcolm, *History of Persia* (London, 1815), Vol. II, p. 487.
[24] *Ibid.*, p. 437.
[25] *Ibid.*, p. 436.
[26] *Ibid.*, p. 435.

7. minister of war (also commander in chief),
8. comptroller of the privy purse,
9. private secretary of the shah.[27]

The increased importance of the prime minister is described by a contemporary British observer: the sadr-i-a'zam "is the alter-ego of the Shah, superintendent of every branch of the administration, and referee on every disputed question. In the absence of a Grand Vizir, many of the functions proper to such a post devolve on the Shah himself." [28] However, in the absence of the sadr-i-a'zam, the mustaufi al-mamalik served as president of the council.[29]

If we cannot credit the Qajar shahs with these changes, we may at least acknowledge that they would have been impossible to achieve without royal approval. It is somewhat more difficult to assess from available sources the responsibility of the prime ministers themselves. The outstanding prime minister of the period under discussion was Mirza Taqi Khan, the Amir-i-Nizam, now better known as Amir-Kabir. There is little doubt that Watson was generalizing from the arrangements under Amir-Kabir and his successor. Nevertheless, we find nothing to indicate that Amir-Kabir reorganized the government at its highest level. He reduced useless ceremonial, he fought bribery and corruption, he credited all the bad debts of the previous administration, he tried to centralize control of the administration, to regularize the military organization, and to provide modern educational facilities.[30] He also reorganized the financial administration, apparently by concentrating all its functions in a single department.[31] However, he does not seem to have attempted to fashion the cabinet into an efficient instrument of policy-making nor into an administrative coördinating board, for he tightly controlled all governmental activities himself; he made the mustaufi al-mamalik directly responsible to himself, he held the ministry of war himself, and he was in direct charge of the intelligence agency.[32] Apparently, he had no interest in organization reforms that might not outlast his own ministry. Rather, he concentrated upon working the existing system to the best of his great ability, and this he did by choosing only "honest and industrious" subordinates.[33]

---

[27] R. G. Watson, *A History of Persia* (London, 1866), p. 17.
[28] *Ibid.*, p. 16.
[29] *Idem.*
[30] Watson, *op. cit.*, pp. 371 f.; F. Adamiyat, *Amir Kabir va-Iran* (Tehran, 1323), Vol. I, pp. 126.
[31] Adamiyat, *op. cit.*, p. 113.
[32] *Ibid.*, pp. 113, 127, 150.
[33] *Ibid.*, p. 121.

The increased rationalization of the highest level of the Iranian administration, which we have noted, is probably to be attributed to the stronger position of the Qajars, to the exclusion of the tribal nobility from higher administrative posts (though certainly not from political influence), and to the predilection of contemporary British observers to put a familiar construction upon an unfamiliar institution.

After leaving the position of prime minister vacant for six years, Nasir-i-Din Shah Qajar appointed the second great Iranian prime minister of the nineteenth century, the Sepah Salar. This was the period in which the Iranian government was most susceptible to Western ideas and techniques. After the shah's visit to Europe, the Sepah Salar proposed a decree to reorganize the Iranian cabinet along the lines of that of France, and incidentally to establish thereby his own precedence as prime minister. The necessity of writing this authority into law may be an indication that the clear superiority of the prime minister which existed at mid-century came to be contested—or more likely that it never implied clear political superiority. The decree which was approved by Nasir-i-Din Shah provided for the establishment of nine ministries and one bureau (sadarat).[34] The ministries were:

1. interior,
2. foreign affairs,
3. war,
4. finance,
5. justice,
6. education (ulum),
7. public works (fava'id),
8. commerce and agriculture,
9. court, and the bureau was the Sadarat-i-A'zami, or the prime minister's office.

This cabinet was called the darbar-i-a'zam. The prime minister was to be the chief of the cabinet, and all the ministers were to be responsible to him for the administration of their departments. Individual ministers were strictly limited to their own departments, except insofar as they might contribute to general consultations, when they might participate in one another's work and share responsibility. The prime minister was to be appointed and dismissed by order of the shah, and individual ministers were to be appointed and dismissed by order of the shah, according to the advice of the prime minister.

---

[34] Nazim al-Islam Kermani, *Tarikh Bidari Iranian* (2d ed.; Tehran, n.d.) p. 110 f.

The cabinet was to meet every Sunday and Thursday at the prime minister's office at four o'clock. The agenda was to be prepared in advance. Meetings were always to be held at the same place, none but cabinet business was to be discussed, and none but ministers were to attend.

The decree went on to provide that every ministry was to have its own building; that every minister should report, from time to time, on the activities of his department, which report would be approved by the prime minister and signed by the shah; that the authority and activities of each ministry would be determined by the cabinet; that all increases or decreases in personnel would first have to be approved by the prime minister in cabinet; that no minister had the right to create new offices without cabinet approval or to dismiss "servants" without permission; and that salaries would thenceforth be dependent upon, and specifically related to, posts, and would have no relation to persons. The salutory principle "name and fame are entirely separate from salary" was laid down.

The last part of the decree presented some of the reasoning behind its proposal. The Sepah Salar held that once the basic foundation existed all the rest of the affairs of the kingdom would gradually become well organized in a natural way. The decree went on to stress the importance of carrying out this program and stricty imposing it upon all the ministers. The prime minister would be responsible for all administration to the shah, and individual ministers would be responsible to the prime minister. The prime minister would be the sole medium of governmental intercourse with the shah; all requests and reports from the ministries would be given to the prime minister, who would bring whatever was necessary to the attention of the shah. The shah's answer would then be received by the prime minister, who would further convey it in a letter to the ministries concerned.

From the emphatic repetition of the section on the prerogatives of the prime minister, we may understand part of the intention of the Sepah Salar. While we may sympathize with his efforts to formalize the executive procedures of the cabinet, to carefully delimit authority on that level, and to rationalize the distribution of administrative functions, we must admit that he hoped for too much on both counts, that of the political possibility of establishing such a system by mere decree, and that of the felicitous results that must naturally follow upon such a reform. While certain prime ministers have been able to dominate their colleagues, the office of the prime minister has never acquired the character insisted upon in the decree. Moreover, it is quite clear that the rigid implementation of this arrangement would have rendered the shah gradually more and more dependent upon his chief minister. However, neither the ordinary ministers nor the shah have since been reduced to so powerless a position. Even the highly formalized procedure preferred by the Sepah Salar has never been rigidly instituted, as we shall see. Of so little effect was this unique effort that the constitutional documents of 1906 and 1907 reflect none of its spirit.

Iranians may be justly proud of their constitution, for it is the oldest document of its kind still in service in the Middle East. If its goal was too ambitious for an underdeveloped polity to achieve, it nevertheless set a noble objective for Iranians to strive for. These sentiments notwithstanding, the Fundamental Laws of 1906 confused constitutionalism and parliamentarism; while even the Supplementary Fundamental Laws of 1907, which much more nearly approximated a constitution, left certain issues in doubt. One of these issues was the status of the cabinet, and particularly that of the prime minister.

The constitution of Iran mentions the cabinet and the prime minister but twice each, and then only in passing. It refers to ministers who are appointed and dismissed by the shah.[35] There is also one reference to the council of ministers, in the clause providing for the dismissal of the cabinet or an individual minister, should the majlis or senate be dissatisfied with either.[36] The prime minister is mentioned merely to indicate that he, too, may propose bills to the majlis.[37]

The constitution also states that the number of ministers will be fixed by law,[38] but this provision had no effect on existing ministers until the single "cabinet statute" was passed by the first majlis. Article 21 of the Fundamental Laws of 1906 states that the majlis must approve any change in the "fundamental laws of the ministries" regardless of whether initiated by the min-

---

[35] *Supplementary Laws*, Article 46.

[36] *Ibid.*, Article 67.

[37] *Fundamental Laws*, Article 33; Article 15 of the same document provides that bills passed by parliament will be forwarded via "the first person of the government" for the royal consent.

[38] *Supplementary Laws*, Article 62; Ahmad Araqi, *Huquq-i-Asasi-yi-Iran* (Tehran, 1331), pp. 362–363, holds that this article prohibits the establishment of new ministries without majlis approval. This is true, but it has not prevented the appointment of ministers of state without special authorization.

isters or the majlis. Apparently this use of the term "fundamental laws" refers to the law which originally established the ministry, and not to constitutional law subject to the special amending procedure or to basic administrative regulations outside the sphere of the majlis. In any case, no such laws were passed for existing ministries. The constitution nowhere defines the scope or powers of the cabinet, and there is no provision that ordinary ministers shall be appointed upon the advice of the prime minister.

Two commentaries on the constitution add material derived from the practice of the cabinet which may be considered conventions. Professor Qasimzadeh writes that in Iran the ministers are organized in a cabinet, at the head of which is the prime minister. The cabinet approves the general policy of the government and determines its relations with the majlis. In addition, every minister must present a report to the cabinet on all important matters bearing upon his department. All bills prepared by ministers and all treaties must receive the approval of the cabinet before being presented to parliament.[39] Mr. Araqi holds, without reference to any constitutional provision, that the cabinet may issue decrees and regulations for carrying out the laws.[40] Actually, the constitution describes this function as "the King's right."[41] Araqi implies that this authority is derived from specific grants of power by the majlis. Cabinet decrees, he writes, may not exceed the limits of the legislation which they implement; they may not regulate those portions of the constitution which are to be further specified by law; they may not contravene other valid legislation; they must be in accordance with the general principles of Iranian law, such as that of equality before the law; they must be discussed at a formal cabinet meeting, and each of the ministers must declare themselves thereupon; and they must be published in the official gazette as well as in newspapers of wide circulation. Mr. Araqi goes on to differentiate other decrees that are really orders relating to the executive branch of government and that do not depend upon prior majlis authorization but apparently require a majority vote of the cabinet.[42] But Araqi does not mention the acquired authority of the cabinet

---

[39] Qasimzadeh, op. cit., pp. 376–377.

[40] Araqi, op. cit., p. 416 f.

[41] Supplementary Laws, Article 49. The quotation is from Browne's translation, A Brief Narrative of Recent Events in Persia (London, 1919), p. 95, still much the best English version. The original Persian may be found in Qasimzadeh, op. cit., p. 449 f.

[42] Araqi, op. cit., p. 419.

to issue decrees which are only afterward approved as law by the majlis.

Other important constitutional provisions make the shah not responsible,[43] require that every act of the executive branch in the name of the shah be countersigned by a minister,[44] give the ministers the primary power of initiating legislation,[45] and permit ministers to appear before plenary sessions and committees of the majlis.[46] Ministers may not be members of the majlis concurrently.[47]

There is some disagreement over the power of the shah to dismiss his ministers, despite the aforementioned emphasis upon the separation of powers. Mr. Araqi offers a prolonged argument to prove that the shah must dismiss the ministry whenever it fails to receive a vote of confidence.[48] Professor Qasimzadeh disposes of the issue with a brief statement to the same effect.[49] However, both sources are silent on the question of whether the shah may dismiss ministers who have not suffered a formal loss of parliamentary confidence. The matter is clearly "internal" to the executive branch, and it may be explained by reference to the clause which prohibits a minister from evading responsibility on the ground of his having followed commands of the shah.[50] This clause does not require that the shah be inactive; it insists, rather, that the relations between the shah and the ministers are beyond the sphere of the majlis, without in any way limiting the power of parliament to compel the dismissal of ministers. The new provision which empowers the shah to veto financial legislation is similar to that which empowers the shah to issue decrees for giving effect to the laws, but it exists alongside of provisions which clearly imply that ministers cannot veto majlis decisions.[51] This new veto power is generally considered a personal prerogative of the shah, though his message will probably be countersigned by some minister or by the entire cabinet.

---

[43] *Supplementary Laws*, Article 44.
[44] *Ibid.*, Article 45.
[45] *Fundamental Laws*, Article 33.
[46] *Ibid.*, Articles 31, 40.
[47] This rule was definitively established in the electoral law of 1911, as amended in 1927, but it has always been a strong convention. See J. Tavallali, *Le Parlement Iranian* (*These*; Lausanne, 1954), pp. 172–173.
[48] *Op. cit.*, pp. 407–410.
[49] *Op. cit.*, p. 377.
[50] *Supplementary Laws*, Article 64.
[51] *Fundamental Laws*, Articles 15, 19, 40, 41.

The constitution did not aim at regularizing the organization of the cabinet, nor at regulating the relations between the shah and the cabinet or between the prime minister and the rest of the cabinet. It seems that the ministers and their relations with the shah were more or less accepted as given at the time. The Sepah Salar's efforts in this regard were ignored, and, if anything, the position of the prime minister was made more equivocal in law than it had been in practice. On the other hand, it was assumed that the various ministers would encompass all government activities. The view of Professor Qasimzadeh notwithstanding, it was not assumed, nor is it the case today, that all ministerial functions would center upon the cabinet. The constitution provides for joint and individual responsibility,[52] thus designating a sphere in which the ministers may not be responsible to the cabinet. Joint responsibility exists for matters of general policy, and this is the sole legal basis for the ministers to meet with one another. Mr. Araqi's views notwithstanding, the constitution does not require that decrees be passed at a formal cabinet meeting, nor can there be any such thing as a *formal* cabinet meeting, under the constitution. Even bills presented to the majlis and senate for approval need not be forwarded by the entire cabinet.

The practice of the Iranian cabinet is not based upon the constitution. It rests upon a preconstitutional foundation and has developed under the impact of extralegal forces, in accordance with the tendencies, trends, and characteristics outlined above.

If the constitution left things pretty much as they were for the cabinet, the majlis did not. The first majlis attempted to assert its authority over the executive branch and

> On March 17 (1907) *it was decided to abolish the post of Prime Minister, or Sadr-i-A'zam, and Mirza Nasru'llah Khan Mushiru'd-Dawla, who held this office since the granting of the Constitution, resigned. The new Cabinet under the presidency of Sultan Ali Khan Wazir-i-Afkham, included the Farman-farma (Minister of Justice), the Ala'u's-Saltana (Minister of Foreign Affairs), the Na'ibu's-Saltana (Minister of War), the Nasiru'l'Mulk (Minister of Finance), and the Muhandisu'l-Mamalik (Minister of Public Works). Amongst the members of this Cabinet all the Ministries (which had hitherto been distributed among some 58 office-holders)*

---

[52] *Supplementary Laws*, Article 61.

were divided, so that a Cabinet Minister was now responsible
for each department of the State, and coördination succeeded
the former chaos.[53]

It is obvious from the reports we have of earlier reforms, that
merely reorganizing the departments of government and declaring
them coördinated was insufficient to realize any real improvement.
The majlis would have had to exert much more continuous
supervision of the cabinet, and to have been much more capable
of controlling the political infighting among the noblemen, who
were then the only eligibles for ministerial positions. Furthermore,
simply to group a number of departments under a single head
does not necessarily bring about coördination, as the experience
of contemporary Iran shows. Nevertheless, in this action of the
first majlis we find another in a long series of attempts to rationalize Iranian administration and to reduce the number of opportunities for administrative profiteering.

The second majlis was without any stable majority, so that
cabinet "crises" were all too frequent. This was the period of
Ahmad Shah Qajar's minority, when there was no one to jealously
preserve the royal prerogative. It was Nasir al-Mulk, the regent,
a man educated in England and anxious at once to rule con-
stitutionally and to avoid difficulties, who instituted the practice
of consulting the majlis before appointing a prime minister.
This practice was the beginning of the now disputed convention
of the preferential vote by which later assemblies presented their
nominee to the shah. Nasir al-Mulk went on record with the
suggestion that the majlis should be organized into majority and
minority parties, the former being capable of sustaining a cabinet
and its policy.[54] For this "innovation" he is much blamed by
Morgan Shuster, who states that the majlis agreed, but that the
ensuing partisanship led to too many cabinet crises.[55] Bahar,
however, records the existence of "Democrats" and "Moderates"
at the time of Nasir al-Mulk's election,[56] though, obviously,
these were not stable parties.

The period during which the majlis exerted some measure
of control over the cabinet was limited. On December 24, 1911,

---

[53] Browne, *op. cit.*, pp. 21–22.
[54] Tavallali, *op. cit.*, p. 87.
[55] M. Shuster, *The Strangling of Persia* (New York, 1920), p. 236.
[56] Malik al-Shu-ara Bahar, *Inqiraz-i-Qajarieh* (Tehran, 1323),
p. 8, illustrating that Shuster's failure was a triumph of good will over
good political insight.

with the approval of the cabinet (which Shuster considered to be illegally in office [57]), the regent dissolved the majlis. The third majlis met only from November, 1914 to November, 1915 before it dispersed, while the fourth majlis did not assemble until June, 1921.[58] During the period of Ahmad Shah's minority, the cabinet was itself the dominant force in the country, and it ruled without much interference from the regent, though under a good deal of foreign pressure. Even after the shah was crowned, in 1914, he seems to have been dependent upon his ministers, until his dispute with Samsam al-Saltaneh, in 1918. Samsam al-Saltaneh attempted to defy the shah's dismissal order but was unsuccessful.[59] However, there is ample evidence that Ahmad Shah continued to control his cabinet only with great difficulty.[60]

The position and power of the Qajar dynasty were greatly diminished by a number of political factors: opposition of the ulama, the merchants, and the intellectuals in the constitutional movement; British support for this movement; the support of non-Qajar tribal leaders and the Qajar-created landed proprietors for the constitutional movement; the deposition of Muhammad Ali Shah after his anticonstitutional coup; and above all, the appointment of a child as the last of the Qajars. Ahmad Shah never regained the power of his predecessors. His reign was marked by the increasing power of the ministers, while the source of ministerial power shifted from the authority of their offices to the social and economic power of the ministers themselves. The culmination of this tendency was achieved in the coup of 1921, when Reza Khan, at the head of the Persian cossack corps, installed a cabinet including himself, without reference to the shah. The cossack corps was the only significant military formation at that time, and while it was not a sufficient lever for the acquisition of unchallenged power, it enabled Reza Khan to succeed Ahmad Shah and to establish the Pahlavi dynasty, in 1925.

The new dynasty was to be based upon an expanded and reorganized army and a new career bureaucracy, the development of both having been begun before Reza Shah's accession. Until these new foundations of power were consolidated, coöperation was willingly received from some groups of the Qajar-created landed class. Thereafter, the landed proprietors were as often the victims as the beneficiaries of the regime, and the tribal nobility

[57] Shuster, *op. cit.*, p. 206.
[58] Tavallali, *op. cit.*, p. 114.
[59] Bahar, *op. cit.*, p. 30 f.
[60] *Ibid.*, p. 37 *et passim.*

was generally suppressed. A new class of influential individuals arose in the army and the bureaucracy; these were essentially of middle-class antecedents, but in the last analysis all were dependent upon the favor of the shah. Both the cabinet and the majlis reflected these changes, and there was a high degree of coöperation between them and the shah. However misguided were the policies of this period, there were some real accomplishments: administrative procedures were established, and the cabinet became a more orderly and coöperative body. Majlis succeeded majlis without great lapses of time, and improvements in the practice of cabinet-majlis relations were realized. However, throughout this period important policies and decisions were made at the court and were only carried out or made more precise by the ministers.

The forced abdication of Reza Shah Pahlavi, the breakdown of his system of control, the occupation of the country by foreign troops, and the intervention of foreign powers in Iranian politics restored the chaotic conditions of 1911 and 1921. Shah, prime minister, cabinet, army, landed proprietors, ulama, new war-rich merchants, old bazaar and craft guild groups, bureaucracy, intellectuals, and professionals—all came undone. Seemingly, there was nothing to bind all these, and the new labor groups as well, in coöperative effort. There were no rules to the game any more; one prime minister might coöperate with the shah, another might not; one prime minister might dominate his cabinet, another could not; one prime minister might receive the majlis' vote of preference, another did not and still acquired a vote of confidence; but no cabinet long enjoyed the support of the majlis. Every position, whether administrative, judicial, military, or legislative, was looked upon as an independent island of power or influence, and not infrequently as a justified means of seeking private advantage.

A social and political system that had always depended upon the official designation of its leaders by legitimate authority found authority speaking with many voices and self-appointed leaders springing up on every corner. Into this confused situation there was brought, almost by default, the strange charismatic figure of Muhammad Musaddiq. His success and his failure were due alike to his unique personality and to his special abilities. He was not the usual bombastic or conspiratorial military figure associated with Middle Eastern coups d'état. He was a sensitive, highly educated lawyer and parliamentarian. He was a passionate nationalist, though his theory was legalistic. He sought political reform; but here, too, his conceptions were clouded by a legalistic emphasis. Above all, he sought to realize his own legal interpretation of the constitution of Iran without regard for Iranian practice, but with firm conviction in French constitutional theory. Instead of putting his energies into the construction of a strong political movement, he purged the judiciary, attempted to place his own men in the important administrative posts, and successfully insisted upon the right to appoint the minister of war in his own cabinet. Finally, Musaddiq acquired full powers to rule by decree from the majlis, and he proceeded to reduce all opposition by the use of those powers. Particularly during his last months in power, Mussaddiq refused to recognize that political influence rested any place but where the constitution, as he saw it, and the decree powers had placed it. Finally, the court managed to rally parts of the army, the ulama, the lower classes of Tehran, the bazaar people, and perhaps a smaller part of the middle classes to its support. Musaddiq never did manage to have the majlis approve an interpretation of the constitution which would have specifically excluded the shah from the determination of the affairs of state.[61] In the event, the counter-coup of August 19, 1953, confirmed the power of the shah to dismiss his prime minister, and Musaddiq's attempt to concentrate all authority in the cabinet failed.

In the succeeding reaction the shah acquired more power than he had previously enjoyed, though he has remained more dependent than his father upon the influential groups that came to his support, immediately after Musaddiq's dismissal. Four ministries have held office since that time, and each has included fewer men of independent influence than its predecessor; the Eghbal cabinet (May, 1959) enjoyed the services of four generals, all of whom owe their rise to Reza Shah Pahlavi, two doctors, at least one engineer, and a number of former civil servants. This cabinet must share decision-making with other groups and individuals, official and otherwise, who have direct access to the shah. The majlis and the senate (both more appointive than elective) still represent a considerable number of interests, but the members of those bodies do not now seek to forward such interests by dismissing ministers. Interests and points of view not so represented, nor having either a traditional basis or an officially recognized organization, have no influence and little access.

Despite the instability of the years 1941 to 1953, the Iranian cabinet has developed, or at any rate maintains, a fairly consistent

---

[61] Wilber, *op. cit.*, p. 119.

set of practices. Of course, the cabinet no longer needs to devote so much time to planning its own defense before the majlis, but there is substantial evidence to show that this function was usually not performed at formal cabinet meetings anyway.[62] Before looking at the procedures of the cabinet itself, it may be useful to attempt a more precise assessment of the instability prevailing before the present period, for part of the continuity is due to the fact that this instability was not as great as is often assumed. This is significant, for as we shall see, there is no permanent cabinet secretariat to help maintain procedural, let alone policy and administrative, continuity.

In the approximately ten-year period between 1941 and early 1952, twenty-six cabinets were officially installed; and at an average rate of 15.5 cabinet posts per ministry, 400 cabinet positions were filled during this period.[63] However, these 400 posts were actually held by only 144 persons, so that while the average cabinet lasted only about five months, the average minister served more than a year. During the same period, only eleven persons served as prime minister, only nine as minister of war, and only ten as minister of foreign affairs. A large part of the turnover among the same people resulted from cabinet reshuffles involving seventy-one changes without requiring a new investiture. One reason for the turnover among different persons was the fact that Qavam al-Saltaneh, General Razmara, and Dr. Musaddiq all brought in a number of new faces. A possible explanation of this policy on the part of three "strong" prime ministers was the hope that it would help in controlling their colleagues. Significantly, each of them was less dependent upon the majlis than was ordinarily the case during this period.

Although these statistics help us to understand how a measure of continuity in cabinet practices was maintained, they should not mislead us into assuming that policy and administrative continuity were thereby achieved. Not only were there numerous internal reshufflings and changes, causing frequent interruptions in the service of ministers; there was also a tendency to discourage specialization. For example, eighteen of the 144 ministers held office 133 times out of a possible 400, in nearly every one of the

---

[62] This problem was sometimes discussed at cabinet meetings, but more often between the prime minister and his parliamentary undersecretary, or between the prime minister and his friends in the majlis.

[63] These statistics have been derived from Araqi's list of Iranian cabinets.

ministries. These eighteen ministers gained a wealth of cabinet experience, yet it is difficult to see how they could have maintained any consistent policy over these years. Moreover, it is almost invariably the rule in Iran that every new minister brings with him his own undersecretary.

When the majlis was in session, during this period, that body had a substantial influence on the composition of the cabinet, though this influence was more often negative than positive. Lacking any stable internal political organization, being debarred from holding ministerial office, and having no more than a tenuous connection with organized political groups outside the majlis, the latter is incapable of agreeing upon and pressing its choice of ministers upon whomever receives the preferential vote. Furthermore, even after approving a cabinet and its program, the temporary majority of the majlis soon dissolved. The "ministrables" themselves often found it more to their advantage to wait patiently as independents, rather than to tie themselves to any of the short-lived "fractions" in the majlis.

This situation had some bearing upon the relationships of the ministers themselves. It will be remembered that the constitution of Iran does not give the prime minister the right to dismiss his colleagues, though during the period under discussion he often chose them on the basis of the short-lived preferences of the majlis. It was safer, in constructing a cabinet, to choose new persons about whom the majlis had no strong opinions, but it was not possible to avoid all parliamentary pressures. The newcomers could be depended upon, more or less, but the others caused friction within the cabinet and might at any moment become political liabilities if and when certain groups of majlis deputies broke up. In the latter case, the prime minister could not compel the resignation of the now useless minister without presenting the resignation of the entire cabinet. This procedure, in fact, was followed twice by Qavam al-Saltaneh, but the majlis was not in session at the time. Perhaps more significant is the fact that out of seventy-one changes not involving a new cabinet investiture, thirty-six took place under Qavam, Razmara, and Musaddiq. Thus it was not so much the position of the prime minister, but the power and personality of its incumbent, which determined the degree of control and coördination in the cabinet. However, if the prime minister and the shah are able to coöperate, the prime minister may benefit from the constitutional authority of the shah to dismiss his ministers. The cabinet never votes on the appointment or dismissal of ministers; the prime minister alone accepts resignations, also introducing new ministers to the cabinet and to the majlis. The majlis itself does not pass upon the appointment of a new minister, during the continuation of a cabinet, though some of his friends may shout their congratulations when he is first introduced.

It is highly probable than any group of individuals meeting together over a period of time will evolve a stable pattern of interaction. When this pattern is handed on to a succeeding group thrown together under similar circumstances, we may say that a stable group culture has been evolved. The nature of that culture is not easily predicted, though among the contributory factors will be the personalities of those involved, the purposes of the meeting, the basis for recruiting the members, the general culture from which they are drawn, and many, many more. In the case of Iran, it would seem that the essential purpose of the cabinet is to legalize certain projected laws and decrees, rather than to decide anything. The basis of recruiting, as we have seen, depends upon the stage of the struggle for control among the shah, the prime minister, and the various powerful families and groups. The development of a set of consistent practices is not evidence of cabinet efficiency, it is merely evidence that the cabinet has been more or less firmly institutionalized. Stable practices are evidences of institutional continuity, of the need for ministers to work out a modus vivendi; but the functionality of these practices depends upon the demands that are made upon the cabinet. As we have seen, not the shah, nor the prime minister, nor the majlis, nor even the educated public have demanded efficiency or long range policy planning and coördination from the cabinet. The cabinet of Iran, except in certain appearances which have been borrowed from the West, has not advanced much beyond the wazirate; it is still essentially a device for delegating authority.

In Britain, the stable culture of the cabinet has been an important factor in producing a measure of continuity between conservative and labor governments. This culture, in turn, has been produced in large part by the necessity of accommodating that institution to those of party discipline, sub-cabinet administrative stability and neutrality, treasury control, and coördination through the cabinet secretariat. All of the rigid procedures of the British cabinet result from the requirements of these extra cabinet institutions, and the informality of the cabinet meeting itself stems from the importance of achieving full agreement.

The British cabinet does not always work as it is supposed to (witness the Suez incident of 1956), but when it does, it works as part of a rationally coördinated system.

As regards the Iranian cabinet, we have found that the reforms of Sepah Salar, of the constitution, and of the majlis, together with the relative stability of the Pahlavi period, have permitted the growth of certain stable practices. But these practices have evolved without regard to the development of other institutions or administrative organizations. It is true that the various ministers and their ministries have much more clearly defined tasks than in earlier periods, and the prime minister does have a more central function. Nevertheless, the cabinet is no more a collective body than it was in the past. Cabinet practices represent a more or less reasonable solution of the problem posed by the need to meet together, to allocate certain resources, and to bear a measure of joint responsibility. Insofar as the individual ministers are concerned, the values to be sought or preserved are:

1. membership in the cabinet itself;
2. prestige within that group;
3. independence in one's own ministry;
4. the maximum of personal patronage; and
5. the minimization of overt conflict or disagreement.

It would almost seem that the meeting is more important than what is decided. None of the cabinet practices contribute to the function of determining general policy or of ironing out differences. All controversial problems are worked out, or not, elsewhere. And all policies are ministry or agency policies. A detailed description of the consistent practices of the cabinet reveals only that the cabinet has been incorporated into the loose bundle, the functional and nonfunctional political institutions of Iran.

The Iranian cabinet meets three times a week, Mondays, Wednesdays, and Saturdays at six o'clock P.M.[64] Usually, the meetings last about three hours, except that of Monday, which the shah attends. The Monday meetings rarely exceed two hours in length. On rare occasions, such as when many unimportant decrees or regulations are to be signed, the meeting may stretch far into the night. On other occasions, emergency cabinet meetings may be called, as a consequence of some important event or intelligence.

---

[64] The following material has been assembled from interviews with present and former cabinet ministers, cabinet secretaries, and others who have attended cabinet meetings.

Attendance at the cabinet meetings is ordinarily limited to ministers and ministers of state; however, there are a number of exceptions. The most important exception is the attendance of the shah with his minister of court every Monday. Occasionally, one or another undersecretary may attend, when his chief cannot, but two and sometimes three of the prime minister's undersecretaries are usually in attendance. One of these is the director of the plan organization, who is undersecretary to the prime minister for the purpose of maintaining adequate liaison between the plan and the cabinet and the majlis. The second undersecretary acts as the cabinet secretary. The third is the director of the government's radio and propaganda bureau. Occasionally, certain experts such as the governor of Bank Melli may be invited to give their views on important questions. Only ministers have the right to vote, but others may express their views, though in practice most of them do not.

It is only in the last three years or so that the cabinet has had the regular services of a secretary. According to one report, the prime minister's undersecretary acted at times as cabinet secretary during two earlier post-war ministries, but this has not been confirmed. Up to three years ago, the youngest of the ministers acted as secretary, and the one who first became a minister (in whatever cabinet) acted as dean, presiding in the absence of the prime minister. The only departure from this practice was in the case of Dr. Eghbal, who always volunteered for the job of secretary, in every previous cabinet of which he was a member. Apparently this job was not much fought over, but certain political advantages may flow from being in a position to let petitioners know as soon as possible that the relevant decree has been approved, or to let the court know of cabinet proceedings, when the shah is not in attendance. The secretary now sits at the foot of the table, opposite the prime minister, passes around papers for signature, records votes, and takes down the minutes of the meeting.

The duties of the cabinet secretary do not require him to have a large staff. No more than fifteen of the sixty civil servants employed in the prime minister's office work under him. Records of cabinet proceedings consist primarily of a list of decisions made, though if an important discussion takes place the names and the views of the participants may be recorded. The minutes themselves are not circulated, but are merely read and corrected at the next meeting. The record serves as a personal reminder to the prime minister whose responsibility it is to follow up decisions and see to their implementation. The text of specific decisions, decrees, and bills are reproduced and circulated only as widely as is thought necessary.[65] There are no regular recipients of cabinet papers, and in reality there are no cabinet papers, in the proper sense. The record of the cabinet meetings is simply kept in a large journal, and when that is filled the volume goes into a secret file in the prime minister's office. Except for annexed proposals, the authentic record is therefore a handwritten affair.

The preparation of a formal agenda is a recent practice, and one that is not too well established. During the ministry of Qavam, no agenda was prepared; the meetings simply began with the prime minister's stating what was on his mind, and it went on from there. Before bills are referred to the cabinet for a decision, they are first approved by the prime minister and then circulated to all of the ministries. Decree proposals must also be approved by the prime minister, then they are passed back to the cabinet secretary, who must check them against existing laws before placing them on the agenda. Often in the past, however, certain agenda items followed naturally from the previous meeting's discussions, indicating that frequently there were occasions on which matters could not be brought to a conclusion. During the progress of such a meeting the prime minister might bring up new items as he liked, but these could be postponed by majority vote. Ordinary ministers could propose items for discussion only with the prime minister's approval, and usually only with his prior approval, even if acquired but a quarter of an hour before the meeting. If a minister failed to get such approval, there was little likelihood of his point being well received.

Under Musaddiq, an agenda was put together as little as half an hour before the meeting and was organized according to the preferences of the "baby" of the cabinet. All the issues or bills presented by a single ministry might be placed together, or their succession might be ordered in accordance with the importance or urgency of the matter. New items could always be brought up during the meeting, by any minister. It seems, however, that the general policy decisions of the cabinet were not taken seriously by Musaddiq, for he sometimes disregarded them, and more often than not did not bring such issues to the cabinet.

At the present time, the secretary draws up the agenda on the basis of proposals for legislation and decrees received in ad-

---

[65] Cabinet decisions are personally conveyed to the shah by the prime minister before being given any publicity.

vance, but there is no rigid time limit on their presentation. Both bills and decrees must be approved by the prime minister, and if they involve some expenditure, by the finance minister also. The practice of the last two cabinets has varied in the placing of decrees on the agenda: formerly they were taken up after all other business was completed, but now they are considered at the start of the meeting, the secretary passing the forms for signature around from his own left. After the decrees (which usually grant licenses, etc.) are finished with, the prime minister asks each in turn for any matters he may want to discuss. Apparently the seating, as well as the order in which the members are addressed by the prime minister, depends upon the length of time each has served as minister in the government of Iran, unless someone possesses some other claim to peculiar respect. After the individual ministers have had an opportunity to bring up certain matters (all of which have probably been cleared in advance) the prime minister calls for the set agenda, of which the only copy is in the hands of the secretary. This agenda has been drawn up by the secretary on the basis of issues postponed, bills proposed, and issues placed thereon by the prime minister. If the agenda is too heavily loaded, the matter is simply carried over to the next meeting.

The agenda for the meetings attended by the shah usually depends upon the matters taken up the previous week, and involves reports on issues relating to broad policy. Detailed matters are not discussed at these meetings, nor is there any voting. Usually the meeting starts with the shah's asking about developments since the previous meeting. The secretary will then read the minutes of the intervening meetings, after which the shah may put some further questions. He may then ask if there is anything new to be brought to his attention, or he may give instructions about things that he wants done. No one has heard of any order of the shah being negatived, but if the cabinet deems it wise the matter concerned may be postponed. It is evident that the shah is briefed for these meetings every Monday morning and that he discusses their consequences every Tuesday morning with his minister of court.

The procedure of those meetings not attended by the shah is informal, and the prime minister does not bear a major responsibility for moving things along. The ministers express their views with a good deal of freedom, and votes are taken only when necessary. Usually, on matters of general policy, no vote is taken, nor does it appear that there are previously prepared policy statements. The implementation of the views of the cabinet requires a nice adjustment between the preferences of the minister concerned and his impression of the sense of the cabinet. Bills and decrees are always voted on, and each member must sign, regardless of whether he favors or opposes the proposal. Despite the fact that the constitution does not insist upon the collective responsibility of the cabinet in this regard, practice has rigidly required that all the legislative activities of the ministers be collective. Decrees not supported by a majority of the cabinet have no legal effect, while individual ministers must channel all proposed legislation through the cabinet, unless they can get fifteen members of the majlis to propose their bill. Every government bill, after approval by the cabinet, is presented to the majlis with the signature of the prime minister and one other minister, usually the one most concerned. Should the minister in whose proper sphere the bill lies refuse to sign, the government would be seriously embarrassed. Occasionally, a minister brings up a matter for general discussion which is properly within the sphere of his own department. His colleagues usually do not hesitate to encourage him to shoulder the responsibility himself. On other occasions, a minister may bring up a matter properly the responsibility of another member of the cabinet, but cabinet discussion of the issue depends upon his proving it to be of wider governmental concern. These practices notwithstanding, ministers are usually very jealous of their authority within their own departments, to the point where rudimentary coöperation is often lacking.

One of the statutory tasks of the cabinet is the appointment of certain higher officials: the governor of Bank Melli, the director of the plan organization,[66] the director of the National Insurance Company, the governors of all government banks, and the directors of the Iran Carpet Company, the Shilat Caviar Fisheries, and the Foreign Transactions Corporation. Usually it falls to the prime minister to find appropriate candidates, and his choices are likely to be approved with little discussion by his colleagues.[67]

The device of cabinet committees is not much employed. Occasionally issues have been turned over to two or three ministers for clarification, but their report must always be acted upon by the entire cabinet. These are ad hoc committees, and they usually report to the next cabinet meeting or to the one following.

---

[66] These two officials must be approved by the majlis.

[67] These choices are in most cases worked out with the court.

The study of a larger problem, requiring a longer period, is usually assigned to a single minister and is carried out at the subcabinet level; or it may even be handled by a supra- or extra-cabinet group. Practice in this regard is extremely flexible, and usually it is not conducive to thoroughgoing cabinet control. Iranian cabinet ministers do not tend to delegate much of their authority, so that they often get bogged down in day-to-day affairs and cannot engage in lengthy studies. Ministers of state may be used in this manner, and the former Minister Teleqani, who resigned, led a group of higher officials in the preparation of an administrative reform and reorganization bill that would affect every part of the ministries. Partial exceptions to the rule of ad hoc committees were the budget committee and the housing committee. The budget committee of 1959 was similar to the one appointed the previous year, before the budget session of the majlis, and that one, too, did not outlast the session. That committee was composed of four ministers and was to complete the task of cutting demands for credits that was begun by a committee within the ministry of finance. The housing committee was made up of the prime minister and the labor minister. Like the budget committee, it utilized the staff of the prime minister's office, but it had much more the character of an operating agency than a cabinet committee.

A third committee was appointed to deal with the problem of extending terms to prospective American participants in a new Iranian development bank. But this group was made up of three ministers and the governor of Bank Melli. Furthermore, this committee reported to the higher economic council rather than to the cabinet. The higher economic council also comprises ministers and non-ministers as does the high council on education, the high council on health, and the high council on labor. These three councils serve as advisory bodies to the ministries immediately concerned, but the higher economic council is the only one that reports to the cabinet. On the other hand, the higher economic council sometimes holds sessions in the presence of the shah, while the other councils have access to the court and are not subordinate to their related ministries.

There seems to be some difference of opinion about whether the decisions of these councils are binding on the ministries concerned. One of the ministers of the Eghbal cabinet insists that they are not, and further holds that the decision of the cabinet on all such matters is final. He has been at some pains to point out that the higher economic council meets with the

shah every Monday afternoon, while the cabinet meets with him
on Monday evenings. The cabinet then approves all that has been
advised earlier by the council. Other views on the matter exist,
and it is difficult to believe that cabinet ministers could oppose
decisions made in the presence of the shah only a few hours
before. Other information on the lack of voting in the presence
of the shah also militates against this argument; however, the
shah does not usually stay for the whole meeting.

In general, it may be said that the cabinet does not control
Iran's economic and fiscal policies, but shares these with the higher
economic council, the plan organization, Bank Melli, and perhaps
even the Foreign Transactions Corporation and the National
Iranian Oil Company. This is a particularly important problem
in a country engaged in a long range development programing,
on the basis of the substantial oil revenues expected in the next
few decades. Economic planning was presumably removed from
"politics" by being placed outside of the cabinet in the plan
organization, which was made only indirectly responsible to
the majlis. Friction grew as the plan organization developed as
to rival existing ministries, and as the funds which it could expend
through the ministries or unilaterally increased to rival the national budget. Matters came to a head during the preparation
of the budget for March, 1959, in a complex situation involving
calculations about United States economic and military aid, pressure to increase military expenditures, the fostering of rival development projects in the ministries, an expected deficit, an
international loan tied to a balanced budget, and plan organization insistence that it receive its entire allotment from the oil
revenues. There was also a great deal of personality conflict.
Finally the shah was prevailed upon to take sides. An announce-
ment followed that the cabinet had decided to present a bill to
the majlis providing for the subordination of the director of the
plan organization to the prime minister, in the interest of efficiency
and more direct responsibility to the majlis. The previously independent director, Mr. Ebtehaj, resigned, which result was apparently the purpose of the whole change. At the present time, it
seems as though the only result has been to resolve the budget controversy in favor of the ministries and against the plan organization. There are, however, other areas of duplication, competition,
and uncoördinated development activity that have not been dealt
with, while the whole administrative structure of the plan organization has been left much as it was.

As yet, the cabinet still lacks full control of economic policy;

development priorities and balance have remained as established by the plan organization when it was independent. The Bank Melli still looks after currency stabilization and anti-inflationary policy; the higher economic council retains primary concern for encouraging foreign investment, while the National Iranian Oil Company handles relations with the International Consortium. Legally, there is no doubt that the cabinet has supreme authority, but in fact it has neither the unity of purpose nor the appropriate organization to properly exercise this authority.

In the sphere of security policy, too, the cabinet does not enjoy complete control. In recent years a security commission has been appointed which often meets in the presence of the shah. The members of this commission are the prime minister, foreign minister, war minister, interior minister, the head of the security organization, who is nominally undersecretary to the prime minister, and the chiefs of the army, gendarmerie and police. Security policy often bears heavily upon foreign policy, so that some international issues are taken up in this commission. It is, of course, most unusual for the cabinet to discuss, much less to determine, the level of defense expenditures in the annual budget. The army is the special province of the shah.

The cabinet itself serves as the principal coördinating body in the government. The supra-cabinet bodies like the security commission and the higher economic council perform similar functions, with the same lack of systematization.

Most Western governments have found the modern budget the ideal basis of government-wide coördination, though more is often needed. In Iran, however, since the abdication of Reza Shah, governments have usually been unable to get the budget through at the beginning of the fiscal year, and have sometimes gone through a whole year on twelve monthly appropriations of one-twelfth of the previous year's expenditures. The year 1959 was the first in a long while that the budget was approved on time, but, as we have seen, not without an administrative battle. It was also the first year that an attempt was made at producing a program rather than a line-item budget, and, while this was a serious improvement, civil servants are not yet used to the system. It is also possible that the severity of the budget struggle was due, in part, to this very reform and to the greater clarity with which the individual ministers could see what they are doing. There has been no difficulty in getting the budget passed through the present acquiescent majlis; the real problem is in getting the ministers to agree. Except under an extremely powerful prime minister, this has always been a problem in Iran, because neither the prime minister nor the finance minister can overrule their colleagues on the budget, and because there is no widely accepted basis for or means of establishing priorities. Despite the shah's finally siding with the prime minister against the director of the plan organization, he did not seem inclined to strengthen the powers of the prime minister to the point of having him dominate the cabinet. It may well be that the recent strengthening of the prime minister was meant to counterbalance the increasing pressure of the military, as evidenced in their part in the removal of Mr. Ebtehaj as director of the plan organization. Nevertheless, the shah insisted that the budget be balanced and readied on time, and the resultant trial was a valuable experience for Eghbal's cabinet.

Below the cabinet level, for coördination purposes, there is only the temporary budget committee in the ministry of finance and a recently organized committee of the stable administrative undersecretaries of each ministry. This latter body is chaired by the prime minister's stable undersecretary, and its duties are restricted to the improvement and standardization of both administrative techniques and management. Its impact on policy making has not been great, nor have the undersecretaries been quite as stable as was hoped. On the other hand, the group has just started working and high hopes for them are entertained in some quarters.

Beyond coördination, modern governments have found it necessary to plan development, services, and ordinary legislative programs long in advance. A concomitant of such planning is a staff to do relevant research and at least narrow the alternatives before the ministers, perhaps even make estimates of the results of such programs. Obviously, the cabinet secretariat of Iran is unequipped to carry out this function, or even to adequately brief the prime minister on matters coming up at the cabinet meeting. At times this small secretariat can help the prime minister follow up operations, but this is not its major function. The main task of the secretariat remains that of checking decrees against the law books and typing up bills after they have been checked in the ministries concerned. From the size of one post-cabinet meeting file of decrees, it is obvious that these routine matters are permitted to take up an enormous amount of the cabinet's and the secretariat's time. But the typing, checking, passing, and signing of decrees seems to be nothing more than a highly formalized "pork-barrel" system which is difficult to justify in an essentially non-democratic system. Most decrees concern matters which should be determined by ordinary civil servants on the basis of more or less objectivized criteria. The absence of policy papers and routine justification procedures is a corollary of imposing problems requiring special study upon the ministers themselves and even upon the prime minister. Under these circumstances, it is understandable that the government has no long range legislative program planned, that it has no objective basis upon which disputes may be settled, and that settling the budget is a pure bargaining process.

So long as major aspects of foreign, economic, petroleum, and security policy (not to mention many minor decisions on personnel, licenses, contracts, and the like) are determined formally or informally by direct representation to the court, the cabinet may not be the focal point for broad policy leadership, control, and coördination. Furthermore, so long as the members of the cabinet lack a collegial character, lack any but the most tenuous kind of personal mutual obligation, and lack any influence except that derived from their temporary designation by the shah, it is highly unlikely that the ministers can coöperate sufficiently to work out and persevere in a long range program.

We have found that the structure, procedures, practices, and internal relations of the Iranian cabinet have grown out of the political history of that country and have only a limited connection with the Iranian constitution. The collegial character of the cabinet, its political power, its policy-making initiative, its administrative control and coördination, even the scope of its authority, are all restricted. If it has failed to develop a strong substructure for staff, secretarial, and communications purposes, this is not only due to the tradition of the cabinet and the unfamiliarity of its members with other methods, but is also the result of the fact that political forces have militated against the dominance of the prime minister and the coöperation of cabinet members.

ADMINISTRATIVE ORGANIZATION

In moving away from the cabinet and taking a broader view of the entire administrative apparatus, we find more of the same lack of ordered hierarchical authority and coördination. At the center of the whole structure are the twelve ministries, with the finance ministry and the prime minister's office looming largest of all. Neither of these two, however, dominates the others, though they may set limits to their authority. Unless some problem rises to the level of a pressing political issue, be it inflation, the supply of meat, the bottling up of a port, or a major strike, the issue remains strictly the business of the ministry concerned. That ministry is not prepared to anticipate problems; it has all it can do to carry out the routine functions assigned to it by earlier laws and decrees. These functions, moreover, become ritualized and are disturbed only occasionally by zealous groups or individuals, in or out of the ministries, who conceive of some new law or revision of the old. The new law may be passed from committee to committee and outlive several cabinets, until the ministry is sufficiently stirred by the rise of a political issue, by the vigor of a new minister, or by the well meant pressure of foreign advisers. The ministers usually do not seek to gain notoriety by having important pieces of legislation pass, and their political lives do not much depend upon getting along with one another.

The picture of twelve jealously independent ministries is further complicated, as we have seen, by a number of high councils existing at a level of equality with, and even superiority over, the cabinet itself. These councils either recognize the independence of some institutions such as the Bank Melli, the security organization, or the army, or the university, or they are meant to deal with pressing problems that involve the security of the regime or the interests of influential groups. At a lower level, there has been a similar proliferation of special bureaus, agencies, and authorities to deal with specific problems or to undertake special projects like village development, irrigation, small-scale industry, religious mortmain supervision, etc. These are further paralleled by a number of enterprises which are nominally subordinate to certain ministries like the railroad, Iranair, the broadcasting authority, or the telephone company, or are presumed to work closely with certain ministries or agencies, for instance the various government banks, the National Export Company, the university, and the Workers Social Insurance Company, or are independent firms like the National Oil Company, the Shilat Fisheries, and the Iran Insurance Company. Or they may be directly controlled by certain ministries, or by institutions like the enterprises of the ministry of customs and monopolies, the plan organization industries, or the Pahlavi properties administration, the Pahlavi Foundation hospitals and orphanages, and the Royal Agency for mortmain properties placed in the care of the "ruler of the age," all under the ministry of court.

This bewildering array of ministries, councils, bureaus, agencies, banks and companies is not very different from what might be found in a number of more highly developed countries, but in the absence of a cabinet which can really unify their operations, and in the face of politically motivated, frequent changes, or the inordinately prolonged maintenance of agency directors, it works out differently. There is a decided tendency for certain enterprises to follow a completely self-determined policy, and for others to become completely demoralized under a series of plundering short-termers. The governor of Bank Melli, the director of the Oil Company, and the ex-director of the plan organization are examples of the former, while the directorship of Workers Social Insurance Company, and the village development agency are examples of the latter. It is not surprising to find that more than one organization may be assigned the same or similar functions with attendant conflicts, buck passing, and concentration upon competing for political support, rather than upon accomplishing the job at hand. There are several statistical agencies doing similar work, both the Iran Insurance Company and at least two banks are involved in relieving the housing problem, and many aspects of plan organization activity compete with similar ministry programs. The enunciation of clear public policy not only runs up against the resistance of vested bureaucratic interest, but is always subject to the most damning kind of "political" interpretation. The tendency for each agency to be treated by its director as a private power base is further enhanced by the way in which many appointments are made and by the financial independence of many of these institutions. The process of making appointments will be discussed below; suffice it here to point out that the minister having nominal authority over the agency, and perhaps even the entire cabinet, may not exert crucial influence in the appointment or retention of an agency director. Not until last year were the budgets for all agencies and the Oil Company reported in the general budget bill, and even then they were reported for information purposes, rather than for approval. All of these budgets were shown to be balanced by the expected income from agency or company operations, and even the bureau of waqfs (religious mortmain) is supported by a fee upon mortmain revenues, rather than out of the ministry of education budget.

Fragmentation among various government agencies parallels that among the ministries. It is true that the consequences of administrative fragmentation at this level is not so great as that at the ministerial level. Two housing agencies are not of the same import as the conflicts on development priorities between the ministries and the plan organization. The difference of approach between the village development agency and the agricultural extension service is not so great as that between the ministries of interior and justice involving a major proportion of all criminal

cases. Nor is the well institutionalized independence of the ministries of war and foreign affairs of the prime minister quite matched
anywhere below. Nevertheless many agencies, like the ministries,
hire their own personnel on the basis of independent criteria. A
number of agency directors report directly to the shah. Many
agencies may also have their own, rather than a ministry of finance,
accountant. Many, too, have their own employee welfare arrangements, hospitals, and coöperative stores.

That coördination is weak has already been pointed out. The
major basis for achieving some degree of coöperation, and the
most effective one, is through bargaining, often accompanied by
mutual favors unrelated to the problem at issue. More comprehensive budgeting, and American encouraged program budgeting,
do impose some sort of coördination, but in the absence of agreed
criteria for determining priorities, balanced programing is achieved
by bargaining. During the last few years, the shah has entered
the budget process only at the final stage, once to dismiss Mr.
Ebtehaj, and therefore has not brought his superior authority to
bear directly upon the bargaining bottleneck. Again, as we have
noted, most agencies are in any case excluded from the budgeting
process, while their continued existence effectively precludes the
ministry most closely associated with each from undertaking basic
policy adjustments with regard to a particular agency's concerns.

Some further measures of coördination may be achieved when
drastic or emergency action is determined upon by the cabinet, an
ad hoc cabinet committee, the higher economic council, the security committee, or by the high council for administrative improvement. Often, mere decrees or laws must be resorted to, and
the measure affects only a single issue, rather than the fundamentals
of administrative organization. Even when some issue requires
drastic action, the lack of adequate research and planning may
result in the failure of the new arrangement or in such a spate
of protests from persons of position who have been unwittingly
injured as to lead to a reversal or simply to non-implementation.

Control and supervision on a government-wide basis is similarly weak and incomplete. In addition to the usual departmental
inspection bureau there is a new royal inspection commission, the
majlis and its court of accounts, the administrative court, and the
ministry of finance. Complaints from the public may not be
referred to the Iranian equivalent of the council of state, and
there exists no clearly elaborated legal principal of the government's responsibility to ordinary citizens for the error or wrongdoing of civil servants. The notion of exceeding administrative

authority is never the basis of a legal proceeding. Such complaints, according to a recent royal decree, may be brought before the travelling royal commission. No reports have yet been published about the accomplishments of this commission. Complaints may also be made in the majlis by deputies favorably moved, and this usually has some effect, unless the complaint concerns a chronic problem: the security agency recently restored the publication license of a religious magazine, but the Tehran meat supply could not be so easily assured. The majlis court of accounts is ineffective, lacking both an adequate staff and the political motivation to carry out its task. The administrative court is charged with cases of grave wrongdoing by civil servants or judges, usually when the victim is the government itself. Complaints may be referred by the ministers themselves. As with the 1959 Tehran meat scandal, the referral of a case may have such important political implications that it is first taken up by the cabinet and even referred to the shah. Treasury control, as exerted by the ministry of finance, is of the most rigid kind, often obstructing programs already approved at the cabinet level. The ministry of education recently rehired retired teachers, with cabinet approval, but the finance ministry refused to pay their retirement benefits in addition to their salaries because of the general ruling that employees may not receive two government salaries. After some delay, the issue was bargained out between the two ministries. Transfers from the various budget subheads are generally not allowed, and these are watched over, along with authorized expenditures, by the ministry of finance accountants, who sit in every ministry and sign all payments.

Departmental organization suffers from many of the defects of interdepartmental fragmentation and conflict. Most ministries comprehend many similar divisions, as well as specialized units, but their growth and their assembly has been haphazard, and their organizational patterns differ. From time to time, a ministry reorganization bill is presented to the majlis for approval, or a "note" to the same effect may be attached to the annual budget bill, if and when such a bill is prepared. At the present time, a general reorganization bill is under consideration for all except the ministry of foreign affairs and the ministry of war, which are in any case quite separate and unique establishments. The intention of the new bill is to gather all of the internal administrative operations under a "stable" administrative undersecretary and to group the specialized operations under a technical undersecretary. A parliamentary undersecretary who will be a political appointee, a stand-in for the minister when he cannot attend parliament sessions, and charged with ministry public relations is also contemplated. The major purposes of the bill are to define the functions of the ministries and each of their divisions, to group related operations, to establish an orderly chain of command and eliminate direct reporting to the minister, and to permit delegations of authority.

The need for such a bill indicates not only the vagueness surrounding the relationship between various ministry divisions, but also the tendency of each section head to refer problems involving interdivisional coöperation to the minister himself. It is clear, however, that the new bill emphasizes the grouping together of internal functions such as personnel, accounting and audit, and new administrative improvement sections rather than staff operations. That is to say, technical administrative goals outweigh program and planning goals, a situation which accords well enough with the need to rationalize the bureaucracy in order to rationalize the entire polity. In place of the usual staff and line separation, the new bill seems to call for a separation of specialized operations and household activities. One gains the impression that household operations have been singled out and placed under the stable administrative undersecretary, in the hope that these tasks will be considered apolitical and not be much disturbed by cabinet changes. It may be doubted, though, that the household division will have any serious influence over the specialized division, unless it adjusts its methods to the substantive work of the ministry, in which case it will not long preserve its neutrality. This compromise, seeking to improve administration for its own sake, in a restricted area of bureaucratic activity, would appear to be weak in both conception and prospects of success. The new arrangement will create new problems, too, for despite the fact that it is to have only a two-year trial and then undergo revision, in some cases its sections describing the functions of various administrative units go beyond or conflict with existing law.

The not entirely successful effort to give a measure of permanence to the administrative undersecretary does offer hope of his being able to manage the household functions and eliminate duplication of such functions for each ministry section. The underlying weakness in planning, however, militates against the unification of other operations which do not necessarily fit together substantively, but, rather, programmatically. The ministries are the primary political arena; therefore some specialized divisions will naturally be the focus of much external pressure, while individual division chiefs will continue to strive to elevate their own operation to that of an independent agency with a legally protected permanent director. The greater the political pressures, the more likely such a change is. Furthermore, the proposed bill attempts, at least by diagram, to bring many agencies into closer subordination to their related ministries, and it thus poses an issue which can be determined only by the political pressures in or out of the courts.

Paper plans do not make an administrative system. The people who have to work the administrative apparatus are, of course, the key elements; and these will be approached from two points of view. The first will be that of formal personnel administration supplying the institutional context, and the second will deal with a number of more obvious aspects of administrative behavior revealing the true import of organization charts. An understanding of the personnel situation should indicate some further effects of the existing political system on administration, and should illustrate how imposing is the problem of bureaucratic rationalization.

The basic personnel law for the government of Iran was passed in 1922, and has since undergone but minor changes. The original law was one of the early moves toward rationalization following the Sayyid Zia–Reza Khan coup and preceding Reza Shah's accession. The law itself lays down some general rules on classification and pay grades, promotions, discipline, and retirement. Later provisions permitted experts or extra employees to be hired on contract or daily wage terms, and there are other sections on suspension with part pay, leaves, and extra allowances for travel, family, provincial posting, and bad climate compensation.

There is as yet no central civil service commission, and every ministry does its own hiring. There is not yet a position classification system, though work is being done on one. Salaries are not based upon the class of work or upon training, except for the broad categories of undergrade menials, overgrade professors, and some others, and higher grade entry for those of some educational qualifications. Estimates of the total number of civil servants in all ministries and agencies run to about 200,000 persons, i.e., over 1 per cent of the population. About 35 per cent of these reside in Tehran. Promotions are based on seniority and they come at regular intervals (or are supposed to). There are only nine regular pay grades, and in time all employees may reach the top.

Government service carries with it fairly high prestige, although work for special agencies, for the university, or for private companies is sometimes considered to offer higher status. Members of the more influential classes regard it as important to hold a higher administrative position, even though the salary may be low. Most members of the educated middle class seek government positions as the only outlet for their more sophisticated talents, but they are usually dissatisfied with the low salaries and the impossibility of getting key positions. Among the lower classes, there seems to be a similar preference for getting on the regular government payroll. In the latter case, security, the absence of close supervision, the opportunity to supplement incomes by petty bribes or tips, share with higher prestige in attracting even the illiterate of the lower urban classes.

The relationship between education and a government position, in most underdeveloped countries, has been remarked on by many observers; in Iran, too, anyone who has finished the first half of the secondary school program looks primarily to the government for a job. Religious students, also, despairing of making an adequate living in religious pursuits, frustrated with the uncharted routes of advancement in the traditional religious institution, and aware of the relatively low prestige which they enjoy among the intelligentsia, seek a method of entry into government service. The government's own halfhearted attempts to rationalize the religious institution have depended upon opening the way to government employment for those who study at the modernized religious academies.

Before the passage of the personnel law of 1922, the hiring of government employees was more or less the prerogative of the head of each administrative division. Since that time, the use of government jobs either as a form of patronage or as a way to take care of one's relatives has not been eliminated, but efforts to rationalize the service have brought newer aspects of government service to the fore. The effort to eliminate "political" interference with employment has resulted in a near practical impossibility of dismissing anyone. The disciplinary code is also largely a dead letter. Uncoöperative or obnoxious persons, even those who are somewhat dangerous politically and for whom a pension seems desirable, may be placed on the *disponible* list at part pay. The higher positions are critical enough so that every new minister or agency director prefers to appoint his own choices, but their predecessors, being regular civil servants, even if at the time enjoying a "political" appointment, cannot be dismissed but only made *disponible*. At lower levels, political pressures have compelled the government at various times to hire more freely, and the regular retirement laws have not been adhered to. The consequence of these arrangements and pressures has been a great overstaffing of the service.

But the Iranian bureaucracy is at once overstaffed and understaffed. That is, it is understaffed in many skilled positions. The need for specialized skills, the relatively low pay scales, and the political pressures to hire more persons have caused too full an exploitation of the provisions for hiring employees by contract or day wage. This practice is still followed, despite the provisions in effect for nearly a decade against any new hiring of regular civil servants. Only teachers, judges, translators and a few technicians are excluded from this prohibition, but engineers and some others prefer the contract setup because it affords them higher pay. For the rest, highly trained and ambitious young men are disinclined to enter government service on contract, so that the loophole tends to bring in less qualified persons. Some young men try to break into the prestige services by starting out as teachers, beginning as employees of the ministry of education and then transferring; but lately the ministry of education has refused to permit transfers. Others are attracted by judgeships, but the only immediately available places are at some distance from Tehran and so do not attract those who are unwilling to wait at least five years to come back to the big city.

With the help of Point Four advisers, the Iranian government has tried to cope with this situation. Recently, bills have been placed before the majlis providing for compulsory retirement with pensions of nearly full salary, for revising salary schedules, and for transferring all contract employees to regular status. A bill is presently under study in the prime minister's office which will provide for the regular hiring of those with B.A. degrees in economics, diplomacy, engineering and some other fields. These bills have not been tied in with the emerging position classification scheme, and the financial base of the retirement system is generally acknowledged to be unsound. Similarly, the general reorganization bill and the suggested reorganization by the new minister of the interior are not tied in with other personnel measures planned or under study. Consequently the current situation is one of great interest and activity, but the lack of order and the absence of thorough planning or any clear notion of the final integrated result is obvious. This disorderliness is not the result of Iranian perverseness but due to a variety of pressures: individual pressures to hire qualified and influential persons; and especially the increasing concern with inefficiency rather than corruption (though the latter is by no means dismissed) as the reason for Iran's lack of development.

Until the recent increased emphasis on development and on military preparedness, the outstanding financial burden on the country was its personnel bill. It is true that Reza Shah spent much on development and on his armed forces, but that was before the time of huge oil profits and substantial United States mutual security grants. Despite these new problems, indeed partly because of them, the monthly payroll still looms very large in the Iranian budget. This is one of the reasons why some people think the personnel system must be rearranged; it has also been the occasional cause of acute governmental embarrassment. Since so many urban residents, especially in Tehran, are government employees, not infrequently one finds the government judged on the basis of whether or not it pays salaries on time, whether these salaries are complete, and whether promotions are given on time. The latter illustrates the common attitude that promotions should be automatic, based on seniority rather than performance, despite the widespread complaint that top positions always go to influential or otherwise favored persons. Promotions are, of course, merely increases of pay and pay grade, rather than movements to positions of greater authority. Presumably, the new position classification plan will entail new pay scales and a new grading system, but to incorporate these essentials from the very start has been deemed far too disruptive.

To cope with the increasing pressures for higher salaries and greater security, there has been a noticeable tendency in many government services to establish coöperative stores, restaurants, hospitals, and even vacation spots. The Oil Company is, perhaps, foremost in this type of activity, and Bank Melli next; but the ministries, and some of the larger industrial enterprises like the tobacco monopoly, are not far behind. As yet, these special benefits have not had a deep effect in weakening extraorganizational loyalties, just as they have not supplanted demands for higher wages and regular promotions; nevertheless, the incipient tendency toward the creation of an exclusive interest group through these paternalistic measures in each of the ministries and agencies should be noted. As we have seen, there is not yet an unequivocal determination to rationalize ruthlessly and to isolate the administrative services from the rest of society; nevertheless a hesitant start has been made. This start is partly the result of ideological preferences for rationalization, but partly also the result of short range political pressures. The incompleteness of these efforts renders further discussion of this topic more pertinent to our later consideration of groups and interests.

Given these organizational factors, their failure to supersede traditional organization completely, and their inability to deflect extrabureaucratic interest and kinship influences, nonrational patterns of administrative behavior tend to be institutionalized within the Iranian bureaucracy. Much attention has been focused upon these digressions from "ideal" bureaucratic practice, and pejorative judgments abound in rough proportion to the failure to realize that such textbook ideals are not part of a universal heritage, nor necessarily imbued with the sanctity of natural law. The problem of administrative behavior once again illustrates that bureaucratic rationalization is dependent upon either isolating the bureaucracy or achieving far-reaching social and political changes throughout the polity. In either case the task is formidable, but the former solution seems somewhat simpler, and consequently more tempting. Isolating bureaucratic personnel from their society is all the more attractive to higher civil servants, since these tend to be more highly modernized and more desirous of breaking traditional ties and family obligations. They also have a clearer conception of the values of rational hierarchy and tend to feel uneasy in a situation where two quite opposed patterns of behavior are acceptable.

While the textbooks have for several decades described ideal bureaucratic behavior, we have also, in the last few years, benefited from several useful attempts to describe how traditional bureaucracy works, or at least how traditional patterns are maintained, even after recent efforts to rationalize the bureaucratic hierarchies of underdeveloped countries.[68] It remains only to be pointed out that Iran is more or less typical in this regard. Overstaffing, lack of coördination, failure to delegate authority, inadequate salaries, the absence of professional "esprit," and the like, are manifested in a general lack of courage and willingness to accept responsibility. All manner of minor orders and expenditures require the signature of the minister or agency director. Sometimes several signatures are necessary, to validate some instruction, so that responsibility is spread. Disciplinary measures are generally not used, except indeed for acts of commission. Acts of omission are not blameworthy. Long delays in carrying through private applications

---

[68] Siffin, ed., *Toward the Study of Comparative Administration* (University of Indiana Press, 1958).

result from the need to await word from the top or from the need to go from office to office, collecting signatures.

The overwhelming emphasis of the individual civil servant is upon job security. Advancement in grade and salary is in any case automatic, or should be, and there is little or no reward for meritorious work or initiative. Sometimes the pattern of inactivity is justified by rejection of the government, and civil servants proudly report that they were paid for a day's work but did nothing. Others insist that they are doing their jobs effectively, despite lack of support from above and below, and despite external political pressures. The latter almost always add that they may be forced to quit, but that they can find other jobs or have property from which they can derive sufficient income. They usually have prominent family support, too, but do not stress this.

Even where some degree of courage and willingness to accept responsibility does exist, it is usually accompanied by acute distress arising from recognition of the inadequacy of one's training or information.[69] Traditional tendencies persist too, in suspicion of strangers or foreigners, extreme formalism, a notion of courtesy which forbids allowing callers to wait outside, a tendency to favor friends or relatives or people from the same town, a predilection to arbitrate rather than rule in cases of conflict among applicants, and an acceptance of bargaining over substantive decisions with agency or division directors at the same level as the normal basis of administrative coöperation.

Suspicion is usually manifested by withholding information. Even more or less routine information is not divulged unless the bureaucrat is absolutely sure that it will not be used against him, or unless he is trying to ingratiate himself. Sometimes information is withheld to enhance the importance of the functionary, even if he is only a file clerk, and sometimes it may be withheld to sabotage the efforts of a disliked official or director general. Foreign advisers run into this problem, in addition to the usual language barrier, but there are numerous occasions, too, in which the required information simply does not exist. Formalism in social relations is, of course, a well institutionalized protective mechanism for handling the stranger or the distrusted colleague, for finding out his purpose and, if appropriate, for putting him off without antagonism. The ritual of greeting, asking after one's health, and expressing first solicitousness, then gratitude, can be

---

[69] For much of the following I am indebted to my colleagues in the "Social Research Seminar," for a time held weekly at the house of ex-Senator Khajeh-Nuri of Tehran.

so skillfully accomplished that following it with a specific request is all but impossible unless one knows the official so well that it is possible to draw a chair up close and whisper the rest. Formalism is still tied to the residue of a monarchically or militarily oriented aristocracy, and persons enjoying this status, or those whose names indicate their high religious ancestry, are often the beneficiaries of this technique. For those unfamiliar with the usefulness of such formalism or unappreciative of the verbal virtuosity that accompanies it, formalism is a quaint, inefficient, and time-consuming practice that must be eliminated.

Part of the same behavioral complex is the admission of all callers who can get the doorman to present their cards. It is not rare to see five or six persons sitting in a director general's office while one tries to work out one's affairs. In some places, whole crowds squeeze into a small office to get their pieces of paper signed. Where callers are seated, those taking chairs closest to the official's desk are most honored, while those farther out must shout out their business for all to hear, or wait till the others leave.

Favoritism and nepotism are the bases of frequent criticism of the Iranian administrative system, but it is really only recently that these practices have been deemed at fault. In earlier times, the staffing of an agency was considered purely the affair of the minister concerned, and he wisely employed those whom he could trust to coöperate with him and keep his confidences. The control of a top level administrative post and its peculiar authority was similarly considered an independent prerogative or "concession" held by the official so appointed. If this view is frequently criticized today, it is nevertheless much in evidence in practice. It is not at all rare to sit with several persons in an official's office and hear him recommend a friend or relative over the phone to some other agency head. To walk into any office without a letter of introduction is downright foolish. Employment is now open only to contract workers, but the recruiting system is still so decentralized that personal recommendations help considerably. Even where the individual functionary is determined not to favor anyone, he may be convinced that the whole task in which he is engaged will suffer if he does not bow to pressure.

Among those who have some notion of modern professional standards and who prefer rationalization, their conceptions are almost invariably legalistic. At lower levels this is manifested in strict adherence to routine and "proper channels," and at higher levels by strict application of regulations that is sometimes carried so far as to penalize those who would seek favors by hardship working interpretations of the regulation. The official at the lower level may also seek to avoid responsibility by adhering to routine, but the general tendency of higher officials is to seek interpretations which are compromises between the letter of the law and the desires of an applicant who is both suitably dressed and suitably recommended. Where two or more such applicants are competing with one another, the traditional pattern is to seek to bring about a compromise agreement between the applicants, with little reference to the regulation. Of course if one of the applicants has some special claim on the official, then his task is more clear. On the other hand, where various applicants cannot always agree, the application of some regulation, or even the execution of an entire project, may be held in abeyance. Not infrequently, a person has access to someone in the bureaucracy who has nothing to do with the business he wishes to accomplish. Bureaucratic influence is, however, exchangeable, and from the point of view of the applicant, it is diffuse rather than specific. The problem of coördination has already been referred to, and its operative solution suggested in the practice of bargaining. Bargaining takes place among bureau directors, not only in order to expedite decision making and to coördinate program implementation, but also to acquit one's self of pressing social and political obligations. Favors done by officials for officials establish further obligations which are usually honored when occasion demands.

These practices indicate the general absence of a special bureaucratic *esprit de corps*. It is not simply that there is a lack of appreciation for instrumental as opposed to ultimate standards and objectives, but also that no single agency or bureau, let alone the entire service, represents the strongest interest attachments or basis of successful achievement for the functionary. The bureaucracy is not supposed to be neutral, rather, it is expected to be loyal to the government of the day. It *is* the government, and it determines all but the highest policies. The cabinet is no more than a logical extension of the rest of the service, and it operates in much the same way. The issue is not that of loyalty to the cabinet any more than it is of loyalty to any other bundle of administrative offices. One must fulfill the obligations of loyalty to persons and not offices. One repays the favors granted by individuals, and one fulfills one's bargain with a person not an agency. Coöperating individuals, regardless of the basis of coöperation, form cliques, and regardless of where these individuals spread throughout the bureaucracy as their careers advance, they remain obligated to one another. Advancement to positions of authority, success in carrying out assignments, even majlis approval of one's projects, depend upon maintaining loyalties and building obligation credits. To refuse to participate in a clique or not to do favors is to refuse to work the system by means of its only effective mechanism. The idea of appointing permanent administrative undersecretaries runs counter to the entire system, in which all positions are fluid and only grades and pay rates fixed. Fixing personnel in positions of relatively high authority is not to rationalize the administration but to legitimize for long periods the influence of power structures built upon nonrational hierarchical bases, the systemic function of which depends upon their exercising only temporary authority. That is to say that the present administrative system must be capable of exploiting a variety of power structures through granting concessions of temporary authority. If administrative personnel cannot be replaced, then certain tasks will remain beyond the government until the administrative system itself can be rationalized.

The practices that have been described are the mechanisms by which the existing administrative machinery works; they are not the causes of its malfunctioning. These are dysfunctional practices only in the sense that a political system differing from the existing one is preferred. Keeping this view in mind, even the relatively simple problem of bribery and tipping becomes complicated. Here again, we have one pattern of neutrality and anonymity written into law and another of personal loyalties and bargaining manifested in practice. Tipping is perhaps a euphemism for the payment of petty bribes at lower levels for the expediting of applications, for finding papers in the files, and for getting an appointment with the boss. The custom of tipping is one of long standing and is seen by many as a right or duty, often not accompanied by penalties for failure to conform. Few people seem particularly irritated by the practice, and more well-to-do persons may even remark on the poor fellow's need to supplement his meager income. Bribe taking is more generally condemned, especially when it involves the purchase of lucrative privileges. It is not merely a vestige of the old practice of paying directly for government services but is either the purchase of a concession for public service from the government or the substitution of a cash payment for the repayment of such favors in kind. The latter, in addition to being contrary to long-established values, admits of a new kind of social power based on accumulated wealth rather than noble birth and military or religious service.

In discussing the machinery of rationalization, we have thus far concentrated upon its own lack of rational-hierarchical organization, and we have briefly discussed some of the attempts at reform. The suggestion has been made, despite much irresoluteness, that the government of Iran would like to effect the transformation of its presently mixed political system to a more rational one, primarily through manipulation of the bureaucratic apparatus. But merely rationalizing the machinery of rationalization does not guarantee its effective control over and ability to alter the political system. There is, first, the problem of the social isolation of the bureaucracy; then that of giving it adequate facilities, skills, and enforcement capacities; and finally, that of so managing groups, associations and individuals that they will be responsive to bureaucratic efforts. There are precedents for the isolation of the bureaucracy, and the specialization of their training going far back into Eastern history, culminating in the temporarily effective Ottoman system. The earlier method of utilizing specially educated family-clique groups, or the current Soviet system of combined direct party administration and close party supervision, are other possible examples. Facilities, skills, and enforcement are problems of finance and education, as well as that of rationalizing the military and security forces. These forces will be briefly discussed below. Assuming, however, that the bureaucracy can be isolated from external influences, that it can be indoctrinated in some rationalizing ideology, that it can be adequately trained, that it can be given enough facilities for gaining intelligence, planning, computing, communicating, keeping records, and the like, also that it has the support of an efficient and loyal military force, successful achievement of rationalizing social goals will still be obstructed by widespread illiteracy, poor inter-regional communications, widespread distrust of government, poor standards of health, and the lack of many of the skills necessary to a modern industrial society.

Education may depend in part upon economic development, and economic development, in turn, may depend in part upon rationalization; but rationalization depends to a far greater extent upon education and economic development. This problem will become clearer when it is related to a further hesitant tendency, not without historical precedent, for the government of Iran to recognize, legitimize, and set the organizational pattern for a number of interest groups. Obviously, this is a step in the direction of rationalizing the entire political system, but the mixed results of such attempts evidence the influence of these groups upon the bureaucracy, the lack of bureaucratic rationalization, and the inaccessibility of these groups to economical measures of bureaucratic control. Illustrative examples may be drawn from some current problems of the government of Iran. In a recent strike of brick kiln workers it was evident that no one knew how many workers were so employed. It was also evident that no one could speak authoritatively for all the workers, that no one knew exactly what the workers' grievances were, that the government was unable to communicate directly with the workers, that the workers did not know or were not powerful enough to take advantage of the various social welfare facilities offered them. The issue was resolved by the use of force, without going to the root of the problem and without the development of better machinery for communication with and control of the workers.

A similar situation exists with regard to the new income tax law that requires all taxpayers to make out returns; for the first time, penalties are imposed for failure to comply with the law. The finance ministry officials have no idea of how large business profits are. Corporation boards are not responsible to stockholders, so their reports cannot be used as an adequate check. Taxpayers do not feel they ought to pay taxes, or at least not in the legal amount. The situation is further complicated by a general distrust of the assessing officials and a fear of victimization, and by the government's desire to tax petty artisans, who are difficult to locate and whose income it is nearly impossible to guess. The absence of standard prices and standard services, the wide variation in rents, the practice of banking funds abroad, the difficulty of getting and communicating information, the fear and suspicion of taxpayers, and the tacit agreements to resist, all preclude effective tax collection, short of phenomenal government expenditures. As it now stands, it seems unlikely that the government will have the facilities to process all the returns which will come in claiming losses for the past year.

The efforts of the ministries of commerce and agriculture to establish grading and sorting standards for export products runs into the same problems of ignorance, poor communication, and suspicion of government intentions. The distribution of crown lands has not only met with difficulties arising from lack of coördination among the government agencies dealing therewith but also from the peasant's ignorance, his unwillingness to join coöperatives, and his inability to manage his own farm. All sorts of well meaning government programs to improve public welfare fall short of hoped for results because the public itself is not sufficiently aware of its interests, doesn't understand what the government is about, or assumes (probably correctly) that government statements must not be believed and acted upon lest one's employer or landlord, or lest a government official himself, penalize the citizen for his impertinence. The magnitude of the task of rationalization cannot be measured simply in terms of rationalizing the internal administration of the bureaucracy, and administrative reforms such as those that are now being pressed are primarily of the latter nature.

SECURITY

THE IRANIAN SECURITY and enforcement organizations are the army, the gendarmerie, the police, and the security organization. In general, all except the last of these share the characteristics of the bureaucracy, being composed of much the same type of people (though generally of lesser education) and still retaining many elements of traditional organization and emphasis upon status and prestige. Unfortunately, it is not given to us to investigate organizations of this type closely for their internal political structure, and the present writer thought it of little use in the wider context of this study to attempt to probe fully into their formal organizational characteristics. Yet despite the incompleteness of our knowledge of these forces, their social composition, and their power structures, they may not be ignored.

The Iranian army is, of course, charged with defense of the country from external aggression, but its domestic political function is much more crucial. Reza Shah built up the army from a weak, ill-clad and ill-disciplined conglomeration which was incapable of withstanding the single Cossack brigade of some 2,000 men. Reza Shah's activist nationalism tried to use a powerful army as a symbol of a reborn Iran, at the same time subduing regional rebellions and tribal uprisings. Not only did he succeed in unifying the country under his rule and in using the army to some extent as a channel for social advancement based on achievement; he also forged of the army an instrument to maintain his control. In Shahrivar 1320, however, the myth of the national army was destroyed by the extremely poor showing made by Iranian forces against the British and Soviet allies. In the widespread condemnation of Reza Shah's dictatorship, following Shahrivar 1320, the army too came in for much criticism, and it has not yet recovered its former prestige. In addition to loss of prestige, the unity of the army was greatly weakened by the division of the country into areas of occupation and by the increased freedom of various commanders to support any of a number of competing groups. In so far as the new shah, Muhammad Reza Pahlavi, was concerned, the army became at once a less effective basis of power and a force less amenable to central control. Many officers became adherents of the new parties and ideologies that suddenly appeared, and in particular an increasing group became members of the Tudeh Party. The shah at first depended upon his father's old cronies, especially the aristocrats among them, but gradually he turned to the younger officers who actually controlled line outfits. The most outstanding of the latter was General Razmara, who led the Iranian troops in retaking Azerbaijan in 1947 and who helped in the election of a group of pro-monarchy deputies from that area.

These events occurred during the latter part of the ministry of Qavam al-Saltaneh. Qavam had been appointed for the specific purpose of solving the problem of Iran's relations with the Soviet Union, and he acquitted himself admirably of this duty. In so doing, however, he took full advantage of his indispensability and tremendous prestige to build his own position and weaken that of the throne. This is not the place to go into the extremely interesting problem of the personal relations of the shah and Qavam, nor into the engaging personality of the veteran politician; suffice it to say that Qavam was at once forceful and discourteous. For a short time he was able to wrest control of the ministry of defense from the shah, but upon losing this control he turned to building up the gendarmerie as a counterforce, while actively trying to split the army.

Qavam's fall was accompanied by Razmara's rise. General Razmara became a close associate of the shah, then he rose to become chief of staff, minister of war, and, finally, prime minister by direct appointment, without the aid of a vote of preference by the majlis. As the story goes, the shah and Razmara then had a falling out, although no specific disagreement is cited. Their estrangement seems to have been due to Razmara's vigorous use of his authority as prime minister and to fears that he planned a coup.[70] The assassination of Razmara, it is said, was not greatly deplored by the shah; certainly it did remove the single most influential military leader.

---

[70] It is rumored that Razmara was supported by a clandestine and conspiratorial group.

Musaddiq's ministry followed shortly thereafter and was marked by the struggle between the shah and the prime minister over control of the armed forces. The issue was temporarily resolved on Tir 30, 1331, by the Tehran crowds. Mussaddiq had resigned, following the shah's refusal to permit him to appoint his own minister of war, and the shah had appointed Qavam again. The National Front, the Tudeh Party and others besides, led demonstrations against Qavam, and Qavam requested control of the army to crush the incipient rebellion. Fearing Qavam quite as much as Musaddiq, the shah refused; Qavam then went into hiding, and Musaddiq resumed office as prime minister and minister of war. Musaddiq did not attempt to make the army loyal to himself, although he had many military supporters. Instead, he tried to limit military influence and he concentrated upon control of the police, especially the Tehran police.

The last year of Musaddiq's ministry was one of almost continuous struggle with the shah over the control or support of groups, parties, ministries, influential individuals, mullahs, army units, and the police. On the 9th of Esfand the shah threatened to leave the country, and he organized a strong royalist demonstration. This test of strength in Tehran was finally decided in Musaddiq's favor by the alert action of General Afshartus, the police commandant who was a cousin of Musaddiq. About half a year later Afshartus was murdered, and General Zahedi went into hiding, from where he tried to rally various groups of the army. The struggle over the support of various Tehran groups continued, though Musaddiq, in his last months of power, had succeeded in alienating many of the more traditionally oriented, and he had become more dependent on Tudeh support. The signal for the final struggle came when the shah travelled to the north and deputed an army officer to deliver an order of dismissal to Musaddiq. The order was ignored, the officer imprisoned, the shah fled the country, and some National Front leaders began to call for a republic. The shah fled, in the belief that he could not rely on the army; however, as things turned out the antiroyalist elements in the army, especially the Tudeh officers, failed to act. On the third day after the shah's flight, as groups of lower class artisans, hawkers, and bazaar people poured out of south Tehran, Zahedi's followers in the Tehran area moved into action. The police remained inactive, some troops joined the rioters, but Musaddiq refused to issue arms to the nationalist parties or to call upon the Tudeh for help. The Kermanshah garrison, under General Bakhtiyar started for Tehran to take the city for the shah, but by mid-afternoon Radio Tehran announced the dismissal of Musaddiq's government, and no further troops were needed in the capital.

The 28th of Mordad brought two new military figures to the fore, Generals Zahedi and Bakhtiyar. Members of the general staff were still there and were still loyal. Reza Shah's cronies, and the officers who had served him well against the tribes, were still influential and ready for any assignment, and the new men like Colonel Nasiri, who had delivered the dismissal order, were promoted. Zahedi became prime minister, and his son married the shah's daughter. General Bakhtiyar was appointed director of the new security organization, and was slated to become the nominal assistant to the prime minister.

It is apparent that Zahedi deserves most of the credit for restoring the shah to power; but once again, the political dominance of a military figure was disquieting. It also seems that only with difficulty did Zahedi himself get on with the older officers, who had been less vigorous in the last month of Musaddiq's rule. Once again, the decision was against strict military rule and against thoroughgoing rationalization. Zahedi was finally persuaded to resign, and he retired to Switzerland.

In explaining to a French reporter why he fled the country, the shah pointed out that he felt he could not rely on the army. Indeed, one of the first tasks of the new administration was to purge the army and render it a loyal instrument of royal power. Many new promotions were granted, salaries were increased, housing plots were sold at low rates, and other fringe benefits were made more freely available. On the other hand, the security organization followed up Zahedi's preliminary purge by a thorough investigation. After more than two years, Bakhtiyar's persistent efforts broke the resistance of the Tudeh officers, and a grand total of more than 500 were identified, tried, executed, imprisoned, or simply dismissed.

The army has been expanded, reëquipped and trained by American advisers, and to a large extent has been rendered politically safe. Undoubtedly, there are still many elements that favor Musaddiq and oppose the shah. Tudeh strength in the army seems to have been entirely eliminated, however. The army is, perhaps, more united than it was half a dozen years ago, but rivalries and dispersed authority remain, along with the old group of leading generals. Vigorous reform, centralization, and rationalization are avoided. The military budget remains inflated by the costs of maintaining the army's loyalty, rather than by the cost of making it an efficient fighting force. General officers rarely become "superfluous," and they are difficult to retire. Many are used as a reservoir for political appointments or cabinet positions, but this tendency is not systematic, and military appointees have no greater security of tenure than others.

The role of the army in Middle East politics has recently emerged as a kind of stereotype. Military training and organization nicely complement rationalizing ideologies or policies, and even where a coup has not taken place, the desire for reform often brings a military man into political prominence. The obstacles in the way of bureaucratic management of rationalizing reform have been developed at some length, but the fact of bureaucratic failure itself is a further impetus to turning the job over to the military. The military may suffer from many of the same organizational defects and interested pressures, but there may be found in its ranks many more who are ready for ruthless rationalization. To some extent, oversimplified reformist ideals are encouraged in the military, both by the heritage of Reza Shah's regime and by the present shah's choice of certain officers for administrative tasks. Nevertheless the most idealistic group is to be found among the younger officers, those who have studied abroad (perhaps in special training assignments in the United States) and who feel that their way to advancement is blocked by older, satisfied men. Thus it is not simply a matter of favoring and rewarding the army, nor of making the army more centralized, unified, and efficient. Salary and benefits will not quell impatience or dispel shame, but efficient organization may simply make it easier to dispense with civilian authority.

Recent experience elsewhere in the Middle East bears out the conclusion that although the military is the major support of the monarchy it is also the major danger thereto. Musaddiq failed to win over a section of the army, thus adding further proof to the widespread assumption that a coup or revolution will have to come from the army, if it is to be. But in Iran, at any rate, the most dangerous military group was that won over by the Tudeh Party. Furthermore, the very serious threat posed to the monarchy was from the Tehran middle classes. The emphasis of the security organization, therefore, has been upon clearing the army of its Tudeh members, breaking up the Tudeh Party, and controlling or keeping a close watch on all the groups and individuals who participated in the hectic events of the Musaddiq period.

The security organization is reputed to be more efficient than other government agencies. Its employees are well paid and have several clubs, coöperative stores, and the like. Some of the best buildings in Tehran house the organization. Its major function is to uncover and suppress subversive activity; but it also handles important counterpropaganda problems, issuing answers to Soviet broadcasts for publication. Supervision of the media of mass communication is also one of its jobs. The people of Tehran generally hold that the security organization has informers in all public and private organizations, and even in all of the less well-to-do sections of the city. These informers are said to be required to present weekly reports on all their colleagues and neighbors. It is also generally believed that the security organization, in dealing with Tudeh members or suspects, uses extreme forms of torture in order to elicit the names of other members. Whatever the tactics used, there seems to be little question about the success of this organization's efforts thus far in smashing the Tudeh organization. It is further felt, however, that the security organization does not have any great influence over the army, and that General Bakhtiyar does not have a military clique of his own. However, he does not, as Zahedi evidently did, pose a threat to the throne. Finally, it should be stated that popular feeling is very much against both the army and the security organization, as it is against the less powerful but more routine organizations of police and gendarmerie. The army is the most derided and despised group, and the security organization is the one most feared. One may expect, though, that the security organization will not be capable of nipping a serious conspiracy in the bud and that a successful coup will renew army popularity.

FOUR

Structures

of Social Power

THE BUREAUCRACY, led by the cabinet and sustained by the military, may be the chosen instrument of rationalizing policies in the Iranian political system, but progress toward that goal depends very much on what is to be rationalized. As pointed out above, simply to rationalize the administration will accomplish little, unless the cabinet is transformed into a rational policy-making body, and unless the security forces are changed into the pliable instrument of resultant policy. Rational policy making itself requires that more than the final desideratum be considered. The rationalization of politics, on the one hand, and of administration, on the other, are complementary aspects of a single objective based on a unified set of assumptions about absolute values. Their complementarity in theory does not, however, establish their causal relationship. The not altogether happy experience of a good many states, in recent years, has illustrated the efficiency of force in transforming a system, and in this ultimate sense there is a causal relationship between rationalizing an administrative subsystem and the rationalization of a political system. Nevertheless, it would seem to be beyond question that the means of rationalization will affect the end achieved: force is but a crude descriptive of something that may be applied in many ways; its unthinking application, often resulting in praetorianism or "revolving door" coups has consistently failed to achieve rationalization; force sufficient to accomplish this objective is not an inherent qualification of every army; wherever rationalizing policies and ideologies have been notably successful, the army has been subordinated to a bureaucratically oriented elite; and, finally, economies in the use of force can be realized only if existing volitional tendencies among the population are exploited.

To apply these arguments to Iran we need only point out that rationalizing goals are still subordinated to more or less traditional system maintenance objectives, and that the major preventative against reversing the relationship of these goals and objectives has been the permeation of both the bureaucracy and military with traditionally oriented personnel. Even should these objectives be reversed, and even if, by some presently unforeseen development, the predominance of the bureaucracy over the military should be assured, political rationalization will not be the automatic result of a declaration that some desired hierarchical positioning of the varied structures of social power exists—say, in a new constitution. The rational planning and the programing of rationalization must be quite as pragmatic as for any other goal; and where the environmental conditions for rationalization do not exist, they must be produced in an appropriate manner.

The term "structures of social power" has been given preference here to that of "groups," in order to emphasize the fact that we are concerned with social phenomena which differ greatly from those of highly developed, industrialized systems. Ordinary applications of "group theory" do not hold so well, when transferred to underdeveloped areas.[1]

Group theory, in brief, assumes that politics is the interaction of social units in greater or lesser conflict over the distribution of political values. Some even go so far as to call various government institutions or agencies groups, as well as to refer to vaguely articulated interests as latent groups. Obviously, the latter tendencies are exaggerations necessary to make the theory "fit," and they are of little consequence in a system where highly organized, articulate groups dominate the political scene. But in underde-

---

[1] See Almond and Coleman, *op. cit.*; L. Pye, "The Non-Western Political Process," *Journal of Politics* (August, 1958), pp. 468–486.

veloped countries, where effective pressure group organization and activity is rare, it is necessary to get far too much out of governmental–institutional groups and out of latent groups. These types of phenomena, marginal to the basic theory, are of primary importance in underdeveloped countries.

Ordinarily, group theory, as applied to government institutions, must assume a degree of unity of purpose and of professionalization of personnel such as hardly exists in Iran. In other countries, some governmental agencies have become so closely identified with the groups most interested in their substantive administrative area as to be classified with these groups for purposes of political analysis. A similar situation arises where geographical authorities support sectional interests. These aspects of certain bureaucratic organizations permit their inclusion in a "group system analysis," but they obscure both purposeful and ceremonial allocations of legitimacy. In Iran, one of the primary political issues is precisely that of giving the administrative apparatus, from cabinet on down, a personality of its own, separate from that of the groups or interests with which its members are unofficially associated. This "personality" needs to have two characteristics: the first is the obvious one of articulating the interests of bureaucrats as a class, and the second is that of identifying the goals of the bureaucracy with some conception of the general welfare.

At first sight, it might seem that the lack of any distinct bureaucratic interest would render the Iranian system closer to the ideal of group theory, thus dispensing with the need for an exaggerated and elliptical interpretation of the role of governmental institutions in politics. When we turn to an analysis of groups in the Iranian system, however, we find that there exists no clear-cut arrangement of interests to which the members of the bureaucracy can be related. It is possible to seek a solution in the second hyperbolic flight of group theorists, the notion of the latent interest group. Latency is a useful concept whenever and wherever the conditions for ready group formation exist. In a system in which communication is generally poor, in which information is distorted, and in which there are cultural obstacles to the growth of a realistic hope to change things, interest groups do not necessarily grow out of manifestly common interests.

In Iranian politics, groups never include all of the activities of individuals. Politics, indeed, is a social pursuit; and if by groups we mean no more than this, then the term is surely misleading. The power relationships of an individual are not usually encompassed by a single group, and it seems to be a most inept circum-locution to dub these person-centered relationships a group. The political analyst may, with as much right, take the individual's power relationships or the patterned power relationships of the group as his central point of view; these are two ways of looking at the same thing. In certain political systems, the group has so much more importance than the individual that it would be foolish to look at political affairs from the individual's viewpoint. In others, the group hardly exists, for political purposes, except as exploited by the individual. In the latter type of system, groups have diffuse goals, regardless of the formal basis of organization, and the crux of their political function is closely related to the individual's political decisions. The very restricted interests thus served by this type of political action naturally place greatest emphasis upon primary groups, though other groups have a function, too.

Iranian politics can best be analyzed from the point of view of the individual. His broad class or occupational affiliation will largely determine what he wants and what he can get, but beyond that the individual scouts his contacts, family, friends and col-leagues to see how and whom he can move to achieve his goal. Groups are social resources to be exploited by individuals or by the government, and this explains why many exist in name only or are really variants of primary face-to-face groups with high-sounding aims. Government exploitation of groups is simply the reaction to private exploitation. Private exploitation is chaotic, and it contradicts the legitimate basis of group existence, that is, service of a broadly shared interest. Government exploitation of groups prevents individuals from so doing, renders group goals less diffuse, and channels group activity into support for the government's general policy. In a word, government exploitation of groups is a rationalizing policy parallel to that of rationalizing the administration, and it is interdependent with it. Above all, it should be noted that the success of the government's modern-izing and nationalizing policies depends upon its being able to make groups rather than individuals the basis of political calculus; but experience has shown group leadership to be irresponsible while the existing political atmosphere indicates that associations of the polyarchal sort will be anti-regime.

Primary groups still form the core of interest associations. The extended family stands at the center of Iranian social organization, and it remains the single most important political fact. Of less importance, nevertheless a consistent feature of

social organization is the primary group dimension of the broad
demographic category in which the individual may be classified.
Here, reference is to the relationship between the villager and
his village community, the tribesman and his clan, the city dweller
of the lower class and his neighbors. As one moves up the social
scale the demographic category becomes less important and
cliques assume greater significance. Even these cliques, however,
usually show strong tendencies to be limited to persons speaking
the same language or dialect, those coming from the same town,
or those of about the same age, having a similar education, or
possibly even working in the same office or profession. It is easy
to see how groups of this sort can work together quite naturally
in defense of their own interests or to help one another toward
some specific benefit. If some individual is of particularly great
influence, it may even be possible to have some effect in determining policy, but usually these groups are on the defensive or are
concentrating upon attempts to benefit from some already announced policy.

Broad demographic categories such as urban-rural, linguistic,
regional, religious, and the like are sure to be taken into account,
but these, currently, have little direct bearing on day-to-day
politics. Efforts are made to win pork-barrel projects for provincial
towns; the government attempts to settle tribesmen or expropriate
tribal leaders; the Soviets try to turn the Azerbaijanis against
the government; the Kurds are propitiated, against eventualities
growing from the Iraqi revolution. Members of the majlis are
often chosen from among provincially rooted aristocrats, even
if they do not reside in their original areas. The Hayat Davud
and Qashqa'i leaders reside in exile in Europe. Whole regional
development programs have been worked upon, and work is
going forward on asphalting the streets, piping the water, and
increasing the electrical power of some three hundred provincial
municipalities. The non-Muslim minorities are granted representation in the majlis, and the big Sunni minority in Kurdistan
has its traditional political and religious leaders recognized. It
is clear that the realities of demographic differentiation are accepted in Iran, and even at the popular level Azerbaijanis are
known as tightwads, Shirazis as pleasant fun-loving people,
Isfahanis as liars and cheats, Kurds, Turkmen and Baluchis as
somewhat stupid, and so on. Nevertheless these demographic
differences, where they are not clearly represented in the influence
of a tribal or religious leader, are manifested in the influence of a

family or clique and not in a popular movement for local benefits or for separation.

Iranian social classes have nowhere been carefully described, and all that can be done here is to give a general impression of those aspects of stratification which seem to have political significance. However, one should avoid the facile oversimplification that Iranian politics can be understood simply as a struggle between the "feudal" and the middle classes, or, even less likely, between the landlords and the peasants. Class lines are not nearly so rigid, nor are class differences so few and simple, as the doctrinaire and educated young man chooses to believe. Again, there are no political movements rooted in class interests, though some may claim to be. These classes are significant in quite another way. In the first place, they cut across the broad demographic categories and therefore set limits to organization on those lines. They indicate traditional bases of leadership in tribe and village. They show where it may be possible to shape common interest groups, should conditions allow and circumstances so determine. They further reveal how advancement in the military and civil services may determine class membership. In the case of the ulama, especially, they indicate how a common general classification ill accords with political tendencies. Most important, social class has a general relevance to ideological orientation. Social classification may also circumscribe, not a pattern of common interest layers, but constellations of existing and potential common interest groups that stand close to one another, whether coöperating or competing. These groups may act without great regard for those further down, either ignoring or manipulating them as the situation allows. Finally, social classes and occupational strata indicate the size of the problem of political rationalization.

Interest groups, as we know them in the West, are more potential than actual in Iran, but knowledge (however partial) of their presence in the West tends to precipitate a variety of attempts at their formation and manipulation. Alongside of groups newly formed in imitation of Western prototypes, there exist more traditional groups, some of which have simply survived and others of which have been revived for some pressing political purpose. Between these two types another hybrid may be discerned, in which an occupational class or grouping without formal organization responds to the cues of a self-appointed leader whose representations to the government are more or less effective (i.e., he has won access). In nearly all cases, in all three categories, the interests represented are diffuse, the membership fluid, the organization informal, the level of activity erratic, the commitments of both members and leaders indeterminate, and the finances precarious or clearly based on personal or external sources.

In the past, these group interests of, say, religious class, guilds, minorities, city quarters or bazaar areas, or tribal groups, were in each case alternatively represented by two or three handfuls of wealthy and respected individuals who were appointed, or at least recognized, by the ruling power. A change in policy almost invariably involved changes in personnel, and was hardly distinguishable therefrom. Access was often controlled by a few favored officials and was restricted to those recognized leaders. Such leaders were not specialized functionaries but leading members of a group, trade, or profession; hence they were the competitors of those whom they represented. In any case, there was little if any control from below, and failing a change of government, there was not much hope of changing group leaders. There was, however, one parallel channel of access that was open to all and that touched every level of government; this was through the religious institution of either the majority community or one of the minorities.

This interest pattern still persists, but some important additions have been made to it. Some of these changes are the increased division of labor and the resulting specialization in the bureaucracy and the army; the encroachment of Western manufactures upon the sphere of the traditional bazaar; the diffusion of the economic interests of the aristocratic and landed elite; the introduction of Western legal systems and the growth of a group of professional lawyers; the development of other professions, such as medicine and engineering, accounting, and teaching; the importation of complete sets of Western political institutions and the effort to construct political parties, increased communication, and mobility; and finally, authoritatively determined policies of nationalizing the outlook of the masses and increasing the scope and power of government.

The consequence of these changes has been the creation of many new groups or interests, many of which have not yet (or not clearly) been articulated. Western political institutions have generally contributed to an increased awareness of the importance of formal organizations, of propaganda activities, and of political access. On the other hand, the actual power structure, as understood in terms of those actually making decisions, has not changed much; rather, the means at their disposal have increased in quantity and in formal legitimacy. Thus the formally organized interest group tends to be inefficient, a prey to "political brokers" who trade nuisance value for political power, an instrument to be manipulated by government agencies, a revolutionary cabal, or quasi-governmental regulatory institutions. For effective access these groups must accept the leadership of a member of the traditional elite or of an adherent, and so their political practices become assimilated to those of the traditional interest system, except perhaps for the publication of a newspaper. Nevertheless, these interests exist and emerge as articulate forces in the political processes, with greater regularity of activity. The increased scope and power of government and its policy of national unification may forestall such a development. The slow growth of governmental paternalism, in group after group, tends to exclude the possibility of the growth of an interest system on the Western pattern.

The place of political parties in any political system varies considerably with historical, cultural, and ideological factors, but, leaving important details aside, parties may be seen either as interest groups or as temporary shifting aggregations of groups. Where the role of parties has been so institutionalized that it can deliver legitimizations to its adherents, the parties usually perform an aggregative function. Where parties cannot grant legitimizations, or where they refuse to admit certain groups, parties more often become common interest associations or become dominated by some ideological outlook. Iran has had both general types of parties and important variations on each theme. The role of parties and quasi-party organizations like the National Front has varied with political conditions. Before the rise of Reza Shah, what went by the name of parties were but loose associations of members of the majlis. After Reza Shah's abdication, a host of new parties were formed in the wake of, and under the organizational influence of, the Tudeh Party. Despite their formal organizational regulations, most of these parties were either the personal support of a majlis member, transformed interest groups, governmental electoral instruments, or small extremist youth groups. Some non-majlis members won personal followings, and the National Front, too, was an exceptional development. In the last five years or so two official parties have been recognized. These are both loyal to the regime, have moderate reform programs, deëmphasize ideology, and attempt to aggregate as widely as possible through existing or newly created groups. The two official parties promised to be able to divide the fruits of the 1960 election between them, but the general incredulity with which these claims were met was manifested in a reluctance to join. Rapid changes in the over-all political situation and the consequent victimization of those who took the wrong side has also served to make people very cautious about committing themselves to a political party unless some concrete immediate benefit may be offered.

In the rest of this chapter detailed descriptions of each of these aspects of power structure in Iran will be presented. While the general characteristics of the family as a political unit may be analyzed, it seems profitless and far too ambitious to enumerate the most influential families. The broad demographic divisions of the Iranian population will also be given short shrift, for these have been described elsewhere, and a new and fairly efficient national census has been reported which will surpass any description we now have. Social classes, groups, and parties will receive more detailed attention. It must be stressed again, however, that each of these aspects of power structure must be seen as the social environment which the individual tries to manipulate in getting a job, a promotion, a license, a contract, title to public lands, or membership in the majlis. There is little common effort for a common objective, instead, an involved procedure of bargaining and mutual favor-doing, clearing of mutual obligations, and lutigari [2] holds these groups together.

PRIMARY GROUPS AND
DEMOGRAPHIC CLASSES

IT MUST NOT BE THOUGHT that the family is any exception to this general rule. While the family is the common interest group par excellence, each of its members must pay a certain price. For political purposes, the nuclear family unit is of little consequence; the extended family, on the other hand, being a much larger and more comprehensive system of mutual obligations, rather than a hierarchy of authorities, fits the Iranian political system much more closely. Each of the oldest males of the related nuclear families is ideally an independent bargainer, capable of disposing of all the resources of his family. His subordinates may act only with his permission. He may call upon uncles and cousins for assistance, but again, consultation is required. In entering upon any enterprise, be it business or marriage, relatives have first claim

---

[2] "Lutigari" is a colloquial term for a kind of chivalric friendship involving the doing of mutual favors.

as partners or spouses. Nepotism, where possible under modern conditions, is a strict family obligation. When one moves up to the families of really important influence, a further obligation is that of accepting, or further recommending, "clients" referred by relatives.

Generally speaking, these obligations stand, despite a good deal of family friction, usually the result of sibling rivalry. On the other hand, one does find examples of branches of a large and influential family that have grown distant from one another. There are also occasions where a rebellious son or an educated Westernized young man will refuse to ask permission, or to consult, or even to benefit from, family "pull." It is very rare, however, to find this sort of thing among the most influential families; it is found, rather, among declining families or those that have been severely penalized politically on some occasion. Among middle-class families it seems to be uneconomical to keep up the extremely wide contacts of the aristocratic families. Where these distant connections are maintained one usually finds some history of mutual assistance. The mutuality of obligation beyond the nuclear family is not often obvious, for it is nicely camouflaged in a pattern of ordered deference which recognizes age, education, wealth, and the like. But this is a surface phenomenon that merely permits the system to work more smoothly.

Some of the most important families have developed, through ownership of land or services to the crown, a strong basis of influence in certain provincial towns. Out of tribal leadership others have developed local influence. The Qajar families, having held influence at the court, extended theirs by acquisition of lands in the provinces; the provincial aristocrats, on the other hand, tried to extend theirs to Tehran by placing members of their families in the ministries or in the army, or by winning seats in the majlis. Nowadays, when most of the important families are concentrated in Tehran, it is not surprising to find several members of one family holding down jobs in a variety of ministries or having seats in the majlis while running a number of enterprises in the afternoon, having left one brother, perhaps, back in the home town. Families in the traditional middle class have also sometimes acquired a permanent relationship of influence within a guild or in one of the smaller towns.

The particular basis of family influence is often connected with aspects of the broad demographic divisions among the Iranian population. Iranian nationalists will agree that there are no

national minorities within Iran, only irredenta or volks-Iran outside, like the Kurds, Afghans, Baluchis, Pathans, Azeris and Tajiks.
Nevertheless, there are significant differences among the population of Iran, and these differences, though they do not reach the
level of competing nationalisms, do affect political groupings.
Demographically, Iran may be seen as two overlapping con-
centric circles, the area covered by the smaller circle being inhabited by Persian-speaking Iranians proper, and the larger outer
area encompassed by minorities of diverse languages and cultures.
The minorities around the outer edge have more dominant tribal
characteristics, except for the Azeri Turks. The tribally, or partly
tribally, organized groups have their own traditional leaders and
their own tradition of political activity. The Kurds have had a
separatist movement only recently, in the Mahabad Republic,
under Mullah Mustafa Barazani; but the Ardalan and other
families based on Kermanshah and Sanandaj have coöperated
with the Iranian government. The Bakhtiaris have helped the
shah, given him a wife and a head of the security organization.
The Qashqa'is, who are Turkic speaking, are the traditional
enemies of the Pahlavi dynasty, as are the Hayat Davudis, and
with less regularity, the Boir Ahmadis. The Arab tribes of Khuzistan, long influenced by Shaikh Khaz'al of Muhammera (Khoram-
shahr) flaunted the government at Tehran until Reza Shah
brought them under control. Since that time, Arab influence in
Iran has declined; the Arabs have never been able to make their
presence seriously felt in Tehran. Other smaller tribal groups exist
in substantial numbers, with more diffused leadership in proportion to the degree to which they are settled.

The Azeri Turks are the most important of the linguistic
minorities, comprising nearly a third of the total population and
inhabiting a fertile if difficult part of the country. The Azeris
have come to Tehran in large numbers, often going into retail
business, maintaining their own mosque and helping one another
in the face of the "Fars" prejudice. Azeri members of the majlis
often speak up for the interests of their own province or to praise
the industry of its people. On the other hand, there seems to
be little evidence that Azerbaijan is an easy prey to separatist
propaganda or that the Soviet effort to establish an "independent"
Azerbaijan reflected the aspirations of the Azeris. The government
of "democratic Azerbaijan" fell without a murmur of support
from the people, though there may linger among some peasants
a fascination with slogans demanding dispossession of the landlords. The younger intellectuals, now as in the past, may seek to

transform or revolutionize Iran from Tabriz, but not to separate the two. Most important, however, is the fact that the Azeris may not be controlled simply by satisfying their traditional leaders. They are not tribesmen, and many of their landlords are not Azeris. The peasants, of course, are still dominated by their land-lords, but the townspeople—and especially the residents of Tabriz—are amenable only to newer kinds of organization and more direct benefits. Nevertheless, it is significant to note that the recent census suggests that Tabriz has not grown in population as expected, during the last decade or so. Apparently, Tehran has attracted many of those from Tabriz, and the attraction continues. In the general distribution of political values it does not seem that Azeris have been discriminated against, and this would appear to be an important reason why both supporters and opponents of the government have thrown in their lot with the rest of Iran.

The urban-rural division in Iran, as in many underdeveloped countries, places the bulk of the population in the countryside and concentrates political power in the capital city. Despite efforts to raise rural living standards and to improve the attractiveness of provincial cities, the villages still remain extremely backward, and the ambitious young man travels to Tehran, rather than to another provincial center. Obviously, the provinces are not disregarded, but the fate of the nation is decided in Tehran. By any yardstick, it would seem that the political action of Tehran street sweepers is more significant for the future of the regime than the pains and pleasures of the elite of a whole host of provincial towns. Reports keep cropping up concerning the awakening of the peasant and his increased awareness of his interests, but as yet there has been no concrete evidence of this. Perhaps the peasant is ready for a change, but he is not ready to produce it himself. Furthermore, for all but the very wealthy, the barriers to frequent travel and rapid communication in Iran are such that most people must be concerned only with local affairs. Where provincial affairs have risen to national significance, it is usually found that newer types of organizations have come into existence, notably labor unions, in both Isfahan and Abadan.

Some religious minorities are geographically based, such as the Armenians at Julfa, the Zoroastrians at Yazd, and the Assyrians at Rezaieh; but Tehran also has its concentrations of these, and of Jews and Baha'is as well. Aside from the expected popular prejudices concerning these minorities, only the Baha'is suffer from serious political disabilities, and only the Baha'is are accused of having some sinister influence on political events. The other minorities, with the exception of the Assyrians, who are very few, have representatives in the majlis, and their personal status law is at least to some degree recognized. These communities usually enjoy higher standards of living than those of the average Iranians, especially those sections of each community which reside in Tehran. There is, however, much poverty to be found among them, as attested by the Jewish mahaleh in Tehran and reports of similar areas in Isfahan and elsewhere. Of the minorities, it seems that only the Armenians count a substantial number of peasants and rural residents, mostly in Azerbaijan. The Armenian community in Tehran underwent a serious strain, about a dozen years ago, when many of their coreligionists left their homes in the provinces to make their way to the Soviet Union. Emigration was suddenly cut off, and many, having sold all their belongings, simply stayed on in Tehran. Most of these have now been assimilated. Tehran has also attracted many Jews from the provinces, in recent years, some to benefit from the economic opportunities to be found there and some to make their way, with the help of the Jewish Agency, to Israel. Nearly ten years ago, the Jewish community of Tehran received into their fold a sizeable number of Iraqi Jews, most of whom were rather well off, so that they found the opportunities in Tehran more congenial to their talents than was the case in Tel Aviv.

The minority communities maintain their own schools, within the framework of the state-determined curriculum, which includes the teaching of Arabic. They also carry on a number of social welfare activities, in most cases through their churches. There is little participation by these minorities in political organizations or in the ward councils in the larger cities, but they are generally accepted in professional associations, guilds, and the chamber of commerce. The minorities are fairly prominent in trades, crafts, the medical and dental professions, and in such pursuits as taxi driving and entertaining. In most instances, important traders must have Shi'i-Muslim partners, if they are to get along with government officials. The minorities, of course, must bargain for cash (i.e., bribes) more often than others, because they have little else to offer. Some individuals have risen to great wealth, and presumably influence, but they remain few and far between. The outstanding example of the owner of the new television station clearly overemphasizes the extent of Baha'i influence.

While there has been some minority representation in the Tudeh Party, particularly of Armenians, the attraction of the Communist Party of Iran for the minorities has not been so exclusive as it was in other Middle Eastern countries. In any case, Shiite Iranians made up the overwhelming majority of the membership. On the other hand, the minorities, particularly Armenians and Baha'is, have been somewhat quicker to learn the English language, and many have found jobs with the United States Operations Mission or with American and British firms. The relatively higher pay of these jobs, and the prestige associated with American power and influence, has attracted Shiite Iranians to them, a situation which has led to some accusations that Americans favor the minorities. The only Shiite Iranians who can qualify for these jobs are usually men of influential family and of some wealth who have been able to study in the United States.

Despite recent emphasis on nationalism and constitutionalism, the minorities remain outside of Iranian society, as popularly conceived. This popular social conception has not strayed very far from medieval class theories and the early Islamic views which placed non-Muslims in a class by themselves. These theories are great oversimplifications, when applied to contemporary urban society, and they militate against ideological clarity in the political struggle over legitimacy. Especially in Iran, where social stratification is very finely elaborated in a subtle gradation of social ceremonial, it is surprising to learn how crude is the generally accepted notion of class structure.

SOCIAL AND OCCUPATIONAL STRATA

THE FIRST MUSLIMS also thought of their society as made of only a few classes. At the top would be the Muhajirun, who fled Mecca with, or before, Muhammad and who travelled to Medina. The next group were the Ansar, or Medina residents, who became Muslims and supported the Prophet. Then came the much larger group of Arab tribesmen who flocked to the victorious Islamic banner and subsequently went forth to defeat the Byzantines and Sassanians. These were followed in importance by the non-Arab converts to Islam who, at first, could not become Muslims without at the same time becoming the client associates of some Arab tribe. Finally, there came the dhimmis or protected non-Muslim residents of Dar al-Islam. This Sunni religious-centered social theory did not have much effect on early caliphal government, and as time passed it reflected more the ideal of the religious institution than the actual practice.

The Shiites, of course, did not accept this social ideal, since they placed greatest emphasis upon descent from the Prophet and otherwise made no distinction between Arab and non-Arab. Consequently, for the Shiites the most honored class was that of the Sayyids, or descendants of the Prophet through his daughter Fatima and her husband Ali. The next most honored group would be the ulama, or those learned in the sciences of religion. Again, from the religious point of view these might be followed by the mass of Muslims, and then the protected non-Muslims.

While these religious theories never lost all their influence on deference behavior, they were, especially among the members of the more broadly educated and the administrative class, supplanted by a conception bearing the stamp of pre-Islamic imperial Iran. The older Iranian theory of the proper structure of society has come to us in two major variations, that placing the religiously trained in the highest class, and another which would see the bureaucracy alone as the highest class. Both variants have divided society into four classes, the more religiously oriented having it that the highest class was that of the men of the pen, including ulama and bureaucracy, who were at least for a time similarly trained. Then came men of the sword, men of affairs, and finally the peasants. The more secularly oriented view placed the men of government at the top, followed by the men of religion, landowners and merchants, and finally workmen. Both of these variations were associated with a more this-worldly, organic conception of society. While retaining a good deal of the nature of a prestige hierarchy, this Iranian theory stressed the functional utility of such a division. Each class was to perform its natural and appropriate duty, and one of the major tasks of government was to prevent any class from encroaching upon the function of any other.

The mixture of prestige hierarchy and organic functionalism came down to recent times and was expressed with special application to Iranian conditions in the constitution of 1906 and in the first electoral law of Iran. The constitution was to provide for a consultative body representing the important classes of Iranian society. The slight variation between the constitution and the electoral law reveals that practical considerations quite outshine any fixed theory, and that the relative superiority of each group was less important than that all be represented. The constitution provided for representation of the following six classes: (1) princes, (2) ulama, (3) Qajar family, (4) nobles and notables, (5) landowners, and (6) merchants and guildsmen. The electoral law provided for the election of representatives of the following six classes:

1. princes and Qajars,
2. ulama,
3. nobles and notables,
4. merchants,
5. landowners, and
6. guilds.

In the electoral law, which was the practical application of the constitution, we may note that the merchants and trade guilds each received separate and equal representation. The rise of a moneyed, urban middle class may thus be noted. It is similarly significant that the ulama retained their prominent position in both classifications, and we note that the relations of the ulama and the merchants and guildsmen were particularly close at the time. Not mentioned in either classification are the unrepresented peasants, tribesmen, and laborers. Election to the majlis by classes lasted through the first three sessions only, that is until 1922. After that time elections were from geographical constituencies, thus indicating the beginnings of a new conception of egalitarian nationalism rivaling the prestige-function theory.

Despite Reza Khan's nationalist coup, his retention of the royal institution militated against the growth of egalitarian interpretations of social phenomena. No one claimed that Iran had a classless society, but the changes wrought by Reza Shah did affect popular notions of class. The Qajars were, with the deposition of Ahmad Shah, rendered little different from the princes and large landowners left over by earlier dynasties. The ulama were severely repressed, and they lost much of their previous influence and prestige. The traditional middle class was expanded by the modern professions and by newer forms of trade, industry, and banking. During the Reza Shah period (and immediately thereafter, under the impact of much leftist and nationalist propaganda) there developed the contemporary popular conception of Iranian class structure. This simple division into three classes is often reflected in everyday conversation, and it certainly informs people's attitudes about those with whom they come into contact. The three classes are simply referred to as the first, second, and third, more or less corresponding to high, middle, and low classes. The high, or first, class is made up of landowners, aristocrats, wealthy people, and above all those with influence. The second class is made up of the intellectuals, smaller business people, most ulama, and even tradesmen. The third class is made up of workers and illiterates. These classes are distinguished first according to wealth, second according to education, and they are finally judged in terms of their nationalist attitudes. On the basis of the last criterion, it is quite clear that the second class comes off best.

Our presentation to this point has been more concerned with ideology than with political sociology, nevertheless it provides us with some notion of how Iranians interpret their own social environment. It is clear that there exists a widely held belief that Iran is ruled by a small group of selfish people who enjoy an all-pervading influence based upon wealth and prestige, that these people restrict the opportunities and limit the rewards of the more thoughtful or less self-seeking middle class, while ruthlessly exploiting the ignorant and helpless masses. It is assumed, of course, that interests coincide with these broad classifications and that the nation as a whole will best be served if the second class takes power in stewardship for the masses.

We have already criticized the view expounded by some "group theorists" that wherever an interest exists there we will find a group, or may in any case pursue our political calculus as though a group existed. The popular Iranian conception of three classes and three interests is, however, much further from the mark. What is required is, first, a close examination of actual classes, in order to see where potential interest groups exist; and then a survey of existing groups to see whether or not they coincide in any way with social and occupational classifications. Our classification, based on concrete social phenomena can then inform suggestions about latent interest groups. But more importantly, it can tell us what kind of social grouping may be exploited in the Iranian political system, and what are the categories of hierarchical organization that may determine governmental policies of rationalization. Class and occupational divisions may represent latent interests, but in Iran a latent interest is not necessarily the same thing as a latent interest group. Under the contemporary Iranian system there is no scope for group formation by interested persons, though occasionally there may be some sort of short-lived spontaneous coöperative action. Above all, these classes must be seen as potential social forces given to movement either by the government or by skillful persons or cliques.

It need hardly be stressed that class or occupational grouping is not a complete guide to the existence of an interest or a unity of ideological outlook. Religion, ethnic community, personality, history of socialization, language, role conflicts, family, and many other factors may have a more direct impact upon the individual's identification tendencies and upon the politically relevant decisions he makes. The only real guide to the existence of a common interest is the existence of a group with certain common objectives. In advanced conventional-polyarchal systems, voluntary associations appear as needs arise, and though generally in accordance with class and occupational differentia, they are not bound thereby. In traditional systems, certain groups, leaders, or institutions are recognized as legitimate, and all newly arising issues must be settled through these means. In rational-hierarchical systems not only are a limited number of associations recognized, but the function and scope of these groups is also fixed. Consequently, the movement away from tradition involves the recognition of new groups, the restriction of the influence and scope of interest of the traditional groups, and the designation of specific functions for recognized groups. Later, we shall see how the Iranian government is hesitantly moving toward the rational-hierarchical pole in its policy toward existing groups. For the present, we would consider what is the new material out of which new polyarchal groups may arise and out of which this or another regime may try to compound "mass-line" organizations.

Unfortunately, we lack the necessary information for an accurate description of Iranian social classes. Little or no material has been published on the problem, and no sociologists have been at work on the crucial problem of Tehran's social structure. Under the circumstances, all we can do is to guess at the answers, on the basis of general observation and conversations with Iranians. Little guarantee of validity can be held out for the following presentation, but it may well be that an impressionistic view is better than none at all. The general criteria of the following classification are prestige, occupation, wealth, political access, and potential (or actual) political coöperation.

At the bottom of the scale we find the tribes. These vary in size from small clan-like groups to large federations of nearly a quarter of a million. Over the years, there has been a tendency for the unit of allegiance to grow, for the customary rights of the tribesman to dwindle, and for the economic scope of the tribe to become more restricted. The tribesman is to all intents and purposes cut off from the political life of the capital. Radio programs are beamed in his direction, and attempts have been made to provide him with a house and a piece of land. Occasionally the tribesmen will stop in a town for a while, some pass close to Tehran, or several hundred Bakhtiaris may parade through the city on some holiday to demonstrate their loyalty to the shah. The ordinary tribesman obeys his khan and is ready to use violence. He is relatively untouched by either nationalist or leftist agitators, and often he despises his fellow countrymen settled on the plateau. Conceivably, tribesmen can trouble their settled neighbors, vex the gendarmerie, even be used against a rebellious urban mob, but they are no match for modern armed forces. The political problem of the tribes, insofar as the government is concerned, is that of the tribal leaders, and not of the tribesmen themselves. These leaders, as we shall see, have largely merged with the landed elite.

The peasants form the overwhelming majority of the population. Living in villages numbering from a handful to perhaps several hundred families, they make a meager living out of land rented from absentee owners. The stereotype of the Middle Eastern peasant applies here: poverty, disease, ignorance, indebtedness, dependence, and exploitation are his lot. In most villages, hardly any vestige of local autonomy is left, and little individual initiative exists. When given possession of the land, the peasant is usually incapable of determining how best to manage it, and he does not easily grasp the importance of village coöperation. Most peasants are illiterate, generally loyal to the shah, and respectful of religion.

It may well be that the peasants are not nearly so passive an element as was once the case. Though most tales of peasant sharpness are concerned with his dealings with the landlord's representative, there is reason to believe that in some areas the peasant is beginning to conceive of a better life. The radio has come to certain villages, some of the young men have been conscripted for the army, various health and welfare projects or educational schemes have carried new ideas to villages, and in a few places the royal and public domain land distribution schemes have disrupted an age old routine. Many peasants, and not only those near the larger cities, have heard that city life offers amenities and a level of living not to be found outside. There has been a considerable migration to the larger cities, particularly Tehran, indicating increasing awareness in the village. Political parties have wasted a great deal of energy talking about helping the peasant, but none have really made a serious effort in that direction. Only the Tudeh Party, in the area of Tehran and Shiraz, and in some parts of Azerbaijan, has tried to agitate among the peasants, with indeterminate results. There is a great problem in communication between the urban intellectual and the peasant, and its solution can come only with great effort and patience.

To discuss the peasants as a single undifferentiated class is to ignore important differences of class structure within the village itself.[3] In general, the village has no important local leadership in matters outside of everyday village affairs. There are, however, both more and less respectable peasants, wealthier and wiser ones, some craftsmen, usually a religious man, the landowners' representative (who may or may not be the same as the village headman), and perhaps a merchant. Specialists such as qanat repairmen, water distributors, owners of oxen and the like, add to the diversity of village society. Yet these distinctions will remain unimportant in general political calculations until serious efforts are made to move the peasants to action, or until more extensive projects for land distribution and the establishment of village coöperatives are carried out. Perhaps we may sometime have to take account of the coöperative director, the village council, and even the village teacher, but those days seem far off now. For the present, the "natural leaders" of the village are no match for the landowner, the kadkhoda, and the local gendarmerie.

When we move to the city we find a kind of Eastern urban "lumpen-proletariat" at the lowest level. Composed to a large extent of new immigrants from the countryside, this is a predominantly male group, often of no fixed residence. Sometimes a group of such men will share a small room, or a family may even live in a hut constructed of boards and tin cans, built around a cave. A sizeable proportion of these people are not permanent residents of the city, but come for the warmer months and return to their villages during the winter. The men try to pick up odd jobs, and at present they are to be seen in the work gangs engaged in laying pipelines and making street improvements, among the common laborers engaged in the current building boom, and among the thirty thousand or so "temporary" laborers in the brick kilns in south Tehran and Ray. While the brick kilns offer fairly regular work for those who are taken on, other opportunities take the form of casual labor. It is also likely that the unskilled labor force in some factories is made up in the same way. It is not unusual to find a group of men waiting at the edge of town for a truck which carries to some job as many as can climb on in two minutes. Others may be found milling in front of a street paving company's hiring office every day. Those who fail to arrive early enough, or who do not get on the truck, must go hungry that day, wandering about the city. With this group there probably merge those who

[3] See A. K. S. Lambton, *Landlord and Peasant in Persia* (London, 1953).

shovel snow off roofs in winter or who clean courtyard pools in summer. These people are not easily given to organization, but once called to work can be used for any purpose. Their usual wage is about fifty cents a day, so they can be gathered in substantial numbers at low rates, if one knows how to contact them. Finally, they add to the considerable numbers of people who simply seem to loiter about the streets of the city, with nothing to do.

Above this lowest class come those engaged in unskilled service jobs or in certain branches of distribution. In this class we may group a number of diverse occupations of low status: hawkers, peddlers who follow vegetable-laden donkeys through the streets, porters who stand around in the bazaar, men or boys with wiping cloths hanging from their shoulders who watch parked cars and wash them, too, if requested, newspaper boys, and the like. All of these people have regular pursuits which engage them daily; their incomes are irregular, but not so irregular as the incomes of casual laborers, and nearly all depend upon some sort of patron. The livelihood of each depends upon having some sort of prescriptive right to a street corner, admission to the Tehran equivalent of the Parisian Les Halles, a newspaper route, or a parking area. At the very least, they depend upon the favor or venality of the local policeman, and in many cases they cannot hold such favor and prescriptive right unless some more powerful person is willing to support them. Generally speaking, servants may also be included with this group, though their relationship with the members of the employing household is a rather more intimate one. This class contains several groupings that may be easily organized for small and short-lived political tasks, for example, demonstrations. Obviously such groups will be small, limited to what a single policeman, market concessionaire, or bazaar quarter leader can handle.

On a somewhat higher level of political awareness, though not necessarily having higher income, is unskilled factory labor. This is a relatively small class, since industry is little developed in Iran. The workers in a factory, seeing one another every day, receiving the same wages and experiencing the same environment, can more easily recognize their common interest. It seems quite likely that some work stoppages have been the result of quite spontaneous reactions to such practices as withholding wages, though people are more ready to believe that every strike is Tudeh inspired. This sort of natural organization and coöperation is limited by the size of the factory, and most of the factories are small. Government factories like the tobacco monopoly and the plan organization food processing plants are larger, and the workers generally have higher status and somewhat higher incomes or important fringe benefits. In general, one may say that the higher the status of the job and the more regular the pay, the less important does natural organization become and the more important becomes the possibility that the employer, whether government or private, will exploit the factory workers. This exploitation even extends, in the case of private employers, to calling a strike in order to increase prices or create a shortage. The government avoids this, but can call the workers to a pro-regime demonstration. Factory workers, especially those of larger government enterprises, are an important target of political parties, though generally speaking, Tudeh Party successes with factor labor have made such workers a political "hot potato."

Semiskilled labor enjoys higher wages, status, and security than do the unskilled. Into this category there may fall a motley group of occupations: journeymen and apprentices in the bazaar, drivers, semiskilled factory hands, mechanics, and so on. Wages for this group may run anywhere from forty to ninety dollars a month, apprentices, of course, receiving less. These groups will usually remain aloof from those further down the line, but wherever the enterprise is large enough they may form micro-groupings. Their dependence on patron employers is stronger, but they are more cautious and security oriented than those of lower classes.

In keeping with the high prestige in which any kind of governmental service is held, low-grade, and even undergrade, civil servants may be placed above the preceding classes. Here we run into comparatively large groups than can be easily and effectively controlled by higher government officials. Of particular importance in this class are those such as police privates, postal employees, street cleaners, office boys, tea boys, railroad workers, and tobacco monopoly workers. As in the case of other government employees, the wages of members of such groups are generally low, but their job security is unusually high and they are not required to work too hard.

We move now into the lowest rank of the middle class, with its small retailers and guild craftsmen. These are no longer concentrated in the bazaar in Tehran, but in each part of the city people of similar pursuits maintain contact with one another and set their prices and hours of service by tacit or explicit agreement. While the education of these people varies, it tends to be limited to that necessary for carrying on a business. They are more tradition oriented than others above them, and many are religious. While the pressure from establishments of a more modern type is increasing, they maintain the bulk of the retail trade with the lower classes. A good deal of the shopping is done by servants, so that few small shops are in immediate danger of losing out to the modern shops; and the bazaar still enjoys a reputation, probably undeserved, for lower prices if one knows how to haggle. Iranian political history is replete with examples of coördinated action by the bazaar people, and even in recent years the threat of closing all the shops has been an extremely strong influence. Behind this threat there was the internal organization of the bazaar, which depends upon respected and influential people in each quarter, or, in areas outside of the bazaar, perhaps the landlord. The old guild organization had largely broken down, though the more successful members of each line of trade retains a special position. In recent years, the government has used threats of military force to control the bazaar, and it has tried to reorganize the guilds anew, in order to better supervise their activities. In this reorganization traditionally influential people, or "political brokers," having some family history of association with the guild have often received official recognition of their connections. But municipal control of guild elections has permitted the government to penalize opponents or to reward friends. Many of the government regulations seriously affect these petty traders; they are rarely consulted about regulatory matters, and they have little access for purposes of redress. Now, however, they may refer to the high council of guilds, or they may try to make themselves heard through the ulama, which they generally support. Failing this, they can only stop supplying their wares to the public.

The next middle-class group enjoys considerable prestige, is much better educated, but is low paid and has little access. We might call this group the white collar intelligentsia, and most important among them are government clerks and school teachers, but the lower ulama and low army officers might be added to their number. Here we find a sharp contrast between the awareness and the ideological orientation of these people and their low level of influence and their poor organization. Their present financial embarrassment is to be similarly contrasted with their high aspirations for advancement. Success is often measured in terms of a house, a car, or furniture, but the obstacles are seen as favoritism and nepotism. The white collar intellectual is keenly aware of his superiority over those below him in education, but he refuses to recognize any valid basis for his own inferiority to those above him. With the possible exception of some of the ordinary ulama, such white collar intellectuals are regular consumers of communications media, they have opinions, and they are ambitious.[4]

Middle retailers and small wholesalers, those persons engaged in services requiring knowledge of foreign languages and some technical skills, and others of perhaps less education than the white collar intellectual but of higher income, form our next occupational class. These are the beginnings of a new bourgeoisie, but it is not yet a free or courageous one. Security and social advancement seem to be prime goals for the commercial middle class. Conspicuous consumption is a growing practice, but not to the extent that traditional family privacy is broken down. It is difficult to find strong ideological convictions among this group, even religious convictions; and as a group they are usually politically passive. Their education and external appearance warrants greater awareness and political activity, but they are content simply to protect their currently beneficial opportunities.

Professional and technical government employees, including doctors and engineers engaged by contract, appear to enjoy higher prestige than do the retail businessmen, but their incomes (when agricultural sources are discounted) are lower. Naturally, this class boasts educational qualifications of close to the maximum to be found among the Westernized segment, the prerequisite for which is at least a substantial middle-class background. We find among these people high aspirations for advancement, and a good deal of confidence. Criticism of traditional methods, of nepotism and corruption, is not accompanied by despair or withdrawal, but by activism and an optimism which generally accords with the spirit of rationalization. They tend to be impatient with politicians or majlis members, but they do not fail to exploit their own good connections, for private purposes. These people are at the lower level of the governmental elite. They can often influence legislation, too, but their organization is poor.

In prestige, wealth, influence, and organization, professional and technical personnel that are self-employed are both higher and lower than those governmentally employed. Though never out of touch with their bureaucratic colleagues, these individuals stand apart for their dependence upon the public for their variable incomes. Some have chosen not to enter government service because they can earn much more outside, or because they are mem-

---

[4] They are moderns, or at least transitionals, in the sense used by D. Lerner, *The Passing of Traditional Society in the Middle East* (Glencoe, 1958).

bers of minority groups and cannot hope to rise in government service, or because in recent years they were unwilling to accept contract, rather than permanent, employment. Others have simply failed to get into government service. Accordingly, some are successful, some are not. Some are well connected, some are not. Some are satisfied, optimistic individualists, and some are dissatisfied, pessimistic, revolutionary, leftist. With the less successful group one might include persons similarly qualified who have taken ordinary administrative, rather than technical, positions with the government. The successful private professional is usually foreign educated, has a high income, caters to a foreign and aristocratic clientele, and enjoys a very high prestige.

Nowadays, the medium landowners are often indistinguishable from some groups both above and below them. Some of these have come down from ancient lines of "country squires," but significant numbers are descended from previous dynasties or tribal-military leaders or local governors. Their lands have grown small by succeeding divisions through inheritance. They are to be carefully distinguished from those who work their own land. These medium landowners are not peasant proprietors, but owners of one or two small villages, secure in their local influence, without important access to the central government, and a little concerned about the dwindling share of landed income that, in the future, will be able to supplement each family member's city salary. Medium owners are gradually shifting to other occupations, however, in government, business, religion, and the professions. They exemplify multiple motivations and cross purposes, at present, but the urban, modern orientation among them is gaining steadily. Those that remain behind in the small towns and villages, however, tend to hold fast to tradition.

At the low edge of the higher class, from the point of view of prestige and personal influence, are the higher ulama, but they are usually middle class—traditional in way of life and income. The higher ulama are made of two broad groups, those who have achieved position by learning, social skills, and recognition, and those whose learning may be less but is supplemented by family fame. The higher ulama enjoy much respect from nearly all classes except the Westernized middle class groups, and even they show outward deference. Religious prominence is usually a good basis for intermarriage with those of high social status; thus it sometimes happens that the family connections of the higher ulama extend into the local squirearchy, and even into aristocratic families. In the provinces, their influence is more effective than it is in Tehran, but even in the capital their access is nearly unlimited. They hold a loose authority over lesser ulama and maintain fairly close and coöperative, though unformalized, relations amongst themselves. The ulama, like others, tend to form cliques with those who coöperate more closely.

The newest subdivision of the upper class are the Westernized importers, industrialists, and bankers. Not far removed from these are the big merchants, many of whom are religious and maintain a traditional attitude. Some members of this class have managed to rise from petty trading, under the unusual circumstances afforded by each of the two wars. The others, for the most part, are (or were) important landowners who have diversified their interests. In most instances, success in these enterprises depends upon coöperation from high officials, and some members of this group have acquired their stake as government officials. Another important basis of entry into this class is through the happy circumstance of having owned some land in or near Tehran, just prior to the recent real estate boom. Iranian big business and finance maintain excellent relations with the government, in fact throughout the whole of higher society. The wealth acquired in this way is less stigmatized by the middle classes than landed wealth, and is often equally effective in acquiring seats in the majlis or senate. The organization of these interests through the chamber of commerce gives them some official status, but their normally good social relations with one another and with high officials and the court afford a sound though informal basis for coöperation.

Close to the very top of Iranian society, and overlapping both big business and the aristocratic classes, are the highest government officials, judges, generals, and professors, a group that enjoys very high prestige. Its members have great influence, excellent access, and frequently may determine important phases of public policy. This top bureaucratic elite is roughly organized in terms of the organizations which they serve, but also in terms of family. Their education, though heavily weighted toward Western-style higher degrees, varies, the younger and less aristocratic among them usually being more highly educated or having been educated abroad. This class is not closed to those from below, for as in the past, government and army service do afford some opportunity for mobility. Nevertheless, most of the high government personnel are drawn from the class just above.

The highest class is composed of the large landowners, tribal nobility, the wealthy members of the Qajar nobility, and members of the royal family. As a class, its members usually dominate the most effective of the positions just below, though their monopoly was broken by Reza Shah. Newcomers to big business and high government, however, have tended to become assimilated, so that there is little friction between the two. The absence of friction among the highest classes has not eliminated the ambivalence of attitude among its members; at least the younger ones sense the conflict between aristocracy, bureaucracy, and big business enterprise. This is the dominating interest in the country, and while they prefer to present themselves to the public as businessmen or government officials, their family connections and agricultural wealth are prime factors in determining political methods and patterns of coöperation. Admission to this group from below depends both upon the acquisition of land and upon intermarriage.

There are members of the highest class and of the ulama who are reactionaries, in the true sense of desiring to return things to what they were two or even five decades ago. Most Iranians, including the highest classes, favor change, and they recognize that they are living in an era of rapid change. Thus many of the higher classes and the upper middle class are "conservatives," usually adhering to a vague nationalism or patriotism and desiring moderate change within the existing political framework. The "traditionalists," who would seek only minor improvements in the present setup, are for the most part made up of the petty retailers, guildsmen, ulama, rural, and small-town landed gentry, and some of the larger, older, landowners. The nationalists, who desire revolutionary change, though not necessarily leftist change, are the clerks, teachers, government employed professional and technical personnel, and some of the big business, high government, and top army people.

The foregoing "impressionistic" presentation of a variety of class and occupational strata in Iran can tell us only some general things about how individuals feel, what they are trying to get, and how they may go about reaching their objectives. These classes do not represent collective interests that are expressed in purposeful political action. They do, however, indicate the lines along which organization is possible, should political conditions permit. For the highest classes, organization is neither necessary nor desirable, for purposes of benefiting under the existing system. The members of these highest classes are already highly effective in influencing the government, and formal organization ill accords with the diffusion of interests of each of the leading families. The middle classes are capable of organization and would doubtlessly benefit much therefrom. Polyarchal organizations of this type would demand important changes in the existing system, however, and their attempted formation has led to strong reactions and consequent distortions toward either quasi-governmental agencies or sections of political parties. Lower-class organization on a poly-archal basis is not yet possible, due either to ignorance or to the traditional outlook of these people. Both the government and middle-class political groups have tried to organize low-class groups for their own purposes, with some success. The government has always been more successful with its own low-grade employees; and more recently, through regulation and the official parties, it has extended its control to both labor unions and guilds. During the chaotic era from Reza Shah's abdication to Musaddiq's fall, other organizations of government employees and professionals sprang up under self-appointed leaders with very small followings but very large claims. Some of the latter have held on to serve whoever happens to be in power.

INTEREST GROUPS

A SURVEY OF EXISTING interest groups, then, will tell us how Iranian social class structure is exploited for political purposes by the major political protagonists. As we shall see, these formal groups are not themselves protagonists, and in the foreseeable future they do not seem likely to become so. They are, rather, polyarchal symbols to be manipulated in a system which, while manifestly undemocratic, pays lip service to the universally approved ideal. Before Musaddiq's fall, these groups were more than symbols; they were volatile political forces that could often be moved, but not controlled. Thus far, the government has refrained from destroying them as symbols, but has stripped them of independent power. The government must now choose whether to move on to more effective rationalization by giving social and political substance to regulated groups, or whether it will leave this task to its rivals or successors. There is some indication that the government is hesitantly approaching this task, but the example of other Middle Eastern states suggests that it will be seriously undertaken only by a government from which the highest class has been separated. It has been strongly argued that the medieval conception of Islamic-Iranian class structure had an important foundation in fact. Each individual was identified as a member of some corporative group having a useful social function to perform, and all his relations with the government were carried on in this capacity. On the other hand, these corporative groups had fixed functions, obligations, and rights, according to tradition, and sometimes according to law. The classes which we have described in part coincide and in part cut across those traditional corporate identities, but our insistence that these are classes, rather than groups, further illustrates the breakdown of the old corporative society.

A number of professional associations exist in Iran, encompassing doctors, dentists, lawyers, engineers, and even psychologists. Membership in these groups is voluntary and for most professionals is not crucial to successful practice. For doctors and dentists, the usual procedure has been for a group, often with some connection with Tehran University, to set up an association, to publish a monthly, quarterly, or occasional magazine, to hold an annual meeting at which some foreign specialist delivers a lecture, and to collect dues from those who decide to join. These associations do not attempt to set down a code of ethics, nor are they watchful over the qualifications of those who are licensed to practice by the ministry of health. Their journal usually contains translations from foreign periodicals, but it is not a substitute for keeping up with foreign literature. It is thought by some that such associations are closed cliques for the purpose of enhancing the importance and prestige of their founders and in order to improve their competitive ability in Tehran, where there is fairly fierce strife over control of the carriage trade. Sometimes medical associations appear for a single day in order to welcome a foreign lecturer, and then immediately die, a newspaper ad signalling its birth, and prolonged inactivity thereafter indicating its demise. The ministry of health also holds an annual conference for doctors at a beach resort, at which papers are given by invitation. The invitations indicate the particular medical leadership which the government prefers, and the opening session is attended by the prime minister. Government regulation controls entry into the profession, and the government allocates prestige. Since the minister of health is usually a doctor, the government can often choose the "head" of the profession, as well. Though there is no tendency for the medical profession to organize to run its own affairs, the government abstains from thoroughgoing interference. There is a great need for doctors in the provinces and villages, and a comparative oversupply in Tehran, but thus far little has been done to disperse those living in Tehran. Many doctors are employed by the ministry of health, by the army, and some, too, in ministry or agency hospitals. Those on government salary, except for the medical personnel of the National Oil Company, are not organized, but small informal groups of the more prominent do bring occasional pressures to bear for salary improvement.

Of the engineers, many more are in government employ than in private work, and some of them are organized, in two associations. The first and more vigorous group of those who are organized are in the Oil Company Engineers, and the second group belong to the Association of Engineers. Most government engineers are employed on contract, but they would like to become permanent employees. As contract employees, their salaries are often higher than the salaries of permanent employees, though much lower than those of foreign engineers employed by the government or by contracting firms. At the present time, it is said that the Oil Company Engineers are extremely dissatisfied with their pay and their lack of authority, and often they express this dissatisfaction by criticism of the policy and personal behavior of the officials of the foreign Oil Consortium. The Association of Engineers was established about ten years ago by government officials, in order to rival a similar private association that had developed into the reformist Iran Party of Allahyar Saleh. The Association of Engineers, led by Khosrau Hedayat, was effective in eliminating the older association through its monopoly of patronage, and it has since lain dormant. By contrast, the Oil Company Engineers have a working organization, recognized by management, and are capable of electing delegates to negotiate grievances. The director of the company has responded but slowly to the grievances of the engineers and other professionals, whose only recourse has been to spread criticism and tales of foreign exploitation.

There are a great many outstanding Iranian political figures who have been trained in the law, but lawyers have not played the same role here as in colonial countries. Iranian legal reform has imported Western codes, but not a truly independent legal system. The introduction of new codes was accompanied by the creation and development of the ministry of justice, and all judges are employees of that ministry and are more or less subject to its minister. Iran has been turning out its modern-trained lawyers for only twenty-five years, since the establishment of Tehran University; before that the country drew upon the religious classes and the small product of an evening school. Enrollment in the faculty of law, as elsewhere in the University, is paltry compared to that of other colonial countries, while French- and Swiss-trained lawyers are few, and they are usually drawn from wealthier families. Admission to the bar was further strictly controlled by the ministry of justice, first directly and later through the Bar Association. Most law graduates have found government jobs, often outside the ministry of justice. Practice at the bar therefore remains an honored and fairly lucrative profession of quite restricted proportions. The stereotype of the starving lawyer agitator does not hold true for Iran. Musaddiq made some effort to reform the judicial situation, but not by making sweeping legal changes. He tried to clean up the whole judicial service by bringing charges of bribe-taking and the like against many of the high-court judges. The consequence was hardly distinguishable from a political packing of the courts and was reversed by General Zahedi, his successor. A second attempted reform by Musaddiq was that of making the Bar Association independent of the ministry of justice. Despite the abrogation of all laws passed by Musaddiq, the law providing for the independence of the Bar Association was renewed. The renewed law requires the Bar Association to elect its own officers and establish its own disciplinary courts, and it describes the duties of the Association as granting licenses to lawyers, supervising lawyers, investigation of offenses by lawyers, coöperation with the judiciary, and providing for the practical and educational advancement of the profession.[5] Detailed rules relating to the first three duties were laid down, and the Association was instructed to coöperate with the minister of justice whenever he had complaints against a lawyer. Should complaints be brought against the officers of the Association, the high court for trying judges would handle the case. In the matter of determining how many lawyers were required in each area, three representatives of the Association would consult with the chiefs of the judicial districts of the central province, of Tehran district, and of Tehran city.

Admission to the bar remains highly restricted, though older persons who have practiced for a long time are still licensed, despite poor qualifications. The positions of Association officials are similarly limited to older and more experienced persons. The leadership of the Association tends to be conservative, as are, of course, their best clients. Ministry control is fairly unobtrusive, but as in the case of other groups it is nevertheless effective. The very detailed rules of the Bar Association Law belie the independence of the Association. Its officers and library are in the ministry of justice building. Cases argued by lawyers the minister disapproves of are always subject to prejudice. The Association is closely con-

---

[5] *La'iheh-yi-Qanuni-yi-Istiqlal Kanun-i-Vukala va A'in-Nameh-yi An* (Ministry of Justice, 1333 A.H., Solar).

trolled from the top, and the minister of justice may closely supervise and harass the officers of the Association.

As a matter of practice, the Association officers and the government get along very well indeed. The officers elected under Zahedi's ministry have remained in office, and at that time the credentials of all lawyers were reviewed. The Association was not so much purged, at the time, as brought under respectable and safe leadership. Had the wrong people been elected, the chances are that a purge might have resulted. The present leadership is well represented in the majlis, and it has excellent access. Even in the new law to prevent members of the majlis or government officials from carrying on any business with the government, lawyers were permitted to fulfill existing contracts and to perform all legal business except to appear in court. The Association has not been vigorous in pressing for judicial reform, nor even for the relatively minor improvement of establishing more provincial courts. The provincial Associations are especially reluctant to share their business with others, and the establishment of new courts would inevitably lead to the granting of new licenses.

In recent months, a new Iran Psychological Association has been formed, primarily of recent foreign graduates in this new field. It is early to say whether or not this will become a really independent professional association, and we must note that most of these people receive government salaries. Thus far, this Association has concentrated on translating terminology and drawing up a code of ethics. The ties that bind the psychologists and the allied graduates are still very loose, and there is every chance that present high aspirations for raising the prestige of the profession may degenerate into the more usual exploitation of the Association for raising the prestige and the competitive potential of its officers. The government has not yet indicated any serious interest in so innocuous a group.

The Chamber of Commerce is the most important, influential, and broadly interested of all groups. Actually, the Chamber functions as a branch of the ministry of commerce, but some of its members are so influential as to permit them to direct the policy of the ministry. The ministry and the Chamber leaders are generally in agreement in support of the regime, so there exists no particular pressure to implement more strictly the Chamber of Commerce Law of 1333 or to make the Chamber independent.[6]

---

[6] The Chamber of Commerce Law and supplementary regulations are contained in *Majalleh-yi Otaq-i Bazargani* (no. 66, May 3, 1958—Ordibehesht, 1337), p. 41.

Chamber leaders have access at the court, they may refer to the higher economic council and the prime minister, and of course they are by law directed to report officially to the ministry of commerce. The minister of commerce may attend Chamber meetings, and when he does so he presides as honorary chairman. The budget of the Chamber is presented to the minister for his information, but actual expenditures must be approved by him. It is the further duty of the Chamber to present reports on Iranian trade to the ministry, and a list of merchants and their lines of specialization must also be prepared. The ministry is similarly directed to consult with the Chamber on matters of trade, tariffs, transport, and banking.

Here there is no pattern of hierarchical control, but rather one of coöperation through a traditional bargaining process. The Chamber of Commerce Law is to be implemented by the ministry of commerce, but the choice of a president is apparently a matter of the highest patronage. It is said that the recent election of a new president was due to the shah's dissatisfaction with the past president's objection to some new banking policy. Both gentlemen are senators, and the Chamber has fine representation in the majlis as well.

Bigger business is not only dominated by aristocratic and generally satisfied elements; it also depends to a very large extent on government policies regarding taxes, tariffs, aid to industry, the granting of licenses, and bank credit. It is also suggested, though at present this has not been confirmed, that competition is restricted, for patronage reasons, by manipulation of registration rules.

Chambers of commerce have been established in Tehran and in twenty provincial cities. The Tehran Chamber has thirty members, and the others vary from seven to fifteen. All duly registered companies, banks, and brokers may, under certain conditions, become associate members, whereupon they are given cards which are necessary for releasing imported goods from customs. Officers are elected for one year, according to detailed regulations and under the supervision of the ministry of commerce, but most members who were interviewed held that the electoral decisions were for the most part made from above. A further regulation provides for the formation of special committees to deal with tariffs, transport insurance, and the like, and another provides for the formation of twenty-five trade federations.[7]

---

[7] *Ibid.*, p. 50.

The twenty-five trade federations are to be organized much like the craft and the retailer guilds. The president of the Chamber of Commerce, together with the ministry of commerce, call for a meeting and elections. The elections themselves are supervised by the governor of Tehran and the municipality. These federations cover the most important branches of trade, also industry, banking, and transport. The Tehran Chamber dominates the other branches which have not established federations. It is apparent that these federations amply supply the needs of the highest levels of each of these lines of endeavor, for no other important interest groups of this kind exist except among the guilds or, in the past, in groups registered with the ministry of labor.

Coöperation and consultation between the government and the Chamber appears to be frequent and fruitful. The emphasis is upon foreign trade and banking, and in both major areas the government appears to have satisfied the desires of Chamber leaders. Despite the present ambitious development program, its huge capital requirements, and the growing number of foreign loan obligations being built up, the government has set no restrictions on luxury and nonessential imports, nor are there significant limitations upon transferring capital out of the country. In banking, opportunities have mushroomed with the growing demand for credit. Private banks, and banks with large amounts of foreign capital, have been established under the new banking law, but interest rates have not dropped appreciably. Furthermore, it seems that recent regulations will continue to reduce the Bank Melli's share of banking and credit operations from its dominant 80 per cent control. Banking is at present much more attractive than industry, for liquid investors. As yet, banking is neither widespread nor separately organized. A few individuals are influential, as a result of banking only, but most others are substantial importers, industrialists, or landowners.

To be noted for their special organization under the Chamber of Commerce are: various classes of merchants in textiles, carpets, electrical goods, plumbing and hardware, pharmaceuticals, leather goods, industrial equipment, watches and jewelry, and glass; also brokers, bankers, and money changers; and finally dealers in paper and stationery, tobacco, lumber, tires, sewing machines, bicycles, and the like. These groupings are organized under commissions, which seem to represent the influence of leading businessmen rather than important lines of business. Some of the federations regulated by the commissions cover a host of disparate lines, indicating the diversity of goods that any merchant may handle. Manufacturers are not separately grouped, but are considered, rather, as merchants of the articles they produce. Raw materials are generally excluded, though mining is one of the industries to be handled by Chamber commissions. A recent development is the plan of the new minister of commerce to classify merchants and to restrict the number of lines imported and marketed. The reaction to this effort at rationalization and control has been mixed, though the top leadership of the Chamber has expressed itself in favor of the move.

The restricted membership and the foreign trade emphasis of the Chamber renders it of little service to the smaller business people. Moreover, the Chamber is a Tehran organization, with little but a statute-giving function in the provinces. Consequently, smaller merchants are not consulted about new government policies, and they cannot use the Chamber to redress grievances. We find, therefore, an occasional demarche of a group of local merchants to both the minister of commerce and the prime minister, failing which they may approach the court. These are not organized interest groups, and their functions are mainly negative. They appear to join forces for a particular protest and then to fade out of existence until some pressing need brings them together. A group of tea distributors protesting a ruling of the ministry of customs and monopolies fell into this category. Another example was that of a group of textbook publishers in Tehran, who tried to combine in order to seek representation of their interests to the ministry of education; the latter, it was asserted, was not fair in allocating its book business. The matter was apparently not so pressing, and the organization never got off the ground.

Newspaper owners and publishers have no formal organization. At present, strict control is maintained over the press, and while certain types of criticism (primarily of administrative laxness) are permitted, there are no anti-regime papers. Once a month, those owners and publishers that are recognized by the court are permitted into His Majesty's presence for a press conference, at which Senator Mas'udi, publisher of *Ettla'at*, presides. Mas'udi is the unofficial dean of the publishing trade and the leading press lord. Seating and permission to present questions ranks the rest. Aside from this most informal organization, both official political parties claim the support of a number of newspapers, and the Melliyun Party has held an editors' conference and claims to maintain liaison with its press support.[8] There is also some sort

---

[8] The secretary general of the party presented the author with a list of 53 affiliated newspapers published in 14 cities and towns.

of journalists' association, but it appears to be neither active nor greatly supported by working journalists, most of whom hold down other jobs as well.

The status of guilds in Iran today is perhaps the best illustration of the current tendency to convert traditional corporations into legally recognized organizations operating under the close regulation and control of government authorities. Guilds of craftsmen, petty merchants, and service sellers have a long history in Iran, and they have played their part in important political events. Regulation of the activities of guilds, and even attempts to control their choice of officers, are not new, either, but never has such success been achieved as in the last few years. Guild regulation is also a good example of the tendency (the word "policy" might be too strong) of the government toward more closely controlled lower-class interest group formation, while permitting a wider area of freedom to upper-class groups.

In the past, guilds were the only form of economic interest organization, and they appeared in each town as a natural outgrowth of common needs, of location in the bazaar, and for other reasons. The number of guilds was variable, and their formation generally voluntary. The status of each guild, vis-à-vis the government, was determined traditionally or by special ad hoc arrangement, and little evidence of a consistent government policy can be found.[9] Regulation, outside of general arrangements relating to taxation or royal service, was the duty of the muhtasib or the market police, on the basis of general Islamic law. To such practical organizational features might be added some special religious beliefs, rites, or mysteries resembling those of a lodge. Leadership was often accorded on the basis of wealth, age, and influence with the government, and frequently it stayed in one family for several generations. The guilds always worked very closely with the ulama, and often do so today. It is especially worth noting that the guilds were helpful in the constitutional movement, and that the bazaar was well organized by pro-Musaddiq people, during his time.

During the first half of this century it has been apparent that guild organization is breaking down. New types of enterprises, foreign manufacturers, the growth of towns, the inadequacy of the bazaar, and other reasons have contributed to this decline. Nevertheless, some sort of guild coöperation was maintained, and wealthy and influential members still represented guild grievances

---

[9] See A. K. S. Lambton, *Islamic Society in Persia* (inaugural lecture given March 9, 1954, School of Oriental and African Studies, University of London).

to the government. Guild organization was always informal; thus the change was gradual and hardly noticeable. Since Musaddiq's fall, however, the government has made a concerted effort to bring the guilds under control.

According to a law of 1336, guilds could be legally established and would be organized under the high council of guilds.[10] If, in any town, a sufficient number of craftsmen in each line did not exist, a simple guild of all traders might be formed (in a complete breach of tradition). Every shop owner must have a valid license, and may trade only in the line and at the place for which he is licensed. The governor of each town will summon all the licensed traders in each line, to form a guild and hold elections under an election supervision commission comprised of the three oldest and the two youngest members. Five members of the executive committee will be elected immediately and will be introduced to the governor. The guild must then be registered with a notary, within three days, and no other guild will be recognized. The guild may be registered only on the basis of representation by the governor to the notary. Federations associated with the Chamber of Commerce are specifically excluded. In every town, a high council of guilds will be formed of one representative from each guild. The governor will, in each case, be the honorary chairman of the high council. The bylaws of each guild must receive the approval of the high council, and both these bylaws and those of the high council must be approved by the governor. New guilds must be approved by both the high council and the governor. The governor will cover the expenses of elections and pay 10 per cent of the license fees collected to the high council, and he must approve the budget of the high council. The governor may send representatives to the high council or guild executive committee meetings. The high council is also empowered to set holidays and closing hours, which will be enforced by the governor.

The control of the ministry of the interior through town officials over the guilds is fairly complete. The recent example of the breaking off of the elections in the Tehran bakers' guild illustrates how this supervisory power may be used. In the latter situation, however, complications arose from the conflict between the governor of Tehran (an Eghbal man) and the minister of the interior. The two official parties were also trying to get their own followers elected, but the bakers themselves were somewhat con-

---

[10] A'in-Nameh-yi Tashkil-i Itihadiyeh-yi Sinfi va Tanzim-i Umur-i Isnaf va Pishehvaran (Mehr, 1336).

cerned over the new machine-baking company established by relatives of the minister of customs and monopolies. The bakers have still not held their elections, and probably will not be permitted to do so until the governor is fairly sure of the results.

In many other guilds, however, traditional leadership has been retained, or enterprising influence brokers have managed to work their way in and hold on. The coffee and tea sellers' guild offers a good example of slowly changing leadership. The present legal adviser of the guild is a young man who completed a law degree at Tehran University, but whose father was a leader of the guild for twenty years. The incumbent head of the guild is a religious man who was a close friend of the former chief. The legal adviser was associated with one of the nationalist parties. It is probable that he could not have won out over the older man, had he not stepped aside in return for the new position of legal adviser. Despite his nationalist tendencies, he admits to the necessity of coöperating with the governor, the police, and the high council when called upon for political demonstrations and the like. While his legal training stands him in good stead in dealing with the government, the religious background of his aged and inactive chief is undoubtedly required to hold the support of the membership. There are some three to four thousand members in the guild. They have a suite of offices and two full-time employees, besides the leaders, who no longer sell coffee or tea. It seems unlikely that the government could easily replace the present leadership, but neither side is ready to alter the uneasy coalition. The government is obviously satisfied with regulation and surface coöperation. The guild will withdraw its coöperation only if a powerful rival to the government arises. We see, therefore, how failure to rationalize the top level of the government results in incomplete rationalization of interest group organization at lower levels. The ambivalence and hesitation of the shah with regard to cabinet and political party organization is reflected in the ambivalence and hesitation of the governor of Tehran with regard to the bakers and the coffee and tea sellers.

The high council of guilds in Tehran reports some ninety guilds under its supervision.[11] These cover every kind of small shop and trade: barbers, grocers, smiths, auto mechanics, flour sellers, bus agencies, battery sellers, shirt makers, liver sellers, droshke owners, paint sellers, tanners, secondhand dealers, book binders, hat makers, and so on. In the official list of only eighty-

---

[11] Interview; only 87 are listed in *ibid.*, pp. 12 and 13.

seven guilds, no guild is listed as having more than thirty members. While some simply ascribe this to an error, it would seem that the low number of officially registered members is the key to effective control of elections, by either the traditional leadership or the high council.

The leadership of the Tehran high council has not changed during the two elections held thus far. The director is Mehdi Kushanfar of the grocer's guild. He is a member of the Melliyun Party, a close associate of the governor of Tehran and a supporter of the prime minister. One of Kushanfar's special projects has been the establishment of the Guild Bank, an entirely private enterprise which happens to share a building with the high council. Shares were sold to guild members, but control is in the hands of Kushanfar and Gulbadian, the assistant director of the high council. It seems fairly certain that Kushanfar, Gulbadian, and the others are appointees of the traditional sort, who have some status among guild people, can perform services for them, and in so doing will not rock the political boat, and will find ways of receiving generous compensation while acting as influence brokers. Aside from the Guild Bank, another Kushanfar project has been the opening of a supermarket, with financial help from the municipality and the grocers' guild. The interest of the municipality has presumably arisen from its desire to hold down prices, but it is hard to see how the grocers will benefit. Of greater importance to guild members has been the successful action of the high council in legalizing "key money," and thus making it more difficult for landlords to refuse to renew shop leases.

Organized labor in Iran is the least powerful of all categories of interest groups; it is also the least recognized, the most controlled in theory, and potentially the most dangerous to the regime. The ruling authorities are generally uncongenial to the existence of labor unions, but they have been compelled to admit their organization by two circumstances. The first of these was the success of the Tudeh Party in organizing and manipulating workers in Abadan, Mazandaran, Isfahan, and later Tehran. The second is the continuing interest of the ILO, the WFTU, ICFTU, ECOSOC, and the labor division of ICA in the condition of labor in Iran.

The ministry of labor, established in 1946 but always the least important of the ministries, was meant to control labor organization, to draw workers away from the Tudeh, and to deal with interested international parties. In the first year of its existence the ministry was highly successful, in terms of these limited goals. The Tudeh unions in Tehran were broken up by threats and promises, a government-sponsored federation was set up, a Labor Law was passed to regulate the organization and registration of workers, improved conditions of labor were set down, and a kind of workers' social insurance was established.[12] Tudeh Party protests brought a commission from the WFTU to investigate the new unions, but artful double-dealing, coupled with the rivalry of the communist and noncommunist commission members, obviated a negative report.

From this time on the government tended to neglect the affairs of labor and the ministry of labor, though the ministry and its basic law remained in being. The regulations regarding labor conditions and workers' social insurance have been implemented in part only, in large government establishments. With impunity, private employers have neglected to comply. Even regulations regarding the proper settlement of strikes are disregarded by the ministry of labor, and strict interpretations of the laws legalizing a union or its strikers are infrequent. Pressure to improve existing labor laws or workers' insurance regulations either come from foreign organizations or are the results of enterprising individual efforts. Not a few Iranians have tried to gain influence or recognition as representatives or spokesmen for the workers; however, the dominant powers, whether royal or aristocratic (i.e., Musaddiq and Qavam), have stanchly refused to admit that any such interest is worthy of a top bargaining position. Only Khosrau Hedayat, of all the would-be labor leaders, was elected (appointed) to the majlis, presumably as labor representative, for his services in taking the teeth out of the Tudeh-led labor movement. The goal of recognized and legitimate labor leadership is to demonstrate the loyalty of the workers while preventing them from acquiring more efficient leadership. Labor regulation has been symbolic only. Such regulation attempts to paper over the cracks in the traditional system, rather than to implement a program of political rationalization. Nevertheless the existence of the ministry of labor, the willingness of political parties to include workers in their organization, and the growing industrialization of Iran point the way to the more effective use of this group. Should the government's unity and control falter, experience shows that attempts will be made by a variety of political leaders to mobilize this force, but if government organiza-

---

[12] Mimeographed copy of Labor Law, and supplementary regulations, published by the ministry of labor.

tion and control is improved, the laws may be strictly implemented and rationalization approached.

At the present time, the sphere of labor is one which the government limits but does not control. Labor ministry officials frankly admit that they lack information on how many workers there are, on violations of the labor laws, and on how strikes get started. Apparently the suspicion of the potentially disruptive force of labor organization is so great that even government sponsored organizations are given limited support. Thus ESKI (the Central Council of Workers and Peasants and Tradesmen of Iran) was formed in 1946 and the Tudeh CUCTU was weakened, but the promise of that period was not fulfilled.[13] Tudeh influence, unofficial and opposed by the government, slowly reasserted itself, even among workers that the government paid to do no work. Khosrau Hedayat withdrew his interest, and ESKI languished. Some of his associates set up a rival organization, EMKA (Central Union of Iranian Workers), in their own bid for political influence. Later still, another group known as the "ESKI breakaway" was formed and was duly registered with the ministry of labor. After the attempt on the shah's life, in 1949, renewed efforts were made to eliminate Tudeh influence, and the CUCTU was declared illegal. Shortly thereafter ESKI, EMKA, and the ESKI breakaway were all encouraged to unite in the trade union congress. This group, too, dwindled upon receiving almost no political support. New rival noncommunist groups appeared under Musaddiq, but were not encouraged. Some of Musaddiq's supporters, notably Hussain Makki, tried to organize the workers in Tehran and in Khuzistan, but Musaddiq himself banned strikes; he feared that giving recognition to labor would only strengthen the Tudeh. Following the return of the shah and the establishment of the security organization, the workers' groups came under closer surveillance, and all overt Tudeh Party activity among them was suppressed. Noncommunist "paper" federations were not suppressed, nor were they legalized and registered. Several such federations exist in Tehran, and in early 1956 claims were made that others existed in Meshhed and Isfahan. A new labor federation, the Central Organization of Labor Unions, has been set up in Tehran by the Mardum Party, claiming some twenty-five affiliated syndicates. At best, some of these syndicates exist, but none are officially registered, nor is the Central Organization itself. Except for the Mardum Party's labor liaison man, a university lecturer, Tehran labor leaders are known as an ambitious

---

[13] See H. Vreeland, ed., *Iran* (New Haven, 1957), pp. 166 ff.

and unscrupulous lot whose only capital is a claim to represent the workers. When recognized by the government and given permission to lead workers in government factories, they can perform a useful function, under the existing regime. Several of these men worked with the Eghbal government and the Melliyun Party, which claims the affiliation of all the legally recognized unions.

Registration with the ministry of labor is the formal basis of legitimacy for a union. The ministry registers workers' groups, guild groups, and employers' groups. Presumably, only if a union is registered is its strike legal. A further assumption is that if a union has not been registered it does not exist. An examination of the registration records, however, shows something else.[14] From 1946 to 1956, about 180 unions were officially registered, and at the present time only about 27 retain legal recognition. Slightly less than half of all unions registered were those of guild or small employer groups, though at present only six guild groups hold live registrations. All validly registered unions are located in Tehran. The continued validity of registration depends upon whether the union concerned maintains a certain minimum number of meetings, and the semiannual report of the district labor offices is the evidence of such activity. It is apparent that recognition may be withdrawn by a simple administrative maneuver. Some leaders of de-registered unions protest that their unions still exist, though in most cases withdrawal of recognition is apparently justified. Mardum Party unions have not been registered because they are not "politically independent."

Registration was opened with the passage of the Labor Law of 1946 and the establishment of the ministry of labor. It is claimed that the original ESKI unions were immediately registered, but this claim is disproved by the written record, for no more than seven workers' unions were registered to mid 1949, while 32 guild groups were registered. A perusal of the list of registered unions also reveals that the most important and volatile groups of laborers were never registered, while a large number of guilds formerly with the labor ministry are now under the high council of guilds. Some examples of the latter are: coffee sellers, tea and spice grocers, beef butchers, central tea house proprietors, carpenters, cereal wholesalers, textile merchants, mutton butchers, shoemakers, bicycle and motorcycle repairmen, sweetshop proprietors, tailors, cold storage proprietors, bakers, practical dentists, driv-

---

[14] Carbon copies of these records were given to the author through the ministry of labor.

ers, watchmakers, and taxi drivers. The taxi drivers were considered a workers' group, until their recent strike. This was settled by the intervention of the high council of guilds. Registration was closed for about a year, until late 1958, when the new minister took over. Mr. Amuzegar [15] reopened registration and reviewed some earlier valid registrations, but the changes are few and of small consequence.

It is obvious that registration of unions has neither curbed union formation nor encouraged it. Registration is not a device by which the government has tried to rationalize labor groups and subject them to regulative control. Registration seems to serve no purpose other than to show the outside world that unions are legal in Iran. Control is sought in another contradictory provision of the Labor Law, which requires that in each workshop or factory a workers' representative be elected. Occasionally these representatives are union leaders, but more often they are hand picked by management. They are supposed to seek redress of grievances, pass on information to employees, and negotiate in case of a strike. The workers' representative may do nothing at all, however; he may act as a spy for the boss or, as supplicant, he may be able to redress certain minor grievances. The representative is not freely elected, nor does he have the support of the workers. In many cases he is not even an effective channel of communication, but simply part of the false façade of organization. Consequently, the device of workers' representation, too, fails to provide a basis for the control and rational regulation of labor. The result is that labor groups are simply manipulated by management, by political parties, or by the government, or, when they strike, they are suppressed by force, since no other effective method has been provided.

The most usual explanation of strikes is that they have been fomented by management in order to raise prices. This explanation may be an exaggeration of certain actual events, but other causes are discernible. Political strikes inspired by the Tudeh Party have taken place in the oil fields and at Abadan, at the textile factories in Isfahan, and at the brick kilns in South Tehran. Even some recent strikes, after the suppression of the Tudeh Party, have been credited to the CUCTU; but this may simply be an example of extreme rejection of the regime by these informants. Other causes of strikes have been the withholding of traditional holiday bonuses, or even the failure to pay regular wages for

---

[15] Then minister of labor, and later the minister of agriculture.

several months. A ministry division chief holds that most strikes are spontaneous, unorganized affairs, in contradistinction to those who argue that either the bosses or the Tudeh are behind them.

The Labor Law also sets forth a complex procedure for the settlement of strikes, a procedure which involves consultations with the district labor office, investigations, mediation, and reports to Tehran. As a matter of fact, this procedure is rarely followed. When the strike is an important one, that is, one involving Oil Company employees or the brick kiln workers, rather than the strike of a small factory or guild type organization, it almost immediately comes to the attention of the cabinet and the security organization. The minister of labor being the least important of the ministers, and security being the most important governmental preoccupation, it is the minister of interior who has much more to say and do about the strike. The police, and perhaps the army, will be called upon to maintain order, and, failing a rapid settlement, they will compel the workers to return to their jobs. The recent strike of the brick kiln workers affords a good example of how strikes are regarded and how they are handled. For two months before the strike, the workers' representatives had been giving notice of a demand for higher wages. This demand was announced as requiring a 20 per cent increase. It was supported by the Central Organization of Unions, which claimed to have organized the workers' representatives. The strike broke out one day before the first attempt at mediation was to take place, and the newspapers blamed the contractor bosses. On the following day, a small group of representatives carrying lists of some 500 names of workers agreed to the ministry of labor's 20 per cent increase suggestion. The newspapers announced the strike as ended, and the Central Organization claimed credit for the settlement. The next day it was learned that all of the 300 brick kilns were still cold and that the 30,000 to 60,000 workers were demanding a 35 per cent increase, payment in cash instead of scrip (good only at designated stores), and full implementation of the Social Insurance Law. People on the street began to suggest that the Tudeh Party was behind the strike, and the ministry of labor came in for editorial criticism for its handling of the strike and the implementation of the Labor Law. Violence erupted and trucks carrying bricks were stoned; it is said that as many as eighteen workers were killed, and some also say that two soldiers were killed before the workers were compelled to go back to work at a 20 per cent increase. The ministry of labor defended itself against criticism by proving the strike to be illegal, since it began before mediation was tried. It also argued that while the workers claimed a 35 per cent raise they did not put forth their leaders to discuss the matter with the ministry. It was pointed out that while efforts were being made to include all workers in the Social Insurance scheme, workers excluded had the responsibility of complaining; besides, 90 per cent of the brick kiln workers were temporary employees taken on only in warm weather, and so were not entitled to full benefits. The near solid support behind the fixed claim of 35 per cent lends some credibility to the suggestion that the Tudeh CUCTU was behind the strike, but no documentary proof of this exists. On the other hand, the inability of the ministry of labor, the workers' representatives, the central organization, and the Mardum Party to control the strike or to guide it so that force would not be resorted to is evident. The potential disruptiveness of this large group of workers and their alienation from the government is also clear.

Labor legislation in Iran is certainly progressive, and it is at least adequate for the purpose of making an international impression. Each successive revision of the basic law, in 1949 and again in 1959, has registered a "progressive" advance, but none has been effectively implemented. The forces behind these revisions have not been the workers themselves, but ambitious ministers or undersecretaries. The first Labor Law was largely due to the ambitious, possibly seditious, activities of Muzaffar Firuz. The first minimum wages were set by Ahmad Aramesh, the third minister of labor. The second Labor Law was devised by Habib Nafisi, who had been charged with labor affairs in the ministry of industry and commerce and later served as undersecretary of the then minister of labor. The third Labor Law was originally prepared by Dr. Alimi, Musaddiq's minister of labor, and it was slowly revised and studied under his successors and was brought out shortly after the appointment of the present minister of labor. The absence of urgency or pressure behind the latest revision indicates that it was merely the product of the slow grinding of governmental machinery. Both parties claim to have prepared, or to be preparing, labor programs, but neither was involved in the new Labor Law.

Governmental organization of labor unions as part of a rationalizing policy is still a long way off. Quite sensibly, the government realizes that it does not have the skill or the resources to do the job, and there is also the strong prejudice of the security organization to overcome. Tradition, still the dominant characteristic of the regime, militates strongly against legitimizing the claims of workers to recognition. Nevertheless, the ministry of labor invites ICA labor division advisers to help create a strong labor movement. In the absence of either effective suppression or effective control, the inability of the government to cope with serious political change is powerful evidence of increasing instability.

Associations of government employees are not as acceptable as guilds, but not quite so unwelcome as labor unions. In the past, these have taken the form of trade unions,[16] but they were led by employees and supported with greater awareness by the rank and file. Only a few were ever registered with the ministry of labor: the Association of Representatives of Government Employees, and other groups such as the Women Employees, Tehran Teachers, the Railroad Technicians Club, Tehran City Electrical Workers, Employees of the Bureau of Statistics, the Tobacco Workers Syndicate, Government Chauffeurs, Telephone Company Employees, and Tehran Street Sweepers. The larger of these organizations were the associations of teachers, tobacco workers, and street sweepers, and these are still in existence. There were other groups, too, especially in Bank Melli (this organization has since been suppressed) and in the ministry of finance (a group that still exists in name at least). For the rest, we find only cliques of coöperating government employees with no formal organization, or the workers' syndicates in the larger government industries that are claimed by one or another party, but all fall into the pattern described above.

Government employed laborers are perhaps better organized than any others, more accessible to control, and more responsive to government wishes. These workers are better off than the others: they are better paid, are regularly included under the Social Insurance Law, have more holidays and shorter hours, and enjoy higher prestige. These workers not only do what they are told on the job but are used for demonstrations and other political purposes. The street sweepers are also a well controlled and obedient group, part of their tasks including the pasting up of political posters and the signing of petitions of loyalty.

The teachers are one of the few groups of government employees that have survived the fall of Musaddiq. Many of these groups had been deeply infiltrated by the Tudeh Party, which had great success among the white collar intellectuals. As the poorest paid employees, the teachers were an especially good target of the

---

[16] See note 14.

Tudeh, and many of them sympathized with Tudeh objectives, even if they did not join outright. However, the teachers' association, Mehregan, was formed before the emergence of the Tudeh, and its leader, Mr. Derakhshesh, strongly opposed their taking over his organization. Opposition to Tudeh infiltration also led Derakhshesh to oppose Musaddiq. Derakhshesh was on the *disponible* list for fourteen months, under Musaddiq. These events gave him a clean bill of health when the shah returned, and he was then elected to the majlis for one session. His speeches against the new Oil Consortium and in favor of land distribution cost him favor again, nevertheless, and a rival teachers' organization was established. Derakhshesh and Mehregan returned to good grace with Eghbal's minister of education, possibly because of that minister's failure to get along with the prime minister. The rival organization's leader is a member of the Melliyun Party and a friend of Mr. Eghbal. It is said that the majority of the teachers belong to Mehregan. Derakhshesh himself became minister of education in 1961 after an important demonstration by the teachers, demanding higher pay and protesting the killing of one of their colleagues by the police during a previous demonstration.

Originally, Mehregan was set up as an association of the licensees of the Danesh Saray-i-Ali (École Normale Supérieur), in 1932. During its first ten years it gained in members, while its leadership gained in prestige. It was then a typical false front association, controlled at the top and manipulated as the special constituency of its leaders. Its headquarters were in the Danesh Saray-i-Ali itself. After the abdication of Reza Shah, the old leaders were overturned, the Tudeh tried to take over the organization, and Mehregan membership dwindled. In 1946, however, Mehregan called a strike to win for those teachers holding the license degree the extra pay that other licensed civil servants had been granted. After a successful fifteen day strike, the organization began to grow again, and political groups became more interested in the teachers. Derakhshesh himself insisted on the no-political-activity clause of the constitution of the teachers' group, but he was hard pressed by the Tudeh Party.[17] In 1950, the Tudeh teachers left to set up a rival organization, and the conflict culminated in a battle at the Danesh Saray-i-Ali. Both groups were evicted (under Musaddiq) from the school, and they then set up separate clubs. After Musaddiq's fall, the Tudeh group

[17] *Dah Sal Mubarizeh dar do Jabheh* (Jameh-yi Lisansihah-yi Danesh-Saray-yi 'Ali, Tehran, 1335), and *Asas-Nameh* (same publisher).

was declared illegal, and only Mehregan remained. Membership was opened to all teachers, regardless of qualifications, and the organization became active both in social activities and in helping individual teachers with problems of salary, rank, and placement. After Derakhshesh's ill-considered criticisms in the majlis, a new Association of Teaching Licensees was established under a Mr. Ma'rifat. Derakhshesh was deeply insulted by this development, and he compared the situation to that of a dispute between a master and his former servant. Another interesting sidelight on this history is the fact that Derakhshesh considered himself to have been "elected" to the majlis, not as a Tehran representative but, in reality, as the representative of the teachers.

Other associations of lesser importance than those discussed include various foreign university graduates and women's organizations. The foreign university graduates are usually grouped by countries and are primarily interested in the recognition of the validity of their degrees. Perhaps the most recently active of these groups has been the Association of American Graduates, who have yet to receive the full recognition and prestige of French graduates. As yet, the American graduates have hardly made a dent on the university, and they seem unlikely to do so. A variation on this theme has been the formation of a group called Iran-i-Now. This is primarily made up of American graduates, most of whom have worked for Point Four, and are known familiarly as Amuzegar's boys. This group is now associated with the Melliyun Party, has excellent access, and its members are busily trying to position themselves for top bureaucratic posts. Insofar as they have any ideals besides personal advancement, they seem to stress promptness, efficiency, administrative initiative, and political conservatism. They are, of course, optimistic and loyal, in sharp contrast to most young men of their age and approximate training. Most come from well placed families.

There are about fourteen women's organizations in Tehran, some charitable, some social, some professional, and some political. The charitable organizations include the Soraya Charities, the Social Assistance Association, and the Council for Working Women. The social groups include the Women's National Sports Association, the Soraya Youth Club, and the Rah-i-Now Association. The professional groups include a Doctors' Association and a Nurses' Association. The political groups include the Supporters of the Declaration of Human Rights, and the Council of Women, which is the most vigorous in favor of equal rights for women. During the past year, most of these organizations were federated in the 17th of Dey Society, the Iranian date of the anniversary of the official emancipation of Iranian women.

Most of the women who are leaders in these groups belong to several organizations, usually including the alumni association of some foreign school. Many have jobs in the government or serve on the boards of government social welfare organizations like the Red Lion and Sun. All of them are highly educated, emancipated women, and a good many have attached themselves to the Mardum Party. The reasons for the latter connection are that the Mardum Party got after them first, and that the Mardum Party has outspokenly favored women's rights.

The women leaders are all from influential families, but they do not have the access of their male relatives. Their numbers are small, the total membership of all the organizations having been estimated at from 3,000 to 5,000. Nor are the women very aggressive in demanding equal rights. Their social positions largely determine their loyalty to the regime, though some high-born women are known to have been stanch Tudeh members. These women do not try to reach out for mass support, but are mainly preoccupied with winning favors from the government by supplication. The celebration of the last 17th Dey is a good illustration of their political effectiveness: planning an important street demonstration, but knowing full well they had not the personnel to bring it off, the women requested that the ministry of education mark the day by closing all the girls' secondary schools and permitting the girls to march in the streets. The ulama having heard of this plan, promptly protested. The government was then deep in a propaganda campaign aimed at discrediting the new Iraqi regime as being both anti-Islamic and especially un-friendly to Shiite Islam. The prime minister paid a visit to the leading Shiite dignitary at Qumm, one week before the 17th Dey, ostensibly to introduce the new Iranian Ambassador to Iraq (which country encompasses the Shiites' holy places). It was later announced that the schools would not be closed and that the demonstration would not be held. Instead, under the auspices of the Mardum Party, the women placed wreaths on the grave of Reza Shah. The issue was taken up in the newspapers, as a result of the publication of two letters from leading ulama to the majlis. The Council of Women also had a letter published in the press. In general, however, the women took their defeat philosophically.

In the political sphere, the Council of Women is the most active of the women's groups, but unlike those women's groups, attached to the parties of the Musaddiq era, or at least names of groups, there is nothing revolutionary about their methods. Representations to the government and the court are the preferred techniques used by the Council of Women. Its members, however, are a long way from their goal, as may be learned from the following list of requests presented to the shah in 1956: [18] reform of laws regarding the status of children and the implementation of divorce; banning polygamy; banning temporary marriage; removing all inequalities between men and women under the civil law; granting women the right to vote in majlis and senate elections; granting women equal opportunities for government employment; removing all traditional or customary inequalities in regard to such employment; eliminating provisions of the penal code which permit husbands, fathers or brothers to kill their daughters, wives, or sisters; enacting a labor law which more nearly equalizes the condition of men and women; establishing social insurance for women as well as men; in educational work, recognition of the equality of women in administrative, technical, and teaching work; where women are qualified, to put them in charge of girls' schools; inviting women to participate in the high council on education; giving women supervisory positions in social welfare projects; and more vigorous protection of the legal right of women to vote in municipal elections.

Lastly, there are three types of religious groups to be considered: formal organizations, dervish brotherhoods, and the broad group of ulama. Several religious organizations of various tendencies grew up during the period between the abdication of Reza Shah and the fall of Musaddiq. The Fidayan-i-Islam and the Mujahidin-i-Islam were the best known of these. Both were for a time under the wing of Ayatullah Kashani, but the first was led by a half-educated fanatic, Nawab Safavi, the second led by a political opportunist, Shams Qanatabadi, who held a seat in the majlis. Both were fundamentalist nationalist groups with a small, fanatical membership, mostly composed of religious students. Alongside of these may be mentioned the followers of Ahmad Kasravi and his Pak-Din movement. Some of these antitraditional followers still survive, though their activities are banned. Kasravi's works, furthermore, are still printed from time to time. Other less sensational groups exist for charitable and educational pur-

---

[18] From a carbon copy presented to the author by the secretary-general of the Council of Women.

poses, notably the Anjuman-i-Islamia which runs a number of schools. One other organization, called the Young Shiites, has gathered about one of the teachers at the Sepah Salar Madrassah. This group is small, but it does have a downtown office and manages to publish a monthly paper.

Many people claim that dervish brotherhoods have a great deal of influence in politics, citing the fact that most of the aristocratic politicians are members of one or another group and that the Murshids (guides) of certain orders sometimes visit the court. It would seem, however, that common membership in an order is more a basis for forming coöperative cliques of the normal type, rather than for some conspiratorial political control. The Murshid does not get deeply involved in day-to-day political affairs. Not only the aristocrats belong to dervish orders; there are many Khanegahs to which lower-class people repair, and even some where members of the white collar intelligentsia come to listen to mystic poetry.

Much more important than either of the previous groups are the orthodox Shiite ulama. These have been made the subject of a special study, and so will be dealt with here only with the utmost brevity. The ulama may be described as an institution, a class, and an interest group. Their organization is entirely informal, and they would argue that they have no organization at all. Nevertheless informality barely covers a fairly rigid tradition of recruitment, training, advancement, financing, and political orientation. Geographical, hierarchical, functional, and linguistic differences combine with interpretive and theoretical schools and subject-matter specializations, to shape their organization and determine patterns of coöperation and communication. Having held a key position in the traditional system, ulama activity, as that of an interest group, is primarily aimed at preserving tradition and their own positions of wealth, prestige, and access, where they have it. As in the case of other groups, though perhaps more markedly here, the government has legitimized the position of the ulama, at the same time continuing to try to transform them into a well regulated organization serving government purposes. The means of rationalizing the ulama are ineffectively pursued; nevertheless we may illustrate this effort by reference to the faculty of philosophy and theology at Tehran University, the Sepah Salar Madrassah, and the new School for Preachers and Proselytizers. Government control of religious mortmain administration, of notary publics, of entry into legal professions, of teaching jobs, of chaplainships, and of religious broadcasts also help to bring this group more under control.

As we have seen throughout the preceding pages, a variety of interest groups exist in Iran, but most are paper organizations left over from earlier periods or established after anti-government groups were banned. The recognized group leaders wield considerable influence, but usually for their own benefit or to redress their followers' grievances. Rank and file members of nearly all groups are generally dissatisfied with their self-appointed or government designated leaders and are usually critical of their poor organizational apparatus. Many such persons would welcome hierarchical regulation of their own interest group and a more rational basis of appointing leaders and carrying on political action. Many also believe that only vigorous action by the government can solve the problem of effective interest organization and representation. The government, for its part, has gone to the extent of establishing, registering, and formally regulating many groups, but it has invariably fallen back on the traditional device of depending upon a designated leadership to keep it informed and to keep the group under control. The similarity to the role of the traditional leadership of corporative groups and religious minorities is obvious, but the groups themselves are modern creations.

The present regime has not as yet evidenced a firm intention of going the whole way toward rationalizing these new groups, but if it does, or if a successor regime does so, then the traditional element of the Iranian political system will be eliminated. In the meantime, the shah has somewhat contradictorily authorized the development of a quite different basis of integrating interest groups into the political life of Iran: the formation of two official parties. The two-party innovation is not specifically meant to bridge the gap between the formation of new groups and their integration into the political system, for here, too, great ambivalence is in evidence. The new parties are primarily a device to satisfy the predilection for democratic institutions, and one cannot yet know how much political initiative will be delivered to them. Nevertheless, it is inevitable that these parties should try to attract either groups or group leaders to themselves, in order to give the impression of popular support. At present, it seems highly unlikely that a competitive two-party system will take deep root, substituting polyarchal aggregation for hierarchical rationalization. But for this we must examine Iranian parties somewhat more closely.

POLITICAL PARTIES

THE HISTORY OF POLITICAL PARTIES in Iran is short indeed. Not
long after the assembly of the second majlis the supporters of
the government in that body were called "moderates," and the
minority called themselves "democrats." These terms did not
refer to parties, but rather to the shifting groups of deputies
supporting or opposing government measures. Some deputies did
become inveterate members of the minority and tried to build
popular reputations for liberalism, constitutionalism, nationalism,
and self-sacrifice. For the most part, these groups existed only
during the majlis sessions, that is, about 36 months out of the
years between 1910 and 1922. From about 1928, there were no
longer, in the majlis, any outstanding personalities identified with
the democrats and the minority. Parties were prohibited by Reza
Shah, and until his abdication in 1941 they appeared only as
conspiracies. The two conspiracies uncovered were a procommu-
nist one under Dr. Arani and a fascist one led by Dr. Jahansus.

After 1941, a large number of parties appeared, most of them
taking patriotic and nationalistic names, publishing newspapers,
seeking representation in the majlis from Tehran, and agitating
publicly. Most of these parties had little permanent effect on
the political scene, and quickly dropped from view. Others have
had a deeper influence, both ideologically and organizationally,
and have contributed to the contemporary Iranian political style.
Considering only the more permanent aspects of the development
of political parties in Iran, we may discern six phases, each revealing some new pattern. The basic framework to be kept in
mind while examining this development is that of the shah attempting to hold his place against aristocratic challengers and
communist threats, amid the strivings of families and groups to
improve their general position.

The first period immediately followed the abdication and
lasted until about 1946. During this period, as in the following
periods, the Tudeh Party dominated the scene. Sayyid Zia's
Iradi-yi-Melli Party (National Will Party) was built up by the
British to oppose the Tudeh. Alongside of these two there existed
a number of parties of notables, both in and out of the majlis,
and a few nationalist parties composed of groups of students or of
white-collar intellectuals or professional people.

The second period begins and ends with Qavam al-Saltaneh,
one of the most outstanding politicians Iran has ever produced.

His rise extinguished the National Will Party and substituted therefor the Democrat-i-Iran Party, which for a while actually formed a coalition with the Tudeh and the Iran Party. With Qavam's decline, the Democrat Party went out and an interesting experiment ended. Other parties continued to appear, and there was added to the pattern of parties of notables and middle-class nationalists the fundamentalist religious party and the popular party used as a vehicle of personal influence.

The third period lasted from the decline of the Democrat-i-Iran Party through the banning of the Tudeh Party to the 1951 assassination of General Razmara. During this time the extremist parties grew more active, the Tudeh went underground, and the possibility of a coup d'état poisoned the political atmosphere.

The fourth period is that of the dominance of the National Front, led by Musaddiq and composed of a number of middle-class nationalist parties, as well as several outstanding individuals. The interesting thing to note is that while all parties tried to copy Tudeh organization and propaganda techniques, most of the National Front leaders, except Musaddiq, had achieved prominence through Qavam al-Saltaneh. Partly to distinguish his own efforts from the now discredited Qavam, Musaddiq refused to change the National Front into a political party.

The fifth period lasted from the fall of Musaddiq to 1957. During these four years, political parties were not permitted to operate. Even parties friendly to the court were restricted in their activities. The Tudeh Party and the Iran Party were forcefully suppressed. Both General Zahedi and Hussein Ala were opposed to the formation of political parties.

After Ala's resignation as prime minister, it was announced that two official political parties would be permitted. The first was founded by Asadullah Alam as the opposition party, and over a year later the prime minister, Manuchehr Eghbal, established the Melliyun Party as that of the government. This situation was unique in recent Iranian history; it represented a complete break with the earlier development of political parties. Perhaps the only previous parallel is that of the National Will Party; but now there are two of them.

The preceding review of six periods of recent party development in Iran gives us a preliminary basis for classifying Iranian parties. Since most of the parties under consideration no longer exist or have much influence, our major reason for examining them is to arrive at some conclusions about attitudes toward parties and about how parties aggregate interest groups. We shall also be

particularly interested in an analysis of the potentialities of the
two existing official parties.

We must bear in mind that the Tudeh Party set the tune and
style for all political parties in Iran. The Tudeh did not announce
itself as communist, but rather as a radical-reform nationalist
party. It organized its members in cells, established organizations
for a variety of interest, age, and sex groups, published newspapers
and magazines for each of its publics, and set up front groups as
well as the all-important Central United Council of Trade Unions.
In addition to its own publications, it fostered a press front of
about twenty-eight newspapers, all following the Tudeh line.
Most other parties have tried to copy some or all of these characteristics, especially the National Will Party, which was set up
for the express purpose of combatting the Tudeh. The Mardum
and Melliyun, the two official parties, are also superficially similar
to the Tudeh in organization. These similarities should not mislead us into placing all of these parties in the same political class.
Only the Tudeh had a coherent ideology, attempted to aggregate
through its own organizations, and was truly conspiratorial. The
Tudeh shared with other parties emphasis upon the intellectuals
and popular agitation. The Tudeh also shared willingness and
readiness to fight in the streets.

Though long the most effective party in Iran, the Tudeh has
now been crushed, but not quite out of existence. It is said that
three remnants are still to be found. One of these is the remnant
of the Central United Council, presumably the only body recognized by Moscow. This group has given up on the intellectuals
and is supposed to be stressing the proletariat as the only trust-
worthy body of revolutionaries. A second group is that of the
Marxist Circles which claim to be the true Tudeh Party. Reference
here is to the sharp split that occurred in the Party during and
after Musaddiq's last phase. At that time, many of the younger
intellectuals favored complete coöperation with Musaddiq, but
the central committee refused whole-hearted support. After Musaddiq's fall there was much soul searching, and mutual accusations
increased the bitterness of defeat. The failure of the Tudeh Party
to aid Musaddiq (even against his will) on the 28th of Mordad
was a costly tactical error, explained recently by Radio Peiping as a
failure due to the presence of British spies among the members of
the central committee. A third group of Tudeh supporters are said
to be a small number of former members who were excluded for
being too favorable to Musaddiq and who are now ineligible for

membership because of the rule restricting membership to workers only.

It is apparent that Tudeh strength was greatest among university students and civil servants. In addition to well-indoctrinated members, the Tudeh had a large number of sympathizers, gained when they were able to organize doctors', lawyers', teachers', and labor groups. Tudeh organization among the guilds was small indeed, and among the prominent ulama only Ayatullah Burga'i of Qumm, now exiled to Yazd, was sympathetic. Efforts were made to win adherents among the religious students, and some success was achieved, but it was apparently short-lived.

At the opposite end of the scale from the Tudeh were the groups of notables which in the post-Reza Shah period took patriotic names and called themselves parties. Often enough no more than a handful of notables, one of them a newspaper editor, comprised the whole party. As is usually the case with such groupings, the party lasted only so long as the members of the clique held common interests or only so long as they trusted one another. Where the clique had been of long-standing vitality, it adopted or dropped the party label as political circumstances seemed to require. A good example is that of the coöperation of senators Jamal Imami and Ali Dashti, the former of an influential religious family and the latter a skillful writer and newspaper editor. Both have supported the shah fairly faithfully. When occasion demanded, as after the demise of the pro-shah National Will Party, they formed their own party. Now they continue in inseparable combination, but they are not connected with any party.

Midway between these two extremes we find variants of the group of notables, so directed by governmental authorities as to be able to rival the Tudeh in mass appeal and group aggregation. Essentially, the political techniques of these parties are traditional, involving bargaining among those enjoying long-legitimized influence and choosing subordinates from among the well placed, so as to put them under a heavy debt of obedience. Aggregation of interest groups takes place mainly through *ad hoc* agreements with their traditional leaders or with the new group of enterprising brokers. Sometimes a broker's influence is first established by government recognition, then he may go out and bring together the members of his interest group. The third major characteristic of these parties is their governmental support. Without such governmental support, it is impossible to conceive of a group of notables so far overcoming their peers in influence, aggregating widely, and, significantly, having enough influence to induce middle-class groups to form coalitions with them. In the light of these three characteristics, it may be noted that the traditional-aggregating-government party is the meet product of the present transitional stage of the Iranian political system, for it illustrates the ambivalence between traditionalism and rationalism. Traditional organizational patterns and traditional political techniques are the most effective, but the exclusive advantage of government approval and the favorable basis for aggregating groups lends to this type of party a rationalizing aspiration. Examples of this category are the National Will Party, the Democrat-i-Iran Party, the National Front and, to a large extent, the existing Mardum and Melliyun parties.

The National Will Party has been well described elsewhere and need not detain us here.[19] Suffice it to note that it attempted to copy the Tudeh Party in all of its external characteristics, right down to its nationalist propaganda. Instead of accusing the Western powers of interference in Iran's affairs, the National Will Party accused the Tudeh of being a Soviet instrument. The National Will Party, however, was too closely identified with the court, and it foundered on the opposition of many of the notables, who then felt they might disregard both shah and masses and return matters to their pre-Pahlavi status. Failing of support in the majlis, Sayyid Zia could not become prime minister, so that the National Will Party never was truly a government party.

The Democrat-i-Iran Party was the creation of Qavam al-Saltaneh when he was prime minister. Its primary purpose was to produce a majlis which would perpetuate Qavam's office, but it also served as a vehicle of coalition with both the Tudeh and the Iran parties. In 1945 Qavam decided to establish his own party to rival the Tudeh and to break the National Will Party. Qavam followed this decision with a radio speech in which he said that parties were necessary for constitutional government. Qavam would take the lead, but everyone could be free to form his own party. The prime minister then proceeded to choose fifty-two founding members, who dutifully elected nine hand picked members as their central committee. Qavam was chosen as party leader, and the other members of the central committee were Ahmed Aramesh, general secretary (later labor minister);

---

[19] G. Lenczowski, *Russia and the West in Iran, 1918–1948* (Cornell, 1949).

Sardar Reza Hekmat, an ex-speaker of the majlis; Mozaffar Firuz, assistant to the leader (later minister of labor and ambassador to Moscow); Mr. Musavizadeh, later minister of justice; Mr. Sadeghi, later minister of roads, and until his death director of Bank Pars; Mahmud Mahmud, the historian; Mr. Hashim Vakil, now head of the Bar Association; Mr. Ha'erizadeh, a man of religious connections, a veteran member of the majlis, and a political maverick.

Various people were sent to the provinces to organize committees by the same procedures. The organizers chosen were those of established influence in each province. A Democratic Youth Organization was also established to attract younger intellectuals, students, teachers, young judges, and secondary school pupils. A women's organization, Sazman-i-Banovan-i-Demokrat was set up. For workers' groups, the newly established ESKI served as a basis for labor organization. Under the central committee various commissions dealt with organization, propaganda, finances, social assistance, and judicial reform. The party newspaper was called the *Democrat*, but the *Diplomat* was the official organ of the central committee, while *Bahram* was the organ of the Youth Organization.

The party was financed by contributions from wealthy persons, some of whom were rewarded with majlis seats, as was Mr. Herati of Yazd. Over a half-million dollars was collected, about half of which was spent on intelligence activities in Azerbaijan, Kurdistan, and Khuzistan. The other half was spent on printing costs, rent and demonstrations.

The most important task of the central committee was to choose candidates for the majlis. According to a well-informed source, the central committee met on this question three times a week, from two to six hours each time, for a period of about three to four months. Some nominees were opposed by the shah, some who failed of nomination applied pressure, and the list was often changed. The ideal candidate sought was someone without foreign connections who was young and liberal; that is, individuals of independent influence were to be avoided as much as possible, and persons who would be indebted to the party would be chosen. In this manner, an entirely new group of younger politicians was brought in by Qavam, and many of the older ones were skipped over. Musaddiq was excluded, as a bull in a china shop. Sayyid Zia was put in prison. Jamal Imami and Dashti were avoided.

Hussain Makki, later to join and then break with Musaddiq, was nominated from the youth group. Dr. Bagha'i, later leader of the Toilers Party was nominated from Kerman. Engineer

Reza'i, who had left the Iran Party, was nominated from the same place. Dr. Shayegan, later a National Front leader, was made minister of education; Amir Ala'i, later of the National Front, was made minister of agriculture.

Dr. Mu'azzami, dean of the influential faculty of law of the University, was nominated from Gulpaygan. From Burujird, Sultan al-Ulama, a relative of Ayatullah Qummi, was nominated to please the ulama. The list of the independently influential was extended by leaders of the Tehran Bazaar, Nikpur (glass manufacturer, steel distributor, land), Akhavan (Jeep distributor, land), and Vakili (foreign manufactures' distributor, and former head of the Chamber of Commerce). Khosrau Hedayat, who had set up ESKI but is also part of the very influential family of General Hedayat, was made director general of the railways. Furthermore, a number of Qavam's younger relatives were nominated. Khosrau, the youngest Qashqa'i was elected for that tribe; for the Lurs, an old chief named Shuja was chosen; Asef Khan was nominated for the Kurds; Rigi Khan was named for the Baluch tribes. The Bakhtiyaris, apparently, were penalized.

All of these people were elected, but such was not the case for those nominated from Azerbaijan. There, Qavam had successfully insisted that the Russians must leave and the Iranian army enter before elections would be held. The army went in under Razmara and supported candidates of the shah against those of Qavam. Finally, only 85 out of 136 deputies were organized under the Democrat Party.

After the rejection of the Soviet request for an oil concession in the north, Qavam's control over the majlis weakened. The party was revealed to have no real unity, and as the independently influential changed sides some of the younger men also decided to leave the sinking ship. A rash of open resignations followed, and the weekly party caucus dwindled from 85 to 36. Then the party headquarters were attacked and the records destroyed. Qavam failed to get a vote of confidence in the majlis. The party funds were confiscated by the succeeding government, and Qavam himself was sued.

It is apparent that all popular agitation by the Democrat Party was stopped, after the elections were completed. Nor can it be said that the Democrat Party made serious efforts at aggregating new interest groups under its own banner. Instead, Qavam concentrated upon weakening the Tudeh through coalition with them and upon packing the majlis. Despite his unusual success in getting a large number of his own young men in, he worked the system faithfully enough so that he returned many former members to the majlis. These people felt no debt, and many of them were angry at Qavam for refusing to extend or to meet with the earlier majlis that had appointed him.

The National Front was primarily the vehicle of Musaddiq's opposition to the government of General Razmara, and its greatest achievement was the nationalization of the Anglo-Iranian Oil Company. The Front got its start in the election campaign for the 15th majlis session. At that time, Musaddiq protested that the elections were not going fairly, and he took traditional refuge at the gate of the palace, just down the street from his own home. In this manner Musaddiq managed to gather a large crowd right in the midst of town, and he was joined by a number of candidates and middle-class party leaders. After receiving certain assurances, these leaders and some others retired to Musaddiq's house, where they formed the National Front. The Front members were about a dozen, some of them were the leaders of parties, and others were either traditionally influential among the lower classes or were persons of moderate prestige who attached themselves to Musaddiq. The group worked effectively on the streets of Tehran and in the majlis, until Musaddiq was made prime minister. The members of the Front, especially those of the Iran Party, became important channels for dispensing patronage, but Musaddiq rarely met with the Front, never consulted it on policy, and permitted it to become gradually defunct. Nevertheless, in the street demonstrations that followed and in the aggregation of bazaar, government employee, and student groups, the symbol of the National Front remained very effective. Hussain Fatemi himself rose as editor of Bakhtar Emruz, which claimed to be the organ of the National Front.

Between the traditional-aggregative-governmental party and the Tudeh, on the one hand, and between the former and the party of notables on the other hand, there are the less important variant types. The first of these is the middle-class party, used as a vehicle of a group interest, and the second is the middle-class party used as a personal vehicle. An example of the first variant is the Iran Party, and of the second the Toilers Party. From each of these there broke off two personal-ideological splinters: the Mardum-i-Iran Party, from the Iran Party, was of little consequence; but the Third Force Party attracted most of the more modernly oriented of the Toilers Party. All of these groups were radical-reformist, nationalist; they favored oil nationalization and, except for the Toilers Party toward the end of Musaddiq's rule, they supported Musaddiq. Both party types tended to be nonaggregative, though the Iran Party became a favored channel of access for both high and low bazaar people, and Dr. Bagha'i's Toilers Party became a clique of opportunistic influence brokers.

The Iran Party was founded in 1942 as the Engineers Association. For about a year, it remained a purely professional organization of government engineers from many different departments. In 1943, at the suggestion of some nonengineers, especially Allahyar Saleh, the association became the Iran Party. It is unlikely that the Iran Party gained many members until the height of its influence under Musaddiq. It has been claimed, however, that it had over a thousand members, and when recently suppressed over ninety members were arrested. When membership was opened to nonengineers they were mostly joined by lawyers and law professors. Even among the host of small parties that existed during those years, the Iran Party stood out as a valuable political ally, though never a potential ruling party. Its value lay in the fact that it was composed of young and vigorous intellectuals bent on a program of radical-reform and modernization; most of these individuals were from families placed well enough so as not to threaten serious revolution. Their ideas included economic development and land distribution, a combination of a vague form of socialism and Islam, and development of a democratic form of government. This was not an aggregative party, but a group of young modernists whose primary interest lay in breaking down the traditional barriers to their own acquiring of positions of greater authority. Most of its members were government employees, and one of their most emphasized goals was administrative efficiency. In view of the fact that they represented no broad popular group, and in view of the further fact that they were among the better trained and more flexible of civil servants, they were attractive allies.

The Iran Party achieved its first prominence under Qavam, when they joined with the Democrat Party and the Tudeh, in a short-lived three-way coalition. From this time on, the Iran Party usually had at least one minister in the cabinet. Though failing to win interest groups to its ranks, the Iran Party dispensed many favors to interested persons and groups, once it had gained greater influence under Musaddiq. On the other hand, it is clear that Musaddiq chose not to exploit all the potentialities of the Iran group as a party; instead, he sent Allahyar Saleh to the United States as ambassador and utilized Zirakzadeh as his chief oil adviser and majlis liaison man.

The split in the Iran Party arose out of personality differences, but it had certain ideological overtones. Nevertheless, one cannot help feeling that some of the rank and file were disappointed by the failure of the party leadership to act independently of Musaddiq's lead. While the party leaders formed Musaddiq's most loyal support, Musaddiq himself was more concerned with benefiting from the coöperation of individual leaders, in traditional style, and not in building the party as a basis of popular organization. The Mardum-i-Iran Party claimed to insist on a more Islamic interpretation of democratic socialism, as applied to Iran. This splinter never achieved great influence and did not appreciably weaken the Iran Party itself.

Though the Iran Party commenced as a professional association, then transformed itself into a party of French-trained higher civil servants, it finally deteriorated into the personal vehicle of a few cabinet and majlis leaders. At the present time, it is the personal vehicle of Allahyar Saleh, who sits quietly at home, surrounded by a few loyal friends, waiting until the shah will be in so great a difficulty as to ask him to form a government.

There now exist two other small groups that show fascinating similarities to the early Iran Party. One of these is the Iran-i-Now group attached to the Melliyun Party, and the other is a "dowreh" (club) of employees of the Plan Organization, which has no official name and no political affiliation. Both groups are made up of young, energetic civil servants, most of whom have been trained in the United States. Some of their members have gained high positions, but their frank objective is to secure the highest positions possible for themselves—in the interest of modernizing Iran, of course. How many other groups of this kind exist is hard to say, but no doubt few, if any, for the simple reason that persons of this level of education who hold down important bureaucratic posts are rare indeed.

Another possible variant of the nonaggregative, middle-class, group-vehicle party was the Hizb-i-Baradaran of Shiraz. Though the personal creation of Ayatullah Sayyid Nur al-Din, and though not deeply involved in national politics, this party was composed primarily of lower middle-class bazaar merchants. Sayyid Nur al-Din's hold over this group was largely a consequence of his religious activity. The importance of the group has lessened considerably since his death, but at the bazaar and in the Masjid-i-Vakil one can still see framed photographs of the leader. After Nur al-Din's death, his brother, his son-in-law, and even his fourteen-year-old son have all been mentioned as possible successors, but none seems to have been able to win such support as he had.

Dr. Bagha'is Toilers Party is a good example of the personal vehicle appealing to the nationalist middle class. As a personal vehicle, however, its policies depended to a large extent upon the political deals made between the party leaders and other influential persons. Such deals give the impression of aggregative activity, but in reality all that was involved was the coöperation of a number of individuals who were influential with the Tehran mob.

Dr. Bagha'i was first a member of the Ittihad-i-Melli Party, a group built by his father as a means of winning the majlis seat from Kerman. In the elections for the 14th majlis, the Ittihad-i-Melli Party formed a coalition with the Vahdat-i-Iran and the Socialist Party, two similar small personal parties formed for similar reasons. Failure in the elections meant two years of political inactivity, until the 14th session ended. Then Dr. Bagha'i was invited by Qavam to establish a branch of the Democrat Party in Kerman. Bagha'i worked in Kerman for about a year, and he was rewarded with the seat for that constituency in the 15th majlis. After arriving in Tehran and seeing the direction in which matters were going, he split with Qavam, but he could not win over a substantial part of Qavam's organization. Throughout the 15th majlis, he tried to build himself up by vigorous opposition and strong nationalist statements. In preparation for the elections to the 16th majlis he organized his supporters (most of them from Kerman) into the Organization for Supervising the Freedom of Elections, presumably as a safeguard against the government's falsification of returns. Bagha'i also published a paper and identified himself with Musaddiq and the National Front. He was elected to one of the important Tehran seats where elections were more honest and more bitterly fought than elsewhere in the country. At this time he transformed his electoral organization into the Organization for Supervising the Implementation of the Laws. This group supplied Dr. Bagha'i with information on military and bureaucratic excesses, which he brought to the attention of the majlis. Razmara was a particular target of Bagha'i's attacks, and much of Bagha'i's later fame stems from his courageously outspoken attacks on the then prime minister. Bagha'i's newspaper was frequently suspended and his print shop sacked, so he next established a group known as the Organization of Free Constabulary, to protect the shop. This organization was suppressed, but shortly thereafter Razmara was assassinated, Musaddiq became prime minister, and the Anglo-Iranian Oil Company was nationalized. Bagha'i now converted his various organizations into the Toilers Party of Iran, carrying on an anticommunist tradition begun with Qavam, and seeking to attract the oil workers, at least with slogans.

Despite the obviously personal orientation of the Toilers Party, Dr. Bagha'i showed much greater political skill and had greater potentialities than did the more sophisticated leaders of the Iran Party. Both groups, in boasting of their ideologies, claimed to be real parties. These ideologies were essentially programs rather than reasoned systems of values, and they resembled each other. In retrospect it is clear, though, that the Iran Party was bound to eschew aggregation due to its poorly articulated ideal of bureaucratic rationalization; Dr. Bagha'i, however, wished to achieve power through coöperation and bargaining with existing, even traditional, leaders of groups or interests. Bagha'i's own political style opened wide possibilities for the aggregation of many interests, but these were not fulfilled. Primary emphasis was laid upon labor groups, strong connections were developed in the bazaar (Bagha'i and Ayatullah Kashani remain good friends even today), students were to be attracted through the collaboration of Khalil Maliki, and a women's group was to be formed.

Musaddiq was willing to accept the collaboration of the Toilers Party, but apparently he was apprehensive of Bagha'i's ambition and was unwilling to grant the Toilers the official support that he had withheld from the Iran Party. Bagha'i joined with the growing group of Musaddiq's critics, and on the crucial day of the 9th of Esfand he joined (though not openly) with the court. At this point Khalil Maliki split off to form his Third Force Party. Maliki took with him the students and the new women's organization, to which Bagha'i's more religious followers objected anyway. Musaddiq's victory on the 9th of Esfand, through the alert action of General Afshartus, went far toward winning the bazaar leaders of the National Front (Shamshiri, Hajj Muhammad, Hussain Ettifaq, and Mr. Rasekh) away from Bagha'i. Through Kashani, Bagha'i maintained coöperation with some bazaar groups, and with the Mujahidin-i-Islam group of Shams Qanatabadi. It would also seem that his relations with the Vanak cement workers, the shirt tailors, and some hawkers remained good. After 9th of Esfand, relations between Musaddiq and Bagha'i deteriorated to the point where Toilers Party militants were detained or harassed. It is said that Bagha'i now commenced closer coöperation with the court and, further, got deeply involved in the plot which led to the assassination of General Afshartus. For implication in that murder, Bagha'i was sentenced to jail, where he remained until the 28th of Mordad, on which day after Musaddiq's fall he regained his freedom. Dr. Bagha'i still insists that his group exists, and he implies that it is antigovernment. There is no doubt that the security organization discourages groups of this sort from operating, but Bagha'i retains a circle of friends, among whom Kermanis are still prominent.

Khalil Maliki was one of the early members of the Tudeh Party and was even numbered among the first group of alleged communists jailed by Reza Shah. For reasons which are a matter of bitter dispute, Maliki broke with the Tudeh Party and established the Iranian Socialist Society. He claimed his was the true representation of communism in Iran, but Radio Moscow declared the opposite. Maliki promptly dissolved his group and wandered a while in the political wilderness. During this period, Maliki began to write in criticism of Tudeh policies, and gradually he turned against communism. His new line was Titoist, and more recently he has come to follow what he calls "Nehru Socialism," as well as Western European Socialism of the anticommunist type.

Maliki's rise to prominence began with the articles he wrote for Bagha'i's *Shahid*. Maliki did manage to attract many students, and he was capable of organizing the party in a more formal manner. His split with Bagha'i is probably the result of differences in outlook and political techniques, in tactics regarding coöperation with Musaddiq, also, undoubtedly, of interference by both the court and the National Front. Maliki kept the name Toilers Party, but he added Third Force in parentheses. It is apparent that only the students and some civil servants came with him. Maliki now started to publish his own paper, trying to win prominence as the most formidable opponent of the Tudeh Party. His organization was patterned closely after the Tudeh, having small cells, front groups, indoctrination meetings, direct action groups for street demonstrations, and a number of publications aimed at various target groups. Maliki claims that his group was very active on the 30th of Tir, that they sided with Musaddiq on the 9th of Esfand, but were inactive on the 28th of Mordad. The financial support of the organization came primarily from members' fees, from a few bazaar people, and from a prominent member of the Qashqa'i family. Because of the violent anticommunism of Maliki, the court was favorably disposed toward him, and some of his publications, in more recent times, have been indirectly financed from that source. After the 28th of Mordad, the

Third Force was broken up and its leaders jailed for short periods. Maliki is now receiving full pay (or nearly so) from the ministry of education, but he does not go to work. He is also able to publish a thick magazine, made up mostly of anticommunist translations, which is financed from unknown sources. He still claims that the nucleus of his party exists and that the leaders meet regularly.

The Third Force obviously aspired to something more than serving as a personal vehicle for Khalil Maliki's political ambitions. His emphasis on a noncommunist socialist ideology was his only ammunition, for he lacked the traditional basis of influence that was Bagha'i's. His outlook was closer to that of the Iran Party, though he has much greater dialectical skill than Iran Party leaders. His approach fulfilled a real need, and many young men have responded to his presentation of a noncommunist ideology of reform. Consequently, Maliki's Third Force for a time exemplified what may be called the ideological party, though this is true no longer.

The ideological party, as it appeared in Iran in the Tudeh Party, in the various fascist type parties, and in fundamentalist-religious parties, has spent its major appeal among students, especially those students of lower middle-class connections, from government clerks up through professional and technical personnel. Ideological parties have refused to recognize existing structures of power and have therefore failed to aggregate effectively. The major exception to this pattern was the Tudeh success among certain groups of factory and petroleum industry labor, and this was the result of a special effort specifically related to Tudeh ideology. Otherwise, we must associate the phenomenon of the ideological party with a class orientation, rather than with a group interest.

Every Iranian party has claimed a distinctive ideology, and nearly all political party leaders insist that none of the rival parties (except for the Tudeh) are real parties, because they lack an ideology. The programs of the ideological parties, even of all parties, are almost identical, once we have put both ideology and constitutional conceptions aside. This is a further confirmation of the educated middle-class and antitradition orientation of these parties. The same program could be justified through Marxist, nationalist, and religious arguments; and it could be implemented, it was contended, through a people's democracy, a constitutional democracy, a dictatorship, or an Islamic state. It was easy enough to form such a party; a little more effort was needed to start a party newspaper; the traditional connections of the self-appointed leaders would be exploited to give the semblance of wide appeal; and then the new party would spend its efforts in defending itself against the anxious attacks of similar groups, none of which had been able to consolidate its position. Some ideological parties would last throughout the schooling of their leaders, others would persist in the personal circle of one leader, and still others might last until suppressed or until the leader could bargain away its independent existence for a legitimized position for himself in the traditional system.

Despite the nonaggregative character of these parties, and their very limited appeal, some of them did succeed in winning the support of labor groups, of certain guilds, and even of some influential individuals. The bases of such coöperation were usually personal friendships; sometimes there was a cash nexus, sometimes the party newspaper might be used to press for some benefit for a guild, sometimes coöperation was the short-lived result of police machinations. No party was without some affiliates, but in every case these were weaker or less influential than the party itself. The party, being for the most part composed of a volatile student group, was a matter of serious concern to the government of the day. Yet the distinction between an aggregative and an ideological party is one of emphasis and degree only. However, the most extreme ideological parties were the poorest aggregators.

The ideological extremes were represented in the fascist and fundamentalist groups. The Tudeh Party, it must be remembered, did not put its Marxist foot forward in public. The fascist groups came under the general heading of Pan-Iranism, of which there were a number of varieties: the Sumka Party, the Pan-Iranism Party, the Arya Party, and others. The fundamentalist parties were only two, both very small. The Fidayan-i-Islam became very famous for its assassinations, and the Mujahidin-i-Islam was a later near carbon copy of the first.

The Sumka, like the other Pan-Iranist parties, traces its origins back to the sedition of an officer named Jahansus, in the mid 30's. Forty-five men were arrested with Jahansus, and ten were executed for what was called a communist plot. From 1941 to 1949, the Pan-Iranists were inactive and had no organization. In 1949, at the time when the Tudeh Party was declared illegal and most party activity had been stopped down, the Pan-Iranists formed an art group which published *Jami Jam* (Jam-i-Jahan-nema), a journal presenting a "nationalist and anti-Marxist" view of art. Within a relatively short period, this unlicensed journal was suppressed. In the same year, a secret organization called Nationalism Inqilabi (Revolutionary Nationalism) was set up, its membership numbering about thirty army officers and forty others. This group was organized in cells of five members pyramiding up to the five-man executive group called the "nationalist council." The secret organization had a legally recognized magazine called *Nationalist Publications* and about eighty secondary school students organized as the Geruh-i-Najat-i-Melli (National Salvation Group). The leadership of this group approached Razmara, proposing that Bahrein be invaded, a la D'Annunzio, but Razmara's assassination intervened to prevent agreement.

In the meantime, in Germany a number of Iranian exiles and students who had served in the Nazi army formed a party resembling that of the Nazis. Dr. Mukri, of this original group, came to Iran in 1948 and tried to establish the party in Iran, and he was finally successful in May, 1951. At this time the new Führer of the party, Dr. Munshizadeh, was invited to return to Iran from Alexandria, where he was a professor of Persian studies.

From that point on the history of this party, the Sumka (National Socialist Workers Party of Iran), is one of internal struggles and splits, of conflict with the Tudeh Party, attacks by other nationalist parties, struggles with the police, and erratic coöperation with the court. The Revolutionary Nationalists joined with Sumka, as did some members of the secret Anjuman (Pan-Iranist). These people helped Munshizadeh oust Dr. Mukri and his group (those who had originally invited Munshizadeh, and who still tried to control everything from behind the scenes). Munshizadeh also tried to become free of the close supervision of these students (for most of the army officers had dropped out), but in this he was not successful. The party fought the Tudeh in the streets, criticized Musaddiq, and defied the police. On the 30th of Tir, though they did not oppose Qavam, they claimed to have done so as individuals; and again, on the 9th of Esfand, they acted against Musaddiq and for the shah. Under Musaddiq, Munshizadeh was twice jailed, but he was released at last on the 24th of Mordad, presumably to be on hand to embarrass the Tudeh if necessary. As far as can be judged, the party did nothing of consequence on the 28th of Mordad. Under General Zahedi, all party activity was prohibited until just prior to the shah's birthday, when the Sumka was invited to march with others to place a wreath on the grave of Reza Shah. This was the last great demonstration by the Sumka, who were wearing black shirts paid for by the court. After this, the party was suppressed and Munshizadeh was pensioned off and sent to travel in North and South America.

Sumka membership was composed of about 15 University students, possibly as many as 500 secondary school students, and it is claimed that 2,000 to 5,000 workers and small shop keepers were also members. Also associated with the party were the ice sellers, the drivers of two bus lines, and the noncommunist employees of the then unfinished Chitsazi textile factory. The ice sellers were later manipulated against the Sumka by the police and very nearly broke the party.

Aside from the party's connections with the court, there is strong evidence that the Sumka coöperated with the retired army officers' group, especially Generals Muzayani and Zahedi, and with Shams Qanatabadi, then leader of the Mujahidin-i-Islam, and anti-Musaddiq member of the majlis. The Sumka did not favor the Shiite clergy; nevertheless some mullahs frequented their headquarters, notably Ayatullah Qaravi.

Party unity was always strained by internal struggles for power and external attempts at manipulation. The Arya Party was formed by the Sipehr brothers after Hushang Sipehr was put out of the Sumka. Arya has now affiliated with the Mardum Party. The Fidayan-i-Iranshah Party was formed by Abbas Amini in reaction to the ice sellers' dispute. The party also developed a group of Musaddiq supporters, but these were kept in the dark to the bitter end, even through the incident of the 30th of Tir.

Sumka ideology presents few surprises.[20] Patterned after the German National Socialist Party and embracing irresponsible dictatorial leadership as a principle, the Sumka Party published pamphlets glorifying the struggle for power above all else, stressing racialism, attacking capitalism and imperialism, attacking democracy, but never attacking the shah, and always falling short of really grappling with serious contemporary social problems. Its organization also revealed some of the influences of its prototype. The Sumka constitution is a long and involved document describing all the party formations and their regulations. The most important of these were the leader's office and his bodyguard (the Geruh-i-Javidan), the Attack Group for street fighting, and the youth group. There were also sections for affiliated organizations and for tribes, but these had little to do. The internal struggles

---

[20] *Asasnameh-yi Hizb-i Sosialist-i Melli Kargaran-i Iran* (Sumka) (Daftar Sevvum, Seri Yekkum, Tehran, 1331); and *Barnameh* . . . (of the Sumka Party) (2d ed., Daftar Yekkum, Seri Yekkum).

took place among the leaders of these formations and a few section chiefs such as the one in charge of education, sometimes culminating in battles between the rank and file of the Attack Group and others.

None of the Pan-Iranist parties had much influence, nor is it likely that they or others like them will determine the future of Iran. Nevertheless the continued existence of the "Iranian National Party founded upon Pan-Iranism" requires a few additional remarks. This is the party that is, and was, known regularly as the Pan-Iranism Party. It emerged from the same group, followers of Dr. Jahansus, and from among anticommunist students. A former leader, who lost an internal (and violent) struggle for control, is quite extreme in insisting that Pan-Iranism, like all the fascist parties, was supported and manipulated by the police when they were pro-shah.

Pan-Iranism attracted the same student and secondary school pupils; it had a semi-military organization, fought communists in the streets, and had a few affiliated groups. Most important among the affiliates were the coffee sellers' guild, the fruit sellers, the chelo-kababi guild, the painters, and a group of petty merchants called Jam'eh Bazarganan. Relations with the first of these groups remain especially strong, and it is claimed, but not convincingly, that the rest are still affiliated in addition to a group of government tobacco workers. Casual observation indicates that at present the group is no more than the personal following of an energetic and charming young man named Foruhar. Some of his leading supporters were about to split away in 1959, if they had a chance of receiving solid support from the Mardum Party, and the former leader that he ousted seeks to move closer to what is left of the party in order to have a public for his forthcoming ideological treatise.

The most important activity of the Pan-Iranism Party today is the occasional publication of a mimeographed sheet criticizing the government. Even while it is felt that the government is not unfriendly to Foruhar, and even though his mimeographed columns may be used to settle the private political scores of certain influential persons, the general tenor of his attack on the government has won him some favorable attention among young educated radicals. The party's program is also one which reflects the preferences of the same classes, but the Pan-Iranists have not yet managed to inspire confidence in their ability to achieve this program. The most recent version of this program insists upon political, economic, and social independence; on human rights;

on nationalization of industry and agriculture; on a planned economy; on limiting private ownership to that necessary for securing a livelihood for a family; on national service; on the right of children to education and health service, the right of farmers to land, and the rights of workers to jobs and the tools necessary for their livelihood. Other demands are for increasing the population of Iran,[21] for equal rights for women, for abolishing polygamy, and for reviving the ancient culture of Iran. The scope of the future Pan-Iranist state is carefully not alluded to, but the expansion and irredentism which is back of the basic idea of Pan-Iranism is not unpopular in Iran today. Sometimes these aspirations appear in the form of baseless rumors about a federation of the countries of Iran, Pakistan and Afghanistan, but more often they are unexpressed wishes.

At the present writing, all political activity is closely supervised by the security organization, and none but the acts of the two officially recognized parties receive any attention in the press. As we have seen, some individuals still claim that their parties exist, even hinting that they exist in spite of government desires to suppress them completely. Beyond the two or three Tudeh groups, the Toilers, the Third Force, and the Iran Party, there is a group known as the Iranian National Resistance, and sometimes also as Rah-i-Musaddiq (in the Way of Musaddiq), or simply as the Nationalists. This group is made up of younger people from all the older nationalist parties who are somewhat disappointed in their former leaders and seek some active group to which to attach themselves. Though associated with Foruhar, he is not the most outstanding among them. Despite their dangerous opposition to the present regime, they seem to be losing their revolutionary ardor and may find themselves coöperating with the official parties. Some of these people think, or rather hope, that they are being kept in reserve for some severe internal crisis when they will be able to save the throne by bringing about swift and radical reform.

Of the fundamentalist groups we still know very little. Both the Fidayan and the Mujahidin were very small groups, the Fidayan gaining notoriety by violence and the Mujahidin through their coöperation with Ayatullah Kashani. Both groups contained a good number of religious students but also had lay followers.

---

[21] *Hizb-i Millat-i Iran bar Bunyad-i Pan Iranism* (A'lamieh shmareh 1 & 2).

Their general goals were at once nationalist and religious. As nationalists they favored purification of the Persian language, specifically the elimination of Arabic, and as fundamentalists they sought strict application of the letter of Shiite law. They felt that all the ills of Iranian society would be eliminated if the state were run by religious men, and they identified imperialism with Western social practices. The Fidayan opposed the ruling dynasty, as well as the politicians, and they practiced assassination. They accepted the support of Ayatullah Kashani only briefly, but their opposition to traditional leadership, as well as their political intractability, led to a split. Despite the religious orientation of the group, they were opposed to the traditional ulama, whom they claimed compromised with an un-Islamic regime. The leader of the Fidayan was a young man in his twenties or early thirties, of strange disposition and of only slight religious education in which he did not distinguish himself. The Mujahidin were a competitive group, almost a splinter group, controlled by Shams Qanatabadi and Ayatullah Kashani. There is no indication that either group had a wide following or that they attracted many religious students or young bazaar artisans. And today, there does not seem to be a strong fundamentalist tendency anywhere in Iranian society.

The small, impotent remnants of the parties of the Musaddiq period form the backdrop to the farce of the recent officially approved party system. To understand the why and how of the organization, ideological statements, aggregative techniques, and political style of the Mardum [22] and the Melliyun [23] parties, it is important to note that they were striving to present images of what had become the generally accepted notion of a political party. At the same time, the new party system was supposed to intrude new Anglo-American political styles upon the previous continental practices. The consequence has led to many gratuitous criticisms, none of which are important, in the face of the overwhelming fact that the bulk of the educated classes have refused to accept these parties as anything but the creation of the court. In this light it is difficult to get anyone to discuss the two-party system seriously, and hardly anyone considers it worth his while to speculate on the probable future effect of these parties on Iranian politics.

---

[22] *Maram-Nameh va Asas-Nameh Hizb-i Mardum* (Komision Tablighat va Intisharat).

[23] *Maram-Nameh va Asas-Nameh Hizb-i Melliyun* (Dabir-Khaneh, Hizb-i Melliyun, 1337).

The generally held opinion is that the parties do not matter, that decisions will be made much as before, and that the parties will remain so much window dressing.

It is difficult, on the basis of the evidence at hand, to dispute this generally held opinion. In a way, we are faced with a self-fulfilling prophecy, for the parties will never amount to anything unless they serve to draw the political efforts of the educated classes. But the restricted sphere of party influence, the failure of the parliamentary fractions to function as such, and the exaggerated support of the shah by both parties serve to lower confidence. The idea of imposing a two-party system from above is, on the face of things, ridiculous, but it is also futile if no real political function is delegated to the parties. Affiliation with one or another party is not even an effective method of gaining patronage. When the majlis was in session, prior to the last elections, the cabinet had no party identity, parliamentary divisions were not made on a party basis, and the senate ignored the parties almost completely. The opposition rarely opposed, and the majority claimed credit only for implementing the shah's program. Despite all these negative considerations, the contention of the former prime minister, Dr. Eghbal, that the elections of 1960 would be on a party basis and that the next cabinet would be a party cabinet, does indicate the way in which the political importance of these parties could have been increased.

The idea of establishing a two-party system grew out of the desire to permit renewed public political activity while retaining control. The matter was discussed during the Ala ministry. Ala opposed, but Asadullah Alam, then minister of the interior was in favor, as was Dr. Manuchehr Eghbal, then court minister. Ala thought it was too early to permit party activity, Alam agreed to lead the opposition party, and some say that Eghbal favored a one-party system. Shortly after the Ala government resigned, however, Asadullah Alam and fifteen of his friends announced the founding of the Mardum Party. As an opposition leader, Alam took his new function very seriously and in his program stressed land distribution, labor welfare, equal rights for women, and social insurance. For a while, Alam was looked upon as the prime minister–designate, as a result of his "initiative," but then the Melliyun Party was formed by Eghbal. Eghbal's criticism of the opposition was much more severe than the Mardum Party's criticism of his government; and in many ways the Melliyun Party was the more energetic and confident. Still, the Mardum Party has kept doggedly to its praiseworthy reform program, even though its leaders tend to have a correct estimate of the poor prospects for implementing these reforms. The Melliyun Party, on the other hand, insisted that everything was going well and that things were getting better all the time.

Before going into further details and formal matters, the problem of internal party government can be briefly disposed of. The two party leaders were almost absolute rulers of their organizations. Leaders of both parties admit that opportunistic ambition was the sole reason for membership, although failure to win benefits from the government led some groups to become affiliated with the opposition. Consequently, those who had satisfactory positions tended to join the Melliyun Party in order to keep those positions or to move ahead. Those without satisfactory positions, or those who had an exaggerated opinion of Alam's chances for the prime ministership, tended to join the Mardum Party. Hopes for patronage hinge upon the incumbency of the prime ministry, thus making the party leader the most powerful figure in the party. It is further understood by all that no one will succeed to the prime ministry without the shah's approval, so there is no struggle over party leadership. Mr. Alam controls the Mardum Party, though it is the founding committee which has full constitutional control until the long-delayed first party congress is held. This committee of fifteen men was originally hand picked by Alam; it includes close personal supporters, persons from Alam's own home town, as well as a couple of distinguished university professors. In addition, about one-third of the party budget comes directly out of Alam's pocket. Eghbal controlled the Melliyun Party by virtue of being the prime minister. The founders' committee, in the Melliyun, is relatively unimportant, and presently has over two hundred members. Eghbal himself kept aloof from everyday party tasks, leaving these to the minister of state, Dr. N. Kassemi, who was the secretary-general of the party.

It is clear that Alam has built an organization that is loyal to himself personally, and that Eghbal built one that was loyal to the prime minister. Eghbal, however, has become identified with the Melliyun to such an extent that it is difficult to picture it continuing, now that he has been forced to resign.

Outwardly, the two parties are similar. Each is built up from small local cells through local, provincial, and national committees. Each is to be governed by a biennial congress. Each party has a set of organization committees and another set of policy committees. The Melliyun Party has a somewhat stricter system of control, but the Mardum Party insists more specifically on party discipline. The policy committees are supposed to work out the party lines and suggest specific legislation. This has been taken more seriously by the Mardum Party, where legislative proposals have little chance of passing. The Melliyun Party has not permitted their committees to interfere with the normal sources of legislative proposals. Both parties claim to be supported out of initiation fees and dues, which are variable, but the Mardum Party balance sheet shows large "loans" from Mr. Alam, and it is widely held that much of the Melliyun funds came from certain government sources. Both parties have tried to win editorial adherents, in addition to publishing their own organs, but the Melliyun Party has been more successful in winning support and has even organized its editors and held a conference for them. Most of the regular members of these two parties are civil servants. The Mardum Party has from three to four thousand members in Tehran, while the Melliyun claims a much inflated twenty thousand members.

Both parties claim to have ideologies, but these may be quickly reduced to a few principles and a vague program. The programs and principles of the two parties are similar: independence, constitutional monarchy, Islam (the Melliyun stresses Shiite Islam), legal reform, expansion of educational facilities, private ownership, improvement of the status of labor, decentralization of the administration, civil service reform, tax reform, and foreign relations based on the United Nations charter and reciprocity. The Mardum platform differs in specifically favoring land distribution, in favoring political rights for women, and in the greater detail of its presentation. The Melliyun Party program lays greater stress on labor benefits, on free medical service, on the Persian language, and on physical exercise and scouting.

Despite these variations in emphasis, neither party has won the label of a truly reforming and liberalizing organization. Nevertheless, the Mardum Party has not only pressed for land reform and has not only won most of the support of the educated women's organizations; it has also been more active in organizing labor. The Mardum Party's Central Organization of Iranian Workers now claims twenty-seven affiliated unions, but not all of these are active and not all encompass all the employees in such enterprises. About one-third of these unions are closer to the guild variety too. Nearly all were previously organized by Tudeh and were under ESKI, and the Mardum Party simply revived them, though, it is claimed, under new leadership and through democratic means. The support of such groups is a perpetual headache, if not an embarrassment, for the Mardum Party can do little for them and Alam stanchly refuses to come out into open attack on the government. Furthermore, the security organization is very suspicious of all labor activity and the labor ministry reflects this same attitude. As a consequence, the workers tend to have little faith in democratic politics or in the Mardum Party. The record of the Mardum Party is none too good, either; they lost influence with the taxi drivers when they insisted on certain formalities when the guild association took up their grievances; they alienated the printers when they refused to publish an article criticising Senator Mas'udi in the party paper; they backed out of a May 1st celebration in 1958; they were unable to reinstate six silo workers who were dismissed; and they completely lost control of the brick kiln strike.

The Mardum Party has placed emphasis upon land distribution, but it has made no effort to work among the peasants. It is argued that the government is suspicious of agitation among the peasants, and so the party has even turned down a few peasants who came in looking for help.

Guilds have shown an interest in the Mardum Party only to the extent that their interests have not been served by the government. Thus a section of the Bakers' Guild came in after the new machine-baking scheme was approved. The Ittihad-i-Pishehvaran va Bazarganan, petty traders opposed to the Chamber of Commerce, and one other similar group have become affiliated with the Mardum Party. Certain local councils, when unsuccessful in their appeals to the government, have also had conversations with Mardum Party leaders.

Nearly all of the women's groups have some connection with the Mardum Party, and joint demonstrations are held on occasion. Primary school teachers and a group of principals have affiliated. Two or three Bashgahs (sports clubs) are also identified with the Mardum Party. As with most other parties, a few fairly unimportant ulama visit the party headquarters, but the Mardum do not have strong religious support.

Perhaps the most significant effort of the party has been to win over the so-called Nationalists. Thus far, there has been little success, but the prospect of legitimizing the nationalist opposition while winning their endorsement of the present regime is worth the effort. Eventually, the price of such a political shift will probably be a change of cabinet—a price which the Mardum Party is not in a position to pay. Thus far, the party has won over the Sipehr family's Arya Party and has had discussions with a dissident Pan-Iranist. Apparently, the Mardum Party is even willing to discuss forming a broad (anticommunist) nationalist front with these groups.

The Melliyun Party has made no similar effort to win over groups, rather, it has concentrated on key individuals. The most outstanding affiliates are the (quasi-official) leaders of the Chamber of Commerce, of the High Council of Guilds, and of all the officially recognized unions (variously recorded as 18 and 27 unions). They also claimed the membership of half a dozen ministers, about as many more directors-general, and the same number of agency heads. A number of important bank officials and industrialists are members, too. Most of the landlords are said to be Melliyun members. Large numbers of professional personnel, as well as hawkers, are claimed to belong as individuals. The different function of the two parties is clear, even from this brief recitation, for the Melliyun Party represents the traditional modes of organization by gathering in individuals already enjoying excellent access, and often much influence. The rank and file is disregarded, or perhaps more accurately may be considered as dependent upon this upper echelon. The Mardum Party, in its effort to legitimize and control opposition, seeks to reach the less influential, and tends to find them coming in as groups. The Melliyun is comprised of a good number of recognized political bargainers who can usually manipulate their followers, unlike the Mardum Party, which is supposed to act as bargainer for its smaller, less influential group affiliates. It is more than likely that most of the principal bargainers have already left or will leave the Melliyun Party since it has lost power.

FIVE

The Political Functions

BARGAINING

THE IRANIAN POLITICAL SYSTEM is a predominantly traditional one, and its principal mode of operation is through bargaining. The characteristic feature of the traditional system is an apparent absence of rationality or system. Superficially, tradition is chaotic and contradictory. Traditional theory, or rather ideology, is not so chaotic as traditional politics, and its strict application transforms the traditional system. In the traditional system, power is its own justification, but no single structure of power controls sufficient resources to extend itself to include the whole polity. The power structures themselves are much more self-contained; there is less overlapping, and the hierarchy of personal loyalties is well understood. These power structures may be involved in any issue whatsoever, or they may fail to become involved in matters of the most crucial interest. Multiple memberships mean little, in the face of primary loyalties, and the notion of a public interest is extremely weak. Each power structure, each interest formation, stands alone in the general struggle judging when and how to act and with whom. No outside group can move it by any claim of right or duty. There is no obligation, only a market place where buyers and sellers may bargain.

In examining the structure of power in Iran we have attempted to identify the principal bargainers. Parties, and even formalized interest groups, are the results of such bargaining, and they are therefore of limited duration and valid only for certain purposes. The principal bargainers do not lose their identities or their independence by making an agreement, and they may also shape their following in any form deemed desirable by circumstances or prejudice. These bargainers are not only leading participants in structured power relationships; they are also individuals who enjoy delegated administrative or judicial authority.

Bargaining is not an exclusive feature of the traditional system, it occurs to a very large degree in the conventional system as well. Bargaining is the technique of achieving coöperation between independent power structures, but in the traditional system it is also the basis of granting legitimizations. This is best exemplified by the lack of fixity in what are generally thought of as rigid legal systems. The interpretation and application of the law is the result of a bargain, whenever any of the principal bargainers are concerned. In the conventional system, the area of bargaining is often restricted to electoral and parliamentary operations, but in the traditional system it permeates all phases of political life.

In Iran, then, it is useful to look upon each structure of power as a discrete, independent, self-interested unit. If this unit completes a bargain it will coöperate with others until the pay-off, if not it will automatically oppose the others' efforts or will remain indifferent. Everyone is a bargainer, in Iran, the head of every family, and every clerk, teacher, policeman, and merchant. Most of these are not important political bargainers, but the leaders of larger power structures are important, as are those who wield administrative authority. Every wealthy family, every high army or police officer, every mujtahid, every university professor, every tribal khan, every high official, judge, legal adviser, or accountant is an important bargainer. And after these leaders of stable formations come the more enterprising bargainers whose support is less stable but whose potential influence, in view of the weakening of tradition, is great. These are the self-appointed labor leaders, the editors and publishers, the self-appointed leaders of political parties, the leading merchants in each bazaar specialization, the persons who control the modern markets, and the government-appointed or self-appointed leaders of interest or professional associations. In every case, leadership of individuals is stressed because there exists no accepted basis of controlling leaders from within each of these discrete units of power. There can be no appeal outside of the unit, and no relief except to depose the leader forcibly or to form a rival group—both remedies being possible only in the more modern structures and both running strictly contrary to tradition.

Some examples will illustrate how ubiquitous is the bargain in resolving political problems in Iran. The distribution of seats in the majlis and the senate is primarily the result of bargaining between the several aspirants and the court. In constituency G., a certain aspirant was informed that an outsider was about to be selected. He gathered a number of local dignitaries and made a demarche at the ministry of court. After a good deal of talk and several additional visits, a third person was chosen who was agreeable to the protesting aspirant. In constituency M., the seat was usually granted to the eldest son of the leading family. The eldest son having earned the shah's displeasure, another son was given the seat, by agreement between the family and the court. In constituency S., a mullah was granted his claim to manage a waqf comprising an agricultural village, then he came out in support of the shah and was granted a majlis seat. Under Qavam al-Saltaneh, seats were granted to those who made large donations to his Democrat Party of Iran.

It is not unique that budget allocations are sometimes settled by bargaining among cabinet ministers, but it is rare that no other basis of economizing exists. Despite the fact that Iran is engaged in a long-range development program, that program has not been built upon a system of priorities, but upon a principle of balance. Insofar as can be discovered, the principle of balance pursued has no relation to "balanced development"; it indicates merely a balance among the various fields of development, such as industry or communications. Not only is this balance the result of bargaining rather than study, but it cannot be a sufficient guide to the cabinet on budget problems. The plan was presumably protected by the regulation guaranteeing 80 per cent of the oil revenues to the plan organization, but instead of protecting the plan organization from "political" pressures, this provision has brought on cabinet efforts to get the plan to turn over some of its funds to the ministries. Furthermore, this tendency has been enhanced because of the absence of any basis for deciding disputes among cabinet members regarding the budget and thus renders a raid on the plan organization the easiest way out.

In the realm of foreign security policy we have recently been witness to a gross error arising out of this same bargaining tendency. For years now, the government of Iran has been seeking more modern weapons from the United States and United States membership in the Baghdad Pact. Then, in 1958, there arose the proposal of bilateral pacts between the United States and Baghdad Pact nations. These pacts were meant to reduce such pressures as Iran's demand that the U.S. join the Baghdad Pact, but were to be aimed against Soviet aggression only. The issue developed after the Iraqi revolution, and the Iranian government demanded a security guarantee against attack from any quarter, not solely from the Soviets. When the United States resisted this pressure, the Iranian government commenced simultaneous negotiations with the USSR for a non-aggression pact. Instead of the expected reaction of an American concession regarding the bilateral pact, the United States threatened dire consequences. The Soviet delegation was sent home abruptly, and the USSR began a very severe propaganda campaign against Iran and the shah.

In foreign economic policy, bargaining is everywhere a standard practice; but here again, Iran tends to make exaggerated demands, followed by great concessions. Cargoes shipped to the Persian Gulf ports of Iran are burdened with a 10 per cent surcharge because of the delays in unloading. Iran protested these charges to the International Shipping Conference and threatened to withdraw if the charges were not lowered to 5 per cent, at most, although "they should have been eliminated altogether." The solution was to reduce the charges on cargoes to Bandar Shahpur, which receives considerably fewer shipments, and to leave the 10 per cent charge as it was on shipments to Khorramshahr, the major port of entry for foreign cargoes.

The same sort of procedure has been followed in negotiations with Japan over balancing the trade between the two countries. Iran exports to Japan less than 10 per cent of what she imports. At first the Iranian government announced that the trade must be brought into complete balance, then insisted upon exporting 30 per cent of the value of the goods imported from Japan, and will probably settle for much less.

The implementation of the income tax law has similar aspects. Quite aside from alterations of the law occasioned by demarches from the Chamber of Commerce or artists and entertainers, each tax assessment and payment is the result of a bargain. This is partly due to the fact that the government has no idea of the true income of most taxpayers and begins with an arbitrary assessment. When the tax bill is not simply ignored, it may be settled by bargaining either in or out of court.

The administration of justice often involves far more complicated bargaining. Before most civil cases come up there is, of course, a good deal of bargaining among the litigants. Each then attempts to win the support of persons in the ministry of justice, from the minister on down. The judges themselves may try to get the highest bid, if the pressure from the top is not too great.

We have already seen where administrative coördination is largely a bargaining process. This is true not only between separate departments, but also within a single department. Each of the higher positions is an independent center of power in the hands of an artful manipulator. Administrative undersecretaries are supposed to remain on the job for five years, regardless of how they get on with the minister. Accountants are employees of the ministry of finance. Legal advisers hide behind their professional achievements. Directors-general may be appointed only with the approval of the prime minister. Personnel managers hold the future of lower employees in their hands and are the key to successful patronage operations. Each of these is a key administrative bargainer, each can seriously embarrass the others, or the minister even, and the coöperation of all is necessary for minimal administrative efficiency.

In the preceding examples of typical kinds of bargaining to be found in the Iranian political system, it should be noted that all of these are in the nature of counter-mores, when viewed from the vantage point of either the constitutional or the administrative state. Bargaining by persons in legislative or administrative roles is, however, quite in accordance with the values of a traditional system and it may be institutionalized, in the more highly organized. Bargaining by interest group leaders or by party leaders is the norm in conventional systems; contrariwise, it is a type of counter-mores, in the traditional system. Implicit in the sense of the term "counter-mores" is the expectation that the practice will occur; however, all occupational groups are supposed to have their rights and duties clearly demonstrated by tradition (except perhaps in some primitive societies) while parties which aggregate more widely than among those already bound by ties of kinship, geography, religion, or language are unknown to tradition. Insofar as a party is such a group, known to tradition, it is a party only in name, though a legitimate bargaining unit; but insofar as it may be a party with a distinctive *Weltanschauung* then it has no traditional right to bargain. Ideological parties, in any case, tend to prefer the rationalizing pattern, and hence usually avoid bargaining. Of conventional bargaining practices there are none in Iran, unless the Mardum Party may be said to approximate this ideal. As we have already seen, the area within which the Mardum Party may maneuver is greatly restricted. It does not seek to mediate differences between groups, but may only represent group preferences to the government; and even in the performance of this service it tends more toward the role of facilitating catharsis, or it chooses cases of individual, rather than group, grievances. All of this is without prejudice to the party's character, in part, as the following of its very prominent leader.

Bargaining techniques are employed by all political actors, at times, but when the Iranian political system is examined from the point of view of its transitional character, greater stress should be placed upon developmental trends which illustrate increasing alternatives to bargaining among legislative, judicial, and administrative personnel, and increasing opportunities for bargaining by group and party leaders. At the end of this chapter we shall examine some rationalizing tendencies which are tending to decrease the bargaining practices among the authority-laden classes. We have also noted that some tentative efforts have been made to rationalize the role of interest groups. As yet there is no discernable tendency toward the establishment of a totalitarian party.

Any examination of bargaining by groups and parties is fraught with difficulties in evaluation. Just as a restriction of bargaining may represent either a traditional or a rationalizing tendency, in the sense of nonrecognition of nontraditional groups, or their subordination to hierarchical formations, so may increased bargaining indicate either the growth of conventional techniques or the persistence of tradition. A correct evaluation, in the last analysis, depends upon the individuals concerned and their motivations. Individuals engaging in a bargaining practice may or may not have some standing in tradition; they may or may not make demands based upon traditional rights; and they may or may not look upon one another as persons to whom one must defer by tradition. Actually, in most instances, the alternative is false, for such persons will have dual roles and their performance will usually be anomalous.

This duality of role accounts for the general pattern whereby group leaders rarely press the interests of their groups upon the government but do represent the grievances of individuals. Often enough, the individuals so represented are not members of the group at all; instead, they may be relatives or friends of group members. Insofar as the group leader engages in bargaining without threatening some sanction (as in representing some grievance), he bargains with his own support. His ability to speak for his group is taken for granted, and with good reason. Such bargaining may be carried on with the government, with other group leaders, or with self-appointed leaders of parties.

Bargaining is usually not utilized for purposes of holding a group together. The internal structure of groups is either predominantly traditionally oriented, or else indeterminate, so that divisions are never framed and compromise solutions may be effective. The case is, rather, that the leader acts as judge, in traditional groups. In more modern groups, and in those of less functional diffuseness, there are tendencies toward the extremes of traditional rigidity or anarchy. In matters such as price fixing, for example, the bazaar group concerned will agree on a more or less fixed price with relative ease, and without a clearly designated leader to arbitrate differences. Tradition has imposed a solidarity that manifests itself in a mutuality that is not characterized by bargaining so much as by coöperation. Outside the bazaar (where prices are not fixed as they are in the book trade, or for staple foodstuffs) wide variations of price are found. Such variations are especially noteworthy in the fees of professionals, whose standards are also far from uniform.

Bargaining within groups is, in general, of relatively small importance, because of the governmental orientation of the groups. That is, most benefits (or the removal of hindrances) must be derived from the government. The issue is rarely one of what to demand of the government, namely, an appropriate topic of internal bargaining; rather, it is of how much one can get from the government. Thus, the basic framework of bargaining with the government renders internal bargaining useless. This tendency is further enhanced by the frequency of cases in which the effectiveness of group leadership is directly tied to governmental recognition. As we have noted, such recognition applies more to the individual leader than to the group through the leader. The special and nearly independent position of the leader also militates against the importance of internal bargaining. The issue here is to what extent can the leader be made to represent the interests of the individual member? Joining with his fellows will not help the individual, but if he can strike up a bargain with the leader his position may be improved. The consequence of these considerations is that the group leader is rarely the broker between conflicting interests in his group, though he may act as mediator of interested demands of individuals to the government.

Group leadership is always stable, whether rooted in tradition, based upon government recognition, or derived from self-appointment. While occasional divisions occur, the prevailing attitude is rarely one of demanding that the leader serve the members. Such splits as do come up are to be categorized as based on personal differences or upon a shift in governmental preference. By personal differences we mean an attempt on the part of the dissident to rise to a position of leadership, that is, a prime bargaining position, in his own right. Such attempts are rarely successful, exceptions arising primarily in those situations where governmental officials desire a more pliable representative to deal with. The example of the Bakers Guild has already been given, but it is interesting to note that the efforts of the government to create a new leadership for that guild have not been immediately successful. The reason for this lack of success lies in the solidarity of the group and its fears that the new leadership is perhaps an instrument for weaking the articulation of the bakers' interests. Here, bargaining has obviously broken down, and where bargaining breaks down, where a leader has no access, or where a fairly well-articulated interest is disregarded, we tend to find (at the present time) the group concerned enter into negotiations with the opposition party.

The opposition party, fitting in so ill with the pattern of interest representation through recognized, and hence pro-government, leadership, has little to bargain with. It can only offer the barest thread of hope to those who have nowhere else to turn. Thus, increases of Mardum Party membership come through the adherence of groups excluded from the normal political process, and less frequently from individuals who hope for personal support from the party leaders. In return for such adherence, the Mardum Party is compelled to recognize the legitimacy of the group and its leader.

The bargaining patterns of the two official parties can, therefore, be superficially distinguished by the greater success of the Mardum Party in aggregating excluded groups, as against the success of the Melliyun Party, when it was in power, in aggregating already influential individuals. Of course it was not the Melliyun Party which was engaged in the bargain, instead, it was the government, in which it held all the important offices. The Mardum Party, because of the high position of its leader, can lend respectability both to excluded groups and to individuals, and this ability is its major bargaining power. The group leaders who have joined the Melliyun were already recognized and accepted by the government, so that membership was merely their part of the bargain. Moreover, their excellent access and firm status tends to reduce the tensions within their groups. Generally speaking, there was little need for internal bargaining and mediation by the leadership of the Melliyun Party, its important participants being leading individuals. In the case of less influential individuals, the Melliyun secretariat had on occasion refused to intervene with its own subordinates in the government. There was, however, very little complaining by Melliyun members against their leaders. In sharp contrast, most Mardum Party members express dissatisfaction with the looseness of their party's program, with its failure to take a firm stand on issues, and with its general ineffectiveness. Here, more freedom for the expression of such protests exists, and meetings often take on a genuinely democratic aspect. Vigorous protests are often lodged with the party leader himself, though the usual proprieties of politesse are observed. Nevertheless, it is quite clear that these negative expressions put Mr. Alam under a strain which he bears admirably. The cathartic value of the whole process is self-evident, but the party comprehends no more than a fraction of the discontented. The difficulty in holding the support of this political element is significant, and as a consequence, the party leaders are sometimes driven to make critical statements in the majlis, in their press, or in public speeches. These protests are usually restrained and moderate, even to the point where majlis voting is not along party lines, but on at least one occasion the Mardum labor weekly has been suspended by the censor. Mardum membership is therefore not a title to a recognized bargaining position, and most of those who hoped that the Mardum Party would naturally succeed to the government have been disappointed. The minimum of respectability which is derived from membership is small consolation, except where former members of the Tudeh Party are concerned. In other cases, such as with labor, the validity of leadership claims is so much in doubt that membership in the Mardum Party alone sustains it. For the rest, there is a tendency, albeit slight, for the more respected leadership to be regarded in the light of their followers, and hence to be gradually excluded from prime bargaining positions. This was apparently the attitude of Dr. Eghbal, and it caused misgivings in the minds of Mardum leaders.

Throughout this chapter the ubiquity of the employment of

bargaining techniques has been stressed as a characteristic of the traditional element in the Iranian political system. It will not do, however, to oversimplify this classification of behavior or to overstress the place it holds in the dynamics of Iranian politics. In a limited sense, bargaining is the functional equivalent of the structural factor of access. Those having access to persons authorized to grant legitimizations are the principal bargainers. Looked at from another point of view, bargaining is politically functional activity which is devoid of a normative base or referent, which does not seek structural change, and the goal of which is *ad hoc*. The implication of the last point is that bargaining characterizes the disposition of nonrecurring, short-term issues only. Raising other issues of a long-term nature, with a normative dimension or permanently affecting existing structures of power relationships, is clearly dysfunctional to the Iranian political system. Refusing to bargain is dysfunctional, if complete and permanent, but it is simply a variation, or a part of the technique if partial and temporary. While highly restrictive, in general, the system does permit the admission of new groups or individuals to bargaining status, and it may admit issues in which groups lacking such status, under ordinary circumstances, are interested. The issues and the type of activity implied by the term bargaining must always be of such a nature as not to disturb the political myth, which assumes a static society, a fixed distribution of political values, and a divinely guided source for determining public policy. The admission to bargaining status of groups challenging these principles tends to be dysfunctional.

In the light of the foregoing explication, bargaining has no normative base and is not affirmatively legitimized. It is effective only when greatly restricted, and when obscured by a degree of secrecy. In fact, the technical practice is intrinsically associated with a discontinuous, asymmetrical, and disintegrated pattern of communication. Consequently, this political bargaining technique is not analogous to bargaining in the open market, where supply and demand are assumed to mutually and freely adjust, and where buyers and sellers are assumed to have complete knowledge. The bargaining under consideration here is much more akin to bargaining in an oligopolistic market.

Emphasis upon bargaining techniques should not lead us to neglect other, more legitimate, determinants of political behavior. Reference to wealth, age, descent, learning, eloquence, sincerity, and courage are all important and real factors which hedge bargaining in and often determine its concrete result. Just as the free market implies universalistic-achievement value patterns, so is the kind of bargaining with which we are here concerned largely defined by the particularistic-ascriptive values of traditional Iran.

THE LEGITIMIZING PROCESS

THE LEGITIMIZING PROCESS in Iran entails much more varied and subtle ranges of action than merely that of the more usual legislation, regulation, and adjudication of the formal conventional system. In Iran, typifying a system in transition, these formal conventional patterns of legitimization are known and utilized, but often only to lend further legality to a position already won in the framework of tradition. The pattern of legitimizations outside of this formal triad is lacking in orderliness, but it is united by the same characteristics which hedge bargaining. The tradition of a divinely guided king, a fixed society with roles distributed in accordance with privilege, and a fixed distribution of political values in accordance with rank, occupation, and service to the shah are three central principles of traditional legitimacy. These principles limit the use of bargaining techniques and serve to designate the principal bargainers. The legitimizing process consists primarily in designating the principal bargainers, and only secondarily in implementing by law the results of bargains. Thus, the legitimizing function consists of constantly reaffirming the identity of the principal bargainers and of legitimizing only such bargaining arrangements as are in accord with traditional principles. There are some important exceptions, of course, which are illustrations of the rationalizing tendencies already mentioned. These exceptions occur primarily in the areas which tend to strengthen the position of the shah through enhancing the efficiency of the civil service, and through strengthening the army. Planned economic development is also in part an exception. Though the long-range goal of strengthening the regime through development is by no means assured, the very momentum of a comprehensive program has a logic of its own which requires legal facilitations running counter to traditional privilege in some ways. Another exception to the eufunctional characterization (that is, tending to support the traditional aspect of the Iranian system) of legitimizations is in the area of governmental decisions which are the direct result of, or the necessary byproduct of, the wholesale acceptance of foreign aid and technical advice. The last exception is especially pronounced when connected with the three aforementioned areas of administrative reform, military affairs, and economic development; it also has an effect on specific areas of foreign policy. Here we shall be concerned with the traditional or eufunctionally systemic aspects of legitimization.

One of the most important ways in which legitimization is granted is through the institutionalization of access. Traditionally, access to high government officials or to the court is the privilege of the high-born, the wealthy, the learned, or the leaders of tribes and minorities. Others could and did approach the authorities, but always in supplication. The tradition of the "pious sultan" which has persisted in Iran from medieval times requires that the shah be personally available to even the lowest citizen, for hearing complaints and redress of grievances. It was largely with this end in mind that several special inspectorates were established, and especially the latest royal supervisory commission of the shah, under General Yazdanpanah. This tradition notwithstanding, the usual result of private complaints going over the head of lower officials is unpleasant for the complainant; and the few officials who encourage this activity, like the present chief of the *gendarmerie,* are driven to great extremes to prove their sincerity to the peasants. Furthermore, it is impossible for all of the oppressed to receive private hearings. Tradition is served in other ways, such as the acceptance of petitions by the cabinet, during its tours of the provinces last year, and by the admission of a few complaints at the ministry of court, almost every day. Petitions of the cabinet have led to occasional dramatic pronouncements of intentions to ameliorate conditions and the more reasonable complaints to the ministry of court are rewarded by a note to some ministry. The underlying assumption behind this system is that everything is well run except for an occasional administrative error or for isolated examples of corruption.

Another form of limited, noninstitutional access occurs in the representation of whole groups, or of individuals claiming to speak for whole groups. If representing a sufficiently important group, such as the carpet dealers or the taxi-drivers, the grocers or the artists, the spokesman of the group may be admitted by the authorities, but the demands of such weak and low status groups are rarely met. Since their demands usually relate to some decision already taken by the government, within the framework of a traditional bargain or a rationalizing policy, an "interest group" demand cannot be credited. Such negative responses confirm the merely formal character of this access and help us to classify such demarches as variants of the positive system challenging process (see below).

True, or effective, access rests with the members of military, bureaucratic, landowning, tribal, and religious elites. There is a good deal of overlapping among these elites, and some diffusion of interest between these and the professional and business groups. Within each category there is a good deal of competition, though this is less the case with tribal leaders, the highest military, and minority leadership. Among landowners, competition is also restricted, in many cases, to those from the same geographical area. The overlapping and diffusion of interest results from the fact that many individuals may be classified in more than one category, that members of their families may hold positions in other elite formations, or that they or members of their families are professionals, or are engaged in commerce or manufacturing.

Members of these elites are drawn upon to fill important positions, or they are honored or consulted in such regular fashion as to very nearly institutionalize the positions of influence which they hold. This form of legitimization is considerably more important than the specific grant of a license or legal judgment, for it affords the individual concerned an extremely high degree of bargaining power. In return, the man whose access is thus guaranteed should show complete allegiance to the shah and his closest supporters, and he is usually expected to act as a subsidiary channel of informal but effective access for those of lower status who promise him their own support. Many such individuals, especially the more educated, hold a weekly open house for applicants. This ceremony, which usually takes place on Friday morning, is in itself an institution, and many who aspire to prominence will hold it also. The open house may also serve as a source of information and as a communications facility.

The most outstanding of the ways in which access is institutionalized is by appointment to the majlis or the senate. We have already seen where bargaining enters into this procedure, and there does not seem to be much distinction between the handling of those who are formally "elected" and the senators who are appointed by the shah. Members of the legislature are almost invariably of the elites mentioned, with only a few exceptions in the political buccaneers who have risked their necks for the shah. In other words, these are persons who already enjoy access. Their membership in the legislature makes them spokesmen for their own families, towns, or bargaining partners, and practically assures the success of their efforts. Exclusion from the majlis of a very important family usually indicates the incurrence of the shah's displeasure, and in consequence their deprivation. The recognition accorded those "elected" is of such importance that the prudent will often choose to act in concert with, or through, a majlis member.

This pattern has led a number of groups to seek representation in the majlis, but the early corporative aspect of the legislature no longer obtains. Above all, the admission of new groups to bargaining status has been stanchly opposed. Especially, and at least, labor and the teachers have had enterprising leaders who tried to win seats by demanding access for their groups. Both Khosrau Hedayat and Derakhshesh claim they represented labor and the teachers, respectively, when they were in the majlis, but no such representatives held seats either before or thereafter. Only the Chamber of Commerce, the Bar Association, the university and some bankers are represented by their leading exponents.

In addition to the recognition of the elite concerned and the special quality of the access granted by a legislative seat, members of the majlis and senate have an unparalleled opportunity to see and discuss bills in committee, before they become law. Whereas low status groups and individuals can only protest after the fact, when little can be done, majlis and senate members can and do insert self-protective amendments. When the bill does not have stanch royal support, they may also delay it for varying periods. The latter practice has led the cabinet to prefer single paragraph bills referring at times to a volume of specific regulations, or to prefer temporary or experimental grants of power which may be reviewed only after they are long overdue.

Other aspects of the legitimizing process overlap with the institutionalization of access, if understood in its broadest sense, but it may be more useful to designate these by separate classification. Legitimization is also achieved through consultation. This may often be an obscure procedure, concealed from view, and it is, of course, dependent upon the unequal distribution of information to interested parties. Consultation will be discussed as a political process in some detail below, so that we shall now be concerned only with its legitimizing aspects.

The sort of consultation which is significant is not that associated with the tradition of good government in Islam. It is true that the shah does seek advice on a regular basis from certain honored individuals. There are many more who are questioned about specific problems, and more still who are granted audience. All of these procedures are forms of legitimization, just as is the successful attempt to involve one or more of the royal family in business ventures. Emphasis here, however, is rather upon consultation with interested parties, before the determination of a particular policy, or even the regularization of consultation in the implementation of policy through regulation. The distinctive character of this sort of consultation appears in the specificity of the interests consulted. Majlis members consider all bills, but leading law professors are consulted about legal reform and leading members of the Chamber of Commerce are consulted about foreign trade agreements. Of particular importance for regulatory matters are the high councils which we have already discussed.

Another form of legitimization is through the making of appointments. It should be made clear that appointments to offices of authority are not made in order to grant legitimizations, but in order to fill necessary, or at least existing, positions. There are, however, obvious benefits to be derived from office holding, benefits in terms of access, prestige, bargaining power, and opportunities to participate in important decisions. These benefits lead to considerable maneuvering to win offices or to staff them with one's friends, so it may be possible to discern a distinctive political process in this area as well. This problem will also be dealt with below.

Tensions do exist between the need for qualified and competent personnel and the demands of the influential for the spoils of office. Some persons are appointed on the basis of merit, as for example, many officials of the plan organization were. Others, especially the heads of the independent agencies, certain diplomats, and a number of employees of the foreign ministry, have been granted their positions as rewards for political support or because of their noble birth. When an appointment is made to a member of one of the elite formations, its implications are far wider than in the case of a merit appointment or reward granted to a person without noble status. The added ability to command governmental legitimizations accruing to the power structure concerned, and the expectation that this ability will be exploited, render the appointment itself a legitimization.

Religious ceremonials are yet another means of legitimization. While serving as a means of adding religious legitimacy to the regime itself, the court enjoys a certain degree of freedom in choosing those ulama through whom it will demonstrate its attachment to Shiite Islam. There are many of the ulama whose pious caution prevents them from having anything to do with the government, but this caution is counterbalanced by admission of the importance of repeated assertions that Shiite Islam is the religion of the state. Among both Shiite and Sunni ulama there has long obtained a tendency to equate the establishment of Islam with recognition of their own institution. This is usually accomplished by the association of some ulama with the government, in a variety of ways. Such association often enhances the general bargaining position of the ulama concerned, especially with regard to the maintenance and control of madrassahs, the administration of awqaf, the placing of protégés in government service, and the easing of the impact of government regulations upon relatives and friends. Obviously, those ulama who are so honored have entered into a bargain with the court whereby the religious-legal basis of the regime is strengthened, and whereby they are themselves strengthened in leadership positions within the religious institution. Nevertheless, association with the court remains suspect, and it is used as an argument by rivals of associated ulama. The answer of associated ulama is to point out the value of advising the shah in the way of Islam, regardless of how far he may fall short on certain occasions.

As in other traditional forms of legitimization, limitations are imposed by the social and cultural implications of the specific technique. Thus, the institutionalization of access is limited by the traditional bases of deference and by the need for geographical distribution. Consultation is limited by the interest, knowledge, and power relationships of those who will be involved in the eventual implementation of the decision concerned. Appointments are limited to those who, when appointed, will pattern their behavior in accordance with the *modus operandi* of the system; that is, those who will bargain with others whose bargaining status has been legitimized. The choice of ulama is similarly limited by the task required of them and the value derived from their already achieved notoriety. An alim without status in the religious institution is of no use to the court, while one whose status is derived from learning and piety exclusively cannot associate himself with the court at all.

The religious ceremonials of greatest importance fall into two categories: those of general incidence, observed by the Shiite community as a whole, and following the calendar; and those of restricted incidence observed by the royal family, and following the life cycle of its members. In the first category fall the great holy days of Shiite Islam, especially the month of Muharram, in which falls the anniversary of the death of Hussain. Similar anniversaries of the martyrdom of the other eleven Imams are also important. Ramadhan, the month of fasting, with its great penultimate feast, is another long period of the association of the court and the ulama. The public prayer of the shah at one of the great

Shiite shrines is another ceremonial of importance, but this is usually tied in with an important holy day. On other occasions, the religiosity of the ceremony is established almost exclusively by the number of ulama invited to the palace. Examples of the last are, perhaps, the anniversary of 9th of Esfand or of the 28th of Mordad. Now-Ruz is not a Shiite holy day, though it is universally observed. A good part of its religious character is derived from the annual visit of the shah to the shrine of Imam Riza at Mashhad.

Whenever the shah or the council of ministers travel about the country on official tours they are met by welcoming committees. The composition of these committees is important for discerning which groups and which leaders are, in fact, considered legitimate by the government. Permission to participate in a welcoming committee is often taken from an important local official, and such participation is highly prized. Welcoming the shah or the cabinet does not usually confer any specific benefit upon the one so honored, even as the grant of an audience does not always result in the grant of a petition. Nevertheless, in keeping with the essential character of legitimization in a traditional system, it is important as a confirmation of existing power relationships. It may very well be that some members of the welcoming committee are not principal bargainers, or that they are rarely consulted before a decision is made. This is less significant than the demonstration of the traditionally conceived, fixed, and comprehensive structure of society. Nowadays, governmentally recognized labor representatives (not usually syndicates), guilds, local councils, minorities (except the Baha'is), industrialists, and leaders of the Chamber of Commerce are admitted to such committees.

There are also a number of cases in which a diffuse bundle of legitimizations is granted, rather than one affecting power structures or the temporary distribution of a discrete benefit. Legitimizations of this type occur especially where parts of the government's authority over policy or regulation are delegated to associations or individuals acting in their own names or in the names of associations. The devolution of authority to quasi-governmental organizations brings together elements of feudalistic bureaucracy and notions of corporativism which appertain to political traditionalism, but the extension of the scope of this pattern of legitimization is due to modernizing pressures seeking an expansion of governmental interest, even where the government lacks the necessary resources. It is not only a case of demands

upon government outrunning administrative resources; additionally, we may find that traditional power structures are least affected
when such demands are requited through the use of traditional
techniques.

The best examples of the devolution of authority may be
found in the laws and elaborate regulations regarding the Chamber
of Commerce and the Bar Association. With less official and
merely implicit arrangements, administrative authority for many
local government purposes is delivered to tribal leaders and land
owners. The landowner may also come to administer the village
coöperatives, which are hastily set up without adequate preparation of the peasants themselves.

We have already had occasion to refer to the recurrence of
governmental establishment and recognition of associations of
various kinds. We have seen this to be one manifestation of the
tendency toward rationalization in Iran, but there are also cases
in which the actual persons leading such associations are those
who support the traditional regime. The tension between the
form and general goal of such associations and the aspirations
of their leaders is a typical derivative of the anomalous character
of Iran's politics.

As previously mentioned, the establishment of an association by the government arises as a result of some challenge by an
anti-governmental association, or as a result of as yet unclearly
articulated interest demands. In the first instance, the government wishes to supplant or control a hostile force, and in the
second the government wishes to legitimize more specifically
some power relationship of interest to its supporters. The second,
of course, is a clear case of positive legitimization, and the first
is negative, insofar as the governmentally organized association
does nothing more than support the government or discredit
its rival.

Examples of this form of legitimization have already been
given in our discussions of the formation of labor groups, guilds,
Chambers of Commerce, local councils, city councils, the Bar
Association, and the like. Peasant coöperatives, associations of
government doctors and engineers, even of teachers, are other
examples. The choice of the leader or president of such a group
is often of crucial importance, and is sometimes related to the
determination of specific policies. Thus, at one time labor leadership is chosen on the issue of a revolutionary versus a loyal trade
union movement, and at another time on whether or not existing

labor legislation is to be strictly implemented. At one time Chamber of Commerce leadership is changed because of its opposition to the orientation of the government's foreign policy, and at another because of opposition to credit restriction and the imposition of import quotas.

Issues of specific policy and discrete benefits to be distributed among principal bargainers having good access, and already included in the consultative process, may be associated with the conventional forms of legitimization. These conventional forms are by means of legislation, regulation, and adjudication. Under regulation, we might include decree-making and license granting, especially when the latter, as well as the former, is carried out by the cabinet. The role of the cabinet is central, in all of these outwardly conventional legitimizations, whether the cabinet is carrying out its own will or is merely transmitting decisions already made by some other legitimizing technique.

In general, it is possible to say that no major political issue in Iran is resolved through conventional means, which is to argue that these techniques are employed primarily for system maintenance purposes, or to legitimize the system rather than particular power relationships. This point of view will be elaborated below, but here it will be appropriate to indicate to what extent true legitimizations occur at this level.

Within the general framework of a well-controlled legislature, elected members who are actually appointed, an irresponsible executive, and the absence of an effective parliamentary party organization, there is still a range of freedom for members of the majlis and the senate. Their freedom is least evidenced in matters of the budget, foreign policy, and military affairs. Moderate freedom is exercised in modifying legislation dealing with taxation and the regulation of commerce. The largest amount of freedom may well exist in the field of administrative reorganization and economic planning. If this judgment can be borne out by closer empirical study, the conclusion emerges that the majlis is the greatest active brake upon rationalization, even as its eventual elimination may be justified by a rationalizing ideology.

In the area of administrative regulation, despite the limitations of law and the hierarchical organization of the service, a degree of independence may be found, especially in regard to the bases of administrative bargaining already noted above. This area of freedom is that which permits the civil servant to resist the importunities or blandishments of the highly placed, to deliver in return for bribes, and to do favors for friends or relatives. Paradoxically enough, one of the widest areas of administrative legitimization rests with the interpretation of law. Since Iran does not recognize judicial review, final interpretation of the law rests with the majlis and the senate. This circumstance militates against the court's overruling an interpretation which has a semblance of plausibility. Minimal plausibility is easy enough to achieve, for the further reason that much discordant legislation exists which has never been brought together and consolidated by either the majlis or the courts. Hence, in fact, it is the legal adviser of a bureau who determines the law.

Like the majlis, the courts are to a large degree controlled by the cabinet, through the minister of justice. The double reorganization of the ministry of justice under Musaddiq, and then after his fall, indicates to what extent judges may be placed under cabinet pressures. Nevertheless, when martial law does not prevail, judges put in charge of any specific case can decide as they deem just or advisable. The judge is vulnerable to victimization, but there are consequences here for the government, too, in the sense that the public will more readily believe that a judge has been penalized for honesty rather than for incompetence. A number of judges have asserted, in private conversation, that they have defied either the minister of justice or the minister of the interior. More important, however, is the acknowledged division between older and younger judges, which leads to the older and superior judges legitimizing traditional interests and the younger ones favoring middle-class interests and rational values. The education of the older judges is usually religious; the younger hold degrees from schools of law of the Western type.

The cabinet issues decrees and licenses on the basis of existing ordinary or constitutional law. These conventional means are entirely dependent upon a restricted pattern of access in which friendship with a minister and prior consultation, are almost essentials. In most cases of distributing pork-barrel benefits, the minister most concerned is nearly free to distribute governmental largesse to the extent granted to his ministry. The cabinet is not usually faced with a number of alternatives, but with a single proposal based upon the minister's preference or the best bargain made. Such decisions, however, do not basically affect power structures, but rather determine which of the principal bargainers is to receive the specific benefit in question.

THE CONSULTATIVE PROCESS

ATTEMPTS TO ALTER either existing legitimizations or structures of power relationships have been called politically functional activity. In both cases, the agent or initiator may be either a person holding authority in the government or not. Activity of this kind, it has been suggested, may be classified in accordance with five general processes in the Iranian system: the consultative process, the lobbying process, the appointments process, the system maintenance process, and the system challenging process. *These processes need not be exhaustive, and further study may reveal the usefulness of further classification.* For analytical purposes, however, they appear to be quite comprehensive and seem to explain the nature of political activity in Iran better than the application of the formal concepts of conventional political processes or than the use of the vaguer notion of a single political process.

Having admitted the possible lack of exhaustiveness in our categories, we are absolved of the requirement of explaining all acts of political relevance; nevertheless, it is our hope here to relate the major patterns of recurrent action to stable processes of systemic significance. The consultative process is primarily concerned with policy making. The lobbying process is concerned with disposition of specific benefits. The appointments process is concerned with the problem of administrative efficiency through the choice of either qualified or loyal personnel. The system maintenance process is mostly concerned with the manipulation of the symbols of legitimacy. The system-challenging process is concerned with responses to governmental action at the implementation level. It is impossible, of course, to reduce political activity to such specific components that all acts can be distributed into one of the five process classes. Beyond the analytical difficulty, informed observation alone suggests that there is a good deal of overlapping. Classification into these processes makes sense only when action is reviewed in its total context and in its development from base value through power structure to end goal.

We start with the consultative process. We have already briefly noted that consultation before the determination of policy legitimizes the position of the consultants. But since this tells us little of the outcome of consultation, all we can conclude is that consultative legitimacy has no dynamic aspect or that it merely legitimizes a procedure through which policy issues may be resolved. In the latter sense, the consultative process becomes the equivalent of the policy-making process or the decision-making process, except that the term we have chosen seems the better to convey the empirical content of the process itself.

The essential point to keep in mind here is that only a highly restricted group is consulted before policy decisions are made. Only a very small group are of such political status that they must be consulted about nearly all policy fields; more often, each individual or group is assumed to be concerned with only one or two phases of policy. It follows, then, that this process is unified only to the degree that all participants hold legitimized positions; otherwise interaction occurs most frequently only among those whose interest in the same area of policy is generally accepted. Individual plans of action, therefore, are set within the relatively simple framework of those branches of the government charged with developing a policy and the persons who might or might not benefit therefrom. In other words, though both the ulama and the military are consulted on a variety of matters, the military will not be consulted about the disposition of income from crown properties in Mashhad, nor will the ulama be consulted about the movement of troops from Khuzistan to Kurdistan. The ulama need only calculate the possible action of members of their own institution, of the representative of the crown at Mashhad, of the administrator of religious properties, and of the governor of the province. Similarly, the military will consider members of their own institution, the leaders of the security organization, the minister of court, and the ambassadors of the central treaty organization or their military advisers in Tehran. Major tension arises when a problem which cuts across these or similar lines of interest occurs, such as the general policy of the government toward the revolutionary Iraqi regime or the allocation of resources as between military and development goals. Where problems which cut across the usual lines of legitimized interest arise, it is possible to work out a hierarchy of influence upon the government. Such an investigation would undoubtedly reveal the primacy of the military, the importance of the landowners and tribal leaders, the specific areas of religious significance, and the equally specific areas of industrial and commercial influence. It might also be pointed out that in nearly all cases, except the purely military, the bureaucracy is consulted at some stage; and thus the way is always open to the intrusion of rationalizing tendencies in an essentially traditional process.

The consultative process, then, is a prime determinant of the tactics of already legitimized political actors. These tactics will be determined by the nature of the issue, as well as by the character of interested parties. An important factor to be considered is that despite its predominantly traditional character, the Iranian political system comprehends a written constitution which official political formula is scrupulously maintained in outward formality. This powerful tendency determines that all issues which cannot be resolved within the framework of existing legislation must pass through phases of consultation with the cabinet, selected members of the bureaucracy, and the relevant majlis committee, as well as a high council where applicable, and nonofficial groups depending upon the nature of the issue. Though legal requirements determine the consultants, the process is decidedly not conventional in nature. Legal requirements may add or detract from the bargaining power of participants, and the process itself is strongly characterized by bargaining at every level. Recent examples of this type are the new labor law, the law establishing an irrigation agency, and the law preventing civil servants from doing business with the government. In the first case employers and representatives of the ILO and the labor division of ICA were all consulted at various stages, though the bill has been worked on since 1952 in the ministry of labor. In the second, the bill was meant to increase the powers of the government, vis-à-vis landlords, in areas where domain lands exist or where development projects are being carried out. After ten years of work within the ministry the bill was finally brought out, and it met with very severe resistance from majlis members. The third case was one wherein the lawyers especially sought to find a loophole for themselves in committee.

Where the matter may be settled by the issuance of a cabinet decree, as in the attempt to expand the jurisdiction of the governor of Tehran to include the city's suburbs, the number of consultants may be far fewer. Members of the majlis were not consulted officially, and it is quite likely that the minister of interior himself approved the move, only because he was placed under great pressure. Nor were the members of local councils consulted. This is perhaps an extreme example belonging more to a description of rationalizing tendencies. The more usual decree might grant someone the right to cut timber on domain lands, but would similarly involve a minimum of consultation.

The establishment of a new bank must receive the approval of the board of bank supervision of Bank Melli, but prospective founders will undoubtedly have sought to win over the cabinet, the higher economic council, and the shah. Other banks will seek to have their views taken into consideration, and so consultation will widen.

In general, high councils are consulted in matters officially assigned to them, and by their very nature they tend to widen consultation. In the high council of labor, employers' views tend to prevail. The higher economic council will usually bring in the Chamber of Commerce. The higher council on education exerts its influence on behalf of the old guard at the university.

On all matters military, many financial issues, and where subversion or disloyalty is a subject of concern, a number of senior army officers are consulted. Many of these men are personal acquaintances of the shah, whether they are of noble descent or risen to power through their association with Reza Shah. This circumstance and the shah's emphasis upon the military, in order to assure his personal security, suggest that these generals may be consulted on many other matters also.

Foreign trade is, to a large extent, managed and supported by a foreign trade agency and a foreign trade bank. On the other hand, in the negotiation of foreign trade agreements the Chamber of Commerce is always consulted. Sometimes preliminary statements of the government's attitude toward, say, a Japanese or Brazilian trade agreement are first made by members of the Chamber and then followed up by the representatives of one or more of the ministries.

In all matters concerning petroleum, the directors of the National Iranian Oil Company are consulted. This may be more due to the need to emphasize that the nationalization of Iranian oil has been effective than to the influence of its leading officials. It would seem, however, that the Oil Company is intrinsically of such extreme importance in Iran that its director-general enjoys a status no less than that of a superior cabinet minister. Oil Company matters, especially those of an internal nature, may never reach the cabinet, or alternatively, if Company policy so directs, consultation may be broadened to include the associations of professional employees, or perhaps those of the distributors of petroleum products.

The consultative position of the religious institution has many of the characteristics of conventional consultation of the legislature. The quasi-official status of the ulama, and the view that all aspects of individual and social life are of religious significance, gives them a general claim to consultation on all issues. This claim is rarely requited in full, is only occasionally the subject of an outright demand, and is usually limited to the Islamic legal aspects of the question. As a consequence of these limitations, consultation with the ulama takes place regularly only on certain matters, and exceptionally as matters of special interest arise and ulama whose access may be institutionalized in regular (weekly?) meetings with high officials are informed thereof.

There seems to be a good deal of evidence that certain leading ulama are regularly consulted on matters of their special interest, such as religious and general education, disposition of awqaf, religious radio broadcasts, the beginning of important holy days, the regulation of pilgrimages, the closing of the bazaar for religious purposes, and the holding of religious ceremonies. A matter of outstanding importance to the ulama, as well as to the government, was the 1959 appointment of a new ambassador to Iraq. For support in this, the prime minister himself traveled to Qumm to see Ayatullah Burujirdi. Nor was this the only occasion during the year in which he visited Qumm. The more usual procedure, however, is for regular contact to be made through the visit by officials to ulama, or through the transmission of messages to officials by the ulama. It is rare, and rather undignified, for a highly regarded alim to wait upon an official of the government.

Consultation of the ulama through the majlis and senate is also regular and may be called institutionalized. There are a number of members of the two houses who were themselves members of the religious institution, and who still maintain excellent relations with the ulama. More important perhaps than these individuals (among whom the speaker of the majlis and the leader of the opposition party are included) is the son of Ayatullah Behbahani, who served as spokesman for religious interests as well as for the bargaining partners of his parent.

Our discussion thus far indicates that the major groups included in the consultative process are the military, the bureaucracy, the ulama, and the tribal leaders and landlords who have been favored with positions in the majlis or senate. Other groups of more restricted interests, like the Chamber of Commerce, Oil Company professionals, or university professors, are less regularly consulted. More interesting, however, may be the list of interests for which there is little or no evidence of participation in this process. Those apparently excluded represent both tradition and nontradition, just as those regularly consulted represent traditional and rationalizing tendencies. Among the excluded, however, the traditionals are of low status, while those of more modern interest orientation usually enjoy high traditional status and also enjoy access in the second capacity.

A good example of the latter involved a few bankers in Tehran. This group has already been discussed above. The point here is simply to stress the fact that this group lacks formal organization and so engages in coöperative action only on rare occasion. While banking, as a distinctive interest, exists at the very least as a result of the hostility of the Bank Melli to private banking enterprise, individual bankers act largely as independent members of the diffusely interested nonbureaucratic elites. The approval and licensing of private banks is a specific benefit conferred on favored supporters of the government. In exploiting a situation which currently favors banking enterprise, no conclusions are drawn about structural changes in the total system which may be conducive to regularizing the role of private banks in a stably developing economy. The latter sort of ideas occur, rather, to the rationalizers, specifically the officials of the plan organization and their foreign advisers.

Bankers are not consulted as bankers, in the making of policy, nor are the owners of large amounts of urban real estate, middle-sized landowners, nor, at the present time, party leaders, and the professional classes. As for low status groups, labor, the guilds, the peasants, bazaar and small business groups, as well as field employees of the ministries, are not consulted in the making of policy. In most cases, the members of local councils are not consulted, but recently Senator Mas'udi, publisher of *Ettla'at*, has opened a periodical forum for these councils and has given their discussions so much publicity that it is quite likely that their expressed views are now being taken into consideration. It may be that this is a maneuver to win support for a future minister of the interior or to embarrass the present minister or various governors. In such a case, this action would normally fall in the positive system-challenging process, but the regularity of the forums and the publicity given their results suggests the possibility that some account is being taken of these views before decisions are made.

Senator Mas'udi's position as a leading press lord has been legitimized by granting him the honor of conducting the shah's monthly press conference. Despite the over-all legitimization of the press through the mass audience granted its publishers every month, it would appear that the group as a whole is not consulted on press policies, nor even on propaganda policies. These two areas of policy appear to be firmly controlled by the security organization and the information undersecretary to the prime minister. With the recent success of Soviet propaganda attacks, the counter-propaganda of the Iranian government has come in for severe criticism in the majlis and elsewhere, indicating the narrowness of the scope of consultation.

In the process of consultation, it is not classes or groups that are consulted, but individuals whom we have classified variously as a matter of convenience. Not only does consultation fall short of including all of the members of a particular group, but the policy decision resulting may benefit only a very few of the group concerned. It is in this regard that the consultative process differs from consultation as a legitimizing technique. The problem for the legitimized bargainer is to gain sufficient information and to apply the proper measures so that his views will be considered at an early stage. From the government's point of view, consultation serves a number of purposes, the most important of which are winning support from the classes and groups who can help in carrying out the policy, and gaining more accurate information than is afforded by the practically nonexistant research facilities of the ministries. From another point of view, consultation can also be too wide. Because any specific determination of policy will directly benefit only a few, wide consultation will give advance information to persons whose prospect of benefit is slight. Given the weakness (and vagueness) of the concept of the general welfare, and the absence of any fixed sequence in the consultative process, these persons can open the issue for general discussion among those not legitimized as consultants. Such tactics would, in effect, transmute the consultative process into one of the other processes, insofar as this issue is concerned. The usual consequence of the interruption of the consultative process by positive system-challenging activity is stalemate, unless extraordinary pressure is brought to bear. Examples of such extraordinary pressure may be unified intervention of the military, as in the budgetary dispute of 1959, insistence by the shah, as in the law preventing government employees from doing business with the government, or pressure by foreign advisers, as in a number of administrative reorganization bills already mentioned.

Another feature of the consultative process that is of systemic significance is the general cleavage between the approaches to policy of the major groups consulted. The four groups mentioned are dominated by two points of view. The military and the bureaucracy, insofar as they may be composed of Western-educated, nonaristocratic elements, tend to prefer rationalizing solutions. The ulama and members of the majlis and senate lean toward traditional answers. Thus, at the present time, the consultative or policy-making process in Iran exemplifies the essential dynamic feature of the system and underscores the root of instability.

The preceding discussion may now permit us to summarize the nature of the consultative process in Iran. The first point to bear in mind is that, in accordance with what might be called the law of political inertia, governments will not grant new legitimizations unless compelled to do so by the emergence of pressing problems. The enterprising civil servant who devises a program in order to achieve notoriety or advancement is rarer in Iran than in Western countries; still, every ministry has a number of ameliorative projects on file which are not brought forward for lack of any urgency in the form of non-governmental pressures. Projects such as the new labor law, the "Where did you get it?" law, the new water agency, and even the plan organization are the result of generalized alienation from the government and so fall within the category of the system-maintenance process. The fact that most legislation is of this type indicates that the government of Iran is engaged in trying to win support without admitting to consultation the very groups whose support is desired. In other words, most legislation originates from the machinery of rationalization, is then passed through a process of consultation in which the small group of consultants are permitted to modify the bill so that it will be least injurious to their interests, and then final formal legitimization is granted. It is only after such formal legitimization takes place that the remaining political processes become significant.

Within this process, information control and willingness to bargain are the two critical operative techniques. The nature of the Iranian political system has determined that legislative projects have built into them elements detrimental to the interests of established high status groups. To protect themselves from the effects of such legislation, it is imperative that members of these groups be informed in advance of the government's intentions. On the other hand, members of the government realize that the effectuation of their program depends on not letting too many people in on it. Some support is necessary, if only to avoid alienating the high status groups, so the decision as to how many and which ones are to be consulted depends upon the estimated price of winning sufficient elite support. Not only must enough of the principal bargainers be consulted, but both sides must be willing to bargain to the extent that the program may be permitted to pass with its integrity relatively intact, whereas interested consultants benefit from exceptions or from specific complementary benefits such as contracts, license limitation, or tipoffs for the purchase of land. Areas in which close empirical study may reveal this sequence are in the distribution of crown and domain lands, the new income taxation proposals of 1959, and the studies of possible import restrictions.

THE LOBBYING PROCESS

IN THE LOBBYING PROCESS we are concerned with the equivalent of pressure-group influence in policy making as found in the United States, in its closest functional approximation. The Iranian term for the essential aspect of this most ancient of all political processes is, paradoxically, "parti." That is the French word which stands for our colloquial "pull," or the continental term "protection." In Iran, at any rate, the use of "parti" is so ubiquitous, and the expectations of all parties are so stable, that it does not dignify the term too much to treat of this political phenomenon as a process.

The use of parti for nearly all purposes, other than for affecting policy making in progress, is general. In essense, parti is the usual resource for individuals rather than groups. It is directed at achieving restricted personal benefits or exceptions from general regulations. It occurs only where policy lines have been laid down and when regulations have been enacted. In a system where both administrative and legislative arbitrariness prevail, and where not all of the ramifications of policy can be canvassed, because of the lack of even elementary statistical data, the exploitation of parti is the usual way in which haphazard hardship may be alleviated and injustice tempered.

The use of parti is also the most acceptable (in terms of traditional values) of the techniques by which adjustments and changes in existing legitimizations may be sought. The reasons for this acceptability are, first, that the person employing parti sacrifices the moral basis of his protest against the policy output of the system; second, success depends upon secrecy; third, the most useful consequences may be expected only when individuals, rather than large numbers, engage in it; fourth, the nature of the technique requires special adaptation of the ruling to the requirement of the "lobbyist"; and finally, the use of the technique accepts the underlying basis of privilege upon which the system is built.

A further aspect of parti worth consideration is the fact that it not only sustains the ideological basis of the traditional system but also supports existing structures of power relationships by working through them. Lobbying by means of parti is not only supplementary to consultation; it is also complementary. The use of parti presupposes existing power relationships, and to be effective it cannot be channelled through those who lack access or through any but the principal bargainers in the system. Lobbyists accept and seek to exploit both bargaining arrangements and traditional deference value patterns. Viewed in this light, it is possible to argue that the process is objectively controlled by the principal bargainers, even when they do not actively encourage petitioners to come to them.

Our discussion of this process will be developed from the point of view of the petitioner, rather than from the organizing concept. The reasons for this approach are: first, that the principal bargainers have already been introduced, and second, that it is unrealistic to assume that these persons voluntarily control the process. Before discussing the alternatives open to petitioners, however, it may be best to present some concrete examples of the purposes that lie behind typical uses of parti.

One of the principal goals of parti is to find appropriate employment. From this general category we shall exclude important government and agency appointments, for these seem specialized enough to require treatment as a distinct process. In Iran, as in other underdeveloped countries, government employment is highly esteemed, even at the lowest levels such as office boy and janitor positions. Government is also the major employer of Western-educated young men. But the civil service is greatly overstaffed, and most recruitment has officially ceased. And so parti is used to find or create exceptions to the rule forbidding the hiring of new civil servants.

Parti may also be used to win favors from civil servants whose task it is to administer special programs. The specific goal may be the right to purchase public land, the paving of access roads, the granting of concessions to supply electricity, the granting of scholarships for foreign study, the transferring of subordinate officials from post to post, the more rapid processing of goods in customs, the granting of special marketing facilities, and the granting of permission to erect kiosks on the sidewalks.

Another objective for which parti may be used is in the

seeking of licenses. In the previous instances, there need be no assumption that such favors will be granted to anyone. In issuing licenses or permits, there does exist the assumption that a restricted number will be granted, and the procedure therefore involves an element of competition. The use of parti accompanied by higher level tie-ins has led to the increase of the number of taxi licenses issued. Parti was also an important element in the distribution of permits to buy agricultural machinery on easy credit terms. Business and building permits are similarly affected, but hawkers must depend on special relations with the policeman on the beat. Permits to publish newspapers and long-term loans for industrial purposes may also be included here.

A further goal of the use of parti is to win exceptions to established rules. Objectives of this kind differ from the others in the sense that exceptions are contrary to the rules and call for special justification and interpretation of the rules, or require that someone bear the responsibility. Instances of this sort crop up most often in the employment of individuals as technical experts on contract when they lack qualifications, in the granting of licenses to persons who do not fulfill the requirements of the law, in making low assessments of income taxes due the government, or in failing to maintain adequate inspection and adherence to labor and social insurance laws.

It may be argued with much justification that similar techniques aimed at similar goals are prevalent in more modern political systems, especially at the local government level. The important difference to be taken into consideration in Iran is that the use of parti is traditionally functional. Furthermore, it might be argued that parti may be classified as "counter-mores" only from the point of view of the constitutional façade of Iran, and not when seen as an aspect of traditionally institutionalized value patterns. Finally, it may be noted that there is no other means open to individuals for pressing the difficulties of their special circumstances upon the government. Neither the courts nor majlis questions may be very effective in such an area. Above all, this technique is more efficient, more favorably regarded by government, and more often successful than group or individual action of the positive system-challenging type.

The individual seeking to win one of the benefits described above will act on the basis of the connections available to him, and will use those persons upon whom he has the largest claim. Only if his contacts are poor will he try to work through friends-of-friends or interest-group leaders. His resources are also limited by his social position, in the sense that it is possible for a person of some standing to go directly to certain officials, but a worker or clerk or shopkeeper will have no such access. Within this general framework, a number of approaches may be decided upon, depending upon the specific benefit sought and the resources of the petitioner.

The first channel of lobbying is through relatives. These are the easiest to exploit, and the obligations of relatives are nearly unlimited. Families may be strained by great tensions, especially among brothers, but appeals for help that will tend to strengthen the family's position as a whole, and possibly afford a wider use of parti to all, may not be denied. The family also includes many of what we should consider distant relatives, so it is often possible for middle-class families to find one of themselves with the necessary connections. On the other hand, it is rare that any family has so many well-placed members that they need not rely on and respect the bargaining arrangements of the few who hold influential positions. Not a little of the penchant for political and administrative rationalization stems from the desire of educated civil servants to be rid of these pressures. The judicious choice of mates for the young is, however, an important aspect of the process.

A second important basis of parti is the peer group or clique. These are groups of men who are about the same age, and who started at about the same station in life. Migration from the same town to Tehran, or attendance at the same school, sometimes even employment in the same organization, is the key factor in the formation of such a group. Once it gets started, it is tied further by the exchange of confidences and mutual favors. These friendships seem to be extremely important to the Iranian, even though the general pattern of values internalized runs counter to fully trusting any but members of the family. This is a conflict that often leads to severe disappointment when members of the peer group will not run risks, and contributes to the general feeling that no one can be trusted.

Approaches through family or close friends are open to all, and the key to the effective employment of parti is to work through these contacts to persons in authoritative positions. Once one moves beyond these contacts, however, bargaining becomes extremely important, which is to say that anyone may initiate a petition, but the ball must be carried by those of higher status, when the play gets close to the payoff. Consequently, the problems are fewer for persons of local importance, such as provincial landowners, middle-level ulama, wealthy merchants, or higher civil servants. Those who have some bargaining power in their own right can more frequently and usefully engage in lobbying.

One of the usual means of access for provincial dignitaries is through the local majlis representative. The majlis representative is usually responsive to such appeals, because his appointment depends not only on his wealth, fame, and loyalty, but also upon the degree to which other persons of status support him. Local protests, as we have seen, can lead to the substitution of another dignitary in the seat set aside for the town in question. This channel is usually not open to government officials posted to the provincial town, and will not be used against the interests of the locally influential. Majlis representatives are expected to be responsive to local appeals, and in one case, a disappointed constituent bought an ad in a small newspaper in which he complained of receiving no help from his city's representative.

Appeals through the religious institution are open to a much wider segment of the population, although it would seem that the effectiveness of this means has waned somewhat. Some observers indicate that even the petitions of peasants might be profitably forwarded by ulama and redress of grievances thus won. The humane role of the ulama fits in with their duties of managing the distribution of alms to the poor, and thus tends toward the mitigation of the worst abuses of the system. It is, however, questionable to assign any systemic significance to this sort of intercession. In any case, it seems more relevant at this point to stress their diffuse role as a high prestige class in the traditional social system, and as such they are an important channel for contacting government officials. The lines of communication up and down the religious hierarchy are good, and access by at least certain ulama at the various levels of government is excellent. Moreover, the ulama are very responsive to appeals of this kind. Any use of the religious hierarchy for "secular" goals tends to strengthen the total position of the institution, at a time when it is under severe attack from some quarters and when parts of the institution are subject to governmental manipulation. It need not be stressed, of course, that the ulama do not recognize any distinction between religious and secular affairs, and that they view with grave suspicion attempts to restrict the scope of their influence. The ulama also tend to disrespect the expediential legislation of the majlis, and they prefer to determine the distribution of benefits on the basis of the piety of the petitioner. Piety, all too often, is related to general support of the ulama, financial and otherwise, so that the element of bargaining is not absent here, either.

Government officials may also be approached through legitimized group leaders. In this event the group leaders need not be among the principal bargainers, but must merely give regular support to either high officials, cabinet ministers, or majlis members. The principals who may be petitioning here are usually of low status or else they might use some more effective means. As we have already indicated, the organized group more nearly represents the strength of the leader rather than his obligations, because of the all-important factor of government recognition. The more independent a leader is in his control of his group, the more effective is his intervention on behalf of his followers. To this generalization we might also add that the more the use of parti becomes contrary to the ethics of the group, the more is its use rewarded. Thus, the leader of the teachers' organization is more regularly successful than is the leader of the high council of guilds. Both rules apply under these circumstances.

Another instrumentality of parti is the leadership of the recognized parties. As noted, when in power the Melliyun Party leadership tends to use its great influence sparingly, restricting it to strengthening those who already enjoy a high degree of access. The Mardum Party is less selective about the people for whom it will intercede, but it tends to prefer individual to group petitions. The leaders of both parties are accessible, though the official capacity of the Melliyun leaders renders them harder to catch and more circumspect about their immediate responses. It is also clear that the greater effectiveness of the Melliyun leadership lends premium value to secretiveness, else all members of the party might demand equal treatment. It might also be added here as an aside that even in presumably democratic parties the usual social amenities are observed. The reference is not only to the profuse compliments which hedge conversations with obscure circumlocutions, but also the requirement that those of low status stand head bowed and hands clasped when facing social superiors. Under such circumstances, the party leader need answer only to the extent he deems desirable, and should he feel it unwise to pursue the matter, the low-status petitioner can only gnash his teeth in bitterness and swallow his disappointment. Without real bargaining power, he cannot compel support, and where he may get support from the Mardum Party, it may prove ineffective. This line of approach, therefore, is not the most effective.

For those who have some status, there are a variety of other methods which present themselves to the more enterprising. Cabinet ministers are available for conversations on such matters. The wise petitioner will try to follow up a written application with a visit to the highest available official, preferably the minister. Since so many routine matters are referred to the very top, and since so many petitions require responsible signatures which few underlings are willing to give, access to the minister is extremely important. It is possible to get to see the minister and give him the facts of the case, but it is better to send someone who knows the minister well.

Another possibility, though more applicable to the redress of grievances, is by application through one of the control and inspection bodies. The shah's inspection organization, the prime minister's inspection organization, the ministerial inspectorates, the treasury audit section, and the like are appropriate bodies. Such appeals are more often to be seen as pressure brought to bear after a refusal, but their effectiveness depends upon winning the support of inspection officials through *parti*.

Audiences with the shah, arranged through courtiers or high officials, may be another means of successful petitioning. The shah's broad powers and his need for support render him vulnerable to individual appeals. He seems, also, to share the despotic tendency to affirm his humanitarian ideals by individual acts of kindness, rather than through more impersonal programs alone. The problem is how to get to see the shah, and for this *parti* is necessary.

Persons with official positions or who are associated in some way with industrial, commercial, or even charitable or educational institutions may invite high officials to participate in ceremonies like laying the corner stones for a building, inaugurating an orphanage, cutting a ribbon to open a new hotel, or dining in a ministry restaurant. Such participation carries with it many possibilities, for it permits the high official or politician to stand before the public as a person whose presence is thought to lend importance to the ceremonies. So many people feel that ministerial and high administrative posts are granted for reasons other than merit that such unofficial honors are highly regarded. Besides, the sort of prestige which such participation lends stands high among the traditional values to which many of these officials adhere. It can be expected that the official who participates in the ceremony will continue to favor at least the institution or enterprise, if not its founder as well.

We have already seen where participation in welcoming committees or the presentation of welcoming addresses may be a source of legitimization, but such events are also excellent opportunities for making substantive requests of the travelling officials or ministers. In the absence of such visits, or indeed, visits by the shah, local dignitaries must work through either the governor or military commander of the district. These individuals are primarily charged with maintaining peace and orderly government in their areas. Even though they may command the force necessary to suppress local disturbances, their careers, especially a career such as that of the governor, are not enhanced by resorting to force. Consequently, the role of the governor, and to some extent the role of the less accessible military commander, is a conciliatory and accommodative one. Here, too, we find that successful parti is tied in with effective bargaining.

We turn now from these channels of lobbying to some interesting technical aspects of the process which are frequently in evidence. The first and probably most overrated of these is the use of bribery. Obviously this is an illegal method of exerting influence, and the principals involved will try to conceal the use of bribes. On the other hand, widespread opinion holds that the giving of bribes is ubiquitous, indeed the major means of expediting the machinery of government. Loose observation would tend to confirm that bribery is endemic at the lowest levels of government, and in some cases is even institutionalized. Door men, receptionists, low grade clerks, archivists, and even menials expect and accept bribes. Bribery is also the usual means of expediting goods through customs and of carrying on any business whatsoever with the generally despised police. There are always stories of bribery on a large scale which leave no one untouched, but there seems to be good reason to doubt many of these. Certainly not all political bargains are cash sales. On the other hand, the petitioner must know when and where a bribe is expected, and wherever the benefit derived is in fact a lucrative opportunity it would seem that a number of parties must be cut in on the deal.

Between the level of petty bribery and major graft there is an area where parti is best won by the promise of mutual favor doing. The return favor need not be made explicit, for a man's position reveals his potentialities for helping those who help him. This is an area in which great sacrifices or great risks are not involved, so that little is lost if both sides of the bargain are not upheld. But the possibility of frequent recurrence of the need for this type of favor renders it foolish not to uphold the bargain. The substance of the bargain may be no more than expediting a payment order in return for, say, a doctor's certificate of either good or ill health.

A technique of indifferent effectiveness is that of visiting some potential patron at his home, during his Friday morning reception. Most such dignitaries measure their own status by the number of persons attending them, and would encourage as many as possible to come. Visits at Now-Ruz have much the same value. On the other hand, the benefit is small enough so that the request may not be fulfilled if it is difficult, or if it comes from a person of little status.

Many times the response of the person appealed to is simply the writing of a letter to the official to be approached. In this procedure there is a certain subtlety to be observed, especially when ulama are approached, for they may respond with a note of introduction. One of the reasons for this response emerges from the prejudice that it is undignified for an alim to wait upon an official. The letter itself, however, may convey the actual extent to which the writer lends his support to the petitioner. The alim rarely refuses the request for intervening, but if he is not sincere, the burden of giving a negative answer rests with the official. On the other hand, if the alim is quite seriously concerned, he may write a strong letter or, better still, send the letter with his son.

In every attempt to use parti, the petitioner must exercise some degree of caution. He must choose to work toward a person who can really help, and he must exploit the best possibility. It is generally risky to use several persons connected with the same office or administrative function. If the petition gets caught up between two rivals, chances are that the cause will not prosper. It is furthermore always dangerous to go over the head of the official who should grant the petition. While his superiors may hand down orders, he is the better judge of how anxious they are to grant this favor. He is also a past master at evading orders from above or at granting requests in such a way as to render the result useless.

A variation of going over the heads of officials is the attempt to use foreign advisers for parti. While most technical assistance experts try to avoid such involvement, they do engage in pressing reform or reorganization projects upon the administration. The Iranian officials thus pressed are never entirely sure of the consequences of refusing to accede to these pressures, and usually they procrastinate rather than refuse to accept the experts' pro-

posal. Since there is perhaps some vague sanction in the withdrawal of aid or in complaint to one's superior, the Iranian official
is in an uncomfortable position. The relationship is a complex
one, but in general the Iranian soon comes to resent the source
of pressure upon himself. To use this source for parti seems,
then, to be generally unwise. At best compliance will be delayed
and complicated, at worst rejection of the petition will become a
much desired goal of the official.

THE APPOINTMENTS PROCESS

THE DISTRIBUTION OF OFFICES of authority is one of the subjects
of political conflict in all systems. Despite the wide diffusion
and general acceptance of theories of neutral or anonymous
bureaucracies and of professional or "disinterested" representation, it is generally assumed that the method of distributing such
positions is of political significance. Such significance arises from
the fact that these positions are desired for their remuneration,
for the prestige which they confer, for their instrumental value
in winning other benefits from the system, and for the legitimizations which they tend to fix.

Theories of governmental anonymity aside, in Iran and elsewhere, it is well understood that interests may be represented by
any official, regardless of whether he is formally elected or is
appointed. Even where merit systems have had a history of success,
study of the "group process" in politics has revealed the ways in
which interest groups can influence a bureaucratic group or how
an entire bureau may develop interests complementary to those
of a pressure group. In a predominantly traditional system, however, the consequences of these tendencies are even more important. To understand this importance let us consider the following circumstances in Iran: (1) the stability and impermeability
of most structures of power relationships; (2) the importance of
the technique of bargaining; (3) the difficulty of achieving administrative coördination; and (4) the important role of the
bureaucracy in the formation of policy. If we consider further
the importance in Iran of consultation and the institutionalization
of access in legitimizing techniques, we have then canvassed all
of the major elements that render the making of appointments
to the civil service, government agencies and banks, the army,
the legislature, the cabinet and city councils, and quasi-official
religious posts a central political process in the Iranian system.

These positions, to be elaborated on below, carry with them rewards of varying diffuseness, ranging from job security and a salary affording a middle-class standard of living, all the way to opportunities for gaining great wealth or of influencing major policies in a decisive way. Consequently, such positions are in themselves goals of political action, the bases of bargains, and values to be conserved. Viewed in another light, it is ultimately the interaction of persons in these capacities that will determine legitimizations. Few persons without positions of this kind are included in the consultations of the court and the cabinet. The most successful uses of *parti* will be through these persons.

Such positions represent legitimizations, and the method of appointment thereto may be understood as a distinctive political process in two senses. The first and most obvious of these is the distribution of the jobs themselves, as political values. The second, which is of far greater systemic importance, is in the making and implementation of a coherent policy. The goal of the participants in this process is either to win jobs, to reward supporters, and to gain bargaining leverage, or to establish in key positions persons who hold favored views, who are willing to bargain, or who are bound to the participant by some traditional tie.

In a traditional system, policies are rarely separated from personalities, and the making of coherent policy may not be distinguishable from the perpetuation of a high official in office. The term of such officials is insecure; therefore much of their time is spent in protecting their positions. The most effective means of accomplishing this end is by seeing to it that no hostile person or member of a rival structure of power relationships is in a position to create embarrassment.

In this, as in other processes, there is a good deal of tension between existing traditional tendencies and rationalizing aspirations. The connection between persons and policies is not exclusive to tradition, but it is certainly more pronounced here than in other systems. Furthermore it is almost impossible for individual officials or important political figures to continue effective in their political roles without surrounding themselves with loyal supporters. The tendency to people the political universe with real persons, rather than with anonymous functionaries, is perhaps more realistic than the reverse, but it runs contrary to the aspiration for a neutral bureaucracy, merit appointments, and a mechanical administration acting on the basis of impartial or universal rules. Iran, however, is not closed off from these ideas, and those more modern aspirations lead to the condemnation of traditional practices such as nepotism, empire building, or bargaining.

Despite the existence of this tension, tradition still holds sway in this area. Consequently, it would seem to be most useful to look upon the holders of influential positions as constellations of coöperating actors. These constellations are held together by more than random bargaining and kinship relations. They are the result of conscious effort, and they reflect the major expenditure of political energy in the system.

We have already had occasion to examine the cabinet closely, and we have noted some characteristics of the appointment of ministers. The shah is interested in rendering the key officials in the cabinet responsible to himself. The prime minister, war minister, and foreign minister are not subordinated to one another, as the interior minister also was not, until the ministry of Dr. Eghbal. Even Dr. Eghbal attempted to subordinate all the rest to himself. He also tried to win over the plan organization and a number of agencies and banks. The legislature has little or no influence over who is to become a cabinet minister. There was a good deal of tension between Dr. Eghbal and the minister of court, so it is unlikely that the latter exerted much influence either. The highest of the military still wield much persuasive power with the shah, in all fields, but it is unlikely that such influence is exerted except in the case of the minister of war.

Membership in high councils and in control and inspection boards is in some measure predetermined by the other offices these persons may hold. This is especially true of the higher economic council and the high council on education. Both of these councils are difficult to manipulate for that reason, to the distress of the prime minister and the minister of education, respectively. The high councils on labor and on health are more dependent upon the ministers who participate in their appointment; but when the minister is changed, his successor may be saddled with a recalcitrant council. To a much larger degree, the inspection organizations of the shah and the prime minister are controlled by each of them. The majlis-appointed board of supervisors of the plan organization can be an extremely troublesome body, but until his dismissal, Mr. Ebtehaj was fairly successful in seeing to the appointment of persons who were quite content to collect their handsome salaries without interfering in the organization. Some members of the majlis tried continuously to discredit the former plan organization chief, but only one of the board members was foolish enough to stick his neck out, and he was dismissed.

Positions as governors of government banks, state company directors, or agency chiefs appear to be used primarily as political rewards. In each category there seems to stand out at least one exception, in the sense that the enterprise concerned is so important that incompetence cannot be tolerated, despite tremendous political pressures. These exceptions are the governor of Bank Melli, the director-general of the National Iranian Oil Company, and the director of the Social Insurance Agency. The first two have emerged, in recent years, as both independent and influential consultants. The third, representing a critical area of system-maintenance activity, has been characterized by frequent changes indicating the conflicting pressures of royal prudence and aristocratic greediness. The shah's interest here is too small to overcome the large problems of implementing a scheme at present too advanced for Iran to bear. On the other hand, the Oil Company and Bank Melli are of such significance that the shah is personally involved in their appointments.

The appointments of members of the majlis and senate are prepared by the prime minister within the framework already discussed above; however, these nominations are subjected to careful scrutiny by the shah, and not infrequently the right of veto is exercised. There are some indications that senatorial appointments originate in the ministry of court, rather than with the prime minister. In any case, it is clear that the legislature, like the cabinet, is kept fragmented and representative of diverse structures of power relationships by the shah. The majlis is not an independently manipulated constellation of coöperating persons, just as it is not controlled by its party groups.

City councils are presumably elected, but there seems to be little doubt that these elections are manipulated. The election of city councils is a new and experimental affair in Iran.[1] The goal is to try to encourage popular participation at fairly safe levels, and with regard to welfare and service issues rather than ideological or constitutional matters. The councils do not yet replace the governor, but it is hoped that they may as their competence is demonstrated. Much of the pressure in this direction comes from the ICA program, but it still has not overcome prejudices against decentralization in Iran. The success of the program

---

[1] All city councils have been abolished, according to a recent report. The change is directly related to a change of ministers of the interior.

depends upon the council members commanding respect in their cities, acting in a responsible way on the matters placed before them, but not on other matters, and upon their learning to take the initiative under an elected mayor, in matters of local planning and development. When we consider that tradition is still firmly entrenched in provincial cities (the plan has not yet been extended to Tehran), it follows that persons commanding respect are those who control traditional deference values. Sticking to the business placed before such councils, rather than trying to win wider notoriety or to play to the educated gallery, can only be assured if there is an element of dependence on the farmandar (city governor). And learning to take initiative depends on the growth of a still embryonic civic pride. For the time being, at any rate, the councils are training grounds for hand-picked local dignitaries, with the lines of control running directly to the minister of the interior.

Appointments to the civil service involve the most varied array of positions, of extremely diverse significance. Most of these jobs have a primary significance as rewards, though some are not regarded as very attractive rewards. The less attractive positions are those which are, in general, filled in connection with rationalizing goals, and their incumbents tend to feel under-rewarded and hence may engage in system challenging behavior. Efforts to build a coördinated administrative machine do not extend to these positions, even though school teachers, as one example, are of crucial importance in the political socialization of middle-class urban youth.

As we have already noted, the regular civil service of Iran is no longer open to new recruits. The bold step of admitting great overstaffing and closing off the major source of employment for the Western educated, may be administratively sound, but it is politically risky. Happily, the present period is one of economic expansion and relative opportunity; nevertheless there are many over-qualified young men who are compelled to accept the less highly regarded government positions that are open to them. The major exceptions to the rule of no recruiting are teachers and subordinate judges. Even these two classes of positions require that the new recruit spend five or more years in the provinces before standing a chance for employment in Tehran. The supply of candidates for such positions falls short of the demand, first because the number of qualified law graduates is small, and second because teaching is held in low esteem, when compared with other government positions or positions with private companies. Law graduates have tended to prefer to practice, rather than to serve as judges, but the recently increased difficulty of admission to the Bar Association may change matters somewhat. Teachers, too, have until recently been recruited on the basis of the expectation that they might transfer without loss of seniority to other branches of the government service, but this loophole has now been closed.

Contract hiring as experts or specialists has continued until there is now a huge number of these persons. A small number of contract personnel enjoy salary and conditions superior to what they might earn as civil servants, but most have smaller allowances and lack guarantees of tenure or seniority benefits. Consequently, most contract personnel clamor for regularization of their status. The merging of contract personnel with the regular service has taken place a number of times. Obviously, these positions are often filled as rewards or nepotistic benefits. Usually the contracting employee is not fully satisfied, but it appears to be rare that contract employees are dismissed, even though their "parti" may fail them or their superiors be changed.

A special category of exceptions are certain classes of foreign ministry personnel, including translators and legal experts and certain others. These may be hired on regular terms. However, it seems that the control of recruitment here, and its restriction to members of influential landed families, is quite strong.

Salary increases in the civil service are accorded with automatic regularity, with little attention paid to merit. Advance in position and responsibility is, however, quite another matter. At the level of the appointment of the director of the legal, financial, personnel or line divisions, the heads of field offices, shahrdars, farmandars, and ostandars, directors-general, and undersecretaries, the politically functional aspect of this process becomes most apparent. Each of these positions represents a key bargaining power, so that such appointments form the basis of both efficient policy making and coördinated implementation. For the most part, the minister himself is the prime mover, and it is generally felt to be quite just that he puts undesirable bureau chiefs and the like on the *disponible* list and raises others of his own liking. The minister's choice is nevertheless limited by the number of positions that may be filled by non-civil servants, by the existing employees of the ministry, and by the pressures that may be brought to bear upon him by the court, his cabinet colleagues, or members of the legislature.

University professors are also civil servants, but though the law does not prevent additions to their number, there have been no appointments to full professorships in recent years. Appointments at the daneshyar (assistant or associate professor) level are made from time to time, on the basis of an extremely searching procedure which includes a written examination, an oral examination, and a trial lecture. Notions of curricula are fairly conservative, and the existing body of professors tend to be highly self-protective. Whatever hiring does take place is carefully hedged by additional political precautions.

University professors, especially those from the faculties of law and letters became politically prominent after the abdication of Reza Shah, and especially during the Musaddiq period. The political activity of the university students was an additional factor tending to identify the faculty with political radicalism. Since Musaddiq's fall, efforts have been made to exclude the students from all political activity, and only those professors who stanchly support the government have become newly active politically. Only one professor was dismissed, so that the prestige of the group has been maintained. When candidates for jobs are considered, their political respectability and family affiliations are carefully considered. A further recruitment problem arises from the high prestige of university positions and the demand for nominal or part-time appointments by prominent political and official figures. All too often, this demand is acceded to, with the result that some of the younger men are hired on a part-time basis only. A change in recruiting regulations is now under consideration.

The ulama have only a semi-official status arising out of tradition and the establishment of Shiite Islam. In addition, there are a number of fields in which government officials, sometimes the shah himself, have the power to appoint ulama. The recruitment to leadership of the religious institution itself is largely an autonomous process and an internal one, though it is legitimized in great measure by partial recognition by the government. This recognition is partial, in the sense that the government may also recognize persons associated with and graduated from the university's faculty of theology.

Government appointments of ulama to official, paid positions are essentially rewards for past or expected future coöperation. Such coöperation is usually not made explicit, but acceptance of a government appointment is itself considered an act of recognition of the government by the ulama. The only twilight position in which the degree of the alim's commitment to the government is in doubt is that of mutavali or trustee of a mortmain property willed, under religious law, for some charitable or educational purpose. The trustee may or may not be indicated in the will, but if he is the government may not interfere. Where he is not, the government will appoint a trustee. The trustee usually receives ten per cent of the income of the mortmain, which can amount to very substantial sums. The ulama usually hold that it is their duty to manage these awqaf, and that they should also be in charge of distributing the surpluses. Consequently, the ulama do not feel selfconscious about accepting financial support from these sources. When the trustee is not named, however, the government intervenes and names a trustee, usually from among the ulama. The most lucrative of these awqaf are always the subject of political pressures from those who would rent them at nominal fees and reap huge profits therefrom (just as government lands may be rented). Such arrangements fit into our system maintenance process, but the alim-trustee is the indispensible middle man here. Bargaining is the usual method of working out a three-way deal, and the alim quite naturally becomes associated with both the government and the person who leases the land or buildings.

A far smaller number of persons are associated with the ministry of justice as religious judges. Their tasks are essentially to examine marriage documents to ensure their legality, and they thus have little political significance. Nevertheless, their association with the government puts them apart from the nonassociated body of ulama, helps to legitimize the government, but reduces their influence among the ulama.

The Imam Jum'eh, or Imam of the Friday Mosque, in Tehran and in a few other places, is appointed by the government. The only important official of this kind is the one in Tehran, who also performs the necessary religious services for the royal family. The present incumbent is also a university professor and has travelled and studied in Europe. The rewards of this position in wealth and prestige are very great. The prestige of the Imam Jum'eh is limited to the more or less governmentally associated ulama of which he is the closest. His personal tie with the shah is very close, and he was one of the very few who stood by the shah even on the day he fled from Iran, in August, 1953.

The notary public offices in Iran are usually run by ulama or ex-ulama, and are one of the important sources of revenue for them. In former times, these public registry offices were run by enterprising ulama as a private service, for which there was no governmental equivalent. The basis of uniformity and authenticity of these records was Islamic law and not statute law. Now, the number of such offices is limited, their proprietors are licensed, and their operations regulated by statute law. Under Reza Shah they were secularized, but still maintained by ulama, who doffed their religious garb. At the present time, the registry offices are run by the same kind of people, and their establishment and licensing represents a special form of indirect reward to the religious institution, especially outside Tehran.

Appointments in the army are of considerable importance in Iranian politics, but this area is one in which it is difficult to get accurate information. It is clear that certain of the highest military officers have a significant and, in some areas, decisive influence on policy. On the other hand, there has been a marked tendency to create generals as a means of maintaining or rewarding the loyalty of influential officers. The chief of staff and the active general staff and heads of line units are probably the most influential. The military commanders of the various provinces are critical appointments, too, in the sense that they are often in competition with the ostandar and are charged with maintaining security against both urban uprising and tribal disorder.

At the present time, it appears that the most significant patterns of integrating the officials we have discussed are through calculated ministerial action or that of the minister's immediate subordinates. The thoroughness with which a minister will pursue this goal is generally limited by the security of his position, and depends upon whether he was appointed directly by the shah or by the prime minister. The minister's goals may be predominantly traditional or rational, but, even as in the outstanding case of Mr. Ebtehaj's attempt to rationalize the appointment of the plan organization's personnel, his efforts will fail of complete realization and be eventually defeated by the minister or bureau chief's removal. More stable, if less comprehensive, integration occurs in the few cases of large influential families whose members hold positions in the higher civil service, the army, the majlis or senate and at times in the cabinet. The few families having such traditionally significant, diffuse influence are those who best exploit the appointments process in Iran.

THE SYSTEM-MAINTENANCE PROCESS: THE USE OF CONVENTIONAL SYMBOLS

To THIS POINT we have discussed functionally political activity merely as though it existed in a non-selfconscious system. The major foci of this discussion have been the distribution of rewards and the making of policy. While some of the tensions between traditional and rational goals and instrumentalities have been noted, we have juxtaposed rational instrumentalities and traditional processes, but we cannot similarly present rational processes in contrast to the traditional structures of power relationships elaborated above. To the extent that hierarchical practices are pursued, they are rooted in tradition or else incomplete and discontinuous.

The transitional polity, however, is essentially one in which legitimacy confusions exist and in which the conflicting tendencies of the diverse components of the system lead to selfconsciousness. Under these conditions, the actual performance of institutions is constantly under examination and subject to criticism. The different conclusions reached by active participants leads to additional forms of political activity intimately related to the problem of system legitimacy. The two major processes into which this activity may be divided are the system-maintenance process and the system-challenging process.

The system-maintenance process is primarily composed of symbol-manipulative techniques which, in Iran, fall rather naturally into two categories. The first category is that of simulated conventional techniques that, since the revolution of 1906, have become an intrinsic part of Iranian political life. The second is the use of traditional symbols, either to exploit a residual emotional attachment to the monarchy or Islam, to appeal most effectively to the non-Westernized, or to enhance the persuasiveness of traditional symbols by associating them with the national culture or some national peculiarity.

We shall turn first to simulated conventional techniques and the system-maintenance process. It is easy to put aside the whole paraphernalia of conventional institutions as a meaningless façade, asserting that they are nonfunctional in the Iranian political system. This procedure begs the question of why so much effort is currently being put into the maintenance of this façade; and whether the game is worth the candle. One of the answers to this question has already been suggested above, where it has been pointed out that the shah can trust neither the major exponents of tradition nor those of rationalization, so he doggedly maintains the similitude of conventional legitimacy. Another answer lies in the fact that, despite the strengthening of the throne under the Pahlavi dynasty (except for the period 1941–1953), these institutions were already in existence from 1907 to 1928, and could not be eliminated without weakening the shaky legitimacy of the new dynasty. It was, of course, the majlis which invested Reza Shah and formally conferred the crown. The majlis, moreover, was al-most a monopoly of the traditionally influential, and its abolition would have alienated not only Qajars, but all of the landed aris-tocracy. The continuation of conventional institutions has afforded a wider latitude to the Pahlavi dynasty by offering a legitimate basis for the association of the landed aristocracy with the new rationally-inclined dynasty. It has thus developed that the tradi-tional classes have a vested interest in the maintenance of conven-tional institutions, while these same institutions may be used as restraints upon rationalization by the military, the bureaucracy, and the noncommunist intelligentsia in general.

The amount of effort put into simulated conventional tech-niques, and their wide array, suggests the serious commitment of the government thereto. In most instances, the kinds of activity which may be classified under the system-maintenance process have already been mentioned in other contexts. Nevertheless it may be useful to regather these dispersed references in order to illustrate our point.

The formation of political parties is an outstanding example of a simulated conventional technique with system maintenance as its goal. Under Reza Shah, no parties existed, but their forma-tion was encouraged after the abdication. Party agitation during and after the war established the principle that a parliament could not function democratically without parties, so that after Musad-diq's fall and despite his own unwillingness to form a party, there were legitimizing benefits to be gained from establishing parties. In 1957 it was announced that parties would be licensed for po-litical activity, and later it was explained that the need for political stability required that a two-party system be created. It was hoped that the two parties would channel some of the energy demon-strated under Musaddiq into "constructive" channels, but both parties would be unequivocally loyal to the existing constitutional framework and to the dynasty. As it has since developed, the parties do not control the cabinet, they do not organize the majlis, they have not penetrated deeply among the electorate. In both cases, the party leaders were designated by the shah, and they will both be removed by the shah.

An important technique, now partly subordinated to the parties, is that of holding popular demonstrations. These developed as an especially important technique after 1945, and until August, 1953. During this period new radical parties and leaders drew the masses into political activity, by these means, and the court countered by organizing favorable demonstrations of its own. The

Tudeh Party was particularly adept at this technique and used it in attempts to coerce or intimidate the majlis. The culmination of this development occurred during Musaddiq's premiership, when he was able to play upon the crowd's emotion and when the court took countermeasures to assert its own popularity. The 30th of Tir, the 9th of Esfand, and the 25th and 28th of Mordad are all examples of decisive political action by means of organized street demonstrations.

Some four months after Musaddiq's fall, on the shah's birthday, the government organized a demonstration of loyalty to the dynasty. The principal participants were the members of the Sumka Party and some peasants brought in from the Gilan-Azerbaijan area. Since that time, demonstrations have been held regularly on the shah's birthday, the 9th of Esfand, the 28th of Mordad and on 15th Aban, the anniversary of the shah's narrow escape from death by an assassin's bullet. Other demonstrations may be held from time to time, to protest Soviet propaganda or welcome the shah on his return from some trip.

The size of a demonstration depends upon the amount of effort put into it by the government and the parties, and upon the general knowledge that the demonstration is called into being by the government. A less decisive factor is the residual fear of any popular demonstration and the nervousness of the police. This nervousness may be genuine, or it may be used as reinsurance against a very small turnout, as when the shah announced that he did not want a mass welcome because of the heat. The police then announced that people might gather to welcome the shah only in certain areas, though the parties and some guilds had announced that all groups would assemble to greet the shah on his return from a European trip.

The parties are important in organizing demonstrations. Both groups of leaders have many contacts among guild, hawker, and labor leaders. These are given instructions, often by telephone, as to where and when to gather their men. The police see to it that the bazaar and all stores are closed. Government employees are either let off for the day or dismissed early, and school children may either be dismissed or organized at their schools for participation. If the parties are anxious to have a good showing they will hire busses and trucks to carry demonstrators from the slum districts to the points of assembly. If less anxious, they may ask guild and other groups to supply their own transportation. If the government is very anxious, they may commandeer the equipment of the Tehran bus authority and throw in some army busses as well. Sound trucks have been used by the Melliyun Party to whip up spirit and gather crowds. These demonstrations are frequently pointed to as the equivalent of democratic support of the government.

The parties were to add an element of sophistication to the use of the electoral technique, to establish the legitimacy of the majlis. In the past, however, it is generally acknowledged that the victor in each constituency was determined by the government, and the results of the preëlection decision were communicated to the farmandar or provincial commander of the armed forces for implementation. The major exceptions to this rule were the elections to the twelve majlis seats for Tehran, and the winners often took pride in asserting that they were the only democratically elected members. In some cases, stories are told of gross manipulation and ballot box stuffing in Tehran; and we have before us the example of Dr. Bagha'i's Committee for the Defense of Free Elections, the predecessor of his Toilers Party.

Elections are theoretically accepted and at least equated with a theoretical good, although taken in different ways by the Westernized and the uneducated in Iran. The Westernized tend to hold that this democratic practice is corrupted, but the uneducated see it as a matter of no consequence.

Since these lines were written, the elections of 1960 have been held; but so many complaints of falsification were received that the results were abruptly invalidated by the shah. In late December, 1960, the shah once again called for elections. It is obvious that such events defeat the purpose of elections, as we have here described that purpose. However, it is not unlikely that a second goal became overriding: i.e., that of preventing the former prime minister from gaining too much power.

Eghbal was in fact dismissed, and the "two-party system" described above went with him; but grave damage was done. The subsequent elections of early 1961 were cancelled by a now aroused Tehran public which was additionally incited by Bagha'i's revived Free Elections Committee. Bagha'i was imprisoned, Ali Amini was appointed as prime minister, and no majlis has been elected as yet. It appears that conventional legitimacy was sacrificed in order to get rid of Eghbal. Elections, the party system, and the majlis are all in abeyance. In their place the shah has put a "liberal" prime minister, for the time being.

Even though the cabinet is dependent upon the will of the shah, and though cabinet decisions are not publicly announced until they have been communicated to the shah, parallel efforts are made to attribute all the characteristics of the British cabinet to that of Iran. Cabinet meetings are regularly held, and they receive a good deal of publicity. Cabinet ministers themselves strongly assert the supremacy of the cabinet, but no one will hold long to the proposition that the cabinet is a coördinated, collegial executive.

It is apparent that most policy-rooted legislation, other than that aimed at rationalizing the administration, is decided upon without the cabinet, communicated thence to the appropriate ministry for working up into a bill, and then approved by the cabinet for being placed before the majlis. In the majlis itself, the rules of the house are adhered to, though without the strictness that characterizes Western parliaments. The speaker makes short shrift of many tangled procedural questions, and the government is often enabled to force its measures through. The one rule adhered to, in all but the most exceptional cases, is that bills be referred to the appropriate committee before any important debate takes place in the majlis plenary. In committee, and consequently at some remove from public observation, there is a last opportunity for key consultants to try to have modifications accepted by the government. After being reported out of committee, the bill is duly read for the second and third times, whereupon a final vote is taken. On rare occasions a bill may fail of passage, though in the only recent example, it received prompt reconsideration.

The majlis debates are extensively reported in the press, and such reports are often accompanied by serious discussion and comment, as though the legislative process were in fact politically functional. On several occasions, after the 28th of Mordad, deputies have asserted the sovereignty of the majlis under the leadership of the shah. Deputies have also insisted upon the dignity of the legislature vis-à-vis real or supposed slights by members of the cabinet. On the other hand, Dr. Eghbal plainly told the deputies that they had no freedom of choice and that he was not responsible to them.

The discrepancy between the asserted character of the courts and their actual subordination to the executive branch is analogous to the situation of the majlis and cabinet. The press, the radio, and official public addresses deal with the judicial system as though it were independent, but persons high and low, including some judges, readily declare the whole system corrupt. As indicated above, several members of the judiciary go to great lengths to insist upon their own honesty and to show with what courage they have withstood pressures from the police, the minister of interior or the minister of justice. Few will admit to what extent such defiance represents or is protected by a bargain made outside of the ministry of justice.

Such exceptional defiance of hierarchical controls, whether in the courts or majlis, seems to substantiate, at least in part, the contention of a few that the conventional superstructure is in fact constitutive of real legitimizations. It must be remembered, however, that the sort of explanation usually offered in Iran for the failure of conventional institutions draws its assumptions from a hierarchical model. The actual effectiveness of traditional power structures is generally misinterpreted. The apparent inconsistency of the working of these institutions is to be explained by reference to the exploitation of these conventional institutions by traditionally-oriented persons. One of the usual ways in which these institutions are exploited is through the traditionally sanctioned positive system-challenging process. This process will be discussed more fully below, but here a few examples will suffice to establish the relationship between the various processes. These examples will also help to explain the apparent contradiction between the assertion that conventional institutions are a mere façade and attempts to exploit such institutions as though they were really effective.

Among the incongruent kinds of action that seem to lend credence to the assertion that the majlis has power of its own is the statement of a majlis member which is critical of the government or one of its policies. While this does occur on occasion, it is nevertheless surprising how brief such statements are. There has been at least one occasion in which the opponent of a bill refused to state the reasons for his opposition, lest trouble be caused thereby. On other occasions opponents have spoken for no longer than five minutes. More elaborate opposition arguments appear when, in fact, the interests of the member or one of his allies are injured, as in the case of the irrigation agency. Criticisms of the bureaucracy are naturally much more frequent, and the majlis is the best place to carry on a feud between two or more groupings of majlis members and allied bureaucrats. The recent shortage of water in Tehran, as a result of a pipeline break, is such an example. However, there is no longer any permission for majlis members to criticize foreign policy or the shah in any way, and on critical matters such as the recent brick-kiln strike, inquiries are not held.

Statements of protest in the majlis are not limited to the

squealing of those caught in the wheels of higher policy or the harassing of those who will not bargain. To some extent, these statements are veiled threats to expose the whole conventional system as a sham. Since everyone knows it is a sham, the real purport of such statements is to dissociate their speaker from the fakery; that is, their speaker may be trying to win popularity among those partially or totally alienated from the system. Casual observation would seem to indicate that persons who make such statements are dissatisfied with the extent of their influence. They are not of the traditional aristocracy and were appointed to the majlis to enhance its outwardly conventional character. Two examples of such action are the Derakhshesh protest against the agreement with the Oil Consortium and a senator-journalist's opposition to the Baghdad Pact.

Parallel to statements of this kind by members of the majlis is the reading of letters of complaint addressed to the speaker of the majlis. It is difficult to say how many letters of this kind are received but never read. A recent example suggests that the comparatively highly respectful consideration given to such letters is a function of the status of the writer. The letter in question was written by leading ulama in protest against a suggested women's demonstration on the 17th of Dey. Since the government had already acceded to the wishes of the ulama, sending this letter was, in effect, capitalizing on a victory achieved through consultation. The fact that the speaker of the majlis had certain close connections with the ulama was also a point of pressure. Since the ulama had already won their point, having the letter read and published was not playing the traditional game. It was, rather, a veiled protest against the system as being of such a nature that it might permit a women's demonstration if not held in line by the ulama.

Newspapers are also used for purposes of this kind. The usual news article is often a government handout, or a loose quotation of an interview. Reports are often incomplete, and sometimes artfully indirect. Much more innuendo appears in editorials, and some newspapers calling themselves "in opposition" engage in open if restricted criticism. No newspaper criticizes the shah, but many criticize the cabinet, and nearly all criticize aspects of the administration at times. While the prime minister works asssiduously at identifying all he does with the shah, thus giving the impression of a strictly hierarchical regime, the newspapers are at pains to separate them. The court is generally in favor of having a dispensable prime minister bear responsibility, and it is suspicious of any politician building too much popularity. Established policy would also seem to permit the letting off of steam, in small quantities, through the newspapers after this fashion.

Newspapers may also carry advertisements in which battles are fought out between groups of merchants, or between real estate owners and the bureaucracy. Often these ads take the form of open letters to the prime minister and call attention to some misuse of administrative authority. Those who sign such an ad are not usually among the principal bargainers in the system, but they have a higher status than guildsmen or retail merchants. In buying an advertisement, these men have reached the borderline between lobbying and system challenging by using a simulated conventional technique.

A more positive manifestation of the system-maintenance process occurs in the efforts of various government departments to suggest the participation of the average professional (but not layman) in the laying down of policy goals. This effect has been achieved in recent times by calling conferences of government professionals. The most important of these conferences are the educational congress held by the ministry of education, the annual medical conference held by the ministry of health, the recent conference of judges held by the ministry of justice, and the recent conference of mayors held by the ministry of the interior. Only the latter was not composed of professionals. In every instance the ministry in question took the lead. The newspapers reported these conferences fairly well, and the minister's opening speech was quoted at length. On all occasions the shortcomings of Iran were compared with the difficulties in the way of improvement. Resolutions were offered and duly passed, and the conferences all ended on optimistic notes. The attitude of several participants was that these conferences were not manifestations of democratic participation, however, and that the resolutions represented either confirmations of ministry policy or utopian hopes.

THE SYSTEM-MAINTENANCE PROCESS:
THE USE OF TRADITIONAL SYMBOLS

TRADITIONAL SYMBOLS are also used for system-maintenance purposes, sometimes right along with conventional symbols, so that one can easily discern superficial inconsistencies in the statements of government leaders. The prime minister may talk of the Constitutional Monarchy and the ancient imperial tradition of Iran in the same speech. The ancient imperial tradition will be associated with Shiite Islam, in a majlis statement. And on posters seen on the walls in all cities the slogan "God, Shah, and Fatherland" will declare the legitimacy confusion the government wishes to prevail.

There are three aspects of tradition which may here be considered: The imperial tradition, or that of the omnipotent shahinshah; Shiite Islam; and the dominance of the landed and tribal aristocracy. Of these three the last is strongly exemplified in the behavior of all participants in the system, but aristocratic or tribal symbols are notably absent from the Iranian political scene. At the very least, we may say that under conditions of increasingly wide communication and participation, aristocratic symbols are not considered effective in system maintenance.

The value of royal and religious symbols stems from their being still respected by the peasants and the less sophisticated of the lowest urban classes. Among the more educated of the urban classes, Musaddiq reduced the sanctity of the royal symbol, but he never openly suggested its abolition. After the 28th of Mordad, the few persons who did advocate a republic were given short shrift, death or exile. Still, it is clear that the effectiveness of the symbol is limited and that there is an air of over-conviction in the way in which the shah is praised and the royal government too frequently acknowledged to be the only form of government which accords with the national tradition of Iran. Shiite Islam sits lightly on the educated middle class, but even if they have rational doubts, their emotional attachments are strong. There are, further, pockets of potential fundamentalism among these people, and the appeal of a reformed Islam, or the appeal from the communist threat to Islam, does not go without some response.

As for the use of the royal tradition, its reaffirmation is mandatory at all public ceremonies, at the opening of the school day every morning, at the opening of all conferences, before the showing of movies at the cinema, in the speeches of all party leaders, at the laying of cornerstones, upon the opening of hospitals, and during the dedication of factories. Every public place, every government office, and most places of business have a painting or photograph of the shah hanging in a prominent place. All public holidays, except those that are specifically religious or the Now-Ruz, are associated with the shah. Most of the posters hung on the walls contain either pictures of the shah or his name.

Newspapers usually publish at least one photograph of the shah daily and describe his participation at public functions, but practically no material is available on his private life and attitudes.

Translations from the dispatches of foreign correspondents are the best that the Iranian public can get, aside from inconsequential or damning hearsay. In most public appearances, the shah is extremely well protected, often preceded by large numbers of police and the military, and inaccessible to onlookers. Other observers have noted that the shah does appear in the city of Tehran unannounced, and on occasion relatively unaccompanied, but such an appearance seems to be rare. His manner is superior and distant, and he is always represented in the most formal of circumstances. The image thus created is that of the ancient shahinshah and not the loved ruler who is the father of his people. The shah is represented as omniscient and rather more than human. He is certainly more feared than known, and more a symbol than a real person.

It is interesting to note that there has not yet been a formal coronation of the present shah. It is openly said that the shah did not want to hold this formal ceremony until his throne was secure. In 1959 it was rumored that he might hold this ceremony on the twentieth anniversary of his attaining the throne, that is, in 1960, during which year the shah ordered the commemoration of the 2,500th anniversary of Iranian royalty.

The commemoration is in itself an interesting indication of the attempt to associate the present dynasty and the constitutional monarchy with the pre-Islamic imperial tradition of Iran. Not all the plans for that celebration were announced, but it was hoped that Iran might be visited by a number of crowned heads. A series of cultural activities were also to take place to which foreign scholars were to be invited, and ceremonies were to be held at a number of archaeological sites. This was the most ambitious of the activities by which the stability of the throne is still being pursued.

The sternness of the image of the shah is somewhat relieved by attempts to associate him and members of his family with various charitable projects, especially those supported through the royal properties (Amlak-i-Pahlavi) and the Red Lion and Sun Society. The receptiveness of the court to individual complaints by the poor is another attempt to soften the image of the shah. More significant efforts than any of these, however, are the association of the shah with land reform, with the law barring government officials from dealing with the government, the "Where did you get it?" law, and the new royal inspectorate. These and other activities are meant to identify the shah with the ancient ideal of the ruler as the dispenser of justice. For the educated classes, such efforts are as yet unconvincing; for the uneducated they may not be necessary. Some people are charitable enough to say that they will wait and see how these laws are implemented, the rest answer the inquirer with derision.

Despite occasional reference to the constitutional aspect of the monarchy, no attempt is made to hide the great and active influence of the shah in all aspects of government. On the contrary, it would seem that in the attempt to attribute traditional legitimacy to the shah, conscious efforts are made to stress his personal involvement in the decisions that are made. At any rate, such is the inevitable conclusion to be drawn from all explanations of major policy from the literacy campaign to "positive nationalism" in foreign affairs. Even foreigners making polite speeches refer to the shah's leadership. Melliyun Party posters declared that Prime Minister Eghbal was carrying out the shah's program. The newspapers record as fact that decisions of the cabinet must be approved by the shah. Both the cabinet and the higher economic council meet in the presence of the shah. Only the leader of the opposition can afford to declare openly that the prime minister is doing a poor job of carrying out the shah's program.

On the religious side, a variety of attempts are made to lend the legitimacy of Shiite Islam to the government. Not only is the shah associated in some vague way with religion, almost as though he were divinely appointed; he is also represented as being personally religious. Even though the board of ulama, as proposed in the constitution, has never been established, individual members of the majlis have declared that theirs is an Islamic institution and that they may not pass any bill which contravenes the law of Islam. Furthermore, the government poses as both defender and supporter of religion.

The shah himself participates in a number of religious ceremonies, as already indicated. These activities, such as visits to shrines, and hearing the story of Hussain recited at the palace, are usually published, and the names of prominent ulama participating are mentioned. In addition, the shah may have his personal representatives act for him at other ceremonies, and even represent the government in a general way at Friday prayers. The ulama are also prominently represented, if indirectly, in the majlis and senate, and the presence of prominent ulama at the formal holding of court is quite usual.

At least as important as these ceremonial and propagandistic associations of religion and government are the various ways in which Shiite Islam is institutionalized through the government.

We have already mentioned the constitutional provision for a board of ulama. Though the board does not exist, the fact that certain members of the majlis and senate speak for the ulama at times is considered to suffice for practical purposes. Yet one hears few references to the clause as a dead letter.

There are no more religious courts in Iran, though ulama are employed as adjuncts to the civil court, for marriage and divorce cases. Nevertheless, it is strongly asserted that the civil code is predominantly Islamic, even if the technique of codification is somewhat alien to Islamic legal theory. This assertion is not contradicted by the ulama, though some may feel it essential that such laws be interpreted by ulama rather than lay judges. The failure to codify and adopt Islamic commercial and penal law does not seem to disturb the ulama very much.

Government control of mortmain, endowed for religious purposes as awqaf, is a sore point with the ulama. They are not entirely satisfied with this arrangement, because the bulk of the income from such awqaf goes to renters or to the ministry of education. Only those awqaf endowed for very specific purposes produce income for the support of religious institutions. On the other hand, the government respects these endowments, often appoints ulama as trustees, and usually employs pious Muslims in the awqaf bureau. Except insofar as the testament may lack explicitness, Islamic law is the basis of dealing with awqaf, and even then there is room for divergent interpretations of pious purposes and pious trustees.

There are a large number of awqaf for which the "Shah of the Period" is the trustee. These are principally in Mashhad and its vicinity and the endowments tied to the support of the Sepah Salar Mosque and madrassah. The shah has appointed special functionaries to carry out his responsibilities with regard to these, and in the course of so doing a large number of ulama and religious students are supported. The shah also makes contributions for religious learning from his own resources. The role of the shah as trustee of awqaf enhances his position as a pious ruler and also recognizes the establishment of Shiite Islam.

Part of the regular budget for the University of Tehran goes to support the faculty of philosophy and theology. This institution was originally established to create a new clergy, but it was not strongly supported and it closed after a short period. Its tendency, after the abdication of Reza Shah and its reëstablishment, has remained the same, though its efforts in this direction now seem much more tentative. The fact of government support for such an institution is nevertheless a form of recognition, and the special privileges of theology students enhances the institutionalization of Shiite Islam.

Students are admitted to the faculty of theology under easier entrance requirements than those of almost any other faculty. Graduates of this faculty are especially permitted to become secondary schoolteachers and judges, even though they lack special training in education or in secular law. Students may or may not wear religious garb, as they like. Another employment for graduates is in the army chaplain corps, where they tend to predominate.

Other ways in which the government associates itself with Islamic symbols are through providing the facilities of Radio Tehran for religious broadcasts and by desisting from all government business on religious holidays. There are a great many religious broadcasts during the week, of which the most important are the noon prayer and short sermon and the Thursday evening sermon of Rashid. During the holy months of Muharram and Ramadhan, or at least most thereof, there are longer broadcasts of prayers and sermons every day, and no music is played. The large numbers of Shiite holy days in which the bazaar is closed are very nearly matched by the government offices. It is generally admitted that these cut grievously into government business, but no one seriously suggests limiting them.

While not an explicit part of Islamic tradition, the old Iranian ideal of a strict classification of society into occupational groups was gradually accepted. Today these ideas still persist, and even though no explicit attempts are made to justify this view, the prevailing prejudice is either exploited or appealed to in many ways. Originally, it may be recalled, the majlis was established to represent six classes of people, and the first electoral law also spoke of six classes of people. While it is common to speak of three main classes in Iran, occupational groups are generally recognized as having a corporative status of their own. These aspects of tradition are exploited indirectly for system-maintenance purposes, whenever references are made to the support which the government receives from "all classes of people," or welcoming committees are made up of members of these classes, or the government recognizes or consults one of the class groups. The corporative view of society is rarely explicitly elaborated, yet on the basis of casual observation it seems to be deeply ingrained in the culture, and to be widely accepted as just. This view was also generally accepted by most political parties, and it is at the root of any interpretation of "pressure group activity." It also lends legitimacy to those delegations of authority that the government makes to selected groups, even when they are as modern as the Chamber of Commerce or the Bar Association.

THE SYSTEM-CHALLENGING PROCESS: NEGATIVE

THE LAST OF THE PROCESSES to be considered is the system-challenging process. This, too, may be conveniently divided into two major variants, which approximate distinct processes. The first variant we may call the negative system-challenging process, and the second the positive system-challenging process. The essential distinction between the two lies in the goals of the actors and the degree of their alienation from the system. Those engaging in negative challenging do so in the hope of altering the system, or at least in order to manifest their unwillingness to coöperate in any way. Those who challenge the system positively do so as a means of increasing their influence within it. Positive challenging is a kind of bargaining tactic in which the possibility of causing some deprivation is substituted for the promise of a gratification under a mutual arrangement. The positive challenger is always ready to withdraw his threat and to work within the rules of the system, if gratified. One of the consequences of positive challenging is the appearance of hypocrisy, both on the part of the challenger and on the part of those who accede to his pressure. The negative challenger is especially proud of his consistency, and though he may not be able to resist all temptation he strives to avoid all implication with the government. The importance placed upon consistency is a reaction against the unprincipled bargaining which is so ubiquitous, but it is also a partial result of the fact that positive challenging is generally inefficient, in proportion to the number of those engaging in it. That is, the system simply cannot supply the demands of all of those who are politically aware. Consequently, for many, negative challenging is but making a virtue of necessity. The logical connection between consistency and a preference for rational solutions and a rational legitimacy should be obvious, and it is especially among negative challengers that conventional institutions are thought to have bankrupted themselves.

In the discussion which follows, we shall try to distinguish between the techniques employed in each of these variant processes. As has already been demonstrated, we shall draw upon many of the details and illustrations given in other contexts. Thus it may be as appropriate here as at any point to note that the development of similar materials from many points of view merely states the truism that the analytical framework is after all a conceptual scheme, while the phenomena to be described are many-faceted. More significant than such platitudes is the, by now, well demonstrated point that all of the processes discussed are closely interrelated, so that specific action or the employment of a specific technique may be analyzed with regard to more than one concurrent process.

We turn first to negative system challenging. The most extreme form of the negative challenge is membership in a subversive party; that is, a party which conspires to overthrow the regime by force. Under Reza Shah two such conspiratorial groups were discovered and punished; the first was the forerunner of the Tudeh Party, and the second the predecessor of the Pan-Iranism Party. The latter has now shifted to positive challenging, but the former, since the 28th of Mordad, has been broken up. Other negative challengers were the Fidayan-i-Islam, but probably not the Mujahidin-i-Islam. The Iran Party was treated as though it were extremist, though it was probably not. At any rate, there remain four ideological orientations toward which negative challengers may be attracted: the Tudeh, the nationalist, the militaristic dictatorship, and the fundamentalist-Islamic. At the present time, none of these views is represented by strongly organized groups, although there are considerable numbers of persons, in and out of the government, who hold such views. If there are any truly military groups, rather than individuals, seeking to establish a rational-hierarchical regime, theirs are clandestine conspiracies and may not be known to outsiders except insofar as they may issue illegal announcements. In the case of the Tudeh Party, we have already seen how that group has been broken, although we cannot know how many are secret members. The Tudeh Party came close to an internal split over the question of whether to support Musaddiq, and after failing to support him, on the 28th of Mordad, and being strongly suppressed thereafter, the split was consummated. This time, the Moscow-trained leadership pressed the split as a form of purge, accusing those who tended to be more nationalist than Marxist of being British agents. The hard core went underground or into exile. The abandoned nationalist Tudeh members established their Marxist circles, and the discouraged majority have quietly sought to find their places in the system. Aside from these card-carrying members, the Tudeh Party also made use of a number of prominent persons who were not known as communists. Sometimes these were cryptocommunists, sometimes misguided reformers, and sometimes traditionalists who merely extended the bargaining area to include foreign representatives in Iran. The latter tendency has been frequently known in Iran, ever since the mid-nineteenth century, and is in accord with tradition if it contravenes nationalist prejudices. From the foregoing classification of types of adherents of the Tudeh Party it seems probable that many persons who are actually engaged in negative system challenging are outwardly acting as though they accept the existing system.

While only the Tudeh Party and the Iran Party were forcibly suppressed, and large numbers of their adherents arrested, all of the political parties of the Musaddiq era were compelled to restrict their activities and to cease publication of their newspapers. In nearly every case, small groups of those who had gathered around the original leader still exist, and even meet occasionally. The government knows of their existence and watches them, but it does not suppress them. Outwardly, all of these groups engage in negative challenging, though there is evidence that some may engage in collusion with the government and that others hope to make a deal. Of this nature are the remnants of the Iran Party, the Toilers' Party, the Third Force, and two Pan-Iranism parties. In addition to these groups, which seem to be partly in collusion with the government, there are several more persistent challengers calling themselves simply Nationalists, or the National Resistance Organization, or the Rah-i-Musaddiq group. The leadership of these groups cannot be narrowed further than the actual publishers of occasional unlicensed political tracts or news sheets. For the rest, it seems that any number of adherents may attempt to negotiate on behalf of the whole class of alienated youth. These young men differ from those still holding to the old party name in that they have rejected their older leaders. No evidence is available to the effect that this group is well organized, or that it may have an efficiently conspiratorial inner core. The little knowledge we have would seem to affirm that a small number of people publish tracts using the names referred to, and that many young men consider themselves sympathetic to the points of view expressed.

At present, there is little doubt that most of those who engage in negative system challenging are unaffiliated individuals. Many are persons who know one another, are members of informal cliques, or are related to one another. As such, they sustain one another's attitudes, so lending credence to an image of reality which equates the present system with organized criminality. It is difficult to estimate how many people share this negative attitude, but casual observation indicates that alienation is widespread among middle grade civil servants, government professionals, schoolteachers, students, nongovernment factory labor, ulama and tulab, and guildsmen. So widespread, in fact, are negative attitudes that it is not rare at all to hear them expressed by some among the highest beneficiaries of the existing system. To praise or justify the existing system is generally considered an act of extreme naïvete or hypocrisy. On the other hand, "self-criticism" by the beneficiaries of the system is more readily expressed to foreigners than to fellow citizens. Those who really mean it are somewhat more circumspect in their behavior. Obviously, it is not always possible to believe what a man says or writes.

Each of these individuals must decide for himself the extent to which he will try to realize his opposition to the system in concrete action. For most, the means at their disposal are meager. The most frequent response is simply the refusal to believe. The lengths to which simple disbelief are taken are almost incredible: as a general rule, anything which the government says, all official newscasts, all newspaper comment and editorials, all speeches by official party leaders, all statements by officially recognized interest group leaders are dismissed as vicious lies. Furthermore, anyone who purports to believe in these statements must defend himself against the presumption of stupidity.

For accurate information one turns to the rumor based on Radio Moscow or the clandestine National Voice of Iran. Even Radio Peiping supplies some of this material. The fact that rumors are also used by traditionalists to slander a rival's reputation or to win popularity simply reinforces this tendency. All damning rumors are passed, and the more damning they are the more readily believed. Among co-workers in a ministry or among a peer group of ulama, such explanations will be offered. Frequently, when information is not available, complete stories are somehow fabricated and passed on with embellishments or changes, in accordance with the particular kind of interpretation favored by the rumor-monger.

In more critical situations, silent resistance is the only means a man dare employ. He does not externalize his alienation from the system lest he suffer some deprivation, but he evidences his attitude in a quiet stolidity that is all the more suspicious for the absence of the more usual open criticism or profuse and artificial praise. The educated man with no openly expressed political opinions is often the one with strong feelings of alienation.

Disbelief has, as its natural complement, cynicism. The cynic is not so serious about his disbelief, but he lightly expresses the view that all things may be explained by two answers, greed and incompetence. More serious and doctrinaire disbelievers will not even grant the mercy of incompetence.

Another frequent manifestation of negative system challenging is in reputation slander. This sort of behavior is not new to tradition, but in tradition it is meant to achieve a specific end, as interpreted in terms of persons. Negative challengers pass on defamatory information indiscriminately, to show that the whole system is rotten.

Those who are somewhat better organized and who have some financial resources may go a little further and publish unlicensed news sheets which criticize the Western powers and which complain of administrative bungling and corruption. The Pan-Iranism group mimeographs such a sheet regularly. The Rah-i-Musaddiq, or Resistance Group, publishes its tracts from time to time. University students have recently started a new mimeographed sheet. The Marxist circles have published at least one poorly printed handbill. A retired army officer distributed a mimeographed open letter, a few months ago, which received moderate attention. The content of these publications runs all the way from criticism of the shah's land reform program to attacks on the Oil Consortium. Commemorations of martyred heroes alternate with explanations of the German department store scandal, and majlis manipulations of the "Where did you get it?" bill may share some space with a discussion of the Bahrain or Shatt al-Arab problems.

Groups that are somewhat better organized can more effectively pursue a policy of noncoöperation. Among the more important of these are the ulama, as a class. Admittedly, there are a good many ulama who coöperate with the government, who accept state funds, and who bargain with the traditional aristocracy. It is, however, rare to find an alim who will give the government unqualified support. There are also a good many ulama who, while firmly believing that the present form of government is more favorable to Islam than a nonroyal form, are prevented on principle from associating themselves in any way with it. A smaller number argue that the government is absolutely un-Islamic, that it is fostering the corruption of Shiite Islam, and that its leading exponents are sinful men. Regardless of the specific position taken and of the few ulama who directly benefit from the coöperation of the government, the weight of religious opinion rests on the conclusion that pious caution requires that the ulama and all religious men refuse to associate themselves with political authority.

Political noncoöperation occurs principally in the general refusal of alienated groups to lend credence to the government's use of conventional symbols. These people refuse to believe that the majlis will become a free agent, they do not believe that the elections are fair, and they are certain that the two official parties are complete fakes. Both parties try to win members from all classes, but the Mardum Party has sought more assiduously to win over the disillusioned members of the old semisubversive groups, and even some extreme left wingers. Its success in this regard has been poor, and suggestions that the party be given a chance are rejected out of hand.

There is a good deal of noncoöperation within the ranks of the bureaucracy also, though some of this is due to prudence and unwillingness to accept responsibility. There is no question of their refusing to carry out an express order. Yet we have seen where certain key administrators hold solid bargaining positions; their coöperation is often necessary to consummate arrangements made outside the administrative framework, but negative challengers may not play the game. Important licenses can be delayed, application blanks lost, required signatures omitted, illegal requests reported to the wrong superior, and in hundreds of other ways the alienated bureaucrat may refuse to coöperate with the principal bargainers in the system. Noncoöperation of this kind may be rooted in either antagonism for the specific applicant or from a desire to punish those of higher status as a class. Whatever the reason for his attitude, the bureaucrat may protect himself to some extent by insisting that he is acting in accordance with the requirements of his job, that he is following the rational principles of a neutral civil servant whose duties are defined by law. The fact that he may be inconsistent in upholding those principles throws some doubt upon the abstract value orientation of his behavior, and it lends greater credence to the assertion that he is engaging in system-challenging activity. The example of the judge who resists the blandishments of the minister of justice or of an influential litigant is similar. Lest this interpretation be overstressed, it should be added that there are some who consistently adhere to the administrative or judicial ideal, and do so on the basis of conviction. While it may not be intended, it is quite clear that such behavior is just as surely system challenging, though the challengers may mistake the true and purported natures of the political system.

Outright disobedience, as a form of negative system challenging, is fairly rare, usually occurring in inconsequential actions which cause the government little anguish but which give the actor some psychological benefit. One young man told me how he consistently disobeys traffic signals, another refused to appear to sign a petition circulated among all the employees of his office, another refused to dismiss a case involving disorderly conduct.

The ultimate in disobedience is, of course, actively engaging in conspiracy against the regime. As already noted, we cannot know whether such conspiracies are now being formed, or by whom. Clearly, the conspiracy is the means by which governments are most efficiently removed in this part of the world, and we have been several times surprised by the sudden appearance of small conspiratorial groups in the armies of the Middle East. Such may exist in Iran, except for a single bit of inconclusive evidence: alienated groups engaging in negative system-challenging behavior are very pessimistic, very pessimistic indeed.

THE SYSTEM-CHALLENGING PROCESS: POSITIVE

THE POSITIVE SYSTEM-CHALLENGING process is manifested in two forms of political action. The first of these may be described as the refusal to bargain, and the second involves the use of coercive rather than accommodative methods. We shall examine the techniques employed in this process more specifically below, but these two classes of action require further explanation at the outset. Refusal to bargain, as a positive rather than a negative tactic, is the equivalent of holding out for better terms. Its effectiveness is dependent upon the willingness of the actor to forego benefits to himself, and its rational employment implies that the second party stands to gain more out of the bargain than the holdout. Viewed in this light, there are many cases in which the difference between the negative and positive aspects of this process is no more than a question of the time period considered. That is, the specific form of negative system challenging may be the refusal of a civil servant to coöperate or the refusal of a guildsman to act as though he believes in the declarations of the high council of guilds. When the price is raised, however, the civil servant or guildsman may change his mind, and in retrospect his system challenging becomes positive.

The coercive aspect of positive system challenging does not, at the present time, involve the use of force, though it did so during and before the Musaddiq period. Tudeh demonstrations and

The Political Functions   293

street fights with right-wing groups, during that time, might best
be seen as negative challenging. The "mugging" of majlis members, the burning of party headquarters, and the like fall within
the positive system-challenging process. In the post-Musaddiq
period, coercive bargaining techniques derive their effectiveness
from the prevailing legitimacy confusion. The fact that the conventional institutions are a façade leads to the partial employment
of conventional standards as a means of protecting the holdout and so embarrassing the traditional bargainer. There are also
many occasions where such system challenging is used to gain a
specific benefit, as when the majlis rejects a bill and gets away
with it. The technique may also be used to gain a bargaining position, as when a complaint which is embarrassing to a high official
is made public. The use of publicity itself is coercive and has a
system-challenging effect.

From this brief discussion it is possible to conclude that the
goal of positive system challenging is not to change the system,
but rather to derive greater benefits from it. Simple refusal to
bargain is system challenging, but it is the least dysfunctional class
of techniques. The use of conventional responses is the most damaging way of challenging the system, both because it throws traditional practices into sharp and unpleasant relief and because it
permits groups with little or no traditional status to engage in
effective bargaining action.

Most of the specific techniques of the positive system-challenging process have already been introduced, but it may be useful
to recall some of them, in order to facilitate understanding. The
simplest and least disturbing technique is that of private representation of a grievance to a high official, a majlis member, or
merely some influential person. Such representation may be accomplished in the midst of enlisting parti, however; at some point
along the line the petitioner becomes aware of the fact that his
gracious listeners are not going to comply. It is then that the petitioner may choose to make more explicit the threat that he will
publicize his grievance, leave some organization, or resign suddenly from his office. Even if such private representation can be
justified on a legal basis, there may be little hope from recourse
to the courts, but even moderate publicity serving to reaffirm
common negative attitudes toward the government are unwelcome
enough. The challenge need not succeed, and most of the time it
probably does not succeed. The net result is to strengthen both
criticism of the government and cynical judgments, hence to

weaken the stability of the system. It is only the willingness of the petitioner to compromise that lends some positive value to his action.

Of greater significance, despite the low repute of the majlis, is the public statement of a grievance or a criticism of the administration in the majlis. Negative statements of majlis members are more readily credited than praise of the government, for the reason that the prevailing judgment of the government is negative. Majlis members are surprisingly free to use their positions for spot criticisms of the cabinet and administration, though criticisms of the shah and the armed forces are never voiced. There was only one recent criticism of the security organization, after a religious magazine had been suspended for using a photograph which had originated in a communist magazine several years before. But the license of the magazine was promptly restored. In other cases, majlis criticism reveals conflicts and jealousies within the executive branch, as in the feud between Dr. Eghbal and Mr. Ebtehaj when the latter was director of the plan organization. Some of Dr. Eghbal's majlis supporters were perennial critics of the plan. Even though the majlis eventually passed the "Where did you get it?" bill, and the bill to prevent officials from doing business with the government, it first expressed public doubts as to whether this bill might be implemented. The shortlived tax on commercial paper was also criticized in the senate, as was the surtax on property transactions. The new income tax regulations have been attacked, and emphasis was placed upon the arbitrary power which it gave to tax officials in gouging honest businessmen. The debate on the key money bill, similarly, strengthened the guilds and vilified rental property owners. Majlis members have also criticized newly projected roads, the winning contractors, and the conditions of the contract. The attempt to delimit urban Tehran, so as to include more suburban underdeveloped lands, has also resulted in sharp discussions. Majlis criticisms are very few, however, and oftentimes the criticism is voiced indirectly. Furthermore, as we have already noted, foreign policy, the budget, and matters on which the shah is adamant are seldom seriously debated.

There are occasions on which a public protest may be raised and given publicity. Under present conditions, this area of technique exploration is strictly limited, in terms of persons, subject matter, and manner of expression. The use of paid advertisements in newspapers has already been discussed here; if the issue is serious enough, there may be system-challenging repercussions. More important than advertisements are demonstrative protests, for instance, the march of the actors and singers on the ministry of finance, in protest against the new income tax regulations. Before Musaddiq's fall, the most demonstrative form of protest was that of closing the bazaar. This is a traditional technique, but it has taken on the increasingly modern aspect of a democratic protest, for earlier, in the days of the constitutional revolution, the bazaars were closed. The closing of the bazaar, for political purposes, has not been permitted since General Zahedi threatened to destroy the roof of the main bazaar street. Nevertheless, not all public protests have been eliminated, for some bazaar merchants did close shop and did create a stir when they opposed the establishment of the large German-managed department store.

A more conservative and acceptable form of public protest occurs in the demarche of an aggrieved delegation to a high official. Any sort of issue may be at the root of the matter, such as the protest of a group of carpet dealers at the unconscionable use of a foreign machinemade carpet in the new airport terminal at Mehrabad. Or local councils for some of the Tehran districts may be formed for the explicit purpose of demanding better lighting and street asphalting of the minister of the interior.

Like the closing of the bazaar, the expression of a religious grievance by the ulama has a long traditional history, but sometimes the demonstration takes on a modern guise. The details of the protest regarding the last 17th of Dey have already been related. To recapitulate, the opposition of the ulama to a women's demonstration and the closing of the schools was expressed by Ayatullah Burujirdi, during the prime minister's visit to Qumm. It was restated in two letters, one from a group of prominent ulama and one from majlis member Behbahani, that were addressed to the speaker of the Majlis. And it was voiced to a representative of the ministry of court, when he called on a prominent Tehran mujtahid at the latter's request. The success of these protests may have been due to aspects of Iran-Iraq relations, but the publicity given the protests seems, rather, to be a function of the influence of the ulama. The visit of the ministry of court official was not publicized. Generally speaking, the ulama do not engage in system challenging, because they are apprehensive of the consequences of a change in the regime. On the other hand, they cannot remain silent about further encroachments on their authority. Before Musaddiq's fall, they were more outspoken, and Ayatullah Behbahani, as well as Ayatullah Kashani, voiced open criticisms of Musaddiq himself. After the 28th of Mordad, Ayatullah Kashani opposed several of the decisions of the Zahedi regime, which resulted in his being placed under house arrest. The 1955 attacks on the Baha'is, by Falsafi, were not direct criticisms of the government, though they caused the government serious embarrassment in challenging it to demonstrate its orthodoxy. The government was stampeded into supporting the ulama here, but withdrew when the issue died down. Falsafi was not again given the privilege of radio broadcasting, though he still addresses large audiences, as during Ramadhan, 1959, when he criticized the government in a subtle and indirect way.

A strike or service stoppage is an effective means of protest having an even stronger system-challenging effect than the closing of the bazaar, even though the latter is always more likely to precipitate a situation in which large-scale violence results. A strike of workers such as that of textile-factory labor, oil-company labor, the brick-kiln employees, or the Ab-i-Ali (carbonated beverages) employees are examples of the most incongruous of political acts. Technically, in all recent cases, these have been illegal strikes; for they all inspire the fear of subversion and increased Tudeh Party activity, they suggest the most uncompromising kind of opposition to the regime, and they represent the demands of groups which are least recognized by tradition. Labor unrest arouses in everyone's conscience an awareness of the grossest inequities of the system, and as such it is one of the most disturbing of challenges. Usually, efforts are made to prevent general knowledge of the occurrence of a strike, and several of the strikes of the last two or three years have not been reported in the press. The strike of the Tehran taxi drivers has been discussed above. It is clear that this strike, though disturbing because of the inconvenience which it caused, elicited neither a strong nor an emotional reaction. The willingness of the drivers to be organized as a guild rather than a labor union is an indication both of the positive character of their protest and of the reason why the strike was not considered subversive. Of roughly the same nature was the service stoppage by the butchers in Tehran, in protest against municipal control of the centralized slaughter and distribution system, and against the price ceilings set by the municipality. The revelation of malfeasance in the slaughterhouse monopoly led to an easing of controls, and butchers commenced selling meat at around twice the fixed price.

Not only were these strikes and service stoppages technically illegal, but in many cases the very groups engaging in such actions were not licensed. We have seen where all of the unions led by the Mardum Party lack official licensing. The taxi drivers, too, were not officially organized, at the time of their strike, though the butchers have a guild of long standing. The very formation of unauthorized groups, especially of unlicensed labor groups, is system challenging, but because much of this activity is carried on by the Mardum Party, it has a positive rather than a negative system-challenging effect. The ministry of labor has made no move to break up these unions; it simply refuses to recognize them. The unions do participate in government-ordered demonstrations, and have even presented gifts to the shah, so it is clear that the government does not intend to make an issue of their existence.

The opposition party, which is to say the Mardum Party, shares with majlis members of both parties the major responsibility for most of the positive system-challenging activity. The role of the Mardum Party as a safety valve has been explained, and it may not be doubted that its duties require that it engage in system-challenging activity. The very existence of parties is itself challenging to the system, and the more active the party the more challenging is its existence. From the latter point of view, the marginal existence of the remnants of the parties of the old Musaddiq era really constitutes less of a challenge than does the Mardum Party.

Contrary to expectations, the Mardum Party does not lead the expression of criticism in the majlis. It is, in fact, hard to discern any party influence, in the functioning of the majlis. The Mardum expresses its criticism in the addresses given by party leaders, in the party press, and in some of the party's public demonstrations. The addresses of both party leaders and the party press are largely internal media, so that they impose moderate stresses only. We must recall, though, the case where one issue of the Mardum publication was suppressed for printing a picture of a destitute laborer. In public demonstrations, the party inadvertently presents a more serious challenge. The two most important demonstrations, in this respect, were the one on the occasion of the 9th of Esfand, when the unions presented gifts and an address to the shah, and the one on the 17th of Dey; Asadullah Alam on that day led many of the representatives of women's organizations in the laying of wreaths on the grave of Reza Shah.

The Mardum Party organ is not the only newspaper, nor the most important one, claiming to be in opposition. *Kaihan* is the newspaper with the largest circulation of those claiming to oppose the government, though it does not oppose the present regime. Criticism is not limited to the opposition press, however, though it is more consistent with them. Nearly all papers join in criticizing administrative scandals, which again, in view of the prevailing attitude toward government, has a system-challenging effect. The meat shortage, the break in the water pipes, the failure of the ministry of education to acquire a sufficient number of stoves for the schools, the slowness in handling ships at Khorramshahr, the financial manipulations of the German management of the Forushgah-i-Ferdowsi, the failure of various foreign firms to live up to their contracts with the plan organization, the controversy over how many fertilizer factories are needed, the downgrading of the priority of a steel mill, the spending of municipal funds on fountains and squares instead of on social welfare, the small number of hospitals in Tehran—these and many other issues are discussed and bemoaned, though in somewhat guarded language, in all the newspapers, but especially in opposition editorials.

Within the government itself we may find significant illustrations of the positive system challenging process. At the cabinet level, this takes the form of refusal to bargain, as in the almost classical incident of the budget for 1338. Our study of the cabinet has already revealed how fixed disagreement is a nearly integral part of the structure of that institution.

Below the cabinet level, bureaucrats and judges may carry out their functions in accordance with either traditional or rational values. Should they choose the latter, in order to improve their bargaining position, then they are, in fact, challenging the system.

RATIONALIZING TENDENCIES

THIS SECTION of the present study began with a discussion of the practice of bargaining in traditional political processes. Throughout the subsequent elaboration of the characteristic forms of politically functional activity in Iran, we have frequently noted how this general practice found application. And the prevalence of bargaining is the most important factor in assimilating these processes to the traditional model. Yet such processes are not completely traditional, for in passing we have noted many conventional techniques. The major ideological tension in the Iranian system is between traditional and conventional symbols, and this tension has tended to discredit both. In any case, traditional techniques are inapplicable in the solution of the newer problems of development and mass political participation. Conventional techniques are largely demonstrative and not instrumental. Alongside both of these, rationalizing policies are being applied in a gradually widening sphere of governmental activities. Should we reëxamine the political processes already introduced, we would find that hierarchical techniques intervene to limit bargaining, to restrict the use of conventional symbols, and to pose the issues which stimulate political activity. Rationalizing policies are not an independent variable, rather, such policies are themselves limited by traditional practices and by the need to relate all government acts to conventional formulae. These are the elements which determine the transitional character of the Iranian system.

Faced with a variety of demands and with a variety of challengers to the system itself, the administration, the military, and the cabinet, or what we have called the *machinery* of rationalization, have the major responsibility for policy proposals. Essentially this, too, is a form of system maintenance, but it differs from the two varieties discussed; the latter two were composed almost entirely of symbol manipulations, but here we are concerned with rational attempts to maintain the system by requiting more demands, by providing for developing situations through planning, and by increasing the efficiency and professional character of the bureaucracy. Increasing the physical security of the government is one of the more explicit goals of rational policy and a system-maintenance technique.

Rationalizing policies are not merely of system-maintenance significance; they are also to be seen as the result of demands made upon the system by certain classes and groups. Such policies cannot be taken simply as legitimizations accorded to a variety of groups not recognized by tradition. Actually, these policies tend to be implemented through the establishment of hierarchical institutions, and only to the limited extent that traditional influence has been ineffective. As a consequence, adoption and implementation of rationalizing policies tends to legitimize power relationships in which the bureaucracy is dominant, rather than legitimizing the originator of the demand which brought forth the policy. We may further assume that there is among the bureaucracy a high valuation of rational techniques, and a desire to limit traditional interference. The latter assumption leads naturally to the expectation that many rationalizing policies are not the direct result of the demands of essentially nongovernmental groups, but the result of demands made in the first instance by the bureaucracy itself. As many of these policies as are implemented may be taken as legitimizations won for the machinery of rationalization. Nor can we exclude, here, the effect of the environment on stimulating rationalizing tendencies. Foreign affairs, the communication of ideas from abroad, natural catastrophies, economic competition, and demographic trends all produce issues that are brought to the political level by various means and that are responded to by the machinery of rationalization in its proposals of reform, regulation, and development.

To get at the essential systemic significance of rationalizing policies poses an impressive analytical problem. We have indicated that these policies tend to requite more of the demands of those lacking access, especially those who are not ordinarily consulted; but we have also asserted that rationalizing policies actually result in legitimizations of the machinery of rationalization itself, rather than the uninfluential beneficiaries. It has been implied that demands are pressed by these beneficiaries of rationalizing policies, but it has been stated that it is the bureaucracy which responds to issues rising to the political level from environmental causes. In addition to these two paradoxical statements, we must acknowledge that the machinery of rationalization is not itself a socially sealed structure of power relationships. To resolve these issues we must reconcile our paradoxes and explain the present use of the term machinery of rationalization. First, political issues rise to the political level as demands of the uninfluential through the lobbying and system-challenging processes, which is to say, essentially as responses to policies already approved, though not all of the consequences were foreseen. The administrative history of Iran during the last century is replete with examples of supposedly simple technical reforms sought through simple rule-making, which foundered for lack of complete understanding of the necessary sacrifices to be made in a traditional political system for such reforms to succeed. We have noted elsewhere with what naïveté the reform of the royal cabinet was sought. Attempts to render the traditional regime more efficient, but essentially unchanged, led to responsive demands on the part of various groups and social strata which up to that time had merely been the passive subjects of royal policy. The Tobacco Regie is the classic example of an attempt to transform a group of merchants from passive taxpayers into active executors of policy, in a rationalized framework, in other words, a foreign-managed monopoly. In that case, the monopoly was simply rescinded; but at a later date a government-controlled monopoly was established which enhanced the authority of the bureaucracy.

It is difficult to extend this incident to the unexplored possibility that the economic welfare and security of the tobacco dealers has been increased; but our model does not require such a conclusion. All that is required is that the issue be resolved; that is, that the question of the control of the tobacco trade no longer be the subject of representations to the government. It is our further hypothesis, however, that such resolutions tend at least to enhance the economic security of the groups concerned, but in so doing renders them subservient to the bureaucracy.

Despite great changes in the last four decades, the bureaucracy in Iran is neither an independent group nor a homogeneous class. That is to say, the transformation of the bureaucracy has been only partial, and its power relationships are to a considerable extent simple projections of traditional power structures. Yet the increasing size of the bureaucracy and the increasing scope of bureaucratic competence have contributed toward the emergence of professional bureaucratic values, among a great many civil servants. These values have been strengthened by the demands made upon the bureaucracy by the second major group upon which it is dependent, the military, especially the military created by Reza Shah. Consequently, legitimizations of the power relationships of the bureaucracy can only partly enhance the rationalization of the Iranian system. Such rationalization is residual to the indirect protection of the interests of groups and individuals included in the consultative process.

It is difficult to say whether rationalizing policies are the product of a distinctive process, or simply practices alternative to bargaining and preferable to including lesser bargainers in the consultative process. The latter alternative appears to be the more correct one, but we must note that the eventual effect of such policies is dysfunctional. This is not to argue that bargaining with those who lack consultative access would have been eufunctional, for it would seem that the environmental prerequisites of the traditional political system no longer obtain.

We turn now from our explanation of the alternative character of rationalizing policies to some illustrations of their application.

One of the areas of growing demands and of increasing relevance to the success of other government policies has been that of education. We have not the space here to elaborate fully the pattern of administrative control of the educational system of Iran; nevertheless we may indicate briefly the nature of this control. The entire governmental system of education is administered by the ministry of education from Tehran. A single curriculum is planned in Tehran and is imposed upon all parts of the country. All textbooks are prescribed from Tehran. Similarly, supervision and inspection are hierarchically organized. All teachers are government trained and are employees of the ministry of education, and they consider themselves as much civil servants as do the administrators in their bureaus. These teachers follow the set curricula and administer the examinations drawn up under ministry auspices.

The only independent educational establishment is the traditional religious one. We have already noted briefly how certain government institutions have cut into this monopoly of religious education, and the important measure of control achieved thereby. With this control has come the provision of regular teaching positions, judgeships, and chaplaincies affording the graduates of the government religious schools more employment opportunities, higher standards of living, and higher prestige than those of the average talib. These benefits are reflected in certain demands among traditional ulama for greater rationalization of the orthodox religious institution, along with the granting of degrees and formal diplomas, and job placement.

Urbanization, especially since the Second World War, has created an acute housing shortage. Those hardest hit have been the lowest income classes, but it has been the lower middle class which has made the more vigorous demands. The weakness of these demands is matched by the ineffectiveness of government housing policy. Perhaps the only group to have succeeded in articulating this demand is the lower and middle bureaucracy itself, and certain factory labor groups. The issue has been dealt with in the familiar paternalistic way, with individual ministries, employers, and the National Oil Company building housing units maintained for some of the company's employees. Insofar as newspaper reports are complete, there are no plans for housing programs not tied to specific employments, and consequently looked upon as a form of wages as well as a means of stabilizing a labor force.

Particularly during and after the war, retail prices have tended to rise steadily and rapidly. There have been only partial attempts to deal with the causes of inflation. In the face of rapid inflation, high consumption, and high rates of interest, Bank Melli has simply restricted its currency issue and maintained a high reserve fund therefor. Rising budgets and increasing development expenditures have also played their part in inflation. Naturally, inflation is superficially reflected in higher retail prices, and the government has tried to meet this problem by trying to keep prices down. Arbitrary attempts to hold down meat prices resulted in either disobedience or the closing of shops. Bread prices are kept down by subsidies. But the technique by which the government has sought to hold down drygoods and processed food prices is typical of the traditional approach: a large department store and a supermarket have been established in Tehran. Rather than compete with the bazaar, however, both stores have tended to cater to higher income groups and to ask higher prices than those of the bazaar.

More effective attempts to hold prices down appear within the broad context of policies for the improvement of the employment conditions of civil servants. Once again, this group has made more vigorous demands than others, and its control has been more crucial to the government. One hardly knows whether the non-aristocratic parts of the bureaucracy are more rationalizers or rationalized, though they have certainly benefited from these policies. Unlike nonbureaucratic groups, however, these benefits are also legitimizations, because of the better access of the bureaucracy, because there is no clear institutional division between aristocratic and nonaristocratic civil servants, and because of the bargaining power of civil servants at all levels, as the necessary instruments of policy.

Many of the problems of urban life, housing, inflation, shopping for Western-style goods, medical care, and even the organization of leisure activities are made simpler and cheaper for civil servants by ministry policy. We have already canvassed the variety of special facilities provided for the personnel of the ministries, agencies, banks, and government enterprises, and their description need not be repeated here.

Since the reign of Reza Shah, the government of Iran has from time to time made concerted efforts to settle certain tribes on the land, and thereby to weaken the control of tribal leaders and decrease the possibility of disorders or tribal risings. Success in this line has been limited by the opposition of tribal leaders and by the government's unwillingness to allocate sufficient resources to this purpose. The continuing problem is dealt with, rather, at the level of palliatory propaganda, subventions, legitimizations of the tribal leader, and occasional suppression.

On a longer term basis, it is possible to note a tendency to insert the officers of the local *gendarmerie* between the tribesmen and the chief, and between the peasant and the landlord. The *gendarmerie* was created in order to increase the central government's control of outlying districts, but in the past it has usually functioned as an executor of the will of locally influential landowners. Over recent years, however, the force has been strengthened and its technical skills improved. Foreign advice and assistance have also tended to enhance the rationalization of the *gendarmerie*, and the force has lately been directed more at maintaining the security of the shah's government rather than the stability of the traditional system. The greater recent prestige of the *gendarmerie*, and the clearer distinction between their purpose and the interests of the landowners, have permitted some energetic officers to redefine their own roles. Greater protection for the peasant has resulted, but in rural areas the *gendarmerie* have come to wield new influence.

Islamic governments have for many centuries supervised the administration of awqaf. The major responsibility in this regard has been that of the qadi, appointed by the shah or the governor. Awqaf were, of course, a most important source of income for the ulama, and a basis of their influence. Under Reza Shah, the administration of awqaf became the task of a special bureau which was later incorporated into the ministry of education. The ulama were not ousted from trusteeships of awqaf, but some were encouraged to leave off their religious clothing. The trustee's control over expenditure of the proceeds of the waqf was limited, and his choice of renters for the property restricted. Waqf income was used increasingly for secular, rather than the religious, education, and for repairing archaeological monuments rather than the mosques currently in use. Even simple almsgiving is now partly channelled through the Bureau of Awqaf. The result here, too, has been to rationalize awqaf administration and to limit the depredation of the trustee, but some ulama have been brought under the control of the bureau.

Earlier, we had occasion to discuss the tendency favoring policies of organizing, controlling, and setting standards for occupational groups. This tendency is more pronounced and more complete in post-revolutionary systems like the United Arab Republic, but even in Iran it may be easily found. Some groups, such as the Chamber of Commerce and the Bar Association, have a large measure of autonomy; others, like the guilds and labor unions, are closely controlled. In the case of the groups of lesser influence, certain benefits flow from recognition, but the officials in the government usually gain the upper hand.

In the realm of community development in the villages, and

even municipal development in towns having contracts with the plan organization, the way has been opened for significant rationalization. Land reform villages, particularly, are looked upon as areas in which rationalization is the only basis for achieving the system-maintenance goals prescribed by the policy. Land must be surveyed and apportioned according to fertility, location, and the size of an economic unit. Coöperatives must be established, and agricultural procedures standardized and coördinated. Finance, transport, maintenance of machinery, grading, even packaging, must be worked out by the specialists. The peasants must be organized to build their own roads, schools, and clinics. Attempts thus far to accomplish these things through a coöperatives' agent, or through a "dehyar" (employee of the ministry of the interior) have usually resulted in these officials becoming subservient to local landowners. If the plan is to succeed, then the dehyar, or his equivalent, will come to dominate village life.

There are many more areas of government policy in which rationalizing practices tend to prevail: in managing foreign trade, in income tax administration, and in bureaucratic reorganization itself. These topics have already been the subject of discussion and need not detain us here. A full investigation of all the means of rationalization, indeed a more thorough examination of the hypothesis of rationalization itself, is now suggested by these examples. Such an investigation is beyond the scope of the present theoretical analysis, however, but it is to be hoped that more substantial empirical support may be established in the future.

To conclude this section we now turn to some of the consequences of the dichotomous performance of the Iranian political system at the behavioral level. It is impossible, of course, to derive accurate or complete conclusions about prevalent personality types, from a number of generalizations about the political system. Here we are concerned only with political behavior, and then only with certain gross parallels with the most important political practices. We shall, therefore, consider what appear to be widely prevalent images of reality upon which individual social strategies are based.

In keeping with the action frame of reference, it may be acknowledged that the expectations of political actors are the most important bases of their purposeful behavior. Expectations are not always true reflections of the future, but should they be generally grossly inaccurate then no basis for fruitful social interaction would exist. Theoretically, the accuracy of expectations is a function of the diffusion of cultural values and is the test of an integrated social system. We have tried to show the lack of integration in the political system, a lack of integration resulting in conflicting expectations and uncertainties about strategies, on the part of political actors. Having chosen a strategy based on either traditional or conventional value expectations, the actor may be faced with a response based on the opposite value system. This sequence is not only frustrating; it also leads to a sense of arbitrariness and to accusations of hypocrisy. It may even lead the individual to feel that the range of behavior must somehow be restricted.

We may sum up this sequence as the existence of a high degree of behavioral ambivalence, in the Iranian political system, a situation conducive to increased psychological stress and indirectly having a detrimental effect on system stability. Out of the basic ambivalence over whether to pursue a bargaining or a conventional (legal) strategy there flow a number of dichotomies which for the individual Iranian characterize the mental image of the political system. For the influential, landowning aristocrat who moves easily in the higher governmental circles, and who is generally well informed about the personalities and power relationships of key officials, ambivalence is reduced to rational choice between two approaches. For those who lack advance information about some of the officials and influentials they must see, a true ambivalence exists. The divergency in the types of behavior of the Westernized Iranian when "at home" and at the office is a commonplace. It is, however, less well known that he is torn between similar alternatives when he approaches a civil servant or possible patron.

On the surface, one sees the same superfluous courtesies, the same repeated conversational gambits. But will the point be reached? Will the official send the petitioner through proper channels? At what moment should a bribe be suggested? How much? When going through proper channels, should one bring a letter from an influential friend? Which friend? And how is one to understand the official's response? Will he comply, even though he spoke of the fact that the matter is not his to decide? Will he really ask the minister? Might it not be better to threaten the official in some way?

These are some of the questions that will occur to the individual petitioner. How many have offered bribes that were not accepted? How many have brought letters that had no effect? How many have threatened, emptily? What was the reason for such a result? Was it because someone else had stronger parti, or because the official was truly imbued with professional standards and so valued impartial administrative principles? The civil servant, too, and the politician, are also aware of the challenge of conventional values; they also have pride, and they also seek to justify themselves. When must they follow traditional values, and when can they afford the luxury of acting in accordance with conventional ideals?

The ideological context of this behavioral ambivalence is composed of a number of dichotomous explanatory mechanisms. The legal or moral right of a petitioner is frequently contrasted with his prudence and cleverness. The honesty of an official is contrasted with his willingness to take bribes. The vulnerability of an official to influence is contrasted with his efficiency. Often these dichotomies are only apparent; legal rights must be supported by parti, courage requires prudence for success, honesty may even require the admission that certain services are more readily performed if bribes are forthcoming, and efficiency need not be a function of the origin of the directive which the official carries out.

Increasingly, persons tend less to bemoan corruption in government and are becoming more concerned with administrative inefficiencies. Honesty and efficiency are no longer thought of as merely personal dispositions but as the result of administrative technology. The absence of "automatic justice" is bemoaned, and few persons expect to receive "justice" without receiving nonconventional support. All the same, the system is not on the side of those who violate the law. The law is poorly enforced, and some may even openly flaunt it, but from time to time one hears the tale of an isolated, hapless victim of justice. The resultant uncertainties breed alienation, along with a strong sense that no one can be trusted. The transitional system has few supporters and no ideological justification except that of a teleological nature.

SIX

The Politics of

Economic Development

IN IRAN AS IN OTHER underdeveloped countries, economic development programs are but the latest and most elaborate of the plans by which it is hoped to close the gap in international capabilities and welfare between the West and the non-West. There is a kind of progression from the financial and military reforms of the Amir Kabir through the concessions and loans of the Nasir al-Din Shah period to Shuster's appointment, Millspaugh's mission, and the prestige building programs of Reza Shah. From the desire to maintain military equality, in the days of Abbas Mirza, to the determination of the first majlis to economize, and the success of Reza Shah in avoiding foreign loans, a complex pattern of system goals has emerged having greater legitimacy than either the shah or the constitution. Praised equally by shah and schoolmaster, by senator and taxi driver, by the governor of the state bank and by the student, are financial stability, administrative efficiency, patriotism, rising standards of living, industrialization, independence of foreign influence, universal literacy, and simple honesty, sincerity, and mutual assistance.

Reforms were always justified in terms of the regime itself and they had system maintenance as central goals. Only with the rise of Reza Shah did the transformation of the system become the central goal of policy and the praiseworthy secondary goals become the means to that end. The desired system was generally thought of as a nation state, adjusted to the special circumstances of Iran. In time, however, the end goal of system transformation was obscured, and the means became limited goals in themselves. The abdication of Reza Shah was followed by a transitional period of some twelve years, ending with Musaddiq's fall. During this transitional period large numbers of foreign troops and administrators resided in Iran, foreign interests again manipulated much of Iran's politics, and foreign propagandists had nearly free rein. Iranian intellectuals discovered modern art and the novel, they read eagerly of new political tendencies, the world of Marxism-Leninism was opened to them, and the tantalizing paradoxes of truly constitutional government were strongly suggested to them. Above all, they were encouraged to criticize the nature and the achievements of the Reza Shah regime. All of these influences combined to reëmphasize the ultimate goal of a free and prosperous nation-state, to render conventional institutions increasingly functional for a time, to increase the freedom of action of the truly traditional, and to render the rationalizing policies of the previous regime justifiable only insofar as welfare values were achieved. Planned economic development was not a new idea, at the close of the war, and it still had to contend with conservative Western notions of the importance of financial stability and fiscal solvency. Nevertheless, the example of the Soviet Union, the experience of the Western powers in coping with the Great Depression, the new applications of Keynesian economics, and the wartime experimentation with economic controls, all served to create an ideological atmosphere in which it was possible to argue that all the ills of Iran might be healed by planned, comprehensive, economic development. One of the most attractive fallacies attached to this new idea was that somehow politics need not intrude upon this development, a fallacy not directly faced by those who were more concerned with institutional reform of a conventional nature, but one explicitly denied by the Tudeh Party.

The major exponent of the solution by economic development was Mr. Ebtehaj, who won the ear of the young shah, criticized severely the plans of foreign consultants, succeeded in getting his own bill passed, weathered the storm of the Musaddiq period, when funds were not available for salaries, let alone development, and finally became director of the plan organization in time to begin the implementation of Iran's second seven-year plan. The first plan had been cut short by the economic crisis of the Musaddiq period, and the second depended upon the renewed flow of funds from petroleum operations. To be sure that political interference would be restricted, an independent plan organization was established, the director of which reported directly to the shah. The plan organization funds were to be drawn from the profits of the National Oil Company, in fixed proportion to the total of such profits. The plan organization would determine which projects were to be carried out, and in what priority. The plan organization would let construction contracts and supervise the organizational phases, after which projects would be turned over to the ministries or factories sold to the public for ordinary administration.

Planned development involves more than building things, however, and the areas of necessary coördination with the ministries were revealed to be very great indeed. Many of the established functions of the ministries involved development projects that were not given up to the plan organization. The resultant struggle over funds, and hence authority, between the ministries and the plan organization has already been discussed, and the partial victory of the cabinet noted.

The objective here is not to present a detailed account of the specific projects of the plan organization and their impact upon particular groups. Such a study would be of great importance in examining the extent to which economic development has, in fact, been dysfunctional to the Iranian political system, but the research involved would be formidable, and many of the criteria of rationalization in such specific applications remain to be established. Before any success in a study of this nature might be hoped for, the entire issue must be seen in its political context; that is, the points of contact between these changes and the political system must be suggested and tested. *Our purpose here, then, is of a preliminary nature, in keeping with the theoretical orientation which has been maintained throughout.*

The systemic significance of economic development is difficult to assess. As an issue of policy and as an institutional problem it cuts across the analytical categories elaborated above, and might be discussed in part in each of the processes described. In another sense, it is best related to the goals of particular structures of power relationships in which the shah and a group of Westernized upper middle-class bureaucrats and industrialists are dominant. In yet a third sense, economic development is but an ill-suited title for a number of issues which have risen to the political level out of the environment of the system. These three senses are not contradictory; they are, rather, complementary: the environment of the system has given rise to a series of issues; a number of social power structures have identified their own interests with a particular kind of solution; this kind of solution has resulted in the continuous flow of tentative decisions which are then modified and implemented, in accordance with the political procedures described; and, finally, these decisions, as implemented, create new legitimizations or alter existing structures of power relationships such as result in further issues of political significance. The environmental origin of such a pressure is one of the more important determinants of the dysfunctional character of its resolution. External pressures not only give rise to issues that might not otherwise be recognized, but, because of the internalization of certain of the values associated with economic development, any resolution of an issue will dissatisfy either the forces of tradition or the machinery of rationalization. Furthermore, the time lag involved between project idea and increased welfare is such as to enhance prevailing notions of dishonesty and hypocrisy. The latter is true even when the project is successfully handled, and such is not always the case. Successful handling of a project, in accordance with the model herein elaborated, is by definition dysfunctional, in that it involves a reallocation of wealth and security values from the traditionally influential to the middle and lower classes, or a distribution of newly created wealth to the latter classes. At the same time, it enhances the control by the bureaucracy over the distribution of these values and over the determination of the resultants of the power relationships among these latter classes. It may be possible to achieve economic development while enhancing conventional techniques. This, too, would be dysfunctional and unstabilizing, in Iran, but the predilections of the shah and the bureaucracy, and even of the majlis and the senate, render the conventional solution less likely. Economic development is an area of conflict between traditional and rationalizing tendencies, in the transitional political system of Iran. There is no evidence of a serious beginning in democratic planning.

After the fall of Musaddiq, the government of the shah took up the task of economic development in great earnest. This policy was pursued, along with severe repression of the Tudeh and Iran parties, and with increased efforts to win the symbols of nationalism from the opponents of the regime. There is little question of the intention to seek greater security for the throne, and economic development seemed a particularly apt approach. It was argued that Musaddiq had done the country great harm by cutting off its major source of income and foreign currency. Musaddiq had diverted the energies of the nation in a self-defeating adventure, and had retarded development and decreased welfare. Planned economic development, if unexciting, was still the best way of achieving further independence and a better life for all. Development would provide for, and proceed hand in hand with, the spread of literacy, with land reform, and with rural social improvement. It has even been hinted that democracy would increase with economic betterment and the attendant growth of civic responsibility. The funds for development would be forthcoming from the sale of Iran's petroleum, thus necessitating agreement to the consortium proposal. The instability and lack of progress which had prevailed since 1941 were ascribed to the irresponsibility of the politicians and parties, so economic development had to be insulated from politics. To accomplish this end the plan organization would be kept quite separate from the cabinet and majlis. The only ties to those two bodies were the assistant director of the organization, who was also undersecretary to the prime minister, and the appointment of a watchdog group of supervisors by the majlis, the latter reporting periodically on the word of the plan organization.

It is apparent that the goals of this policy were not merely system maintenance; a measure of change was also desired. The teleological-democratic theory, justifying present authoritarian practice on the basis of providing the prerequisites of democracy, is in wide use outside of Iran, but it lacks all empirical basis. Instead, it is apparent that economic development was meant to be an adjunct to the general policy of increased rationalization, to requite the demands which had developed during the preceding twelve years without permitting the control of affairs to leave the hands of those personally loyal to the shah. Rationalization meant resistance to the forces of tradition, as well as control of the rising middle classes, but it also meant increasing the authority of the military and the bureaucracy. We have already noticed the dilemma of the shah, for the higher military and bureaucracy are closely interlocked with the forces of tradition, but the middle military and the bureaucracy tend to favor rationalization extreme enough to change the regime, and even to dispense with the shah himself. In the final analysis, the shah is striving above all to create the kind of situation in which he can keep his place. Practically, this has meant neither the strengthening of tradition nor the support of rationalization, simply maintenance of something in between. The existing transitional system is no longer sustained by a struggle between the shah and his supporters, on the one hand, and the forces of tradition and revolution on the other. The system is maintained, rather, by suppression of outright revolutionaries and by balancing rewards to both the aristocracy and the middle classes. By partially satisfying both, the shah endears himself to neither, and the irrationality of the system is only too apparent to all. Under these circumstances, it is not surprising that many remain unconvinced that development is being seriously pursued. Indeed, there are evidences that the goals of development have been sacrificed to satisfy both individual and institutional demands.

To state the dilemma of the shah in other terms: under the existing counterrevolutionary circumstances, economic development is both the result and the cause of thorough rationalization, but rationalization is itself dysfunctional and results in positive system-challenging activity. The relationship between effective system maintenance and economic development is a delicate one, for a choice must be made between satisfying middle-class demands and creating or consolidating structures of support among the privileged classes. Consequently, economic development cannot be thought of as separate from politics, as some would have it, but perhaps as the most important source of political issues. Barring the chance bullet or the unforeseen conspiracy, the direction and rate of systemic change in Iran will depend upon the balance of choice between the traditionally influential and the middle classes. This is not to argue the centrality of economics to politics, but the centrality of politics to politics. The transitional system is in a state of change, and each decision creates a somewhat different situation which, in turn, defines the next issue. Economic development, however, has a separate logic of its own, though it may be but dimly perceived even by specialists. It is within the realm of possibility that enough progress may be made, even under existing political conditions, so that a point will be reached where private investment in industry, and large-scale scientific agriculture, are relatively more profitable than other less socially beneficial pursuits.

The political and economic conditions for this are obscure and cannot be prescribed. Nevertheless, within the essentially uncontrolled relationship of economics and politics, in Iran, this point may be reached and a considerable change in the political role of aristocratic elites may result. Under such circumstances, the middle classes, too, may come to look less upon the government as the sole source of satisfying their demands. Having stated this possibility, with its conventional political implications, we can turn aside from it as merely indicating a middle range between the unlikely return to extreme traditionalism and the far more likely movement to thorough rationalization. The degree of possibility of some such middle-range result depends on another range of decisions on economic development: that is, within the framework of satisfying the demands of the aristocratic elite, should they be rewarded with positions in the machinery of a rationalized economy or encouraged in private enterprise? The latter alternative, given existing economic conditions and prevailing value preferences, is not much demanded and would probably lead to much greater alienation among nonelite but politically aware groups. Consequently, reaching the takeoff point for simultaneous development toward a free enterprise economy and a conventional political system is highly unlikely. This is not to argue that the latter may not be reached separately, but the former would seem to be impossible without the latter.

There are other areas, too, in which decisions on economic development will be crucial to political change. At the present time, the plan organization still has no plan. All that it has is a collection of projects based upon a variety of specific goals. The nature of some of the goals will be discussed below; suffice it here to say that these goals have not been derived from a comprehensive theory of economic development, applied to Iranian conditions and calculated so that "scientific" decisions on the allocation of resources and priorities may be made. The present goals of the plan organization have been determined by the immediate desirability of certain projects, from a political point of view, and by an arbitrary balance between agriculture, industry, communications, and social welfare projects. Balance, here, means spending about the same under each head. Balance has been sought, in order to avoid political accusations of bias, but balanced development requires not the equality of these four areas but the coördination of all, so that raw materials have factories in which to be processed, so that factories have raw materials, so that processed goods, raw materials, and imported machinery can be moved safely and cheaply to their destinations, and so that fields may be tilled and machinery run by healthy, educated, and hence more efficient, human beings. To make "scientific" decisions to this end, more than theory is needed: accurate statistics on the existing state of affairs are also required. The latter, at least, are presently being gathered, but they are still inadequate.

Nevertheless, even if all of the prerequisites for scientific planning existed, and even if the plan organization were so constituted and insulated that it would pursue scientific development, its various allocations would have political consequences. Not a few Western economists (and some Iranians, too) have bemoaned the fact that "politics" have a way of interfering with economic development. The unwillingness of economists to accept the interference of politics as necessary may be traced to two mistaken assumptions: that wealth may be increased and more evenly distributed without affecting power relationships, and that a more even distribution of increased wealth leads necessarily to a universally desired democratic form of government. Neither of these assumptions is true, nor are we in a position yet to establish that certain economic conditions are necessary and sufficient causes of certain political consequences. All that we can say is that the quantity and distribution of wealth does have an effect on structures of power relationships. That is, there is only a conceptual difference between economic decisions and political decisions. If the economists had their way, legitimizations would be granted by an autonomous development process, by a sort of conventional process, that is, which substituted productivity for legality, as the conventional statement of "power relationship." It is not impossible for such a state of affairs to prevail, but it must surely depend upon the existence of a prior acceptance of conventional values.

The decisions of the plan organization are neither wholly scientific, economically speaking, nor wholly scientific politically. Certain areas, geographic, social, and productive, are being rewarded, developed, or otherwise affected, as determined by the political and economic strategy of a relatively small group of officials, advisers and consultants. For the aristocratic elite, this has meant the redirection of their efforts so as to best exploit the possibilities of this situation. Only on rare occasions have some individuals of great influence sought to affect the basic decisions of the plan organization. The pressure to build a second fertilizer factory at Shiraz is one example. Most of the time the decisions of the plan organization have been accepted as fixed factors. They determine the shape of the pork barrel.

Economic development decisions, therefore, produce politically significant results at three levels. There are, first, the people who will benefit by the welfare value produced, be it improved crops, a road or a school. Second, there is the fellow who gets the contract, who manages the coöperative, who gets the land, or who is appointed to run the factory. Third, there is the increased authority of the administrative structure, the plan organization itself, the ministry of education, the ministry of roads, the ministry of customs and monopolies, or the new administrative organization established to manage the new enterprise. All three levels are important, in examining change in the political system.

Earlier, we referred to specific goals, as the result of the political and economic strategy of a small group of decision makers. It is important to stress that these goals are not parts of a coherent program aimed at a preferred and clearly perceived result. All that may be said is that such specific goals seem to be desirable at this time, and not at some future time, as contributing to an entirely different state of affairs. In other words, these goals are sought on the basis of the implicit assumption that everything else is going to remain as it is.

One of these strategies has to do with the balance between urban and rural development. From the political point of view, the issue is not that of which will result in higher productivity, not even of which is the prerequisite of the other. Rural development counterattacks in the area of accusations concerning the feudal character of the present government, but it tends to waste resources on a social group which is not now capable of making effective political demands, and it will probably render them more capable of so doing in the future. For a government which is unable to satisfy the demands currently being made upon it, this procedure is at least questionable. Urban development would seem to be directly aimed at satisfying the demands of the most troublesome groups, that is, those most often engaging in damaging system-challenging activity. On the other hand, urban development will attract even more people to already overcrowded cities and will leave the government open to criticism for not relieving the most pressing problem of mass rural destitution. The plan organization has vacillated here, but more recently it has tended to stress rural development while concentrating upon middlesized provincial towns, in its urban projects. It has not been revealed whether the cause of this procedure was the desire to render modernizing and urbanizing change more orderly and gradual, or whether the priority given smaller towns was meant to win support against Tehran, or simply to wipe out the blot of backwardness in areas more frequently seen by outsiders and high officials.

The reasoning and motivation behind the choice of projects and assignment of priorities does not seem to be uniform. Balanced scientific development has not yet established criteria, nor is there any reason to suppose that planning has involved such sophisticated considerations as that of creating centers of social power balancing the one of the Tehran middle class. The political aspects of development revolve about such system-maintenance goals as may be achieved through a sudden magical accomplishment, some prestige project, or through "non-political" and generally laudable nation-building projects.

The search for a magical accomplishment must be discussed in terms of the prevailing skepticism of the literate public. Most politically aware Iranians, except for some of those employed by the plan organization, do not believe that anything substantial will be accomplished. Such expressed opinions cover diverse attitudes. Some undoubtedly hope that the plan organization will succeed, but having been so often disappointed in their hopes in the past, they are loath to express them, lest they be accused of naïveté or of hypocrisy. It is not in style for any but cabinet ministers to be optimistic. Others are frankly cynical and do not believe that any public affair can be insulated from the "corrupt" politicans and influentials. Yet a third group disbelieves, as a matter of ideology and of negative system-challenging policy. It may be an exaggeration to say that loyalty to the present regime implies the necessity of an optimistic attitude, but open pessimism is surely detrimental to the goals of the government. On the other hand, we can clearly discern in those alienated from the present regime a pessimism-shame-disloyalty syndrome. A rapid achievement of great magnitude, the "public relations man" approach, might be the solution. A similar attempt was made in Iraq, though the less magical device of housing was used to win support. But development failed, politically, in Iraq. In Iran, the big achievement that has been sought is coördinated regional development. This interesting approach has made some progress only in Khuzistan, where the Clapp and Lilienthal group received, first, a contract to survey development projects in the area, and then a contract to manage the phased development of the entire region. Great hopes are held out for Khuzistan, but official hopes are already more than counterbalanced by the quite general opinion that overhead costs are much too high, that progress has been too slow, and that many of the projects will be uneconomical. The whole program is condemned as being much too ambitious. The former director of the plan organization was acutely aware of the criticism that progress in general was slow. His defense was that all projects had to be studied and carefully checked before being approved. But just at the point where he thought results might begin to show, he was dismissed.

Even if no magical achievement could be made, something on the order of Reza Shah's railroad success might win support by the national prestige which it conferred. The shah is especially interested in carrying through his father's plan for building a steel mill, primarily for purposes of national prestige. Mr. Ebtehaj, listening perhaps too closely to foreign advisers, fought a losing rearguard action against this proposal as an uneconomic expenditure of funds. The ultimate political value of the project is doubtful, but discussion of it without action, over a long period of time, merely feeds the pessimism syndrome. Recent reports indicate that a minimal steel project will be carried out, as a compromise between the need to spread investment funds widely and the desire to capture nationalist symbols.

The alteration of the project will also feed the continuing tendency to complain of delays, changes, and failures in the work of the plan organization. Ebtehaj's excuses were not accepted at their face value. Rather, people questioned the efficiency of the organization, the competence of its experts and advisers, and the honesty of its officials. While there seems to be some evidence that the organization is more efficient than the ministries, and its personnel more competent, there are also time-servers, patronage appointees, and phony experts. Furthermore, the discussion in the majlis of the dismissal of Ebtehaj rendered complaints of delays and inefficiences more or less official.

However debate may rage over the prestige-project, there has been unwavering support of "social" or nation-building projects. Health and education, especially the building of schools, have received continuously increasing portions of the national budget and consistently large sums from the plan organization. The importance of these projects is apparently beyond question, and no serious suggestions for curtailing relevant funds have been entertained. This is the one area in which the government has assumed that it will be severely judged, and it does not intend to be found wanting. In Iran, unlike Egypt or India, there is still little pressure on the land, and an increased population is looked upon as an unmixed blessing tending to increase both national power and importance. The possible dysfunctional effect of education, especially through a standard program which increases the demand for university training, is either ignored or felt to be a necessary price. Perhaps it is not fully realized to what extent teachers fall short of inculcating loyal attitudes, or it may simply be that literacy is thought of as the necessary adjunct of a rationalizing policy. More simply, this emphasis can be understood as required of any government claiming to be national and essential to an attack on the shame aspect of the pessimism syndrome.

Though presumably not directly affecting development funds, the established policy of maintaining a large and well equipped army has tended to reduce funds for development. Despite the fact that the plan organization's income is guaranteed, we have seen where it has been forced to give up some part of this for regular budgetary needs. The ordinary budget would certainly have shown a smaller deficit, if military expenditures were more moderate, but it is, further, the unwavering policy of the government to give the army whatever it requests, and not to rely, at least not for purposes of domestic security, on either the police or foreign support.

Economic development is similarly indirectly affected by the utilization of foreign advisers. The need for special skills in development is widely acknowledged and easily justified, in the abstract. When the issue is reduced to concrete cases, however, we find certain recurrent attitudes expressed which cannot but be detrimental to the progress of development. These attitudes seem to be general, though some are more frequently expressed by those with whom the foreign expert works, and others by poorly informed outsiders. Iranian counterparts almost always refer to their advisers as completely incompetent, or as rather harmless fools. Outsiders tend to look upon advisers as sinister representatives of foreign imperialism. The counterpart's views are easily related to his impatience to gain his adviser's position, or to be free of a living declaration of his own lack of competence. The outsider's attitude is but another expression of the pessimism-shame-disloyalty syndrome. Plan organization advisers, especially, are thought to be expensive forms of waste. It would seem that Iranians must evidence a good deal more of personal security and optimism before they can take advice in their stride. As for the impact of these attitudes on development, aside from the fact that the benefits expected from the foreign expert are not realized, there is some evidence that certain projects are held up simply in order to spite the foreigner, to defy him, or to ridicule him.

This has been but a brief and incomplete review of some of the political implications of economic development. Enough has been presented, it may be hoped, to illustrate how the issues involved fall within the processes already described, and how they involve the same practices. On the other hand, development is more than a series of loosely related issues, for it represents a deep policy commitment on the part of the government, and it injects a dynamic into the system as a moving-changing entity. Regardless of how successful Iran may be in its economic development, this policy commitment will result in continuously increasing social mobilization, increasing political awareness, and increasing political participation. It will be further understood, from the preceding discussion, that the projects being pursued, while calculated to be of political significance, are too crudely conceived to serve the delicate task of controlling and channelling the new political forces which they will create. As for most governments, Iranian policy is aimed at dealing with the existing situation, not the one which it is creating.

SEVEN

External Pressures

IN REVIEWING the international pressures upon the Iranian political system, our aim here is to go no further than to indicate the variety of environmental forces acting upon that system and to suggest whether these tend toward stabilizing or changing it. As in the case of the systemic components mentioned earlier, precise predictive value cannot be assigned these environmental factors. All that can be shown is the general direction of the influence of these factors, and orders of magnitude must be substituted for exact relationships.

As a secondary actor in international politics, Iran is interested in but few of the nearly one hundred recognized states. In some, Iranian interest is based on its own claims; for the rest, upon the claims of others upon itself. Aside from considerations arising out of concrete claims, Iran stands in a position where it is compelled to interact with the leading exponents in the major bi-polar system, as well as in the subordinate Middle Eastern international system. Though concerned with, and involved in, bi-polar politics, Iran, unlike neutralist states, is equally concerned with both major blocks. Iran is an adherent of the Western bloc, but not so irrevocably as, say, the members of the North Atlantic Treaty Organization. As an underdeveloped, non-Christian, formerly subjected, nondemocratic state, Iran's adherence to the Western bloc is tenuous, and its relations characterized by excessive demands, bargaining techniques, skepticism, and fear of exploitation. It is not only the indignities of the past and the indifference of the leading Western bloc nations that lead to these attitudes, but also at least a vague awareness of the fact that Western ideals undermine the legitimacy of the Iranian regime and that a clear Western victory in the cold war could not but redound to the detriment of the present government.

Iran might prefer to be neutral in the cold war, since it certainly does not favor a Soviet victory, but the neutrals, too, have a kind of ideological bloc which tends to comfort revolutionaries and antitraditional groups. In challenging the leaders of the Western bloc, while being a member thereof, Iran continues the pattern established by Reza Shah. Now, instead of seeking third powers to break the see-saw of British-Russian pressures, Iran looks to secondary members of the Western bloc, who are also hopeful of improving their influence vis-à-vis that of other bloc members. This tendency is enhanced and best exemplified in Iran's oil policy, for both the United States and the United Kingdom have petroleum interests which are considered more important than those associated with Iran. Certainly, neither country is any longer under great pressure from private companies to make great concessions to Iran.

In general, Iran's relations with the Soviet bloc are unfriendly and highly colored by suspicion. Russian and Soviet pressures on Iran are not forgotten, and the Azerbaijan affair and the role of the Tudeh Party are still vivid incidents. At present, relations between Iran and the Soviet Union are strained, and Soviet broadcasts attack the existing regime with vigor and success. Despite these facts, which predispose the present government against the Soviet government, Iranian political leaders have stubbornly persisted in the belief that the only effective defense against Western pressures lies in relations with the Soviet Union. Moreover, the government fears that the Soviet Union can move a domestic opposition to dangerous revolutionary activity. The Soviets, however, were strangely willing to compromise their supporters in Azerbaijan, under Musaddiq, and perhaps again in the future. Hence, the best defense against subversion would seem to be good relations with the Soviet Union. These considerations strengthen further the economic reasons for good relations, for much of the agricultural produce of the north can best be exported to the Soviet bloc.

The third orientation of Iran's foreign relations is toward the Middle Eastern system of which it is a part. The ties which bind Iran to its closest neighbors are more than geographic. The common Islamic heritage of Iran and its Middle Eastern neighbors is weakened by Iranian heterodoxy, but it provides elements of common discourse. More important than geographical contiguity and common beliefs is the common ideological frame of reference by which modernized, middle-class Iranians and other Middle Easterners try to understand their environment and their place in history. In this sense, the communication of information about neighboring states leads to the drawing of parallels. When another Middle Eastern state achieves some measure of economic progress, or when it wins an international victory or suffers a popular revolution, Iranians ask "Why not here?"

There are also Iranian minorities in some of the neighboring countries, and there are other groups that are divided by the boundary lines, or that cross them at will. As a producer of petroleum, Iran is a competitor of its neighbors. Iran is also dependent on some of these neighbors for the means of transporting its petroleum to foreign markets. The boundaries themselves, between Iran and its neighbors, are subject to dispute in many cases. Iranian expansion is not now a vital issue, but nationalist historians, and some political activists, have made suggestive references to the historical boundaries of Iran and to the area inhabited by Iranian peoples.

From the preceding discussion we find that Iran is concerned internationally with three groups of countries: the Western bloc, the Eastern bloc, and other Middle Eastern states. Before examining some of the specific issues with which Iranian leaders must deal, let us first state briefly the Iranian relationship to some of the major countries of its concern.

Relations with the United States are particularly close and complex. In a formal sense, Iran-America ties are many and varied, running the gamut from treaties of friendship and commerce through mutual security arrangements and Iran's adherence to the Eisenhower Doctrine. The United States helped to overthrow Musaddiq, to reorganize Iranian oil production, to plan economic development, to train the Iranian army, and to balance the Iranian budget. American advisers serve in nearly all the ministries, many banks and agencies, in some industries, in municipal governments, in most military formations, and even in the security organization.

The Iranian army is equipped with American arms. Economic development proceeds partly on loans from the Export Bank and from the Development Loan Fund. Recently, the United States and Iran signed a bilateral pact, by which the United States guaranteed to defend Iran, in case of communist aggression.

The United States, however, has steadfastly refused to join the Central Treaty Organization, despite Iranian demands. Short of such membership, there seems to be no way to mitigate Iranian distrust of the U.S. Such distrust of American motives and intentions leads to increased demands for weapons, for investment funds, for loans, and the like. Nor is the United States still seen as the homeland of Morgan Shuster, but rather as the enemy of Musaddiq and the supporter of General Zahedi; as the country which has supported Britain as the balancer of Russian influence; and as the country which has sent thousands of its nationals to live among Iranians, to ridicule them, to exploit them, and to insult their sensibilities.

Close coöperation with the United States, in the face of such stereotyped views of the United States and of Americans, is not an unmixed blessing to an embattled regime. A pro-Western policy in Iran may not be justified by appeal to moral principles, as is the policy of the United States at home. The same moral principles seem to deny the legitimacy of the regime and to require a policy of neutralism. Unfortunately, coöperation with the West must be justified as expedient under existing circumstances. Opposition groups tend to deny that expediency alone motivates such coöperation, or else they condemn expediency and point out that Musaddiq acted otherwise.

The United Kingdom occupies a unique place in the Iranian view of the forces at work in international politics. This view is oversimplified, yet there are so many emotional dimensions to it that it may be put aside only with difficulty. There is little doubt of the respect and fear in which the British are held, feelings which are sometimes expressed as hatred, but more often in grudging admiration. The qualities admired are, in many cases, not those truly characterizing British policy, but rather the projection of qualities which stand high in Iranian culture. Shrewdness, courage, ruthlessness, deliberateness, dissimulation, urbanity, courteousness, arrogance; these are some of the qualities admired. Not all of these qualities are considered virtues, but many Iranians wish they could pursue their own interests in the same manner as the British pursue theirs. They are convinced that in these, rather than in ability or intellect, lie the secrets of success.

The British are, consequently, thought of as the prime movers in Western policy formation. In sheer power, the United States exceeds Britain, but the British have found ways to have American power serve their interests. The United States is only, or at any rate primarily, interested in containing Soviet expansion, but the British wish to gain positive benefits. The British work quietly, behind the scenes. They understand the Iranian temperament. They dress conservatively. They manipulate and may even buy off the most influential of the aristocracy. The British are thought to be the creators of the present dynasty. It is the British that sustain the forces of traditional politics, while the naïve Americans think they can improve matters, teach democracy, and enhance the efficiency of the civil service.

For those who do not believe this myth, the educated Iranian will point to the large share of Iran's foreign trade which goes to Britain, the retention of 40 per cent control of Iran's petroleum exports by the AIOC (now British Petroleum), and the fact that Britain and not the United States is a member of the Central Treaty Organization.

Part of this inordinate respect and fear of Britain arises from the difficulty Iranians have in understanding British policy. This policy has fluctuated widely in Iran, from intense interest to near indifference, from intervention to neglect, and from support of revolutionary movements to defense of established authority. Support of the Qajars against Czarist Russia was followed by indifference to Iran's defeats, in 1812 and 1828, but this neglect ended with intervention to prevent Iran's conquest of Herat, in 1856, despite the exigencies of the Crimean War. The ensuing scramble for economic concessions dropped off to permit the Russians to win almost complete financial domination of the shah, until influences from the Indian Empire led to the support of the constitutional movement. The Anglo-Russian treaty of 1907 ended this support; the revolution was stillborn, Russian influence became dominant again, and the British hardly exploited the opportunities won in the treaty. After World War I, the proposed treaty of 1919 seemed likely to lead to the complete subjection of Iran to British imperial control; but when opposed, the British decided instead to support the nationalist revolution of Reza Shah, however tentatively. Moderate support and nonintervention were underscored by concessions in revising the oil agreement, but the last World War brought the joint intervention of Britain and Russia, and the occupation of Iran. The Soviets were permitted freedom of action in their zone of occupation, and the British evacuated their troops before the Russians did theirs, but Qavam's attempt to negotiate with the Russians and to work with the Tudeh Party brought British-inspired tribal risings in the south. And in the latest phase, the British stubbornly resisted the nationalization of the AIOC, then conceded Iran's right, accepted the participation of the United States in exploiting Iran's oil, became Iran's ally in the Baghdad Pact, but failed to respond in support of Iran against Soviet propaganda attacks. There are, of course, adequate situational explanations of each of the developments in British policy toward Iran, but these explanations are inaccessible to those who insist on personifying international actors and interpreting policies in terms of stereotyped personalities. The fact that Britain retains much of its influence and position in Iran is proof positive of the astute, calculating, self-interestedness of Great Britain. Yet too often, such proofs lead many people to explain all international events in Iran as the result of British manipulation.

Germany loomed large on the Iranian international horizon, during the reign of Reza Shah. Germany was first invited as a relatively weak and disinterested third power, but German technical ability, nationalist fervor, military resurgence, and stress upon an Aryan racial myth all appealed to the Iranian imagination. German exports and advisers supplanted those of other nationalities, and Germany grew to be the most important of Iran's trading partners. At the outbreak of war, Germany appeared to all Iranian nationalists as the heroic opponent of Iran's inveterate enemy. Many people, ranging from religious youths through military officers and bank managers, fervently hoped for a German victory. The wartime occupation of Iran and the subsequent defeat of Germany ended the growth of German influence, destroying the idea of a national rebirth through fascism. Germany was then returned, in Iranian eyes, to the status of a disinterested third power. German capital could help Iran develop, and German experts could improve Iranian administration and industrial enterprise, without endangering Iranian independence. With the near miraculous recovery of the West German economy, however, the attractiveness of "nonpolitical" coöperation was greatly increased, and in recent years many German businessmen, technical experts, and sales agents have settled in Tehran. In general, Germans enjoy a strongly favorable prejudice, on the part of most Iranians, and they are moderately successful in their business ventures. On two occasions, where closer coöperation with the government at an official level was required, the Germans have not fared so well: the German-owned Tehran department store and the engineering contractor, Kocks, Inc., have both come under a cloud. The latter's contracts were suddenly and completely revoked. The Krupp firm is engaged in negotiations on the steel mill project, and they have been instrumental in bringing Iranian authorities to a more realistic understanding of the expenditures and sacrifices involved. It is not impossible that this firm, too, will suffer from a sudden reversal of Iranian governmental attitudes, in an attempt to place the blame for delays on the steel project upon foreigners. Germany has not attempted to win any oil concessions in Iran as yet, and hence is still able to keep its reputation clean, insofar as this delicate subject is involved.

Japan and Italy, on the other hand, have both attempted to win concessions for their oil companies. Italy has made greater progress and a socalled 75-25 per cent arrangement has already been made although no oil has yet been produced. The 75-25 per cent arrangement is actually no better than the consortium's equivalent of a 50-50 per cent profit split, we are told; but the symbolic importance of these figures, when added to the fact that Iran does not fear Italian imperialism, has the effect of winning popular approval and also pressuring the consortium toward a more generous split. Japan has found an increasingly wide market for its goods in Iran, and Italy is seeking to expand its exports. The trade imbalance in Japan's favor is so great that the government has had to take measures to pressure the Japanese into buying more Iranian goods. Iranian efforts in this regard have been of little avail, for low-priced Japanese goods aimed at lower income groups are in great demand, and the government can ill afford to cut off this means of satisfying middle-class groups. Italy has not yet succeeded in winning a broad market for its goods, but it made a considerable merchandising effort with an expensive industrial exhibition in Tehran, in 1958.

Soviet citizens are not often seen in Tehran, nor are they as conspicuous as Westerners. Nevertheless, the Soviet presence is strongly felt. Irano-Soviet relations have been strained since the abrupt dismissal, in 1958, of the Soviet delegation which came at Iran's invitation to discuss the signing of a nonaggression pact. Since that time the full force of the Soviet propaganda machine has been turned against Iran. These radio broadcasts have been supplemented by Tass reprints which have been distributed in Tehran streets by Iranian employees of the Soviet Embassy. Two of these men were arrested, and the Soviet chargé d'affaires promptly demanded their release, threatening dire consequences. This sort of behavior is reminiscent of Russian interferences in Iran during

Shuster's mission and after the dissolution of the second majlis, even to the detail of the West's nearly total lack of response to Soviet pressures.

But the Russian presence is felt not only in its radio broadcasts. The historical and political image of the Soviet Union, in Iran, is important to the general orientation of Iranians to international relations. The Soviet Union is, to many of them, more or less the same as Czarist Russia. That is, the Soviet Union is a powerful neighbor bent on expansion southward, but restrained by distant Western forces. Other Iranians are more aware of the fact that the Western powers support the present regime than they are of Western prevention of Soviet expansion "in the direction of the Persian Gulf." Under the circumstances, where large numbers of urban Iranians are alienated from the present regime, support for the Soviet Union, even where sovietization is not desired, becomes a most satisfying form of system challenging behavior. These activities involve listening to Soviet broadcasts, repeating their contents, praising Soviet scientific achievements, and, for newspaper editors, giving space to Soviet cultural and scientific events in their papers. There are others, too, who feel that the present Iranian regime is so well entrenched, so well supported by the West, and so corrupt, that it can only, and must, be destroyed by the Soviet Union. They further argue that they have nothing to lose anyway. Undoubtedly, there are some well indoctrinated communists who actually desire sovietization, but none express these views openly.

Irano-Soviet relations cannot be considered apart from the role of the Tudeh Party in recent Iranian history. This is not the place for such an historical review, but we can mention the principal events that are of importance in forming prevailing attitudes. It has been pointed out that Tudeh propaganda did not stress Marxism, but rather nationalism and social reform. Tudeh journals were also prominent in stirring wide intellectual interest in Western art and literature. The heady tonic of revolution and release from a hopeless, static tradition won many young adherents. The Azerbaijan incident, Soviet attempts to win an oil concession in the north, and the attempt on the shah's life did not discourage Tudeh support. It grew, during the Musaddiq period, but it came under a cloud when it failed to take decisive advantage of the situation. Musaddiq, in the end, is the true symbol of nationalism, and the Tudeh Party now is measured by its past policy toward Musaddiq. The policy of the Tudeh Party reveals that at that time it was a negative instrument of the Kremlin, at least until Stalin's death led to cautious inaction. As a negative instrument it would be used only if the government of Iran refused to coöperate internationally. At the present time, Soviet-Iran tensions have brought rumors of a revival of Tudeh activity and of the possibility of a change in the cabinet in order to mollify the Soviets. The theme is as old as the Iranian cabinet itself.

But these pressures can and will be turned off when the time for a rapprochement arrives. The Iranians know that the Russians have their price, and if Soviet propaganda efforts are successful enough, the Iranians will pay, if the United States lets them. No one is fooled by such a rapprochement; everyone accepts it as a temporary lull. The only consequence is that Tudeh activity is somewhat lessened. But because no one is fooled, the Soviet Union does not lose its effectiveness as a symbol of revolution.

Iranians are aware of the pressure of China, too. Asians cannot avoid the imposing, possibly threatening, aspect of a China which is increasingly asserting itself. Disturbing though this prospect may be, it is not of immediate impact. Pro-Soviet elements take a cautiously pro-Chinese line, but quite definitely, enthusiasm appears to be lacking. Only a few make it a point to listen to Peking's broadcasts in Persian, though in many ways these land more telling blows than do the Soviet broadcasts. On the other hand, many of those who despise the present government are openly apprehensive of the Chinese. They have no sympathy with Chinese nationalism, nor do they look to China to learn how to solve their own problems. They fear the pressure of hundreds of millions of hungry, crowded Chinese, and hope rather doubtfully that the West will bear the brunt of their emergence to world power.

Iran's nearer neighbors in the Middle East are also cause for concern. Strangely, most Iranians do not appear to sympathize much with other Middle Eastern states. Except for a few, Iranians tend to dislike Arabs and to suspect Arab nationalism; they are formally friendly to Turkey but somewhat contemptuous of Afghanistan; and they are oddly indifferent to Pakistan. Turkey and Pakistan are close allies, but except in official circles one meets with little enthusiasm for them. Both Iraq and Egypt have posed recent revolutionary challenges to Iran, and the neutralist-pro-Soviet policies of both have tended to increase official suspicion.

Iraq is of serious concern because of ethnic, linguistic, and religious spillovers of population, on both sides of the border. Iraq is also an oil competitor, and it was a "constitutional" monarchy. Population spillovers, the annual attraction of the pilgrimage to the Shiite shrines in Iraq, and the frequent exchange of letters with relatives over the border render it much easier for Iranians to get authentic information about events in Iraq than is the case for any other Middle Eastern country. Enhancing the importance of Iraq, in its influence upon the Iranian political system, is the further fact that Iraqi policy has been respectful of the communists and has admitted a number of Tudeh leaders. These leaders are working among Iranians in Iraq, but they may also have contacts within Iran as well.

Egyptian attacks upon the Baghdad Pact did much to sour relations with Iran. Egypt and President Nasser came to epitomize all that was disliked about the Arabs. The Iraqi revolution, the subsequent cooling of Egyptian-Soviet relations, and the rapprochement of Egypt and the United States have rendered Nasser more acceptable. Additionally, it might be noted that the Egyptians sent their king away on a yacht, while the Iraqis assassinated theirs. For a while, Cairo broadcasts spoke in friendly tones to the Iranian people, and the government of Iran responded in kind. Nevertheless, no concrete coöperative action was taken, and none seems to have been intended.

Iran remains suspicious of Egyptian aims in the Persian Gulf, in Bahrain, and in Kuwait. Egyptian control of the Suez canal, and the possible extension of its control over some of the oil resources of the area, are also disturbing. The prospect of an Egyptian victory in Iraq is not yet gone; and this is a matter of considerable apprehension in Iran, though not so bad as a communist Iraq. To balance these fears somewhat, Iran has recognized Israel, permits small quantities of oil to be moved directly to the Israeli port of Eilath, and facilitates the regular movement of persons and goods from Tel-Aviv to Tehran by air. As a consequence, Egypt has broken relations with Iran and has resumed the broadcasting of bitter criticism of the shah.

With Turkey, Iran maintains good relations as a Central Treaty Organization ally. There are frequent diplomatic visits between the two states and there are other exchanges of military missions, parliamentarians, journalists, and the like. Trade agreements have been made, though they are not of great importance to either country; and under CENTO, an agreement has been reached to complete a rail connection between the two countries. On the other hand, there is little coverage of Turkish affairs in the local Iranian press, and the government controlled radio does not give out a particularly favorable picture of Turkey.

Afghanistan relations are often front-page news, in Iran. The

Afghans are Persian speaking, too, but they are Sunnis. Nationalist Iranians feel a strong kinship for Afghanistan, sometimes even considering it an integral part of the Iranian homeland. On the other hand, Iran-Afghan relations are marred by border disputes, by Afghanistan's neutralist attitudes, and by its stubborn unwillingness to enter into serious negotiations with its neighbors.

Pakistan is another CENTO ally of Iran, but relations between these two countries are strangely unbalanced. There is quite as much coming and going of delegations between the two as with Turkey, but Pakistani emphasis upon friendly relations with Iran is only perfunctorily noticed by the latter. The two countries exchange time on each other's radio programs, but Iranians are not enthusiastic about these ties. Nevertheless, Pakistan is thought to be more Persian in culture and more Shiite in religion than is actually the case, so it seems that propaganda emphasis upon the common culture of the two countries has had some effect. Even so, road and rail connections with Pakistan remain poor or nonexistent. Pakistani suggestions that the railroad be extended from Zahidan to Kerman as a means of exploiting the resources of that remote province have fallen on deaf ears. Nor has Iran given Pakistan all the support it seeks in the Kashmir question.

These, then, are the nations with which Iran is most concerned in its international affairs. We turn, now, first to some of Iran's international claims, and then to problems arising out of the Middle Eastern system and problems of bi-polar politics.

Iranian international claims are generally small and do not require satisfaction through any basic structural changes in the Middle East. Small though they may be, they are in some cases necessary to the solution of certain domestic problems, and in all cases they are important as prestige weathervanes.

The Iranian claim to Bahrain, now under a British protectorate and never in recent times controlled by Iran, was revived by Reza Shah. The island itself is inhabited by Arabs, for the most part; but if there is any threat there to British control it would seem to be from Egypt, rather than Iran. Iran's claims are based on one time conquest and rule of the island, but that was long ago. Now the barren, backward place has achieved importance because of its oil production. Egyptian, British, and Iranian claims all overlap here. Iran reasserts this claim, from time to time, but does nothing about it. Such demands seem to be mostly a means of keeping up a nationalist front, rather than a manifestion of a serious policy. Yet one informant holds that his organization was prepared to accomplish a Castro or D'Annunzio sort of invasion in Bahrain, and went so far as to get General Razmara's approval. The project was put off because of the prime minister's assassination.

Iran disputes Iraq's control over the Shatt al-Arab. Iranian ships may use these waters, but the boundary is not held to be in the middle of the river, instead, on the Iranian bank except around Abadan Island. Not only does Iraq control the river; it also collects fees from the ships using the channel, and it does not divide this revenue with Iran. Iran presses for boundary revision and for an equal share of the fees collected, but the Iraqis have put off serious discussion of the matter. Here also, it is hard to say precisely how serious the Iranian claim is, but raising an issue of this kind might well stress the nationalistic differences between the two countries and might even result in concessions from a new and instable revolutionary government.

Iran makes certain other demands on Iraq, growing out of the location of the Shiite shrines and the fact that up to half a million Iranians reside in Iraq. The largest Iranian colonies are concentrated in Najaf, Kerbela, and Baghdad. Iran claims to be their protector, and on the basis of a mutual agreement it does send teachers out to man government schools for Iranian expatriates. A particularly ticklish aspect of this problem arises out of the emphasis upon religious freedom for the Iranian minority. This problem, considering the anti-religious ideology of the communists in Iraq, has some interesting ramifications. Iranian government-controlled media have recently published a good many reports calculated to accuse the Iraqi government of suppression of Islam.

Iran's principal dispute with the Afghans is over the distribution of the waters of the Helmand. Iran desires a larger share of these waters, in order to irrigate part of Sistan. The boundary in the area has been settled, but Iran claims that Afghanistan has not recognized Iranian downstream rights. Afghanistan, on the other hand, has developed an irrigation scheme of its own in the Helmand valley, with American help. Obviously, the Afghans are reluctant to enter into negotiations with Iran on this matter, so long as they remain the beneficiaries in the present situation. Iran continues to make representations, and it plays up its claims in the domestic press, usually asserting that negotiations will soon take place and that Afghanistan is about to make concessions. The continued failure of serious negotiations to materialize, however, simply parallels the failure to realize extreme claims concerning internal reforms. Disbelief is consequently encouraged.

On a number of occasions, recently, Iranians attempting to

enter Kuwait have been the victims of unscrupulous boat owners or have been stopped at Kuwait's borders. Others have entered without visas and have gained the more attractive jobs to be found in that oil principality. The status of nonvisaed Iranians remains insecure, for they may be expelled at any time. The desire of many Iranians to move to Kuwait is embarrassing to the government of Iran, and it has led to newspaper criticism of the fact that adequate sources of employment are not to be found at home. These complaints have been especially pointed after some disaster, such as when a group of Iranians were left to die on a desert island off the coast of Kuwait. The government of Iran would generally like to see a more liberal immigration policy in Kuwait, as well as in the other oil principalities, but finds it awkward to press for this openly. Kuwait and other Persian Gulf protectorates are, of course, somewhat apprehensive that large-scale Iranian immigration might bring serious political problems in its wake, not excluding territorial claims. For the present, Iran does not press its views strongly, though it continues to permit clandestine emigration and it does seek to protect Iranians, once they get out of the country.

The last of the claims to be considered relates to the smaller non-Middle Eastern countries with whom Iran trades. From these, Iran wishes to get guarantees of a better balanced trading pattern. In recent months, Iran has pressed this point more vigorously, but current policies of permissive importing and free adjustment of the bazaar, out of deference to effective demand, do not allow the government much maneuverability. It may well be that foreign currency earnings from petroleum will not keep pace with development requirements and consumer preferences, but it is by no means sure which direction the government will take.[1]

Of those particularly Middle Eastern problems which impinge upon Iranian domestic problems in the most general of ways, the most significant are nationalism, revolution, petroleum, inter-Arab rivalries, and minorities. Iranian nationalism, when and to the extent that it exists, is unique. Nevertheless, throughout the Middle East nationalism has taken on a number of secondary connotations that cannot be easily separated therefrom. Anti-imperialism, state capitalism, social welfare, universal literacy, economic development, restriction of foreign influence, Westernization, even neutralism in the cold war, are considered not merely adjuncts of

---

[1] These earnings have not kept pace with expenditures, and Iran is reported to be facing a foreign exchange crisis.

nationalism, but proofs of its authenticity and sincerity. The nationalist awakening that has occurred throughout the Middle East is a challenge to Iranian leadership and a yardstick by which the politically aware measure their own government. The corollaries of nationalism are widely accepted, or ignored at the risk of losing claim to the most potent political symbol of the day. Despite the magnitude of the problem, it is clear that little intellectual effort is currently being spent in this direction. A few students would like to do theses on nationalism, but their professors are afraid of the results, and no one else dares write on the subject. The problem is being dealt with on the level of slogans which ring false, or else is avoided in preference for such dubious symbols as God, Shah, and Fatherland.

While revolution is not a necessary corollary of nationalism, it is often associated with it. In the rejection of the nationalism of the older generation, in particular, youth tends to think of revolution as a necessary precondition. As one informant put it, the very word is spoken with joy and eager anticipation; young people think of revolution as an unmitigated good. Nationalist revolutions have occurred in the Middle East, in Turkey, in Egypt, and in Iraq, and have brought with them some of the startling changes desired in Iran. More moderate shifts have occurred through the Pakistani and Sudanese coups. Iran itself approached, but hesitated before, its own third revolution. This history and these examples are part and parcel of the image of reality which every educated Iranian has. They are contributors to the prevailing tendency to seek thorough and radical change. The Iraqi revolution was thought by many, both in and out of Iran, to be the signal for a similar event in Iran. That there was no one in a position to accomplish this, at the time, is less significant than the feeling that events in one Middle Eastern country would naturally affect those in another—even beyond the confines of Arab nationalism—and the feeling that the situations in both countries were so nearly the same that one could reason from the Iraqi example to the Iranian.

Petroleum is the third of the problems named. The subject is a complex one, and we shall forego detailed treatment to point out only how its regional character produces environmental pressures on the Iranian system. In the first place, Iran is in competition with other producers. At a time of glut, all must suffer, but for each the relative penalty depends very much on their international positions. The lowering of the price of crude oil in the Middle East was the jumping-off point for an Arab conference on oil, held at Cairo. Iran decided to go it alone and not to try to concert its policy with that of the Arab countries, hoping for better treatment at the hands of the consortium. Undoubtedly, this policy was determined by an unwillingness to alarm the consortium, an unwillingness to strengthen Nasser's control of Middle Eastern oil policies, and fear of being used to further the ends of an alien nationalism. The fact that Iraq withheld full coöperation somewhat eased Iran's position, but both sent observers to the conference, lest they be accused of breaking the non-European "front." Profit-splitting with foreign oil companies is another issue on which external developments can have a profound effect. The Iranian government is bound to get the very best terms offered anybody, or it will be thought to be subservient to the exploiting power. The refusal of the AIOC to work out a 50-50 per cent arrangement with the government of Iran contributed to the nationalization crisis. Should any Middle Eastern state reach the point where it can truly run its own oil industry, unaided, one can easily conceive of the great pressures that will be brought to bear on the government of Iran to break its arrangement with the consortium. Another aspect of this problem is that of transporting the oil to foreign markets. The only important route, which is through Suez, is dominated by Egypt. Other solutions, such as the pipeline to Alexandretta, may yet be worked out, but they are expensive and they may not be important or efficient enough to solve the problem. Rounding the Cape was suggested, and this is a method already used by some big tankers. No one, however, contemplates such a solution with complacency.

Inter-Arab politics affect Iran also. As we have noted briefly, Iran cannot avoid some taking of sides in the Nasser-Qasim dispute. More especially, Iran cannot be indifferent to what occurs in Iraq, and its response thereto predisposes Iran toward a whole set of attitudes regarding inter-Arab politics. Iranians in general may pay no attention to these events, but many individuals do, in fact, hold strong opinions about which of the two, Nasser or Qasim, is the true nationalist. Once a stand is taken on this issue, a criterion is established for judging the sincerity of the Iranian government's policy.

The last of this set of problems is that of the minorities which spill over boundaries to become international minorities. The Kurds are the most outstanding of these, but the Arabs of Iran and the Iranians in Iraq are important, too. The encouragement of Kurdish political activity, under the revolutionary Iraqi regime, had the immediate effect of threatening the internal stability of Iran. Tudeh propaganda aimed at Persian-speaking residents of Iraq was considered a nearly hostile act. The problem of the disregard of the Arab minority, in southern Iran, has not much preoccupied Arab leaders yet, but there is no gainsaying the potential explosiveness of this issue. The political role of the minorities on both sides of the line produces tensions which act quite directly on the expectations and fears of Iranian decision makers. Armaments, border patrols, subventions to tribal leaders, increased respect for the exponents of orthodox Shiism, may all be the results of these tensions. The responses are not necessarily traditional or rational, but whichever they are, they impinge upon the process of transition in ways that are difficult to calculate in advance.

Bipolar politics give rise to numerous problems as well. The most important of these, for Iran, is the country's identification with the Western bloc. Ever since the constitutional movement of five decades ago, Russian influence has fallen short of its earlier dominance. The myth of balancing Russia and Britain beclouds the fact that Russian influence reached its apogee just prior to the revolution, and since that time Iran has never been in close alliance with the Soviet Union. The treaties of 1921 and 1927 did not bring the two states together, but they did limit the nature and extent of permissible British influence. British influence declined, too, after 1921, though the oil concession in the south was maintained. The wartime occupation of Iran brought back both Britain and the Soviet Union, this time with the United States. The government of the shah quite clearly favored the West over the Soviet Union; though Qavam wavered a bit in 1946–1947. Some form of American advice and assistance was accepted throughout this period and up to the present. In fact, if the best interpretation be placed upon Qavam's policy, Iran has steadily sought to eliminate Soviet influence, to withhold any northern oil concession, and to reinterpret the treaties of 1921 and 1927 so that the Soviet Union might have no excuse to occupy Iranian territory.

Iran has been unable to play a truly neutral role because Soviet pressures were far too great. The success of the Tudeh Party and the long undisturbed control of the northern provinces by the Soviet Union were of a more serious nature than British and American control of the southern provinces. Consequently, Iran has been compelled to identify more closely with the West, except for Qavam's short experiment, in coöperation with the Tudeh Party, and Musaddiq's attempt at pursuing what he called a positive equilibrium. In both cases, irreversible Soviet gains were in the offing, and were only staved off when both leaders realized that a Soviet alliance could not be a temporary substitute for close relations with the West. Nevertheless, there is no basis for concluding that Iran must continue to side with the West. Iranian leaders have repeatedly demonstrated suspicion of Western motives or apprehension at Western ideals. They tend to feel that it is easier to make a "deal" with the Russians than with the Americans. In particular, the shah's government is apprehensive at the prospect of bland American acceptance of the Egyptian and Iraqi revolutions. It is evident that the United States is embarrassed by alliances with nondemocratic regimes, and that it has no great respect for traditional royal legitimacy. Furthermore, Iranians do not see their alliance with the West as something inevitable. They refuse to recognize their inability to engage in diplomatic maneuvers. Even if we conclude that closer coöperation with the Soviet Union at this time would start an irreversible trend, Iranians see such action as a matter of tactics only.

Such would seem to be the only context within which Iran's adherence to the Baghdad Pact may be understood. The Baghdad Pact, now the Central Treaty Organization, is not a more modern version of the Sa'adabad Pact, nor is it, for Iran, the application of the "Northern Tier" concept of Middle East defense. The Sa'adabad Pact was signed by independent, or nearly independent, states in a futile attempt to keep out of the last world war. This was a truly neutralist action. The Northern Tier concept admitted not only the difficulty of winning the support of the Arab countries for the Western cause; it also postulated the impossibility of defending the area, once the Soviets had penetrated beyond the mountainous frontier. The Baghdad Pact, insofar as Iran was concerned, was certainly not neutralist, nor could Iran subscribe to the idea of shifting the scene of battle from Europe to the Middle East.

How are we to explain Iran's decision to join the Baghdad Pact, when the United States failed to apply great pressure, and when the goals of the Pact went far beyond Iranian concerns? To this we can only conjecture that the shah was not satisfied with existing American guarantees against Soviet aggression, that Iran wished to strengthen the anti-Nasser forces in the Middle East, and that Iran wished to move the United States to a recognition that special benefits might be derived from helping to preserve the regime, and not merely the independence of the state. The emphasis upon preserving the regime seems, perhaps, too general to be related to a policy as specific as joining the Pact. On the other hand, it must be remembered that often the policies of weaker states must involve such diffuse manipulation of a situation, rather than concrete proposals leading to mutual accommodation. In other words, the United States might not wish, for "ideological" purposes, to guarantee to preserve the regime, but it might also find it useful in fact to do so. Furthermore, there were certain specific threats to the regime, in particular the revelation of the extent of Tudeh inroads into the army and the problems attendant upon removing General Zahedi, that were at least temporarily mitigated by Iran's adherence to the Baghdad Pact.

The establishment of the Central Treaty Organization has not dissolved the Soviet threat. As we have already noted, Soviet propaganda efforts have been increased, and they seem to be remarkably successful. The Soviet Union enjoys a kind of negative support in Iran. All those who oppose the present regime look to the Soviet Union for support, but in general they do not wish to see an extension of Soviet control southward. In a static and rather institutionalized sense, the Soviet threat is established in the relevant clauses of the treaties of 1921 and 1927, which require that Iran may not permit its territory to be used by third powers for aggression against the Soviet Union. Should Iran, on its part, fail to prevent such use of its territory, the Soviet Union would be entitled to occupy parts of Iran. From time to time, Iran has attempted to denounce these clauses or to prove that they are no longer legally applicable. The Soviet Union, for its part, has repeatedly asserted the validity of the clauses.

In a more dynamic sense, the Soviet threat to Iran was represented in its support for the separatist Azerbaijan and Mahabad governments, and by its manipulation of the Tudeh Party. There are many useless "ifs" in international relations, but the two most significant "ifs" for Iran regard these two points. If the Soviet Union had chosen to support the Azerbaijan democrats at the critical moment when the Western powers had withdrawn and Qavam sent government troops into the province . . . ; and if the Soviet Union had moved the Tudeh Party to act in support of Musaddiq, on the 28th of Mordad . . . On the other hand, the actual presence of American forces in Iran, Iran's various treaties with the United States, and the unilateral guarantee of the Eisenhower Doctrine, rather than encouraging the implementation of the disputed treaty provisions, have the effect of restraining direct Soviet intervention.

Under present circumstances, then, there seems to be little fear of direct Soviet aggression, but there is a good deal of apprehension about what the Russians may be able to accomplish through internal subversion. It is possible to suggest that both the United States and the Soviet Union, on the whole realistically, expect some sort of internal upheaval, though neither knows when it may occur and neither will knowingly touch it off. The real problem for both is to limit the other in possible attempts to gain control of the revolutionary movement. From the point of view of the shah's government, both may be tempted to try and end this uncertainty by precipitating the revolt of a friendly group. Nevertheless, the United States is so heavily committed to the present regime, and the present regime so coöperative, that the relative benefits of a pro-Western revolution become less and less. On the other hand, the Soviet Union is continually encouraged to associate the present regime with the West and to incite the people of Iran against both. For the government of Iran, when so pressed, the best alternative seems to be to assert the imperialist designs of the Soviet Union. These assertions are hard to prove, when the Soviet Union is actually encouraging an internal rising. The other alternative, seeking Soviet friendship and ceasing to treat the Soviet Union like an international criminal, is meant simply to have the pressure reduced, but not to resolve the issue.

As a consequence, Iran tries to befriend both the United States and the Soviet Union, under normal circumstances. Were Iran more united and had it a more stable political system, it might win concessions from both sides, like other neutralists, rather than having to grant concessions. This was the argument of Dr. Musaddiq against the policy of "negative equilibrium." Actually, the Soviet Union defeated his purposes, for the Soviets refused to support Musaddiq, either domestically or internationally. *Three* must play at the game of positive equilibrium, and the Soviet Union would not play.

Iran's identification with the West has had many more and complex results than merely a hardening of the Soviet attitude. Iran has had to adjust to many circumstances emanating from the structure of the Western bloc, its particular resource requirements, its strategic position, the pattern of American policy, and that policy's established forms of implementation. The gross differentiation of identification with either East or West is a crude oversimplification of the impact of bipolar politics on the Iranian political system. The place of Britain in the American alliance system, the dependence of Western Europe on Middle Eastern petroleum, the priority of Europe for American security, and the impact of nuclear weapons and intercontinental delivery systems on the strategy of Middle Eastern defense, all are definitive of certain aspects of the alliance of Iran and the United States. While these considerations lead to much tension within the alliance, the mode of implementing current U.S. policy and the philosophy underlying that policy are perhaps the most important of the international factors affecting the Iranian political system.

This is not the place for a close examination of the institutional structure of American foreign policy, so we may merely indicate the lines along which such an inquiry would lead us. The thinking and the organizational paraphernalia of such American efforts as the Marshall Plan, Point Four, the Mutual Security Program, and the North Atlantic Treaty Organization continue to dominate our activities in Iran. We continue to assume, though without any scientific proof, that economic prosperity is both a necessary and sufficient cause of democratic government. We continue to believe that technical assistance can somehow overcome capital deficiencies and also carry a minimum number of political overtones. We continue to disregard the fact that more for everyone means less for some who now have everything. We neglect completely the question of whether partial economic development leads necessarily to partial democracy, simply because we believe that "complete" development is somehow related to "complete" democracy. Mutual security and NATO-type solutions seemed appropriate in the avoidance of overt Soviet aggression and encouragement of the quite substantial anti-Communist "center" groups in Europe, just as the Marshall Plan was based upon the active coöperation of the same political stratum. These assumptions do not seem to apply in the Middle East at all. Furthermore, it is not merely a question of whether such theories and assumptions are valid, but even if they were valid, what is the best organizational mode of application?

It is superfluous to point out the well-known principle that administrative goals will be affected by the structure of the implementing organization, but it is sometimes overlooked that this applies not only to the structure of the Iranian bureaucracy, but also to that of AID, USIS, the Military Assistance Advisory Groups, the Embassy, and other groups like the Gulf District Engineers and the U.S. Educational Foundation. The underlying theory, specific policies, bureaucratic structure, and the personalities and training of personnel assigned to Iran are the four levels of interaction with Iranian government goals, politics, administrative tendencies, and bureaucratic behavior that must be taken into consideration in appraising the detailed impact of the American alliance on the Iranian political system.

In general, this impact, quite aside from the specific projects engaged in jointly, has led to tensions between the Americans and Iranian bureaucratic classes, and at the same time it has strengthened the rationalizing tendencies in the bureaucracy and elsewhere. It is not even that we do not know how to properly combine the eight crude variables isolated in the preceding paragraph. The problem is, rather, that we have not admitted that all of these variables exist. If the preceding discussions of the Iranian political system have any validity whatsoever, they should show how inaccurate and oversimplified are our basic assumptions about the mechanisms of technical assistance, economic development, and mutual security. Perhaps, in the absence of better knowledge, we have no choice but to continue in the way we have gone; but we must seek better knowledge. The way to this knowledge would appear to be through better understanding of the Iranian political system and the nature of the forces of transition within it. The social forces of transition have already been closely identified with the machinery of rationalization and the system-challenging classes and groups. We are strengthening both of these forces by direct and indirect means, and hence hastening the transition to rationalization while hoping to bring about constitutional democracy within a conventional system.

The impact of American assistance is not consistent. One of the primary considerations of American overseas programs is to assist but not to direct. In theory, this mode of operation means that the initiative in undertaking any project must come from the government of Iran. In point of fact, the initiative arises from particular bureaucratic or ministerial groups, as well as from particular branches of the U.S. Operations Mission. There follows, then, a process of political significance in which are involved many rival administrative groups as well as those with consultative access toward the end of choosing among alternative projects and implementive strategies. In the most important issues of this kind the key decisions are made by the leaders of various hierarchically organized formations: the director of AID, the ambassador, the commanding officer of U.S. military assistance advisory group, the shah, the prime minister, the minister of finance, the commander in chief of the Iranian army, and, until recently, the director of the plan organization. Since none of these leaders has a clear idea of where the political system is going and how it is going to get there, decisions tend to be made in such a way as to maintain the relative influence of each of these leaders and their hierarchies. Thus, the presence of the U.S. Operations Mission tends to strengthen the machinery of rationalization and rationalizing tendencies, but it does so without rationalizing the machinery itself, or, we might say, without resolving the shah's dilemma.

The impact of American advice and assistance tends to maintain, and even to enhance, the tension between tradition and rationalization, without any movement toward resolving this issue. The Embassy, insofar as it is possible for an outsider to judge, quite sensibly feels that there is not time to test the solution by development, and it further undertands that progress toward this solution will be obstructed by the defensive tactics of the aristocratic and bureaucratic elites who try to turn development to their own advantage. Success in dealing with Iran depends upon getting along with these dominant elites, the most important of which is the military. For this reason, the Embassy tends to discount the importance of nonfocused AID projects and to submit more easily to the demands of the Iranian military, as channelled through the influential American military. The AID leaders, as a consequence, struggle to show specific economic, technical, and welfare improvements, in order to win greater support and prestige. But their efforts, as we have seen, are disoriented to the central problem of political transition. The Embassy is busily observing the tactical minutiae of transition, while the military are secure in the knowledge that an efficient army will be able to control the situation. It may be doubted, too, that the American military look forward to the Iranian army's playing a specific role in the transition of the country's political system. Rather, it would seem that they are capitalizing on the dominant role of the military in Iranian politics in order to increase their own influence in the American official "family," while trusting too much to their excellent connections with a few of the highest Iranian generals.

The preceding is not meant as criticism, for the simple reason that we do not know how else United States operations in Iran might be organized. Our purpose here is not to correct administrative failure, but to point out how the existing relationship is to be seen. This relationship between the American Operations Mission and Iranian political elites can best be described as a political subsystem in its own right, directly associating the American and Iranian political systems. If improvements are to be realized, this point of view must be accepted as the foundation upon which all changes are constructed. The problem is not that development is politically determined, but that it is not *adequately* politically determined.

There remains for us now to summarize some of the things we have already discussed, as comprising the major lines of Iranian foreign policy. Current Iranian foreign policy has been given the symbolic title of positive nationalism, and the import of this title has been noted above. Its content involves the rejection of neutralism and an emphasis upon the security of the regime, rather than of the state. Domestically and externally, Iran prefers the maintenance of the status quo, and to this end it seeks both to enhance Iranian prestige and to increase the extent to which it can gratify the demands of the population of Iran.

Since the central goal of the shah's government is the security of the regime, Iran's foreign policy is directed at countering the environmental pressures referred to, or at adjusting to them. The security of the regime is threatened from without, both by the Soviet Union and by events in the Middle East. A much more moderate threat emerges from the nonfocused activity of the U.S.O.M. In dealing with these pressures, Iran is being driven further on the way of transition. The army, the propaganda machinery, the bureaucracy, and political institutions are all being bent to the preservation of the regime, and as they bend so does the shape of the political system change.

Conclusion

THE ARGUMENT OF THIS ANALYSIS has been that Iran's is a political system in transition, and the mode of the analysis has been theoretical. At the outset, a crude attempt to identify the major components of a political system was made, and a simple classification of systems was developed. The transitional system here described has been characterized by the juxtaposition of the elements of a traditional system with those of both conventional and rational systems. It may be possible that mixed systems exist, or that our classification of systems is inadequate. Hence, it may well be that the Iranian system described in dynamic terms is not itself going anywhere. If this is true, then it follows that the system is not in transition, and hence is stable.

In approaching the problem of stability, it is well to clarify in just what sense the term is used. Here, we are not concerned with stability of personnel, nor even of the political institutions described in a constitution. The stability of a system is not primarily dependent upon the changing relationships of groups or the emergence of new status strata. Stability, as used here, is an analytical concept, the value of which must be dependent upon the validity of our description of the components of the political system. Such validity, in turn, depends upon whether the particular point of view chosen not only seems to explain the political phenomena with which we are concerned, but also whether useful political strategies can be based thereon. In the latter sense, a theoretical analysis such as the present one cannot be proven. It must rest upon its ability to relate all of the relevant factors in a meaningful way.

Within the limitations of this methodological approach, we must face up to the difficulty that the entire notion of a system and its transition is constructed of definitions, and not of "reality," whatever the latter may be. In seeking a pragmatic determination of reality, the only sure ground we are on is that the earlier ways of approaching political phenomena in underdeveloped countries, and in Iran, specifically, have lacked operational validity. Is the present attempt any more, then, than an exploration of another possibility randomly chosen from an infinite variety of alternatives? In a sense it is not, because it is based on limited observation and limited study; but in another sense it is more than that. The present attempt is not merely based on definitions having no relation to widely observed and popularly described phenomena; instead, it starts from that point and attempts to make more precise what everyone sees in part anyway.

We began, not with a theoretical framework, but with loose nondirected observation. We began with the very notion of instability and change, as these terms are understood by the layman, and we have attempted to give them meaning. The problem is not that of whether the system is in transition, whether or not it is changing, but to find out what is changing, and, perhaps, how. Loose and imprecise observation has already shown us that changes in personnel, and even in constitutional forms, do not underlie the political events in the Middle East, and when consummated do not resolve all the issues. Casual observers report that, despite successful revolutions from Egypt to Indonesia, social power structures are frequently undisturbed, behavior patterns and social strategies remain much the same, and value patterns, insofar as they affect ideas of legitimacy, continue to diverge from actual institutionalizations thereof.

The task of analysis is, therefore, to identify all of the relevant features of the system that was, and to suggest what must be the configuration of these features in order for change to cease. The point at which the preëxisting system ceased to be stable, and precisely when some new system will become stable are purely matters of definition. The important question is to explain the nature of change and to refine that explanation to the point where rational political strategies may be chosen. Change is not the product of the inquiry but its starting point; it is the basic postulate. Theoretically, it may be possible to "define away" change and instability, but that would be to deny the very existence of what most of us would like explained. We have some tentative explanations of this sort, stressing the medieval Middle Eastern governmental pattern of sultan, military, and bureaucracy, and disregarding the recruitment of new elites and the different things these elites are doing. The postulate of stability and no change leaves so much unexplained that it must be rejected, until such time as its exponents can elaborate it to the point of comprehensiveness and pragmatic applicability. To assume, as the basis of a rational political strategy, that the Iranian military is functionally the same as the Tahirid, Buwayhid, or even the Tufangchi military formations, so insults the common sense as to challenge the theorist's claim to an equal hearing.

Throughout this study, the tensions between the traditional and nontraditional features of the Iranian political system have been discussed, and we have taken the position that instability is the result of continuous attempts to resolve specific issues. The resolution of particular issues may be conceived of as continuous throughput, or a flow of energy bringing about interaction (political inputs) which result in new legitimizations (outputs), some of which create new issues or which will affect the way in which other issues will be resolved. It is the latter type of result which we hold to be political change. The sources of instability in the Iranian system, then, are to be discovered, not in the existence of conflict over the distribution of political values, but rather in the dynamics of policy as the resultant of a number of political processes. Our emphasis is upon what people do as well as what they are, and policy is conceived of not as the resolutions of specific issues, but as the institutionalization of techniques for resolving classes of issues. This is a view which can be more thoroughly (empirically) tested than we have here attempted to do.

The sources of instability in the Iranian political system are those dynamic features which tend to reduce the effectiveness of traditional political techniques and to alter the pattern of traditional legitimizations. Most of these have already been discussed in other contexts, so that little remains for us in this concluding section but to draw attention to them again. The whole group of rationalizing policies fall into this category. Perhaps the most important of these is the rationalization of social structures of power relationships. In Iran, these policies have not proceeded very far, but if persisted in they will surely have a profound effect. Especially in the rationalization of the civil and military services, but not insignificantly in interest groups, and even among tribesmen and some villagers, much has been accomplished in this direction. Some details of these policies have been given above, and the contrast with tradition has been suggested.

While successful rationalization can be discerned in the aforementioned areas, it seems to fall short in the broader areas of economic development, social welfare, universal military service, and universal education policies. These are four extremely broad areas affecting larger segments of the population, without admitting any political consequences to be the legitimate result of relevant policy implementation. Through each of these policies, new persons are continually being made aware of the political environment in which they live, and they are constantly given opinions about that environment. As a result of these policies, people learn to make increased demands of the government, even as the government becomes something tangible and describable.

Traditional though they may be in essence, favorable government responses to positive system-challenging activity is another source of instability, for much of this activity is now channelled through conventional institutions. Favorable government responses, therefore, tend to suggest both the possibility of vitalizing these institutions and the weak moral position of the government. Even without these suggestions, favorable responses simply encourage further use of the techniques and attract other groups to their use.

The use of positive system-challenging techniques through conventional institutions is the complement of the government's use of conventional symbols to bolster up its position. This use, alongside traditional symbols, tends to bring both into disrepute and to suggest new forms of system legitimacy and, for those whose values or position will not permit them to engage in positive system challenging, to encourage technique exploration in negative system-challenging directions. The necessity of appealing to two sets of legitimizing symbols has been imposed upon the government by historical circumstances, rather than by any free choice of the shah, but the consequences are the same. To the extent that there is any change discernible during the present reign, it is away from traditional symbols, and, hence, further strengthens the tendency toward instability.

Another important source of instability is the failure of the government to satisfy the demands made upon it. It is not rare that a government cannot supply all the demands made upon it, but alienation does not always follow such failure. Where the limitations of resources or the difficulty of implementation of complex programs are better understood, when those whose demands are unrequited believe that they have themselves contributed to the choice among priorities for the whole system, or where effective controls render demands ineffective, alienation need not result. In Iran, however, these conditions do not obtain, for even if wide popular demands are not considered in the consultative process, they become partially effective in other ways, in the system-challenging process or in the interaction of foreign advisers and government officials. The government's failure is one of not satisfying expectations which it has itself created. Actually, there are two aspects to this failure; the first arises out of the lack of resources under present conditions of development, and the second arises out of the failure to carry out promised programs of specific improvement. Neither difficulty is faced up to in government propaganda, so that expectations have been continuously disappointed.

Other sources of instability arise out of international pressures. These have been reviewed above. The example of other Middle Eastern states, Soviet propaganda attacks, association with the United States, all enhance instability. They all lead to government preferences for nontraditional policies, and all carry with them symbolic overtones affecting the legitimacy of the existing system. These are issues on which people tend to have opinions, even when they are relatively ill-informed on other matters.

These are the major sources of instability. They have all been stated as policies, and they indicate how a government which is essentially bent on preserving a political status quo is being compelled to alter that status quo. Indeed, they illustrate how inappropriate is the term "status quo," and how necessary it is for us to find a more dynamic terminology. Change, then, is our basic postulate, and the government is the primary agent of change. These legitimizations may not, and probably will not, stick. If, as seems the case, the government cannot really control these changes, what is likely to be the nature of the future political system of Iran?

The answer to this question has already been suggested, and it is doubtful whether there is much use, given our present state of knowledge, in trying to predict, rather than note existing trends. There are possibilities, say, of a successful military coup, or even an assassination attempt which might intervene and alter certain aspects of the transition we are studying. Such events cannot be predicted, nor need they be, within the framework here followed; in any event, they will not alter the basic question, nor will they effect the completed transition of the system overnight. Any such event, at most, will strengthen tendencies already in existence within the system.

The dominant tendency we have found to be toward rationalization. It is not inconceivable that an essentially democratic system of government, or what we have called a conventional system, may exist with a higher degree of rationalization than is now the case in Iran. It is also within the realm of possibility that a rationalized system may be changed into a conventional system, under certain circumstances. What we do not adequately know, however, are the conditions under which either of these possibilities may occur. In the absence of such information all we can do is conjecture. One might look to the two official political parties, or to the impact of increased prosperity, or perhaps to the revitalization of the majlis, though none of these seem to provide substantial hopes. The transition to a hierarchical system is not, however, inevitable; or, at least we may equally admit that we do not know under what conditions such a transition is inevitable.

At the end of this study it would be appropriate to be able to append a few words of optimism, to envision a life of greater security and happiness for the Iranian people, and a greater share in determining their own destiny. Above all, one would like to look forward simply to the establishment of a government with which Iranians might identify themselves, and social conditions which would encourage all the industriousness and artistic creativeness of which Iranians are capable. I really don't know if that is what is in the offing for Iran, but I believe that there is more chance of achieving such a highly desirable end through the patient working of the present system than by violently overthrowing it and attempting to rationalize without regard for consequences. It may not be encouraging for those who seek reform to hear that they ought to continue as they have, nor would I suggest that the present transitional system is the best for Iran or that current government policies are the best. All I would urge is that they recognize that the system is, in fact, transitional, that it is changing, and that the outcome is uncertain. So long as traditional elements remain, it is unlikely that complete rational-ization will occur; hence, it is unlikely that all the possibilities of popular political participation will be closed off. I think there is a further possibility that continued tension between traditional and rationalizing forces may lead to compromises of a sort that approximate conventional solutions. To this end, the wider diffu-sion of aristocratic interests in industry, finance, commerce, and the professions will be necessary, and the shah himself will have to modernize the monarchy. There is some evidence that these changes are also coming about; and as they do, these and other traditional social structures, including the ulama, may find in conventional solutions their only protection against the machinery of rationalization.

In any case, those who desire change can take heart in the fact that change is actually occurring, whether they would hasten it or not.

Index